The Rise of the BRICS in the Global Political Economy

The Rise of the BRICS in the Global Political Economy: Changing Paradigms?

Edited by

Vai Io Lo

Professor of Law, Bond University, Australia

Mary Hiscock

Emeritus Professor of Law, Bond University, Australia

Edward Elgar

Cheltenham, UK • Northampton, MA, USA

Published by
Edward Elgar Publishing Limited
The Lypiatts
15 Lansdown Road
Cheltenham
Glos GL50 2JA
UK

Edward Elgar Publishing, Inc.
William Pratt House
9 Dewey Court
Northampton
Massachusetts 01060
USA

A catalogue record for this book
is available from the British Library

Library of Congress Control Number: 2013949868

This book is available electronically in the ElgarOnline.com
Social and Political Science Subject Collection, E-ISBN 978 1 78254 547 7

FSC
www.fsc.org
MIX
Paper from
responsible sources
FSC® C013056

ISBN 978 1 78254 546 0

Typeset by Servis Filmsetting Ltd, Stockport, Cheshire
Printed and bound in Great Britain by T.J. International Ltd, Padstow

Contents

List of contributors	vii
List of abbreviations	xvi
Preface	xviii
Introduction *Vai Io Lo and Mary Hiscock*	1
1. The BRICS: An Indian perspective *H.E. Mr Biren Nanda*	5
2. How solid are the BRICS? An economic overview *Anthony J. Makin and Rashmi Umesh Arora*	11
3. Fiscal policy and China's economic growth *Shuanglin Lin*	27
4. Productivity differences, technology adoption and economic growth: The case of India *Radhika Lahiri and Shyama Ratnasiri*	52
5. Brazil: A soft power rising with the BRICS towards a multipolar world *Raquel Dos Santos*	67
6. Sino-Brazilian trade and antidumping concerns *Muruga Perumal Ramaswamy*	84
7. Joining the BRICs: The case of South Africa *Laurence Boulle and Jessie Chella*	99
8. Implications of the rise of the BRIC countries for Africa *Emmanuel T. Laryea*	123
9. The BRICS: Experiments with state capitalism and institutional investment *John Farrar and Mohamed Ariff*	142

10. The power of the BRICS in world trade and growth, analysing the macroeconomic impacts within and across the bloc 162
Ahmed Khalid

11. The BRICS+: Fault lines and opportunities 191
Umair Ghori

12. The BRICS: A model for living on the earth 219
Dilyara B. Karimova

13. The BRICS and Russia 228
Stephen Fortescue

14. New players, new rules? The BRICS and global economic governance 241
Mark Thirlwell

15. BRICS and mortar(s): Breaking or building the global system? 253
Melissa Conley Tyler and Michael Thomas

16. China's path to development: Does law matter? 268
Vai Io Lo

17. The role of the BRICS in international law in a multipolar world 288
Muthucumaraswamy Sornarajah

18. Conclusions: The BRICS – Ascendancy, decline or plateau? 308
Mary Hiscock and Vai Io Lo

Index 313

Contributors

Mohamed Ariff holds a Professorship currently at the Faculty of Economics and Management, University Putra Malaysia. At the time of this research he was Professor of Finance at Bond University. Prior to this he held the Chair in Finance for over ten years and was head of Monash University's Finance Faculty for six years. He received his undergraduate education at the University of Singapore and his postgraduate education at the University of Wisconsin-Madison and the University of Queensland (PhD). He is co-author of a leading McGraw-Hill text-book: *Investments* by Bodie, Ariff, DaSilva, Kane and Marcus. His internationally published scholarly books and peer-reviewed journal articles on banking and capital markets, liberalization, exchange rates, privatization and tax-compliance costs, all in the Asia-Pacific region, are widely cited in respective fields. He won several competitive Research Fellowships. He has worked as a Visiting Scholar/Fellow/Professor in several universities; Boston, Harvard, Melbourne, Tokyo (twice) and the UCD of Ireland (twice). He served in 2004–06 as the elected President of the Asian Finance Association. He is a recipient of four ARC Research Grants, the latest being a large ARC Linkage Grant (with two others) on banking research.

Rashmi Umesh Arora is a lecturer in development economics at the Bradford Centre for International Development, University of Bradford. She has worked earlier as a Research Fellow in the Department of Accounting, Finance and Economics, Griffith Business School, Griffith University, Australia. In 2007 she was a Postdoctoral Research Fellow at the Centre for Asia-Pacific Social Transformation Studies, University of Wollongong, Australia. She has also worked in the Reserve Bank of India (India's central bank) in its economic policy department for several years. She holds a PhD in Development Studies from the University of Auckland, New Zealand and an MPhil in Applied Economics from Jawaharlal Nehru University, New Delhi. Her areas of research interest are economic development, reforms, finance and development, less developed regions and globalization. She has published in several international journals including *Applied Economics*, *Journal of Developing Areas*, and *Third World Quarterly* among others.

Professor **Laurence Boulle** studied at the Universities of Stellenbosch, London and Natal and has degrees in Arts and Law. He has practised as a lawyer, been a law teacher for many years, and has worked as a mediator since 1990. He has conducted a consultancy practice in negotiation, dispute resolution and conflict management for over 20 years and worked extensively throughout Australia and New Zealand, the Asia-Pacific and Africa. He chaired the advisory council to the Australian government on dispute resolution policy for two terms, was a member (part-time) of the National Native Title Tribunal in Australia from 2002–06 and is currently Chair of the Mediator Standards Board. He was awarded the Order of Australia in 2008. Laurence has published extensively in constitutional law, mediation and dispute resolution. His 2010 book *Mediation skills and techniques – Triangle of influence* (with Miryana Nesic, Bloomsbury Professional, UK) was awarded the CEDR London Prize for the best international dispute resolution book in 2010. In recent years he has also published in the area of international economic law, including *The Law of Globalisation* (Kluwer Law International, The Netherlands, 2010) and as editor, *Globalisation and governance* (SiberInk, Cape Town, 2011). His books have been published in Singapore, South Africa, the US, Canada and New Zealand. Laurence has worked as an academic at the Universities of Natal and Adelaide and as a Visiting Professor at the Universities of Cape Town and Gent in Belgium. He has been Professor of Law at Bond University, Australia, since 1991 and is an Adjunct Professor at the University of the Witwatersrand, Johannesburg, where he served as Director of the Mandela Institute and Issy Wolfson Professor of Law for two and a half years.

Jessie Chella is a Lecturer with the School of Law, University of the South Pacific. Dr Chella is admitted as a Solicitor of the Supreme Court of New South Wales as well as Assistant to Counsel of the International Criminal Court eligible to assist Defence Counsel and Legal Representatives of Victims. Her work experience includes various legal and administrative roles undertaken in Australia, the Netherlands and Zimbabwe. She earned her PhD from Bond University, as well as her LLM (by Research), PG DipLegPrac, and LLB. Her research interests include: Corporate Social Responsibility, International Criminal Law, International Humanitarian Law, Human Rights Law, and Mining and Resources Law.

Melissa Conley Tyler was appointed National Executive Director of the Australian Institute of International Affairs in 2006. She is a lawyer and specialist in conflict resolution, including negotiation, mediation and peace education. She was previously Programme Manager of the International Conflict Resolution Centre at the University of Melbourne and Senior Fellow of Melbourne Law School. She has an international profile in conflict resolution, including membership of the editorial board of the *Conflict Resolution Quarterly*. In 2008 Ms Conley Tyler was selected as one of the nation's 1000 'best and brightest' to participate in the Australia 2020 Summit convened by the Prime Minister to discuss future challenges facing Australia. Later in 2008 she was selected by the Fletcher Alumni Association of Washington DC to receive its Young Alumni Award for most outstanding graduate of the Fletcher School of Law & Diplomacy under 40. Her recent research includes book chapters on Australian foreign policy-making and Australia's role in the G20 and publications on public diplomacy and Australia as a middle power.

Raquel Dos Santos is a lawyer in Australia currently practising in the energy, resources and infrastructure group at Allens for clients in the extractives, electricity and government sectors. She is an active participant in public interest and access to justice matters, and managed the Brisbane pro bono practice at Allens in 2012–2013. Raquel has previously acted in dispute resolution and performed commercial and research roles in Australia. She began her career in Brazil as a public servant in the Court of Appeal of the State of Santa Catarina (TJSC) between 1996 and 2000. Raquel holds a Juris Doctor from Bond University, Australia, with majors in International Trade Law and Corporate Law, and a Bachelor of Laws from the Federal University of Santa Catarina (UFSC), Brazil, with a major in Arbitration.

John Farrar is Emeritus Professor of Law at Bond University. He is also Professor of Corporate Governance and Director of The New Zealand Governance Centre at the University of Auckland, New Zealand. He was Dean of Law at the University of Canterbury (1985–88), Bond University (1993–96) and University of Waikato (2004–08). He earned his PhD from the University of Bristol and his LLD from the University of London. Professor Farrar is the author of a number of books and papers on company and commercial law and corporate governance. He has also been active in law reform in the UK, New Zealand and Australia, and was a member of the Legislation Advisory Committee of New Zealand (2004–08). In 2008 he was made an Honorary Life Member of the Australian Law Teachers Association for services to legal education in Australia and New Zealand.

Stephen Fortescue has a BA (1972) and PhD (1977) from the Australian National University, with a specialization in Soviet Politics. He is an Honorary Associate Professor at the University of New South Wales and his current research themes are the policy-making process in Russian politics, business–government relationships in Russia, and the Russian mining and metals sector. His most recent monograph is *Russia's oil barons and metal magnates* (Palgrave, 2006). He publishes in journals such as *Post-Soviet Affairs*, *Eurasian Geography and Economics* and *OstEuropa*.

Umair Ghori has a background in legal practice both as a litigator and as a corporate lawyer. He joined Bond University in November 2010 as a Senior Teaching Fellow and was promoted to Assistant Professor in 2012. He recently completed his PhD from the University of New South Wales. His thesis examined the policy and regulation aspects of international trade in textiles and clothing. At Bond University, Faculty of Law, his teaching interests include international trade law, international business transactions, public and private international law, business and commercial laws, arbitration and dispute settlement and law of contracts. Prior to joining Bond University, Dr Ghori taught advanced legal research, foundations of law research and some components of international trade law at the Faculty of Law, UNSW. Dr Ghori is also a Fellow of the Tim Fischer Centre for Global Trade and Finance at Bond University, Faculty of Law. His primary research interests lie in international trade law, international business transactions, public and private international law, energy law, arbitration and dispute settlement, corporations law and the law of contracts.

Emeritus Professor **Mary Hiscock** spent many years teaching at Bond University and at the University of Melbourne. Her career has also been interspersed with visiting appointments in Europe, Asia and North America. Internationally she has represented Australia on numerous occasions at the United Nations Commission on International Trade Law (UNCITRAL). For many years she was a consultant to the Asian Development Bank and is an Expert Adviser to the European Bank for Reconstruction and Development. Professor Hiscock continues to be a member of several editorial boards, including the *Australian Journal of Asian Law* and of the *Melbourne Journal of International Law* and is the immediate past Chair of the International Law Section of the Law Council of Australia and a past President of the Academy of Commercial and Consumer Law.

Dilyara B. Karimova graduated in 1991 from Novosibrsk University, Russia as a geochemist. Dr Karimova's field of interests include ecological damage, audit, ecological legal systems both national and international, the mechanism of transformation of the mineral substance and waste, life cycle features of waste and secondary materials, and comprehensive approaches for solutions to environmental problems. Dr Karimova has received a letter of commendation from the Federal Service for Environmental and Natural Resources Inspectorate for her contribution to the preservation of Russia's natural resources.

Ahmed Khalid earned his PhD in Economics from Johns Hopkins University, US. He then worked at the National University of Singapore (NUS) from 1992–2000 before joining Bond University. Professor Khalid has also worked at the World Bank, Lahore University of Management Sciences (LUMS), Pakistan Institute of Development Economics (PIDE). He has also worked as a consultant for leading institutions in finance and economics including the Limburg Institute of Financial Economics (LIFE), the Asian Development Bank (ADB), CitiGroup, Haans Seidel Foundation and the UNDP. He was recently invited to be an advisor to the Ministry of Planning in Pakistan. Professor Khalid is currently Head of Department (Economics and Statistics) at Bond University and Director of the Globalisation and Development Centre at Bond. He is also a member of the UK based International Growth Centre (Macro Research Cluster – Pakistan Chapter) and Director of Quality Assurance Program for Sur University College in Oman. Professor Khalid's research interests are in applied macroeconomics and monetary economics, applied econometrics, financial crisis and financial sector reforms with particular reference to emerging economies in East- and South-Asia and globalization and financial market integration. He is Associate Editor of *Singapore Economic Review* and a member of the editorial board of *South Asian Journal of Global Business Research*. His publications include four books (two edited) published by Edward Elgar Publishing, UK, internationally refereed articles, chapters in books and numerous consultancy/project reports, technical reports, working papers and conference papers.

Radhika Lahiri is a Senior Lecturer at the School of Economics and Finance, Queensland University of Technology. She received her PhD from the Southern Methodist University, Dallas in 1997 and has had academic appointments with the Southern Methodist University and the University of Western Australia. Prior to academia, Dr Lahiri held research positions with the National Institute of Public Finance and Policy and the National Council of Applied Economic Research in New Delhi. Her recent research projects have studied the impact of political economy implications of inequality, the link between inequality and growth, tax evasion and the political economy of spending on public goods. She has published in several international journals, including *Macroeconomic Dynamics*, *Economic Modelling*, *Southern Economic Journal*, *World Development*, *Topics in Macroeconomics* and *Economics Bulletin*, among others.

Emmanuel T. Laryea is a Senior Lecturer at the Faculty of Law, Monash University, Australia, and a Fellow at the Tim Fischer Centre for Global Trade and Finance, Bond University, Australia. He obtained his LLB from the University of Ghana (1992), his LLM from the University of Glasgow (1995), and his PhD from Bond University (2001). Emmanuel taught at the University of Ghana, Bond University and Lancaster University before joining Monash in 2001. His areas of teaching and research interests include contract law, international business law, international trade law, international banking and finance law, law of e-commerce and international investment law. He is the author of *Paperless trade: Opportunities, challenges and solutions* (Kluwer Law International, 2002), and several journal articles and book chapters. He has also practised law with a commercial law firm in Ghana. His research interests include international economic law, and law and African development. He is the author of several publications in these fields.

Shuanglin Lin is Professor of the National School of Development at Peking University, and Director of the China Centre for Public Finance at Peking University. He has also been Noddle Distinguished Professor of Economics at the University of Nebraska Omaha and Research Associate of the East Asian Institute at the National University of Singapore. He obtained his BA in Economics from Peking University, MA in Economics from Northwestern University, Illinois and PhD in Economics from Purdue University, Indiana. His research concentrates on public economics and China's public finance. He has published extensively in academic journals, including the *Journal of Economic Theory* and *Journal of Public Economics*. His policy articles have appeared in the *New York Times* and *China Daily*. He is Associate Editor of China Economic Quarterly. He serves as a columnist for the *People.com.cn* in China. He was President of the Chinese Economists Society 2002–03.

Vai Io Lo is Professor of Law at Bond University and a Co-Director of the Tim Fischer Centre for Global Trade and Finance. She received academic training in English literature, law, business administration and organizational behaviour. Prior to joining Bond, she held teaching or research appointments with the University of Washington, International University of Japan, Waseda University, National University of Singapore and the University of Tokyo. She has also been a Visiting Scholar to Harvard Law School and a Visiting Associate Professor to the University of Windsor in Canada. She has concentrating on comparative and interdisciplinary research, especially on Australian, Chinese, Japanese and US laws, and in the areas of labour and employment, foreign direct investment, health care, law and society, dispute resolution and legal education. Her publications, including books, journal articles, and book chapters, are distributed worldwide.

Anthony J. Makin is Professor of Economics at Griffith University, Gold Coast campus, Australia. Before joining Griffith, he was an International Consultant Economist with the IMF Institute, and previously taught at the University of Canberra and the University of Queensland. He represents Australia at meetings of the Pacific Economic Co-operation Council (PECC), is a member of AUSPECC, and has served in the federal departments of Finance, Foreign Affairs and Trade, The Treasury and Prime Minister and Cabinet. He holds undergraduate degrees in Arts and Economics and a PhD from the Australian National University, and has published widely on Australian and international macroeconomic policy issues. He is the author of *Global Finance and the Macroeconomy* and *Global Imbalances, Exchange Rates and Stabilization Policy*, and *International macroeconomics* and has published widely in economics journals, including *The World Economy, Journal of International Money and Finance, Economic Modelling, Contemporary Economic Policy, Applied Economics, The Economic Record*, and in many explicitly Asia focused journals, including, *Asian Survey* and *China and World Economy*.

H.E. Mr Biren Nanda joined the Indian Foreign Service in 1978 on completion of his postgraduate degree in Economics from the Delhi School of Economics. Mr Nanda has previously served as a diplomat in Indian Missions in Singapore, Beijing, Shanghai, Washington, DC and Tokyo. He was the Consul General of India in Shanghai from 1996–2000, Deputy Chief of Mission in the Embassy of India in Tokyo from 2000–04 and Ambassador of India in the Republic of Indonesia from 2008–12. Prior to taking up his assignment in Jakarta, Mr Nanda was the Head of the Division in the Ministry of External Affairs, which looks after relations between India and countries of Southeast Asia and the Pacific. Since 26 April 2012 Mr Nanda has held the position of High Commissioner of the Republic of India to the Government of the Commonwealth of Australia.

Muruga Perumal Ramaswamy is an Associate Professor in the Faculty of Law, University of Macau. He graduated with a Bachelor of Law in Common Law from India and a Master of Law (LLM) in Labour and Maritime Law. He was a Research Fellow in International Law and subsequently qualified with an MPhil in International Law. His interdisciplinary research interest in law and business management prompted him to qualify with a Master of International Business Management from IIUM, Macau and Portuguese Catholic University. He completed his PhD from the Faculty of Law, University of Hong Kong in International Law,

E-Commerce and Informational Technology Laws. He was a Research Fellow at The Hague Academy of International law, Netherlands and specialized in International Trade Law at the University Institute of European Studies in Turin, Italy. He studied American Constitutional Law at Yale University in New Haven, Connecticut and taught comparative constitutional law in Macau. He has been Secretary of the International Law Association in Hong Kong and a member of the ILA Committee on International Trade Law for many years. He is a member of several other international legal institutions in the UK and the US. His research interests are in the fields of international law, trade and investment laws, international sales and e-commerce laws. In trade law, he holds a specific interest in inter-regional trade involving emerging markets and is currently the principal investigator of a research project focusing on BRIC trade cooperation.

Shyama Ratnasiri is a Lecturer in the Department of Accounting, Finance and Economics, Griffith Business School, Griffith University. She earned her PhD from the Queensland University of Technology, Australia in 2009, for which she received the Outstanding Doctoral Thesis award for her PhD thesis on economic growth, inequality and technology adoption. She obtained her BSc and MSc degrees from University of Peradeniya, Sri Lanka. Her current research themes involve macroeconomic issues such as technology adoption, economic growth, inequality, financial development and food security. She also works in the area of microeconomic issues such as food consumption patterns and demand for water. She has published in international refereed journals including *Southern Economic Journal* and *Economic Modelling*.

Muthucumaraswamy Sornarajah LL B (Ceylon) LLM (Yale) LLM, PhD, LLD (London) is CJ Koh Professor of Law at the National University of Singapore. He is Visiting Professor at the Centre for the Study of Human Rights at thc London School of Economics. He was previously Tunku Abdul Rahman Professor of Public International Law at the University of Malaya, Kuala Lumpur and Head of the Law School of the University of Tasmania, Australia. He is the author of *International law on foreign investment* (Cambridge University Press, 3rd Edition, 2010) and several other books.

Mark Thirlwell is Chief Economist at Austrade (the Australian Trade Commission). Prior to joining Austrade he was the Director of the International Economy Program at Lowy Institute for International Policy and a Fellow at the Institute's G20 Studies Centre. He is also a Visiting Fellow at the National Security College at the Australian National

University. Mark has been tracking global economic trends since he joined the Bank of England's International Divisions in 1990 where he worked as part of the Whitehall Economists Subgroup, coordinating the forecasting of major emerging markets across the Bank, Treasury, the Foreign and Commonwealth Office, and other stakeholders. Mark subsequently joined JP Morgan as a Vice President in Economic Research with responsibility for Central Europe. Before joining Lowy, he served as Senior Economist at Australia's Export Finance and Insurance Corporation, working on sovereign risk with a particular focus on East Asia. Mark has degrees in Economics from Cambridge and Oxford Universities, UK and a post-graduate qualification in Applied Finance from Macquarie University.

Michael Thomas has a Bachelor of Arts/Bachelor of Asia Pacific Studies and a Masters of International Affairs from the Australian National University. His academic interests include international relations theory, historical and strategic dynamics in northeast Asia and Japanese foreign policy. He recently completed an internship at the Australian Institute of International Affairs.

Abbreviations

ANC	African National Congress
APEC	Asia-Pacific Economic Cooperation
ASEAN	Association of Southeast Asian Nations
AU	African Union
BASIC	Brazil, South Africa, India and China
BIT	Bilateral Investment Treaty
CAMEX	Chamber of Foreign Trade (Brazil)
CIS	Commonwealth of Independent States
CMs	Contingency Measures
COMESA	Common Market for Eastern and Southern Africa
DSB	Dispute Settlement Body
EITI	Extractive Industry Transparency Initiative
EMEs	Emerging market economies
FDI	Foreign Direct Investment
FSSBG	G20's Framework for Strong, Sustainable and Balanced Growth
FTA	Free Trade Agreement
FTT	Financial Transactions Tax
GAPP	Generally Accepted Principles and Practices of Sovereign Wealth Funds
GATS	General Agreement on Trade in Services
GATT	General Agreement on Tariffs and Trade
GCC	Gulf Cooperating Council
GDPPC	Annual per capita economic growth based on GDP
GES	Growth Environment Scores
GFC	Global Financial Crisis
HYVs	High Yielding Varieties
IBSA	India, Brazil and South Africa
ICSID	International Centre for Settlement of Investment Disputes
IIAs	International Investment Agreements
IOSCO	International Organisation of Securities Commission
IPFSD	Investment Policy Framework for Sustainable Development

IWG	International Working Group on Sovereign Wealth Funds
LIC	Low Income Countries
LTOGGDP	Openness variable
MES	Market Economy Status
MFN	Most-favoured-nation
NAFTA	North Atlantic Free Trade Agreement
NATO	North Atlantic Treaty Organization
NEPAD	New Partnership for Africa's Development
NIC	New Industrialised Countries
NIEO	New International Economic Order
OCA	Optimum Currency Area
OECD	Organisation for Economic Co-operation and Development
PCA	Principal Components Analysis
PP	Phillip-Peron Test of Stationarity
PPP	Purchasing Power Parity
PSNR	Permanent Sovereignty of States Over their Natural Resources
R&D	Research and Development
R2P	Responsibility to Protect
RBI	Reserve Bank of India
RSA	Republic of South Africa
S&T	Science and technology
SACU	Southern African Customs Union
SADC	Southern African Development Community
SAFTA	South Asian Free Trade Area
SASAC	State-Owned Assets Supervision and Administration Commission
SCO	Shanghai Cooperation Organisation
SECEX	Secretariat of Foreign Trade (Brazil)
SMEs	Small and medium-sized enterprises
SOEs	State owned enterprises
SWFs	Sovereign Wealth Funds
TAI	Technology Adoption Index
TNCs	Transnational Corporations
TPP	Trans-Pacific Partnership Agreement
TRIPS	Trade-Related Intellectual Property Rights Agreement
UNCITRAL	United Nations Commission on International Trade Law
UNCTAD	United Nations Conference on Trade and Development
UNFCCC	UN Framework Convention on Climate Change
WTO	World Trade Organization

Preface

On 10–11 August 2012, an international and interdisciplinary conference on 'The Rise of the BRICS: Changing Paradigms for the Global Political Economy?' was held on the Gold Coast, Australia. This conference was hosted by the Tim Fischer Centre for Global Trade and Finance and co-sponsored by the Commercial Law Centre, both of which are housed in the Faculty of Law of Bond University. Participants from various parts of the world conducted thought-provoking discussions over a wide range of issues, including economics, finance, trade, investment, international relations, foreign policy, development, sustainability, inclusion and exclusion. This book continues and expands the discussions by inviting the conference presenters, and two other academics and one lawyer who have an interest in the BRICS to make contributions. Accordingly this book contains rich contents, analysing and assessing the rise of the BRICS from diverse perspectives. Account has been taken of post-conference developments to 30 April 2013.

Preparing for the conference and editing the proceedings has been a joint effort. The planning committee consisted of Associate Professor Vai Io Lo as Chair, Professors John Farrar, Laurence Boulle and Mary Hiscock, and Dr Umair Ghori. The committee was strongly supported by the Faculty of Law and the Faculty Events Officer, Mairead Courtney. Vai and Mary have edited the proceedings with the editorial assistance of Tonya Roberts and Courtney Olden.

This book would not have come into existence without the collaborative efforts of the contributors. Hence we would like to express our sincere appreciation to everyone in this professional team. Last, but not least, we would like to thank our publisher, Edward Elgar, for turning the manuscript into this book. It is hoped that the book will generate further research interest into the implications of the rise of the BRICS on the global political economy.

Vai Io Lo and Mary Hiscock
Gold Coast, Australia
April 2013

Introduction

Vai Io Lo and Mary Hiscock

The world has been dominated by the West since the eighteenth century, with the empires of the UK, France, Germany, Portugal and the Netherlands dividing up the resources of Asia amongst themselves. The genesis and continuation of such an imbalance in the world order is an intricate account of the economic, historical, political and social developments within individual countries or regions and between countries or regions. Even so a sketch of the global politico-economic history in the past two hundred years can put things into perspective.

In the nineteenth century, owing to scientific and technological advances and the consequential military might, as well as economic prosperity resulting from industrialization, European countries were able to secure resources (such as tea, coffee and timber), open foreign markets (such as those in East Asia) and proselytize the Christian faith through colonization and warfare. The first half of the twentieth century was afflicted with wars. The two World Wars reduced the political hegemony of European countries as they were left with devastated economies, while the US emerged as a super power as a result of its recovery from the Great Depression, late participation in the Second World War and possession of atomic weapons. At the same time, some existing countries were plagued with civil wars (such as China and Korea); while newly independent or emergent countries were left with empty coffers and a group of inexperienced and inefficient low-level bureaucrats. The ensuing Cold War cumulated in a bipolar world with the US and the Soviet Union as the leaders of their respective groups predicated on the ideological divide between capitalism and socialism.

During the 1990s, the ultimate destruction of the Berlin Wall and the collapse of the Eastern Bloc ushered in an era of US dominance. The corollary of US dominance is the acclamation of neo-liberalism (economics), democracy (politics) and the rule of law (jurisprudence). Although the newly industrialized economies in Asia, such as Taiwan, Singapore and South Korea, had impressive economic growth under state-led industrial policies, they were not able to posit a challenge to the US-dominated world order either individually or collectively. Nonetheless, in recent years the Global Financial Crisis (GFC) and the European Sovereign Debt Crisis have cast doubt on the efficacy of neo-liberalism. Meanwhile the BRICS (Brazil, Russia, India, China and South Africa), a bloc of countries which span four continents and have recorded impressive economic growth, has emerged as a powerful group and caused developing countries to wonder whether development models other than the Washington Consensus espoused by the IMF and the World Bank should be adopted.

Against such a background, this book examines the BRICS retrospectively (what factors have contributed to the economic growth of the individual BRICS countries and what forces have driven the 'formation' or grouping of the BRICS), presently (what economic or political conditions the BRICS as a group or the individual BRICS countries have and what kinds of intra-BRICS relations, trade and investment are in progress), and prospectively (whether the BRICS countries will coalesce and expand into a powerful economic and/or political bloc). Although the rise of the BRICS has generated numerous issues, this book focuses only on such areas as economics, finance, trade, investment, international relations, foreign policy, development, exclusion and inclusion. Specifically, this book consists of the following chapters.

In an overview, H.E. Mr Biren Nanda traces the historical developments of the BRICS, highlights the differences, commonalities and complementarities of the BRICS countries, and heightens the potential role of the BRICS in representing developing countries and in tackling the challenges facing the world (Chapter 1). Based on macroeconomic indicators, Makin and Arora outline the economic performance of the BRICS as a group, and at the same time underscore the major differences within the group (Chapter 2).

Looking at the individual BRICS members, Lin, Lahiri and Ratnasiri, and Dos Santos examine the economic developments of China, India and Brazil, respectively. Lin illustrates the impact of tax, government spending and government debt policies on China's economic growth and argues that China's future growth hinges on investment in local infrastructure, investment in private enterprises, human capital and technological progress (Chapter 3). Lahiri and Ratnasiri explain that India has not followed exactly the classical model of economic development – a sequence of growth patterns in the economic sectors of agriculture, manufacturing and services – and underline the correlation between technology adoption and productivity (Chapter 4). Dos Santos depicts the unprecedented economic growth of Brazil, but also points out that Brazil's foreign trade and Mercosur membership may become obstacles to the conclusion of a BRICS Free Trade Agreement (Chapter 5). In the case of Brazil, Ramaswamy also argues that despite the rosy picture of trade between Brazil and China, the Brazilian antidumping law and practice and the antidumping actions taken by Brazil against China will result in trade friction (Chapter 6).

As South Africa joined the BRIC group only in 2010, Boulle and Chella analyse the promises and challenges of its inclusion, while Laryea examines the impact of the BRIC on African countries. Boulle and Chella investigate the reasons for South Africa to join the group, outline the benefits to South Africa upon becoming a member of the group, but argue that South Africa is only a limited player in this transgovernmental network, which lacks the necessary administrative infrastructure to become a powerful bloc (Chapter 7). Laryea explores the benefits (such as the unleashing of African entrepreneurship) and pitfalls for the BRIC countries to engage with Africa (such as slowing the progress of governance reform in African economies) (Chapter 8).

With respect to the BRICS vis-à-vis the non-BRICS blocs or countries, Farrar and Ariff draw attention to two specific issues, namely, state capitalism and institutional investment. They highlight the sources of discord among the BRICS members, compare the BRICS with the EU and the US, and raise the issue of the BRICS' relationship with the non-BRICS countries (Chapter 9). Khalid compares and contrasts the economic performances of the BRICS countries, argues that the BRICS is only a 'trade bloc' due to diversities among its members, and suggests that the BRICS should open its membership to other Asian countries (Chapter 10). Ghori argues that the BRICS can be a trade and investment hub and advocates an inclusive Free Trade Agreement model, under which proximate countries who are ready suppliers of manufacturing inputs may obtain spillover benefits (Chapter 11). From her background as a mining engineer, Karimova explores whether the BRICS can serve as a model for living on the earth (Chapter 12).

On the political side, Fortescue discusses the two possible motives – the 'great power diplomacy' versus the 'new diplomacy' – for Russia to step out of its comfort zone to actively engage the other BRICS countries, and argues that the weaknesses of the BRICS are also its strengths amid the drive towards a multipolar world (Chapter 13). In assessing the impact of the BRICS, Thirlwell maintains that although the rise of the BRICS has posed new challenges for global economic governance by creating a period of 'multipolarity without multilateralism', the diffusion of economic power in the world economy has not yet resulted in innovations in global economic governance (Chapter 14). Tyler and Thomas present the common arguments for and against the rise of the BRICS and conclude that the BRICS countries just want to be included, but not to topple the existing international system (Chapter 15).

As regards law and development, Lo explains that law has played a significant role in China's economic development by providing the necessary regulatory framework for economic activities, and that China has chosen to chart its own course of development in light of its national circumstances by selectively and incrementally experimenting with reform initiatives, rather than adhering to every tenet of the Washington-based approaches (Chapter 16). On the other hand Sornarajah argues that international law has been used by the hegemonic US to achieve its ideological preferences, but the rise of the BRICS will lead to a new multipolar world order, which will, in turn, effect changes in international law (Chapter 17).

Given the differences, commonalities, complementarities and thus possible synergies between the BRICS countries, but in the absence of an institutional framework and a well-defined collective purpose, the concluding chapter explores the central question of whether the BRICS is a loosely formed intergovernmental network, a pressure group to raise awareness of the imperfections resulting from an unbalanced world order, or a powerful economic bloc that can effect paradigmatic changes in the global political economy.

1. The BRICS: An Indian perspective

H.E. Mr Biren Nanda

In 2001, a study by Goldman Sachs predicted that the BRICs would emerge as a major economic force by 2050. In just over a decade that grouping has been institutionalized and enlarged. By bringing in South Africa into the grouping at its third Summit, the BRICs leaders not only expanded their reach to all the continents barring North America, but have also added the strength of a nation of 50 million people with abundant natural resources and a growing economy. Within a short period of time the BRICS has come to acquire a powerful voice in the conduct of international relations.

The role of the BRICS came into prominence as a driver of growth, at a time when the world was trying to cope with the global economic crisis. The BRICS agenda and approach was primarily economic. The BRICS countries sought a reform of global economic governance and developed an agenda of cooperation and interaction amongst themselves. The goal was to build upon the complementarities of their economies and to enhance their influence.

Developments in West Asia and North Africa with their global implications have brought a political dimension into the BRICS agenda. The Delhi Summit delivered a clear statement of the BRICS' positions on Syria, Iran and Afghanistan.

The BRICS has projected itself as an independent grouping in a fast changing world. The BRICS process is relatively new and its forums and formats are still evolving. A number of cooperation mechanisms have been developed, including the Action Plan and meetings of Foreign, Finance and Trade Ministers as well as Central Bank Governors.

The global situation facing us today presents a mixed picture. On the one hand, emerging market economies are growing at a healthy pace and increasing their share in global trade and output. On the other hand, many obstacles have to be overcome if we are to sustain rapid growth in the years ahead.

The BRICS countries have all been affected by the global economic slowdown, the volatility in food and energy prices, the challenge of reconciling growth with environmental objectives, the political uncertainty in West Asia and the rise of terrorism and extremism. Their responses to these challenges may be different, but there is much common interest that binds them all together. There are ten specific issues which are of concern to all BRICS countries. These include:

1. Their unique demographic profiles, each presenting its own challenges of labour and job opportunities.
2. The supply side constraints of the BRICS narrative of catch up growth, notably energy, water and food.[1]
3. The measures for sustained and balanced growth, including reviving progress in the Doha Round.
4. Maximizing the benefits from intra-BRICS complementarities through greater business interaction.
5. Access to capital, especially for infrastructure development.
6. Addressing deficiencies in global governance to reflect contemporary realities.
7. Green growth and sustainable development.
8. Dealing with growing income inequalities.
9. The challenges of urbanization.
10. The geopolitical environment that impacts global energy markets and trade flows, and the concerns of terrorism and piracy.

The BRICS countries are brought together by their shared capacity and will to engage with each other, as well as with the rest of the world, in the global quest for meaningful, sustainable solutions to contemporary challenges.

The original economic rationale put forward by Goldman Sachs in 2001 was the potential of these four countries – Brazil, Russia, India and China – to be drivers of global growth. Members of the BRICS, with a population of 3 billion, are fast growing economies and roughly account for a quarter of the world GDP. Today intra-BRICS trade is growing at an annual average of 28 per cent and currently stands at about $230 billion. Intra-BRICS investment flows – drawing from the complementarities in their economies – are increasing. Consumer expenditure in the BRICS countries as a percentage of GDP, ranges from 35–61 per cent, and there is a strong and growing middle class with rising levels of income.

The BRICS countries today present an opportunity as new growth drivers in a multipolar world. The BRICS agenda is not a fixed one. It is a positive, forward-looking agenda that tends to reflect the main issues and challenges before the world community at a given point in time. It draws from the perspective of five major countries and economies with the capacities to contribute substantively to the global discourse for peace, security, stability and development for all. It is a perspective that seeks practical solutions and ways forward for global growth, through cooperation and policy coordination.

It seeks political dialogue towards a more democratic multipolar order, in a world that is undergoing major and swift changes that highlight the need for corresponding transformations in global governance. It works on the principle of consensus.

At the first two Summits the agenda focused mainly on the international financial and economic situation and reform of the international financial institutions. The central role of the G20 and the role that the BRICS could play in this apex body were considered and emphasized. The reform of the global political and economic governance architecture, to meet the interests and developmental needs of emerging market economies and developing countries, was discussed. There was a special focus on the interests of the poor and towards building a harmonious world of lasting peace and common prosperity.

The Sanya Summit took a major step forward when a framework agreement was signed, which enabled financial cooperation by facilitating grant of credit in local currencies. The agreement allowed use of local currencies for cooperation in capital markets and other financial services. It was of crucial significance as it would help to lay the foundation of any future international financial architecture. This was the first concrete step to move away from the dollar-dominated global financial system.

The Summit took note of the excessive volatility in commodity prices and called for strengthening cooperation, to ensure stability by reducing distortion and further regulating financial markets. The Summit stressed the need to address the problem of a shortage of reliable and timely information on demand and supply, at the international, regional and national levels. The statement issued at the Summit said (BRICS, 2011, para. 17): 'The international community should work together to increase production capacity, strengthen producer–consumer dialogue to balance supply and demand, and increase support to the developing countries in terms of funding and technologies.' And also that: 'The regulation of the derivatives market for commodities should be accordingly strengthened to prevent activities capable of destabilizing markets.'

The BRICS leaders called for a quick achievement of the targets for the reform of the IMF, agreed at previous G20 Summits, and reiterated that the governing structures of the international financial institutions should reflect the changes in the world economy, that is, increasing the voice and representation of emerging economies and developing countries.

In the area of energy security, the Summit decided to deepen cooperation within the grouping and reiterated faith in nuclear energy, saying that nuclear energy would continue to be an important element in the future energy mix of the BRICS countries. The grouping also recognized the important role of renewable energy as a means to address climate change.

Health was identified as an area for cooperation, and a meeting of the Ministers of Health was held in China later that year. The grouping also promised to closely cooperate on food security issues. Leaders took note of the challenge to accelerate sustainable growth in developing countries.

The eradication of extreme poverty and hunger was recognized as a moral, social, political and economic imperative, and one of the greatest global challenges facing the world today.

The fourth Summit in Delhi was an attempt to define the role of the BRICS platform, in articulating issues of concern to the developing world and to demonstrate the capacities of the BRICS in dealing with issues of global peace, stability and development.

The Delhi Summit took place at a time when the world was grappling with the challenges of ensuring a sustained recovery from the global slowdown in an environment complicated by developments in the Euro Area. The Summit followed the Durban Conference on Climate Change last December, and preceded another important UN Conference on Sustainable Development (Rio+20) in June, and the Conference of Parties to the Convention on Biological Diversity in October. The three conferences on interconnected themes were all hosted by BRICS members.

On the political side, the BRICS were witnessing fast moving important developments in West Asia, with far-reaching implications for the region and for the world. The leaders at the Delhi Summit therefore had before them a rich and ambitious agenda, and they focused their attention on addressing these and other contemporary issues. There were also the varied concerns for sustained and balanced development. These concerns included food and energy security and inclusive growth[2] which remain the primary objectives of the BRICS to meet the poverty eradication objective of much of the developing world.

In addition to regular meetings of Foreign Ministers and Finance Ministers, a number of cooperation forums and mechanisms have been developed for deepening intra-BRICS cooperation. These include meetings of the BRICS Trade and Economic Ministers, Agriculture Ministers, Health Ministers, senior officials on science and technology (S&T), and a Contact Group on Economic and Trade Issues. These are areas where synergies of BRICS technological and human capacities can serve the cause of our peoples and those of much of the developing world.

To promote a sense of the BRICS process and the diversity of its activities, what follows is a broad outline of Summit-related meetings in the run-up to the Delhi Summit held earlier in 2012.

In chronological order:

1. The **BRICS Statistical Authorities** met to update the BRICS Statistical Publication for release at the Summit.
2. **Development Banks of the BRICS members** held a technical expert level meeting to finalize the texts of two agreements; the Master Agreement for Extending Credit Facilities in Local Currencies, and the BRICS Multilateral Letter of Credit Confirmation Facility Agreement, which were both signed at the Summit.
3. A number of **BRICS Forums** serve as academic think tanks whose recommendations also feed into the Summit's deliberations. They include two track-II groups, namely the **BRICS Economic Research Group (ERG)**, which brings together economic think tanks as well as economic editors of BRICS countries, and the **BRICS Academic Forum**. The Academic Forum has come up with a number of innovative suggestions, such as:

    a. the creation of a virtual academic community for dissemination of information and ideas,
    b. working together to create an identifiable brand value of the BRICS, and
    c. cooperative action on biodiversity issues in the BRICS.

4. The **BRICS Contact Group on Trade and Economic Issues** met to discuss and consider intergovernmental cooperation in the furtherance of global and intra-BRICS trade.
5. The Trade Ministers also opened the proceedings of the **Business Forum**. The Forum was where business delegations and apex business bodies from the five participating countries were involved in a series of sessions on such themes as enhancing financial connectivity for increasing trade and investment, the role of BRICS countries in ensuring global food security, cooperation for energy security with a focus on green and renewable energy and the role of information and communications technology (ICT) and innovation in improving business among the BRICS members.
6. The **BRICS Financial Forum** brought together Export-Import and Development Banks of the five countries. Its primary focus was on the intra-BRICS Interbank Cooperation Mechanism.

The Delhi Summit also saw the release of the BRICS Report focusing on synergies and complementarities of the grouping. The BRICS leaders had agreed at their second Summit in Brasilia to Prime Minister Dr Manmohan Singh's proposal, that is, to research and produce a compendium on the economies of the BRICS countries, and the synergies and complementarities amongst them that could be put to use. This report – the result of detailed research over two years by a multinational group of economists and experts under the supervision of Dr Kaushik Basu, Chief Economic Advisor to the Indian Finance Minister – was released at the Summit.

It was a unique coincidence that in 2011 all the BRICS countries were also members of the United Nations Security Council. They therefore agreed to intensify their consultations to address the major economic and political challenges facing the world. An important objective remained the reform of institutions of global governance to make them truly representative of contemporary realities.

In a short span of two years since the first Summit in 2009, the BRICS has travelled a long distance. The quality and durability of the global economic recovery process depends to a great extent on how the BRICS member economies perform. The BRICS has reason to be satisfied with the management of its member economies, but there is no room for complacency. The developments in West Asia and North Africa, and the aftermath of the huge natural and nuclear tragedies that befell Japan in 2011 have introduced fresh uncertainties in the global recovery process. At the same time, the world continues to grapple with threats to security from terrorism and piracy.

NOTES

1. 'Narrative of catch up growth' defines the process by which the BRICS nations are growing rapidly and trying to catch up with the income levels of the developed economies. Energy, water and food are supply side constraints or the factors of production in limited supply. The BRICS economies cannot continue to grow unless the supply of these factors of production is augmented in keeping with their resource requirements or the intensity of use of these factors of production or inputs is reduced.
2. Ensuring benefits of economic growth and development to all sections of society, including the poor and the underprivileged.

REFERENCES

BRICS (2011, April 14). *Sanya declaration.* Retrieved from http://www.brics.utoronto.ca/docs/110414-leaders.html

2. How solid are the BRICS? An economic overview

Anthony J. Makin and Rashmi Umesh Arora

Over the last few decades the metamorphosis of many developing economies into emerging economies has significantly boosted global economic output, raised income levels and enabled hundreds of millions of people to escape poverty around the world. The BRICs, an acronym coined by Goldman Sachs economist Jim O'Neill in 2001, originally grouped Brazil, Russia, India and China together on the grounds that they were the most prominent subset of fast growing emerging economies. South Africa joined the group in 2011, turning BRICs into BRICS.

Although they are drawn from four different continents and have alternative systems of government, the BRICS members were combined on the grounds that they were populous emerging economies whose living standards, measured on an income per capita basis, have grown quickly over past decades. As a result they have spawned sizeable middle classes and are each destined to become major players in the world economy by 2050, even though per capita incomes still fall considerably below OECD economy levels.

The BRICS accounts for roughly 40 per cent of the world's population and about 30 per cent of the world's GDP, and according to the IMF (2011) will contribute more than half of the world economy's growth in coming years. The BRICS, like all emerging economies, has generally benefited from the globalization phenomenon of the past few decades, as manifested in increased international trade flows and higher levels of foreign direct investment affecting all parts of the world.

The BRICS economies have proven quite resilient to global shocks due to the flexibility of their product and factor markets and policy frameworks. Through increased trade and investment linkages, the BRICS have also increasingly become growth drivers of Low Income Countries (LIC) (IMF, 2011). Nevertheless the BRICS member growth rates have slowed since the North Atlantic banking and Euro Area public debt crises, especially in Brazil and India, due in part to lower spending on imports by the US and European economies, major sources of demand for the BRICS' exports.

Apart from having solid growth rates and sizeable populations, there are points of difference between the BRICS economies that make their somewhat arbitrary economic alliance all the more remarkable. For instance their economies are dissimilar in many respects and not necessarily highly complementary. China is manufacturing oriented, while India depends relatively more on services. Meanwhile Brazil, Russia and South Africa remain reliant on commodity production. China is the heaviest of the BRICS members, with a level of GDP that exceeds the combined total of all other members and is the world's second largest economy. China is also the world's largest manufacturer and exporter.

In what follows we focus on the salient economic characteristics of the BRICS and the main determinants of its success. However, it should be acknowledged at the outset that there is a degree of arbitrariness about the selection of these economies. Cases can easily be made for expanding the grouping to include a number of other sizeable, fast growing emerging economies. Most notably Indonesia should be included, making it BRIICS, a version of the acronym actually preferred by the OECD in its publications. Other emerging economies that could be considered are Turkey, Vietnam, Philippines and Nigeria.

The remainder of the chapter is structured as follows. The next section presents a brief summary of main macroeconomic characteristics of the BRICS, while the third section examines some of the major underlying reasons for their impressive economic performance. The final section concludes.

THE BRICS: KEY ECONOMIC CHARACTERISTICS

In this section we canvass the distinguishing macroeconomic features of the BRICS, highlighting population growth, production, savings and investment and unemployment.

Population

The population of the BRICS has grown by close to 30 per cent since 1990 (Figure 2.1).

However, population growth over the past two decades has differed greatly within the group. China (with over 1.3 billion people) and India (with over 1.2 billion) account for around 87 per cent of the combined population of the BRICS, now approaching 3 billion. Since 1990 India's population has grown 42 per cent, more than double China's rate of 18 per cent, reflecting the effect of China's one child policy over this time.

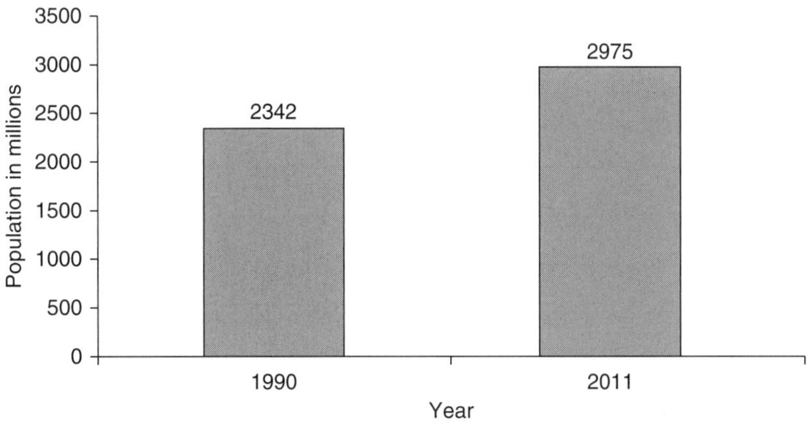

Source: World Bank Indicators and authors' calculations.

Figure 2.1 Combined population of the BRICS

This means India's population is much younger on average than China's, with important future implications for their relative productivity levels. Meanwhile Brazil's population has grown from 150 to 197 million and that of South Africa, the minnow of the group, from 35 to 51 million. Surprisingly, Russia's population has actually fallen over this time from 148 to 142 million.

The proportion of the population in the age group 65 and above in China is almost twice that of India's. Among other BRICS, Russia and Brazil also have rapidly ageing populations. Ageing populations have implications for economic growth due to the associated fall in savings, lower labour force participation and increased expenditure on health care and pensions. To the extent that, with government encouragement, older employees in these economies extend their working lives, thereby sustaining labour force participation rates, the impact of population ageing on economic growth will be less severe (Bloom, Canning & Fink, 2011). In contrast, labour force participation is expected to increase strongly in India and South Africa given their relatively younger populations. Figure 2.2 illustrates the demographic trends in the BRICS on a consolidated basis.

National Income Measures

The BRICS has steadily increased its share of total world output over the last few decades, as shown in Table 2.1. The data reveals that the relative

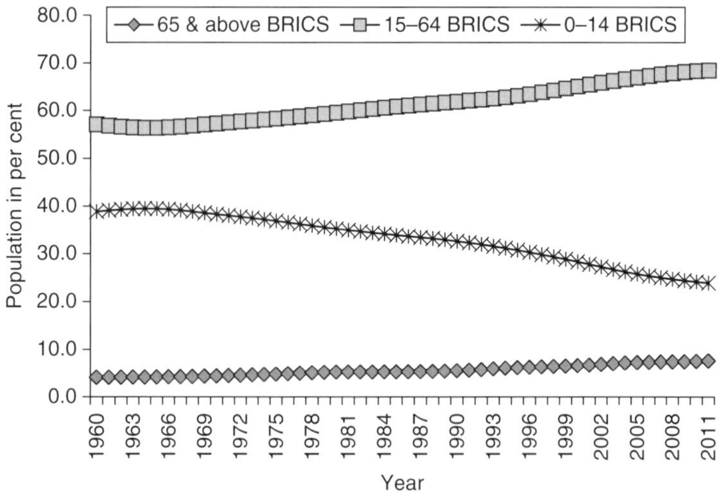

Source: World Bank Indicators.

Figure 2.2 Age structure of the BRICS

Table 2.1 Relative shares of world GDP

	1991–94	2000–04	2005–09	2018
BRICS	5.8	8.5	13.1	21.6
Other EMEs	10.6	10.8	13.3	15.4
United States	26.2	30.6	25.6	22.0
Euro Area	24.8	21.3	22.0	16.6

Source: IMF (2011).

shares of global GDP of the BRICS and other emerging market economies (EMEs) have grown strongly since the early 1990s, while the shares of the United States and the Euro Area of world output have correspondingly shrunk.

The volume of total output produced by the BRICS rose by some 3.6 times from 1990, due mostly to China's superior growth rate over this time, averaging around 9 per cent per annum (Figure 2.3). However, the make-up of GDP in each of the BRICS economies is quite different due to their dissimilar industry structures. For instance Brazil is rich in resources such as coffee, soybeans and sugarcane, Russia is endowed with sizeable energy resources, India has strengths in software development and services

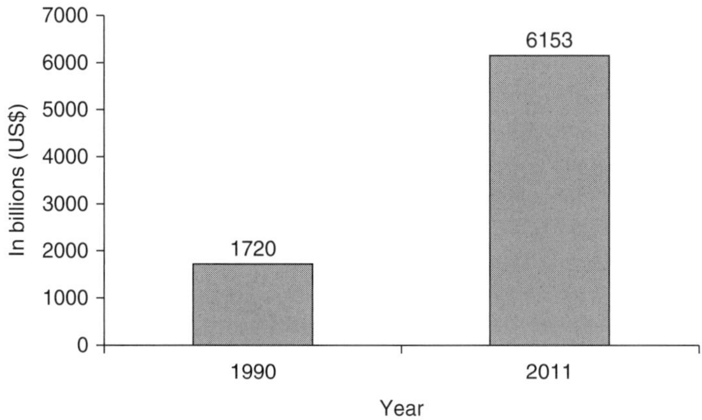

Source: World Bank Indicators and authors' calculations.

Figure 2.3 Combined real GDP of the BRICS

provision and China produces a wide range of manufactures for the rest of the world (BRICS, 2012).

Per capita incomes of BRICS rose from US$9808 in 1990 to US$14 580 in 2010, which is around a 50 per cent increase. Nevertheless per capita income levels within the group vary significantly. India is the outlier among the BRICS economies, with the lowest per capita income and with a significant portion of its population still poverty stricken. The average per capita income of the BRICS members (excluding India) was US$3448 in 2010 (Figure 2.4).

The divergence between the per capita incomes of the two most populous BRICS economies is especially noteworthy since they were at similar levels of development at the start of the 1990s (Figure 2.5). The gap between income per capita in China and India accelerated from the turn of the century, reflecting the combined effects of China's persistently higher economic growth and India's much faster population growth. Indian per capita income is presently only around a third of Chinese per capita income.

Consumption, Saving and Investment

The composition of domestic spending in the BRICS economies also varies significantly. Domestic consumption, the sum of household final consumption expenditure and general government consumption, predominates in Brazil, forming about 80 per cent of GDP with investment around

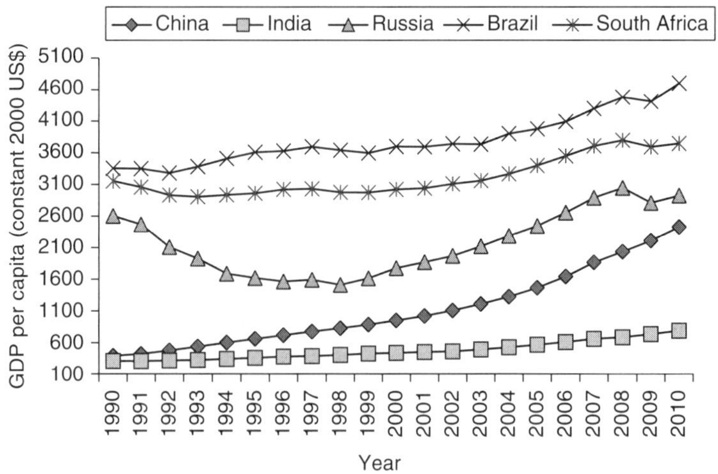

Source: World Bank Indicators.

Figure 2.4 Income per capita in the BRICS

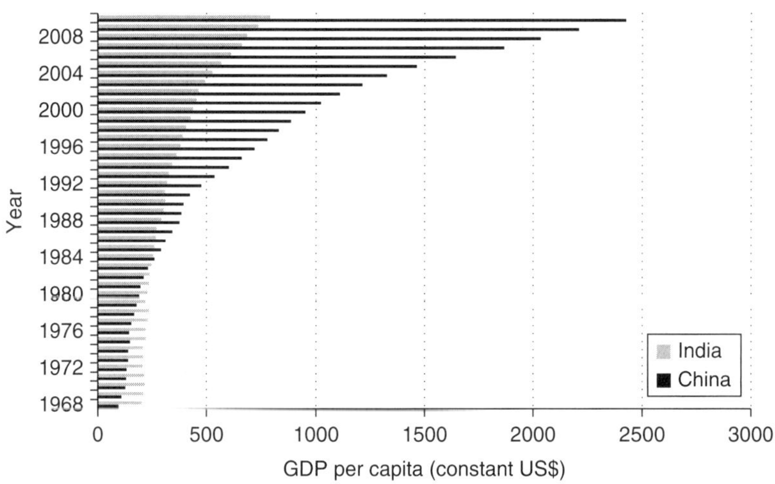

Source: World Bank Indicators.

Figure 2.5 The per capita income gap between China and India

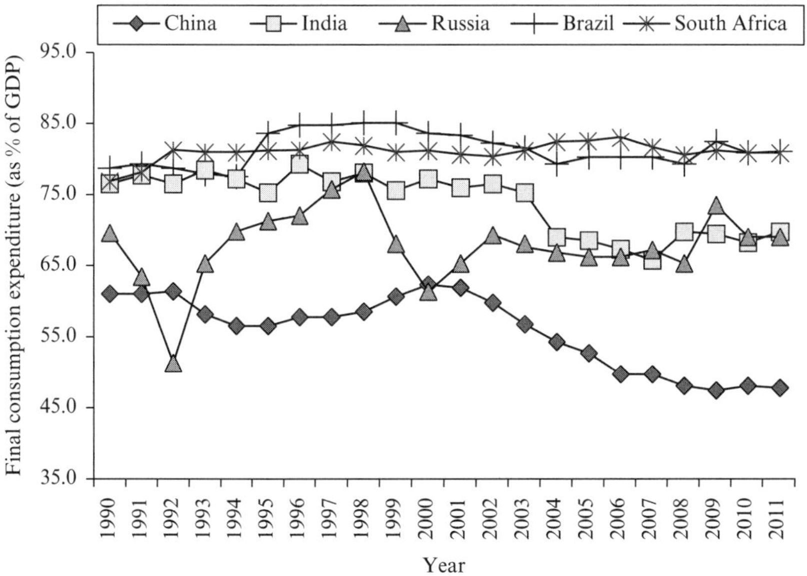

Source: World Bank Indicators.

Figure 2.6 Final consumption expenditure in the BRICS

20 per cent of GDP. In Russia and South Africa domestic consumption also significantly exceeds investment spending. The Chinese economy, on the contrary, is driven by investment financed by high domestic savings. There, household consumption is around 35 per cent, the lowest among the BRICS economies, implying that its savings rate is easily the highest in the group (Figure 2.6).

Employment and Unemployment

Among the BRICS members, the employment to population ratio is much higher in China compared to the other BRICS members. However, this will decline in coming years due to China's ageing population. Strategies proposed to address declining employment rates due to ageing include promotion of lifelong learning to maintain employability in later years and increasing labour force participation. In contrast to China, India's labour participation rate is expected to increase, with its young population expected to join the labour force in coming years, although the labour participation rate has fallen in India due to increased education enrolment by women in particular.

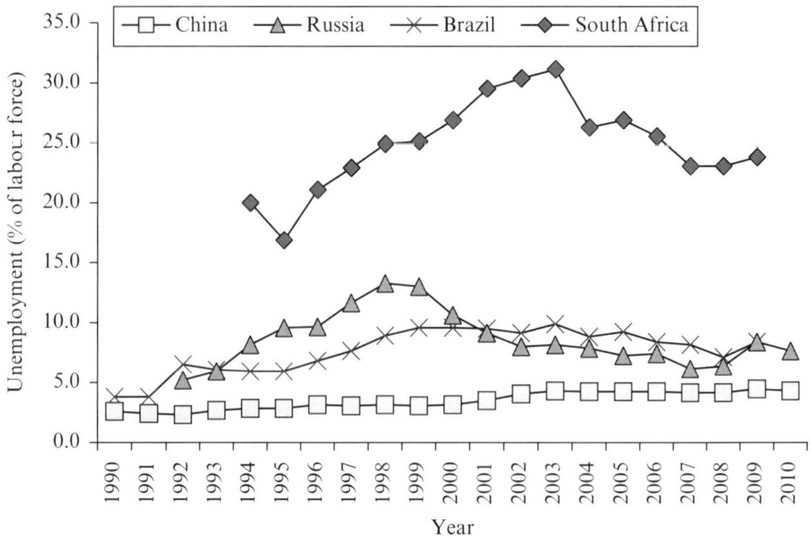

Note: Data for India was not available for all years.

Source: World Bank Indicators.

Figure 2.7 Unemployment in the BRICS

Unemployment rates also vary considerably across the BRICS members. Unemployment has been persistently lower in China than in other BRICS economies, and is especially high in South Africa, as shown in Figure 2.7.

UNDERLYING DETERMINANTS OF THE BRICS' GROWTH

Numerous factors account for the high economic growth rates experienced by the BRICS since 1990. The most notable are its low inflation, economic reforms, increased international trade and investment, increased labour mobility and entrepreneurship, foreign investment, and infrastructure spending.

Low Inflation Environment

Inflation rates fell dramatically around the world through the 1990s from the historically high inflation rates of the 1970s and 1980s. Indeed

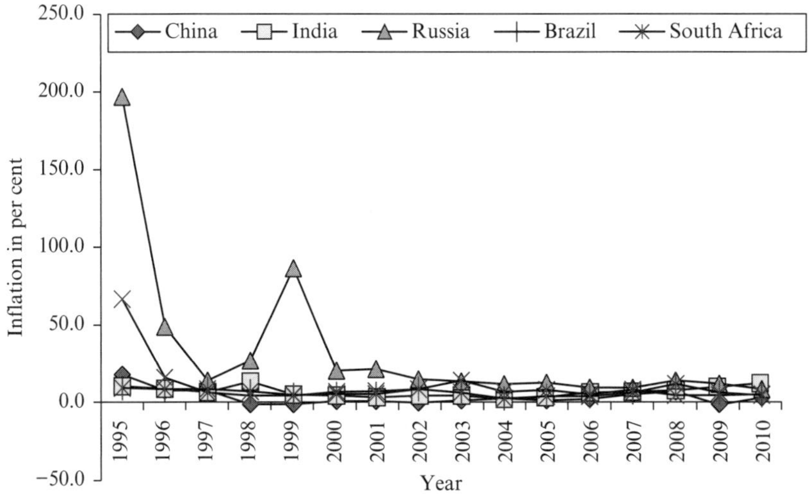

Source: World Bank Indicators.

Figure 2.8 Inflation in the BRICS

the worldwide fall in inflation to the relatively low levels experienced by the 1990s and early 2000s was one of the most remarkable global economic phenomena of the past half century, from which the advanced and emerging economies, including the BRICS, all benefited (Makin, 2009). Low inflation assists economic growth by reducing investment uncertainty and by eliminating the extra real costs that arise when relative price signals become difficult to discern and when resources are misallocated.

Rampant inflation had been a major problem for Brazil and Russia in particular before their economic growth rates accelerated. However, except for India, the BRICS economies have generally maintained low inflation since the early 1990s (Figure 2.8). Hence monetary policy in the BRICS has been pro-growth, but with price stability as a primary objective. Inflation targeting was introduced in Brazil in 1999 and has worked well to bolster consumer and investor confidence (Arestis, Ferrari-Filho & de Paula, 2011; Kamal, 2010). The South African Central Bank also formally adopted inflation targeting as the modus operandi for monetary policy in 2000 where it has also proved effective in anchoring expectations.

Economic Reforms

Major economic reform initiatives sparked economic growth in the BRICS and were mostly introduced in the 1990s, although the reform process had begun from the late 1970s in China under leader Deng Xiaoping. Numerous economic policy reforms in China contributed to its high rates of output and export growth. At the international level, the most important spur was the liberalization of trade barriers and integration with global merchandise markets. Although China acceded to the WTO in 2001, it had previously benefited from export growth at higher rates than experienced by Japan and South Korea during their take-off phases in the 1950s, 1960s and 1970s (Makin, 2007).

India's economic reforms date from 1991 with the abolition of licence raj and other stringent industrial regulations and high taxes and tariffs (Das, 2007). Entrepreneurship combined with low cost advantages enabled computer software, IT related services, pharmaceuticals and telecommunications to emerge as flourishing sectors of the Indian economy.

Reforms were introduced in Brazil in 1994 and the focus lately has been on educational reforms. Russia has introduced major economic reforms since then, which have spurred economic growth and reduced poverty. Major fiscal reforms have enhanced transparency in budget formulation, increased tax collections through better compliance, and improved the pension system (BRICS, 2012).

International Trade and Foreign Investment

Increased international trade and foreign investment in the BRICS has been central to its elevated growth rates since 1990. Over this time the shares of exports and imports have risen significantly as a proportion of their respective GDP levels, as shown in Table 2.2. At the same time other EMEs have also experienced rising export and import shares. However, the opposite has been true for the United States and the Euro Area.

Although China is usually recognized as export focused, Russia has also increased its exports to GDP ratio, as has India. On the other hand other BRICS economies such as Brazil and South Africa noted smaller increases in exports during this period. Figures 2.9 and 2.10 show trends in exports and imports respectively, as a percentage of GDP for the years 1990 and 2010.

Foreign Direct Investment

Foreign direct investment inflows to the BRICS economies have also been relatively high since 1990, particularly into China, as Figure 2.11

Table 2.2 Relative export and import shares as a percentage of GDP

	1991–94	2000–04	2005–09	2018
Exports				
BRICs	4.2	7.9	12.4	20.1
Other EMEs	13.0	15.8	18.6	18.3
United States	13.3	12.0	9.7	9.6
Euro Area	34.7	30.9	29.1	23.0
Imports				
BRICs	4.0	7.0	10.5	18.8
Other EMEs	14.4	14.8	17.2	18.0
United States	14.6	17.1	14.1	12.3
Euro Area	34.0	29.5	28.5	21.9

Source: IMF (2011).

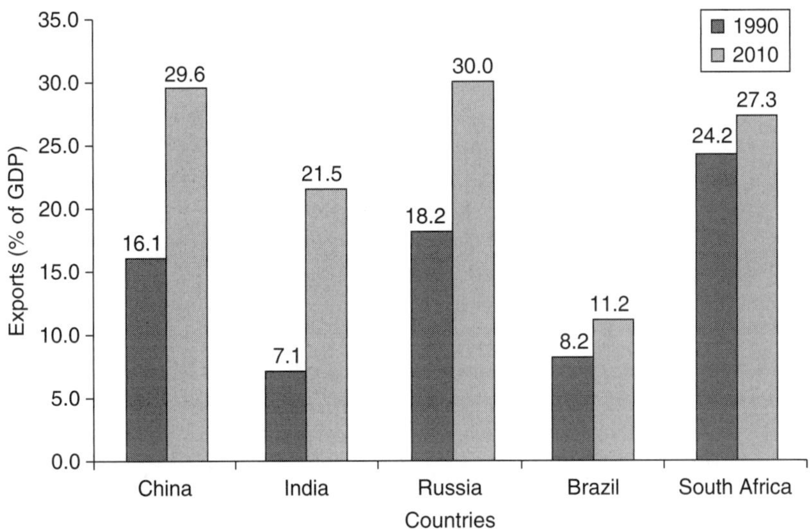

Source: World Bank Indicators.

Figure 2.9 The BRICS' exports to GDP

reveals. This foreign direct investment has conferred productivity gains on the BRICS economies via technology transfer, international management practices and product development, and spurred greater domestic competition and imitative behaviour by existing locally owned firms. As

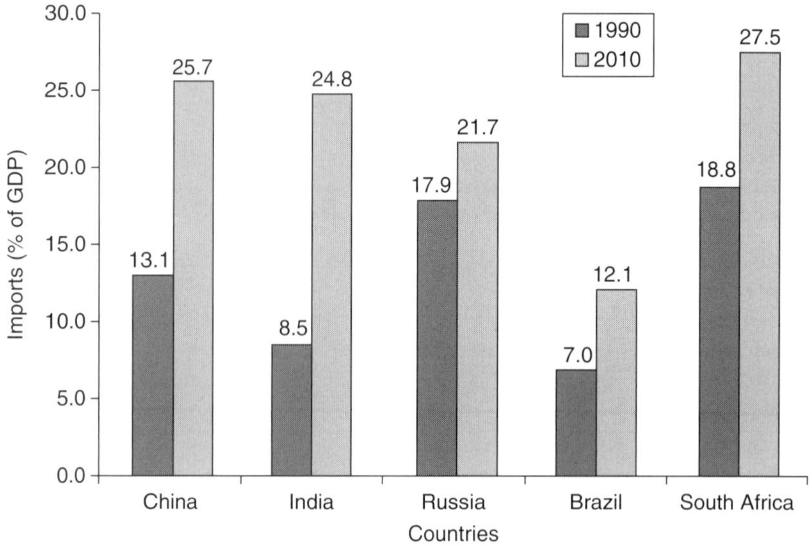

Source: World Bank Indicators.

Figure 2.10 The BRICS' imports to GDP

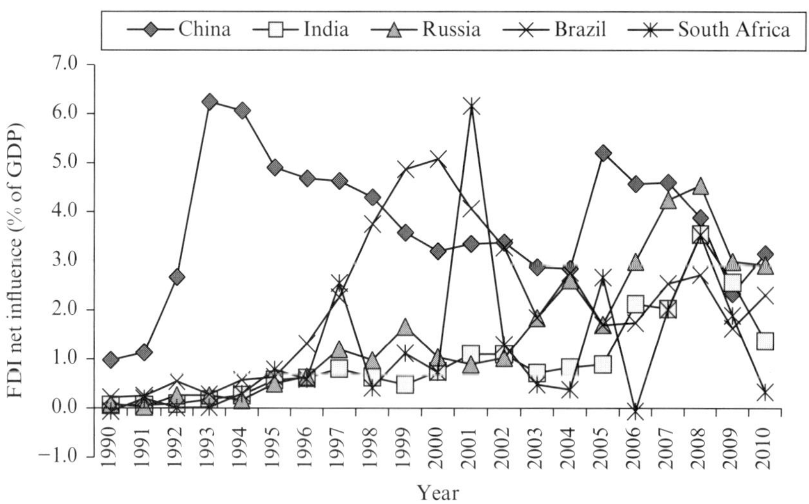

Source: World Bank Indicators.

Figure 2.11 Foreign direct investment in the BRICS

domestic firms have grown, outward foreign direct investment from the BRICS has also increased.

Increased Labour Mobility and Entrepreneurship

Another major factor, although again not unique to the BRICS amongst the emerging economies, has been increased mobility of workers and the upgrading of labour skills through improved education and training. Inter-sectoral or occupational, inter-regional and international labour mobility have all generally increased in the BRICS relative to the 1980s. Inter-regional labour mobility in China is partly restricted by the *Hukou* system, although there has been some relaxation since then (Meng, 2012). In India, where only 30 per cent of the population is urbanized, the movement of workers from rural to urban areas has been considerably lower than in China.

The rise of entrepreneurship has been another factor driving economic growth in the BRICS, fostering higher investment and employment and creating greater product choice for consumers (see Audretsch, Keilbach & Lehmann, 2006; Ghani, Kerr & O'Connell, 2012; and van Praag & Versloot, 2007 for related discussion). At the same time there has been extensive reform of what were once strictly government owned and operated enterprises, most notably in China's broad-based manufacturing sector. Meanwhile, Indian entrepreneurship through innovation and improvisation of existing technology with low cost advantages was particularly evident in computer software, IT related services, pharmaceuticals and telecommunications (Ghani et al., 2012).

Infrastructure Spending

The governments of the BRICS economies have also spent very heavily on physical and social infrastructure, building roads, ports, railways, electricity and telecommunications facilities, while simultaneously improving basic education systems. Efficient infrastructure has proven important to maintaining international competitiveness and for participating in, and reaping the rewards of, globalization.

Modern telecommunications infrastructure in particular has been essential to facilitating transactions across and between the BRICS economies and with the rest of the world. This is because economic transactions between resident and foreign firms, and between consumers and governments, increasingly occur via electronic means, especially in knowledge-based and technology driven industries, and the services sector. Meanwhile traditional infrastructure spending on ports, airports, highways, roads and rail has grown at much faster rates than experienced over the past few decades in the more mature advanced economies.

CONCLUDING COMMENTS

Since 1990 the contribution of the BRICS, especially China, to global GDP has been nothing short of astounding. As a corollary, the importance of the major advanced economy regions, the United States, European Union, and Japan as drivers of global economic growth, has diminished (see Lin & Rosenblatt, 2012; Makin, 2009). In the last few years, the BRICS, along with other emerging economies, has powered the global economy in the wake of the North Atlantic financial crisis of 2008–09 and through the Euro Area sovereign debt debacle that followed.

The development success of the BRICS has many common causes, such as keeping inflation under control and major reform initiatives. Other key reasons for its high growth rates include increased international trade and foreign inward investment, and to varying degrees privatization and reform of state-owned enterprises. Massive sums have also been spent building infrastructure, the demand for which will persist as rising middle classes require more electricity, roads, airports and telecommunication networks. Improved education levels, enhanced labour mobility and the emergence of entrepreneurial classes in these economies have also been pivotal to their ascendency.

Although the solid economic growth performance of the BRICS has been widely acknowledged, it is less well known that except for South Africa, the BRICS has persistently failed to feature among the top 50 countries in the World Bank's *2012 Doing Business Index*. Among 185 countries, Brazil and India continue to perform poorly, coming in at 130 and 132 respectively, and none of the BRICS members were ranked among the top ten most improved countries. This suggests considerable scope exists for improving the quality and durability of their growth by further liberalizing the environments in which businesses operate.

Corruption also detracts from the sustainability and quality of economic growth, with the four original BRICs economies ranked poorly according to corruption measures published by Transparency International. Better governance and greater transparency would encourage more foreign investment and safeguard against capital flow reversals and the relocation of firms to other countries (Smith & Hallward-Driemeier, 2005). In India's case, where the scale of poverty remains greater than in the other BRICS economies, uncertainty about foreign investment policy along with higher inflation and interest rates has worsened the overall investment climate (Reserve Bank of India [RBI], 2012), leading to what may be more than a temporary slowdown in India's growth.

Concrete proposals are now emerging from BRICS Leader's Summits which have implications for the rest of the world. At the 2012 New Delhi BRICS Summit, measures were announced that aim to improve trade links amongst the BRICS as a way of reducing reliance on Europe and the United States. These include easing inter-BRICS visa requirements to facilitate business linkages. Steps have also been taken toward establishing a South-South development bank along the lines of the Asian Development Bank to provide new avenues of funding for member economies. The establishment of this new development bank reflects the BRICS' resolve to be distinctive and to forge a new economic partnership independent of Western dominated economic institutions.

REFERENCES

Arestis, P., Ferrari-Filho, F. and de Paula, L.F. (2011). Inflation targeting in Brazil. *International Review of Applied Economics*, *25*(2), 127–48.

Audretsch, D.B., Keilbach, M.C. and Lehmann, E.E. (2006). *Entreprenuership and economic growth*. London: Oxford University Press.

Bloom, D.E., Canning, D. and Fink, G. (2011). *Implications of population aging for economic growth* (Working Paper No. 64). Cambridge, MA: Program on the Global Demography of Aging, Harvard University.

BRICS (2012). *The BRICS report: A study of Brazil, Russia, India, China, and South Africa*. New Delhi, India: Oxford University Press.

Das, G. (2007). Entreprenuership. In K. Basu (Ed.), *The Oxford companion to economics in India* (pp. 141–5). New Delhi, India: Oxford University Press.

Ghani, E., Kerr, W.R. and O'Connell, S.D. (2012). *What makes cities more competitive? Spatial determinants of entrepreneurship in India*. Washington DC: World Bank.

IMF (2011). *New growth drivers for low-income countries: The role of BRICs*. Washington DC: World Bank.

Kamal, M. (2010). *Inflation targeting in Brazil, Chile and South Africa: An empirical investigation of their monetary policy framework* (Working Paper No. 1004). Ann Arbor, MI: William Davidson Institute, University of Michigan.

Lin, J.Y. and Rosenblatt, D. (2012). Shifting patterns of economic growth and rethinking development. *Journal of Economic Policy Reform*, *15*(3), 171–94.

Makin, A. (2007). Does China's huge external surplus imply an undervalued yuan? *China and World Economy*, *15*(3), 89–102.

Makin, A. (2009). *Global imbalances, exchange rates, and stabilization policy*. Basingstoke, UK: Palgrave Macmillan.

Meng, X. (2012). Labor market outcomes and reforms in China. *Journal of Economic Perspectives*, *26*(4), 75–102.

Reserve Bank of India (2012). *Macroeconomic and monetary developments: Second quarter review 2012–13*. Mumbai: Reserve Bank of India.
Smith, W. and Hallward-Driemeier, M. (2005). Understanding the investment climate. *Finance and Development*, *42*(1), 40–43.
van Praag, M. and Versloot, P. (2007). What is the value of entrepreneurship? A review of recent research. *Small Business Economics*, *29*(4), 351–82.

3. Fiscal policy and China's economic growth

Shuangin Lin

The economic reforms started in 1978 have transformed one of the poorest countries into a middle-income country. Per capita GDP in China has increased from 381 Chinese yuan (the primary unit in renminbi) in 1978 to 38 852 yuan or US$6256 in 2012. Total GDP in China has increased from 364.5 billion Chinese yuan in 1978 to 51 932.2 billion yuan or US$8.363 trillion in 2012 (National Bureau of Statistics of China, 2012 Yearbook; 2013). China has surpassed Japan and become the second largest economy in the world, just behind the US, which had a GDP of US$15 trillion in 2011 (World Bank, 2013).This chapter analyses the role of fiscal policies in China's rapid economic growth in the last few decades.

There is a large amount of literature on China's economic growth in the past few decades. Lin (1997) found that education was crucial for economic development, and provinces with higher average years of schooling in the initial year had higher growth rates of real per capita GDP in subsequent years.[1] Lin (1999; 2000a) examined the effect of exports on economic growth based on the data of 30 Chinese provinces from 1978 to 1995 and the time-series data for the whole country from 1952 to 1997, and found that the growth rate of exports and the growth rate of per capita output were positively related. Rodrik (2010) argued that China should continuously promote modern tradeables and subsidize tradeables directly, rather than subsidize them indirectly through the exchange rate. Lin (2000b) showed that, based on the data from 30 Chinese provinces, the investment share of state enterprises was negatively related to the growth rate of per capita GDP, while the investment share of private enterprises was positively related to the growth rate. Contrary to the literature on economic growth, the effect of total investment share in GDP was insignificantly related to the growth rate of per capita GDP. Lin and Song (2002), based on the data on 189 large and medium-size Chinese cities for the period of 1991–98, found that foreign investment, paved roads, and government expenditure on science and technology are positively related to per capita GDP growth, and total investment share in GDP was insignificantly related to per capita GDP growth. Perkins (2012) pointed out that the difference between China and the industrialized Asian economies was the share of household consumption in GDP, which was much lower in China, and there was a need for large government investment to maintain high growth in China.[2]

Many studies showed that fiscal policies matter for economic growth. Ashauer (1989) argued that government expenditures were productive. Landou (1983; 1986) showed that government size (measured by government spending-output ratio) was negatively related to the economic growth rate. By considering productive services which the government provided for private firms, Barro (1990) showed that theoretically, when government size was small, an increase in government spending would increase the growth rate of output, but when the government size was large, an increase in government spending would reduce the growth rate; empirically, government consumption expenditures were negatively related and government investment expenditures were insignificantly related to economic growth. Lin and Sosin (2001) examined the relationship between government debt and economic growth based on data from 77 countries and found that foreign debt and economic growth were negatively related, but were not always statistically significant. Romer (1989), King and Rebelo (1990), Rebelo (1991) and Jones and Manueli (1990) argued that high taxes led to slow economic growth. Easterly and Rebelo (1993) found that government investment in transport and communication whilst consistently correlated with growth and the effects of taxation were difficult to isolate empirically.

Studies have also shown that tax reforms can improve economic efficiency. Summers (1981) showed that a shift from capital taxation to consumption taxation would increase welfare substantially. Fullerton, Shoven and Whalley (1983), Seidman (1984), Toder (1995), Hall (1996) and Hall and Rabushka (1996) showed that an increase in consumption taxation along with a decrease in income taxes would lower the interest rate and increase capital accumulation. Hall and Rabushka (1985) argued that the flat tax was better for the economy. In the US, President Reagan reduced the highest marginal tax rate from 70 per cent in 1981 to 28 per cent in 1988. Russia adopted a flat income tax of 13 per cent in 2000. Many Eastern European countries have also adopted the flat income tax.

So far there have been limited studies on tax, government spending and debt policies on China's economic growth. However, fiscal reforms and fiscal policies have played a crucial role in China's economic growth. This chapter therefore studies tax, government spending and government debt policies on China's economic growth. After the 1994 tax reforms, consumption taxes have become predominant in China's tax system, which is in favour of investment and economic growth, but not redistribution. On the expenditure side, the Chinese government has allocated a large proportion of its expenditures on economic construction, and a relatively small proportion on public goods and services, which is also in favour of economic growth. After the Asian Financial Crisis, the Chinese government adopted an expansionary fiscal policy by issuing government debt, which greatly stimulated infrastructure development. In recent years, China's local governments have borrowed an enormous amount for local development, which has kept the GDP growth at a high rate. Thus China's economic growth has been largely propelled by the central and local governments through pro-growth fiscal policies. China's future growth will inevitably depend on private investment, human capital and technological progress, along with local infrastructure development.

This chapter is organized as follows. Section two evaluates China's pro-growth tax system. Section three analyses China's pro-growth expenditure system. Section four discusses China's expansionary fiscal policy and government debt. Section five examines China's economic growth in the last few decades. Section six discusses the challenges for China's public finance and provides policy suggestions for equitable and sustainable growth.

CHINA'S PRO-GROWTH TAX SYSTEM

The Chinese government has given up the traditional ideology of low taxation. Traditionally, Chinese philosophers believed that taxes and levies should be low. Mencius, a follower of Confucius, believed that government size should be small, and the tax rate should be 10 per cent of income (Mencius, n.d.). Confucianism has dominated China's philosophy for 2000 years, and the idea of low taxation is deeply rooted in the Chinese people. The establishment of a centrally planned economy in the 1950s in China ushered in an era of strong government intervention and increased government taxation. Today the government revenue share in GDP is more than 30 per cent.

The Chinese government still follows the traditional idea of implicit taxation. More than 2000 years ago, Guan Zhong, the Prime Minister of Kingdom Qi, suggested to the King that the government should not collect head taxes, property taxes and other taxes, to avoid rebellion from his subjects. Instead the government should monopolize the sale of necessities, such as salt and iron, and sell at high prices. The King adopted his suggestion. Throughout Chinese history, even tea and cooking oil were once monopolized by the government. This thought is still influential today, and state-owned enterprises (SOEs) still monopolize many sectors in the economy and play an important role in revenue generation for the government.

Nonetheless China's tax system has followed some of the modern tax principles. Adam Smith (1776) in *The Wealth of Nations* proposed several principles for taxation: (1) Equality, that is, taxes should be in proportion to taxpayers' respective abilities to pay; (2) Certainty, that is, time, manner and quantity of tax on each individual must be certain, and not arbitrary; (3) Convenience for contributors to pay; (4) Economy in collection; (5) Progression, that is, the rich should contribute to the public expense, not only in proportion to their incomes, but something more than such a proportion; and (6) Taxing luxuries not necessities, in other words the necessary expenses of lower income people ought never to be taxed. In recent decades economists have added that the tax system should be designed to promote economic growth, that is, provide incentives for people to save more, and provide more labour and stabilize the macro economy.

After the 1994 tax reforms, taxes have been divided into central government taxes, local government taxes, and central and local government shared taxes. The central government taxes include: tariffs; consumption tax (similar to excise tax in the US); income tax from local banks, foreign banks and other financial institutions; income tax from railways, headquarters of banks and headquarters of insurance companies (for example business tax, income tax, and urban construction and maintenance tax) and vehicle purchasing tax.

The local government taxes include: business tax (excluding business tax from railways, headquarters of banks and headquarters of insurance companies); urban land tax; fixed investment direction adjustment tax; urban construction and maintenance tax (excluding the tax from railways, headquarters of banks and headquarters of insurance companies); housing tax; vehicle licence tax; urban real estate tax; vehicle tax; stamp tax; land appreciation tax; cultivated land occupation tax and contract tax.

The shared taxes include: value-added tax (central 75 per cent, local 25 per cent); corporate income tax (including foreign firms, except railways, banks, etc. central 60 per cent, local 40 per cent); personal income tax (central 60 per cent, local 40 per cent); natural resource tax (only ocean oil resource tax belongs to the central government) and stamp tax from stock exchange (central 94 per cent, local 6 per cent).

Tax revenue accounted for 45.8 per cent of total government revenue in 1978, 57.7 per cent in 1984, 101.8 per cent in 1985, 96.1 per cent in 1990, 93.9 per cent in 2000 and 88.1 per cent in 2010.[3] Total government revenue has increased dramatically since the 1994 tax reform. The average annual growth rate of government revenue was 2.47 per cent from 1978 to 1994, while it was 15.73 per cent from 1994 to 2011 (National Bureau of Statistics of China, 2012 Yearbook).[4] The contrast is unbelievably sharp. The rapid government revenue growth has supported fast infrastructure development in China.

In addition to budgetary revenue, the Chinese government also has extra-budgetary revenue and off-budget revenue. Extra-budgetary revenue is the revenue of government organizations and institutes as well as local governments through fee collection, which is legal and is reported to the central government. Extra-budgetary revenue accounted for 12.26 per cent of GDP in 1978, 16.97 per cent in 1985, 14.51 per cent in 1990, 3.86 per cent in 2000 and 1.88 per cent in 2009. Off-budget revenue (also called the funds in 'the Little Golden Box') is the revenue received by local governments which is not reported to the central government and so is unlawful. Although reliable data is not available, the size of the off-budget revenue is estimated to be 30–40 per cent of local government revenue. Eliminating the off-budget revenue is possible, but it will reduce local governments' fiscal freedom. In 2009, government revenue share in GDP was about 32 per cent of GDP, including 27 per cent from budgetary revenue, and extra-budgetary revenue and social security contribution, and off-budgetary revenue was about 5 per cent of GDP (National Bureau of Statistics of China, 2010).

China's government revenue size is larger than those of many developing countries, smaller than those of European industrialized countries, and about the same as the US and Japan. For example, government revenue share in GDP was 20 per cent in Singapore in 2005, 22 per cent in Thailand in 2006, 32 per cent in Japan in 2005, 34 per cent in the US in 2006, 42 per cent in Germany in 2006, 44 per cent in France in 2006 and 50 per cent in the UK in 2006 (IMF, 2008).

China heavily relies on consumption-type taxes, and its tax system is not progressive. Figure 3.1 shows the composition of tax revenue in China from 1978 to 2011. In 2011, value-added tax (with the standard rate of 17 per cent) accounted for 27 per cent of total tax revenue, business tax (with the standard rate of 6 per cent) accounted for 15 per cent, domestic consumption tax accounted for 8 per cent, consumption tax and VAT on net imports accounted for 5 per cent (see Figure 3.2). All these taxes add up to 55 per cent of total tax revenue! Thus more than half of China's tax revenues come from consumption-related taxes. Producers or sellers then add the taxes to prices of goods and services. Meanwhile personal income tax only accounted for 7 per cent of total tax revenue, and corporate income tax accounted for 19 per cent of total tax revenue.

In the US, individual income taxes in 2010 accounted for 41 per cent of

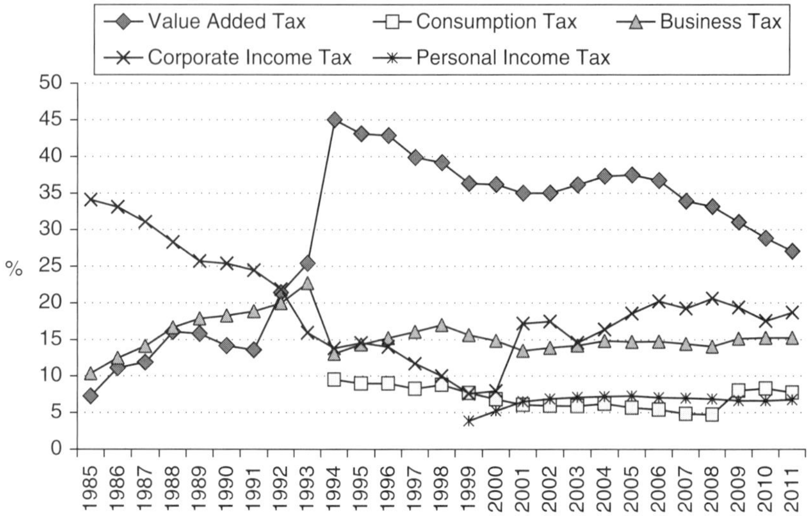

Source: National Bureau of Statistics of China (2012).

Figure 3.1 Composition of China's government tax revenue (1985–2011)

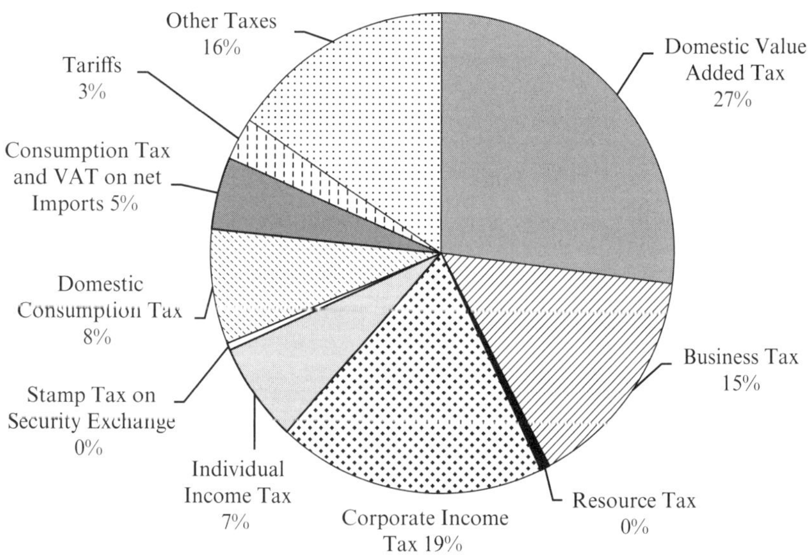

Source: National Bureau of Statistics of China (2012).

Figure 3.2 Composition of tax revenue in 2011

total federal government revenue, payroll taxes accounted for 40 per cent, corporate income taxes accounted for 9 per cent and excise tax accounted for 3 per cent. Clearly the US federal government relies on taxes on income (Joint Committee on Taxation, 2011, pp. 4, 50).

China does not have personal property tax, inheritance tax or gift tax. In some sense China's tax system resembles the tax system US mainstream economists proposed. China's tax system is growth-oriented, not equity-oriented. Many studies have shown that consumption taxes, compared to income taxes, stimulate savings and economic growth, and have supported replacing income tax with consumption tax. Summers (1981) argued that a shift from capital taxation to consumption taxation would increase welfare substantially. Fullerton, Shoven and Whalley (1983), Seidman (1984), Toder (1995), Hall (1996) and Hall and Rabushka (1996) demonstrated that an increase in consumption taxation along with a decrease in income taxes would lower the interest rate and increase capital accumulation. The inference is clear. Income is equal to consumption plus savings. Taxing income is equivalent to taxing both consumption and savings. A substitution of consumption tax for income tax will leave savings untaxed, resulting in an increase in savings, investment and capital accumulation.

THE PRO-GROWTH GOVERNMENT EXPENDITURE STRUCTURE

China's government expenditure increased very slowly in the 1980s due to the slow growth of tax revenue and economic decentralization, but it has increased rapidly since the mid-1990s, along with the increase in government revenue. The share of government expenditure in GDP was 31 per cent in 1978, 22.4 per cent in 1985, 16.6 per cent in 1990, 13.4 per cent in 1993, 11.7 per cent in 1995, 17.8 per cent in 2000, 18.5 per cent in 2005 and 22.4 per cent in 2010 (National Bureau of Statistics of China, 2011 Yearbook).

The Chinese government expenditure structure is also favourable to economic growth. Over the past several decades, the Chinese government has spent a large amount on economic construction, and a relatively small amount on education, healthcare and social welfare. Figure 3.3 shows the composition of government expenditure from 1950 to 2006. Government spending on economic construction accounted for 64.08 per cent of total government expenditure in 1978, 56.26 per cent in 1985, 44.36 per cent in 1990, 41.85 per cent in 1995, 36.18 per cent in 2000, 27.46 per cent in 2005 and 26.56 per cent in 2006.

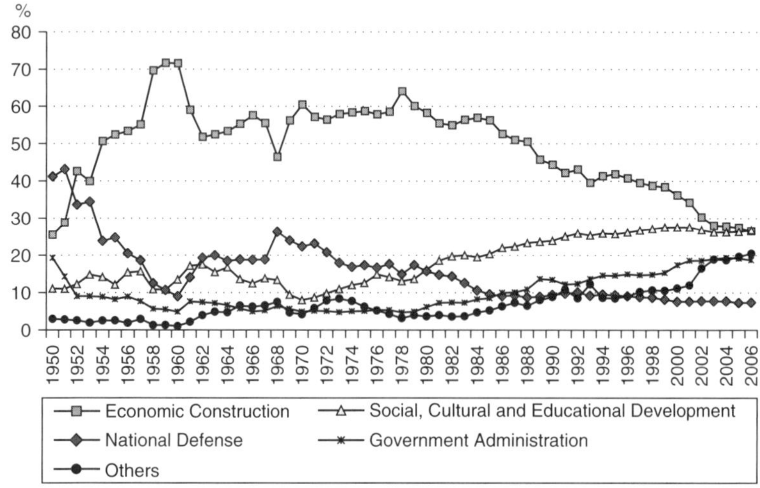

Source: National Bureau of Statistics of China (*China Statistical Yearbook*, 2000–07).

Figure 3.3 Composition of government expenditure (1950–2006)

Beginning in 2007, China's government expenditures were classified into 14 main categories: (1) general public services, (2) foreign affairs, (3) national defence, (4) public security, (5) education, (6) science and technology, (7) culture, sport and media, (8) social safety net and employment effort, (9) medical and healthcare, (10) environmental protection, (11) urban and rural community affairs, (12) agriculture, forestry and water conservancy, (13) transportation and (14) industry, commerce and banking. The shares of the major categories in total government expenditure in 2011 are illustrated in Figure 3.4. The share of education in total government expenditure was 15 per cent, general public services 10 per cent, social safety net and employment effort 10 per cent, agriculture, forestry and water conservancy 9 per cent, urban and rural community affairs 7 per cent, public security 6 per cent, transportation 7 per cent, national defence 6 per cent, medical and healthcare 6 per cent and environmental protection 2 per cent.

The Chinese government spent more on economic affairs than many other countries. Table 3.1 shows the composition of government expenditures for all countries with data available in 2006 and 2007. In 2007, the share of government expenditure on economic affairs was 37.68 per cent in China, 5.36 per cent in France, 7.23 per cent in Germany, 9.81 per cent in Singapore, 9.98 per cent in the US, 10.55 per cent in Japan, 10.15 per cent in Poland and 17.01 per cent in the Czech Republic. Meanwhile the

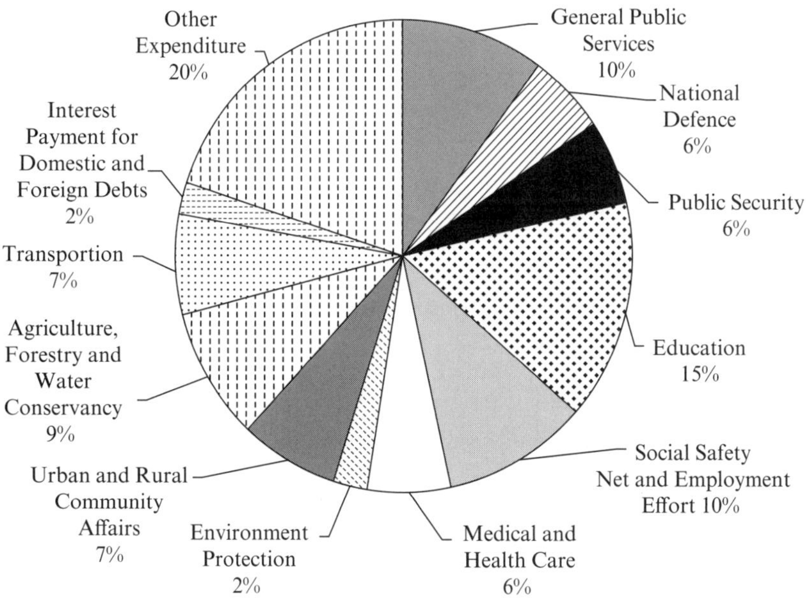

Source: National Bureau of Statistics of China (2012).

Figure 3.4 Composition of total government expenditure in 2011

Chinese government has spent a very limited amount on health, community amenities, recreation, culture and religion. For example, in 2007, the share of government expenditure on health was 13.72 per cent in France, 14.01 per cent in Germany, 6.04 per cent in Singapore, 21.06 per cent in the US, 19.6 per cent in Japan, 10.62 per cent in Poland and 14.24 per cent in the Czech Republic, while it was only 2.51 per cent in China. Moreover the share of government expenditure on community amenities was 3.62 per cent in France, 1.93 per cent in Germany, 12.2 per cent in Singapore, 1.85 per cent in the US, 1.81 per cent in Japan, 1.7 per cent in Poland and 3.57 per cent in the Czech Republic, while it was only 0.44 per cent in China!

A number of studies have shown that government investment expenditures are positively related to economic growth. Barro (1990) found that government investment was positively related to economic growth. Easterly and Rebelo (1993) found that government investment in transport and communication was consistently correlated with growth.

Table 3.1 General government outlays by function for countries with data available for 2006–07 (percentage of total outlays)

Country or Region	Year	General Public Services	Defense	Public Order and Safety	Economic Affairs	Environmental	Community Amenities	Health	Recreation, Culture, and Religion	Education
France	2007	13.28	3.39	2.41	5.36	1.66	3.62	13.72	2.90	11.24
Germany	2007	13.61	2.41	3.51	7.23	1.10	1.93	14.01	1.36	9.09
Italy	2007	15.98	3.14	3.89	10.23	1.83	2.16	12.57	3.05	11.22
Luxembourg	2007	15.74	0.61	2.52	10.80	2.65	2.05	11.90	5.39	13.07
Netherlands	2007	16.11	3.01	3.95	10.48	1.81	2.06	12.54	2.95	11.17
Slovenia	2006	11.38	3.09	4.18	10.68	1.34	1.30	13.66	2.83	14.95
Spain	2007	11.47	2.64	4.86	12.56	2.36	2.45	14.70	4.09	11.28
Australia	2007	11.43	4.85	5.02	12.41	1.61	2.82	18.02	2.43	14.27
Canada	2007	12.52	2.86	4.95	9.09	1.81	2.04	19.01	2.62	15.02
Hong Kong	2006	24.40		10.00	7.47	3.11	6.22	13.23	3.40	19.32
Denmark	2007	12.54	3.08	1.98	6.63	1.11	1.34	14.12	3.07	14.50
Iceland	2007	13.13	0.15	3.46	13.73	1.49	1.15	18.67	8.90	19.18
Israel	2007	14.43	17.07	3.88	6.09	1.49	1.23	11.32	3.09	16.14
Japan	2006	12.91	2.59	3.89	10.55	3.55	1.81	19.60	0.43	10.74
New Zealand	2007	12.58	2.98	4.66	9.58	1.18	1.94	15.31	4.33	15.39
Norway	2007	10.16	3.97	2.23	9.03	1.35	1.44	17.42	2.61	13.31

Singapore	2007	12.37	27.99	6.24	9.81		12.20	6.04	0.48	20.82
Switzerland	2006	13.78	2.89	5.01	11.96	1.71	1.12	12.17	2.62	16.86
US	2007	13.47	11.54	5.71	9.98		1.85	21.06	0.87	16.93
Mauritius	2007	22.25	0.65	7.78	10.70	5.18	2.90	8.84	1.53	15.08
China	2006	18.20	5.24	4.98	37.68	3.21	0.44	2.51	1.27	
Macao	2007	18.32		16.60	13.88	5.79	1.01	10.54	6.51	
Maldives	2007	21.89	5.04	7.24	8.32	1.13	24.90	8.12	4.10	14.22
Albania	2006	21.57	4.42	6.26	15.23	.	5.65	8.24	1.27	10.77
Bulgaria	2007	12.55	6.01	8.12	12.50	0.67	3.17	12.72	2.26	10.19
Croatia	2007	11.21	3.55	6.07	13.99	0.66	4.71	13.84	3.00	9.69
Czech Republic	2007	11.94	3.26	5.22	17.01	2.65	3.57	14.24	2.61	9.65
Latvia	2007	11.48	4.03	7.06	17.23	2.72	3.53	10.09	4.60	16.32
Lithuania	2007	9.67	5.21	4.73	11.65	2.50	1.45	15.26	3.23	15.26
Poland	2007	12.58	3.89	4.72	10.15	1.40	1.70	10.62	2.64	12.72
Romania	2006	12.61	3.56	7.07	19.36	0.98	3.96	9.48	2.63	12.09
Slovak Republic	2007	14.15	3.97	5.50	13.03	1.95	2.03	17.86	2.99	9.55

Source: IMF (2008).

CHINA'S EXPANSIONARY FISCAL POLICY AND GOVERNMENT DEBT

For a long time the Chinese government followed a conservative budgetary philosophy called 'balancing budget with a small surplus'. From 1949 to 1957 the government financed deficits through both domestic and foreign borrowing. In the period of 1958–78, China issued neither foreign nor domestic debt and monetarized budget deficits when necessary. During the period of 1979–93, the Chinese government started to borrow from domestic and international markets, but the amount was small. After 1994, government domestic borrowing started to increase rapidly, while foreign borrowing started to slow down.

In 1997 the Asian Financial Crisis occurred, so China adopted an expansionary fiscal policy in 1998. The government budget was in deficit until 2007. In the beginning of 2007 the government still planned to run an annual deficit. However, because the economy was overheated and the growth rate of tax revenues reached 27.56 per cent, the fiscal account ended with a surplus (National Bureau of Statistics of China, 2007 Yearbook). In 2008, the Global Financial Crisis (GFC) occurred, and the Chinese government adopted an expansionary fiscal policy again, with an aggressive 4 trillion yuan investment plan. To finance the investment, the central government raised 1.1 trillion yuan by issuing debt in two and half years, the local governments raised the same amount, and the remaining part was raised by enterprises, primarily SOEs. Local governments do not have the right to enact tax laws and do not have the right to issue debt, and therefore they turned to banks for borrowing through their investment companies. Enterprises also relied on borrowing from banks to raise funds. Table 3.2 shows government revenue, government expenditure, budget deficit and government debt in selected years from 1955 to 2011.

Figure 3.5 shows the government deficit-GDP ratios from 1950 to 2011. China launched the Great Leap Forward movement to accelerate economic growth from 1958 to 1960. The deficit-GDP ratio was 6.7 per cent in 1960, the highest ever. The deficit-GDP ratio was −0.28 per cent (surplus) in 1978, 1.52 per cent in 1980 and −0.01 per cent (surplus) in 1985. The government budget has been in deficit since 1986. The deficit-GDP ratio was 0.8 per cent in 1990, 1.0 per cent in 1995, 2.5 per cent in 2000, 0.78 per cent in 2006, −0.6 per cent (surplus) in 2007, 0.42 per cent in 2008, 2.2 per cent in 2009, 1.6 per cent in 2010, 1.1 per cent in 2011 and 1.6 per cent in 2012. Clearly the Chinese government has run budget deficits during periods of rapid economic growth.

The government has relied on borrowing to finance the deficits, resulting in an increase in government debt. Government debt increased from

Table 3.2 Basic statistics of China's public finance (billion yuan, percentage)

Year	Government Revenue	Government Expenditure	Surplus	GDP	Government Revenue/GDP	Surplus/ GDP	Government Debt	Government Debt/GDP
1955	24.9	26.3	−1.35	91.0	27.4	−1.5		
1960	57.2	64.4	−7.14	145.7	39.3	−4.9		
1965	47.3	46.0	1.34	171.6	27.6	0.8		
1970	66.3	64.9	1.35	225.3	29.4	0.6		
1975	81.6	82.1	−0.53	299.7	27.2	−0.2		
1978	113.2	112.2	1.02	364.5	31.1	0.3		
1980	116.0	122.9	−6.90	454.6	25.5	−1.5	4.9 (1981)	1.0
1985	200.5	200.4	0.06	901.6	22.2	0.0	23.8	2.6
1990	293.7	308.4	−14.65	1866.8	15.7	−0.8	89.0	4.8
1995	624.2	682.4	−58.15	6079.4	10.3	−1.0	330.0	5.4
2000	1339.5	1588.7	−249.10	9921.5	13.5	−2.5	1302.0	13.1
2006	3876	4042.3	−216.30	21 192.4	18.3	−1.0	3184.9	17.4
2007	5132.2	4978.1	154.00	24 952.9	20.6	0.6	3438.0	16.2
2008	6131.7	6242.7	−111.00	30 067.0	20.4	−1.4	5146.4	20.0
2009	6847.7	7587.4	−739.70	33 535.3	20.4	−2.2	5279.9	17.6
2010	8308.0	8957.5	−649.50	39 798.3	20.9	−1.6		
2011	10 374.0	10 893.0	−519.00	47 156.4	22.0	−1.1		

Source: National Bureau of Statistics of China (*China Statistical Yearbook*, 2000–2012).

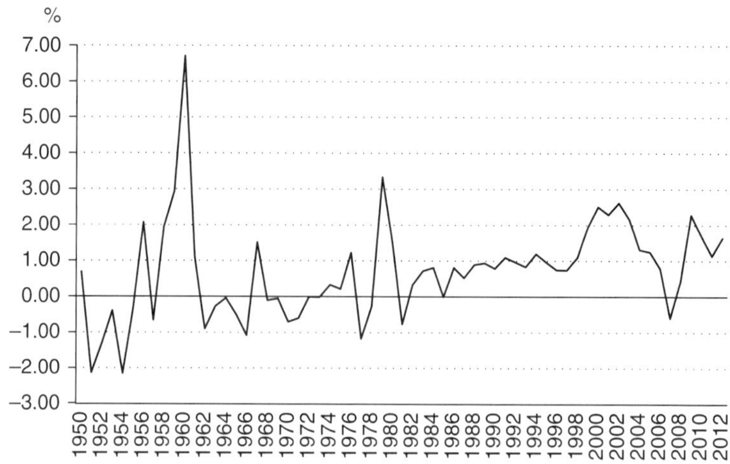

Source: National Bureau of Statistics of China (*China Statistical Yearbook*, 2000–12).

Figure 3.5 Ratio of budget deficit to GDP (1950–2012)

89 billion yuan in 1990 to 5279.9 billion yuan in 2009, an increase of nearly 60 times (National Bureau of Statics of China, 2010)! However, because of the rapid GDP growth, the central government debt-GDP ratio is still not high when compared to many industrialized countries. The central government's debt-GDP ratio was 0.99 per cent in 1981, 4.77 per cent in 1990, 4.36 per cent in 1993, 6.98 per cent in 1997, 13.78 per cent in 2000, 20 per cent in 2007 and 17.6 per cent in 2009. Figure 3.6 shows the government's debt-GDP ratios from 1981 to 2009.

In addition to China's central government debt, local governments in China have accumulated a huge amount of debt. By the end of 2010, local governments' (provincial, prefectural and county) debt reached 10717 billion yuan, accounting for 27 per cent of GDP. In 2010, the explicit debt-GDP ratio was 18 per cent, local government debt-GDP ratio was 27 per cent, foreign debt-GDP ratio was 7 per cent, and the net debt of government institutes (such as state hospitals and state universities) was 5–8 per cent. Adding these debts together, China's debt-GDP ratio is about 57–60 per cent of GDP. China also has debt in social security account, which is explicit, not implicit. Implicit social security debt is the amount government owed to current retirees and those who have contributed to the social security system if the pay-as-you-go system is privatized. The explicit debt is the amount the local governments have borrowed from social security individual accounts. At the moment, the social security account debt is about 2 per cent of GDP (Li & Lin, 2013).[5]

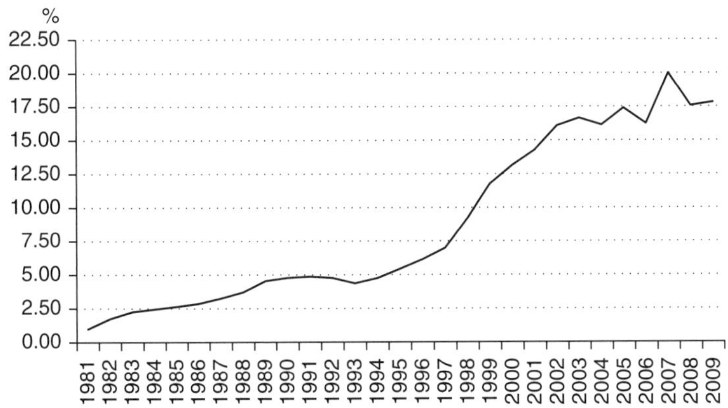

Sources: Data on debt is from the China Commission on Security Supervision and Management (2000); National Bureau of Statistics of China (2010). Data on GDP is from National Bureau of Statistics of China (*China Statistical Yearbook*, 2001–12).

Figure 3.6 Ratio of China's government debt to GDP (1981–2009)

SAVINGS, INVESTMENT, INFRASTRUCTURE CONSTRUCTION AND ECONOMIC GROWTH

With a tax system dominated by consumption tax, and expenditure system dominated by economic construction and a long period of expansionary fiscal policies, China's savings, investment and public infrastructure have increased rapidly, resulting in extraordinary economic growth in the past two decades.

Savings and Investment

The consumption tax dominated tax system encourages savings and investment, while discouraging consumption. China's savings rate has become extremely high since 2000. In the 1980s and 1990s, China's savings rate was in the 35–40 per cent range. The savings rate began to increase after 2000 and reached 53.2 per cent in 2008.[6]

China's total consumption (household and government) expenditure has been decreasing. Figure 3.7 shows China's composition of GDP (shares of consumption, capital formation and net exports) from 1978 to 2011. The total consumption expenditure in GDP was 62.1 per cent in 1978, 62.5 per cent in 1990, 62.3 per cent in 2000, 53 per cent in 2005 and 49.1 per cent in 2011 (National Bureau of Statistics of China, 2012

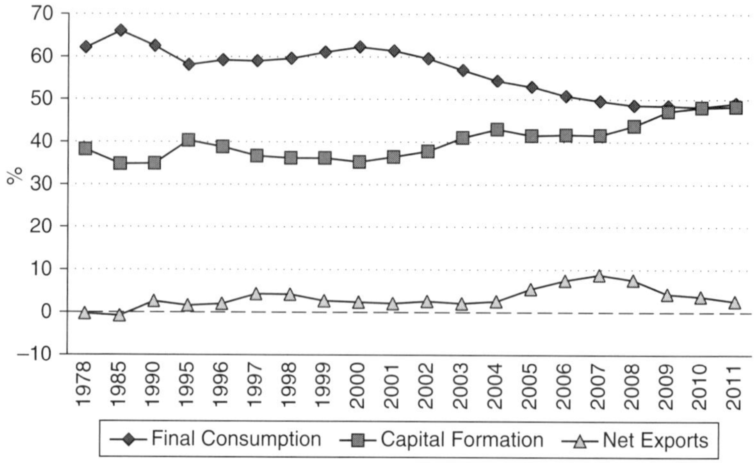

Source: National Bureau of Statistics of China (*China Statistical Yearbook*, 2000–12).

Figure 3.7 Share of capital formation, consumption and net exports in GDP (per cent) (1978–2011)

Yearbook). Meanwhile total capital formation (private and public) has been increasing. The share of total investment (capital formation) in GDP was 38.2 per cent in 1978, 34.9 per cent in 1990, 40.3 per cent in 1995, 35.3 per cent in 2000, 41.5 per cent in 2005 and 48.3 per cent in 2011.

Theoretical studies on economic growth have shown that savings and investment are positively related to economic growth either in the long run (Harrod, 1939; Domar, 1946) or in the transitional period (Solow, 1956). Empirical studies have also demonstrated that investment and economic growth are positively related (see Barro, 1991; Landou, 1983; Levine & Renelt, 1992).

Infrastructure Development

With an expansionary fiscal policy and a large proportion of government expenditure on economic consumption, China has built numerous new infrastructures in the last 15 years. China's infrastructure development was rapid during the period of 1950–78 under the centrally planned economic system. However, the growth of several major infrastructures slowed down after the economic reform started in 1978. The main reasons for the slower growth in infrastructure construction were low government spending on infrastructure, decreased investment incentives to state

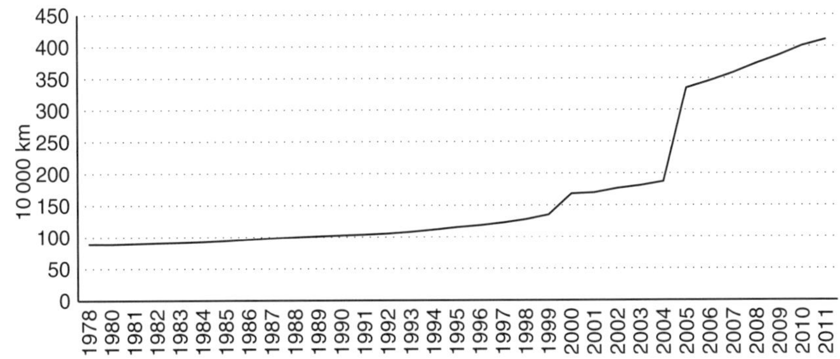

Source: National Bureau of Statistics of China (*China Statistical Yearbook*, 2000–12).

Figure 3.8 Highways in China (10 000 km) (1978–2011)

enterprises on building infrastructure, and the diminished ability of local government in mobilizing rural resources (Lin, 2001). Since the 1994 tax reform, government revenue has greatly increased, resulting in an increase in government expenditure on infrastructure construction. After the Asian Financial Crisis in 1997, the government adopted an expansionary fiscal policy, issuing debt for infrastructure development.

With a large amount of government expenditure on economic construction, many large infrastructure projects have been launched and completed in China. In the last 20 years, many new highways, high-speed railways, bridges, airports, ports and subways have been built. The length of highways was 0.89 million kilometres in 1978, 1.028 million kilometres in 1990, 1.157 million kilometres in 1995, 1.68 million kilometres in 2000, 3.345 million kilometres in 2005 and 4.106 million kilometres in 2011. Figure 3.8 shows the length of China's highways from 1978 to 2011. The annual growth rate of highways was 1.54 per cent from 1978 to 1995, while it was 7.92 per cent from 1995 to 2011!

China has also built many high speed railways, such as the one from Beijing to Shanghai, which has substantially reduced travelling time. Meanwhile the quality of the roads has also improved significantly. Figure 3.9 shows the length of China's railways, electrified railways and expressways from 1978 to 2011. In a similar fashion, the length of railways was 51.7 thousand kilometres in 1978, 57.9 thousand kilometres in 1990, 62.4 thousand kilometres in 1995, 68.7 thousand kilometres in 2000, 75.4 thousand kilometres in 2005 and 93.2 thousand kilometres in 2011. The annual growth rate of railways was 1.1 per cent from 1978 to 1995, while it was 2.5 per cent from 1995 to 2011.

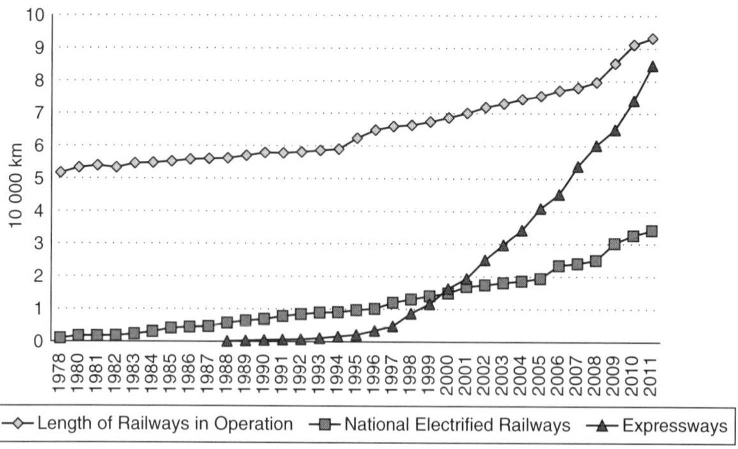

Source: National Bureau of Statistics of China (*China Statistical Yearbook*, 2000–12).

Figure 3.9 Railways, electrified railways and expressways in China (10000 km) (1978–2011)

The length of electrified railways was 1 thousand kilometres in 1978, 6.9 thousand kilometres in 1990, 9.7 thousand kilometres in 1995, 14.9 thousand kilometres in 2000, 19.4 thousand kilometres in 2005 and 34.3 thousand kilometres in 2011. The annual growth rate of electrified railways was 13.4 per cent from 1978 to 1995, while it was 7.9 per cent from 1995 to 2011.

The most amazing achievement is the development of expressways in China. The length of expressways was 0.1 thousand kilometres in 1988, 2.1 thousand kilometres in 1995, 16.3 thousand kilometres in 2000, 41 thousand kilometres in 2005 and 84.9 thousand kilometres in 2011. The construction of expressways started in the late 1980s. The annual growth rate of expressways was 24.5 per cent from 1990 to 2011.[7]

Growth of the GDP

With massive private and government investment, the Chinese economy has grown at an astonishing rate for more than three decades. Figure 3.10 shows China's growth rate of real GDP reported by the government, the growth rate of GDP calculated by using the retail price index and the level of GDP at the 1978 constant retail price. The growth rate of GDP based on the 1978 constant retail price was 7.69 per cent from 1978 to 1994, while it increased to 10.86 per cent from 1994 to 2011. Thus the growth rate of

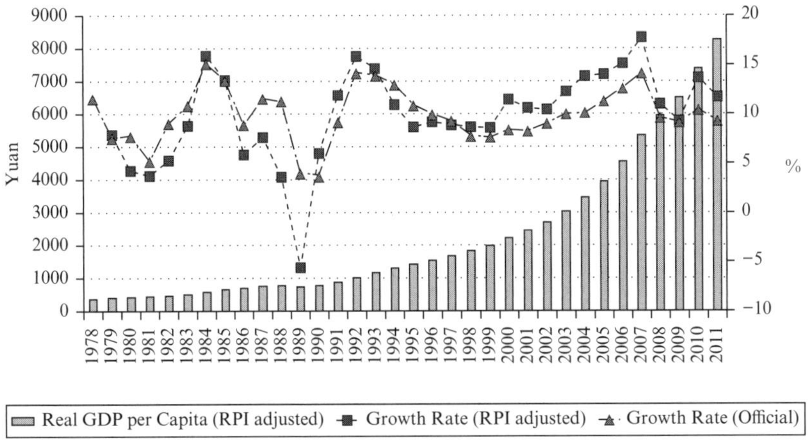

Source: National Bureau of Statistics of China (*China Statistical Yearbook*, 2000–12).

Figure 3.10 Real GDP per capita (RPI adjusted), growth rate (RPI adjusted), official growth rate (1978–2011)

GDP was more rapid after the 1994 tax reform than before the reform. In particular the growth rate of GDP based on the 1978 constant retail price was as high as 12.27 per cent, 13.83 per cent, 14.06 per cent, 15.17 per cent and 17.76 per cent in 2003, 2004, 2005, 2006 and 2007, respectively. Per capita GDP at the 1978 constant retail price has increased by 22 times, from 381 yuan to 8254.6 yuan! China has climbed out of the group of poorest countries and entered the group of middle-income countries. Over the period of reforms and the opening-up starting in 1978, 600 million people have risen out of poverty. There is no doubt that China has created a miracle in economic growth.

When Will China Catch Up with the US in Total GDP?

China has become the second largest economy in the world based on total GDP, just behind the US. The frequently asked question is: Is it possible for China to become the largest economy in the world, and how long will it take? In 2011, total GDP was \$7.298 trillion in China based on the official exchange rate, and it was \$15.094 trillion in the US. We now calculate the number of years it will take for China to catch up with the US. Let t be the number of years it will take to for China to catch the US, γ be the growth rate of GDP in China and ϕ be the growth rate in the US. Then t is determined by the following equation:

$$7.298e^{t\gamma} = 15.094e^{t\phi} \text{ or}$$
$$t = (\ln 15.094 - \ln 7.298)/(\gamma - \phi) \tag{3.1}$$

If the US growth rate is $\phi = 3$ per cent and China's growth rate is $\gamma = 8$ per cent, then $t = 14.5$ years. That is, by 2025 China's total GDP will be the same as that of the US. If the US growth rate is $\phi = 3$ per cent and China's growth rate is $\gamma = 7$ per cent, then $t = 18.17$ years. That is, by 2029 China's total GDP will catch up with the US.

In the same way, we can also calculate the number of years it will take for China's per capita GDP to reach the level of the US per capita GDP. In 2011, per capita GDP was \$5432 trillion in China based on the official exchange rate, and \$48 442 trillion in the US. Let t be the number of years it will take for China to catch up with the US, γ be the growth rate of China, and ϕ be the growth rate of the US. Then t can be determined by the following equation:

$$5{,}432e^{t\gamma} = 48{,}442e^{t\phi}$$
$$t = (\ln 48{,}442 - \ln 5{,}432)/(\gamma - \phi) \tag{3.2}$$

If the growth rate of the US is $\phi = 3$ per cent and China's growth rate is $\gamma = 8$ per cent, then $t = 43.76$ years. That is, by 2055 China's per capita GDP will be the same as that of the US. If the growth rate of the US is $\phi = 3$ per cent and China's growth rate is $\gamma = 7$ per cent, then $t = 54.7$ years. That is, by 2066 China's per capita GDP will catch up with the US per capita GDP. Thus it will take a long time for China's per capita GDP to catch up with the US per capita GDP, even if China's growth rate is kept at a high rate for many years to come.

CHALLENGES FOR CHINA'S PUBLIC FINANCE AND PROSPECTS FOR CHINA'S GROWTH

China's public finance system is favourable to economic growth, but not to redistribution. China now faces many new challenges. First, income inequality is growing. The GINI coefficient in China has increased substantially. From 2000 to 2010, the GINI coefficient was 24.5 per cent in Japan, 28.3 per cent in Germany, 32.7 per cent in France, 36 per cent in UK, 40.8 per cent in the US, 36.8 per cent in India and 41.5 per cent in China (UNDP, 2010). China's GINI coefficient is higher than all the industrialized countries and many developing countries, such as India. If the problem becomes more severe, political unrest may arise. Thus reducing income inequality has become one of the new goals of the government.

Second, the provision of public goods is rather limited. The share of government expenditure spent on education has been low in China. In the early 1990s the government set a goal to increase the education expenditure share in GDP to 4 per cent (Central Committee of the Chinese Communist Party and State Council of China, 1993). However, until 2009 the education expenditure share was only about 3 per cent. The government has waived the tuition fees for elementary and middle schools, but not for high schools. Even for elementary and middle schools, the students need to pay various fees. As discussed, government healthcare expenditure was rather low in China, since local governments at various levels collect a large amount of tolls on highways and fees on public parks, they are inevitably expected to provide more public goods and increase the expenditures on education and healthcare.

Third, while local government revenues are much less than local government expenditures, local government debts are rapidly growing. As China is in a period of rapid urbanization, there is increasing demand for urban infrastructures and other local public goods and services, such as education facilities, public healthcare facilities, environmental protection measures and social welfare programmes. However, local governments are facing severe revenue shortages. The share of local government revenue in total government revenue decreased from 78 per cent in 1993 to 49 per cent in 2010; meanwhile the share of local government expenditure increased from 72 per cent in 1993 to 82 per cent in 2010. The local government self-sufficiency rate was 93.5 per cent in 1990, 61.8 per cent in 1995, and down to only 50 per cent in 2010 (National Bureau of Statistics of China, 2011). In China, local governments have no right to set tax laws and no right to issue bonds. They rely on transfers from the central government to balance their budgets. Thus in 2010 half of the local government expenditure was financed by the central government. As mentioned earlier, China's local governments have borrowed a large amount of funds from banks to finance local infrastructure projects, resulting in a huge amount of implicit local government debt, which is threatening China's financial system.

In the near future, the Chinese government must reform its tax system and expenditure system for equitable and sustainable growth. First, reduce the tax regressiveness by lowering consumption taxes and increasing income taxes. Second, provide more public goods and increase government expenditure on education, healthcare, environmental protection and social welfare. Third, increase the fiscal capability of local governments, that is, the central government should allow local governments to establish local taxes, such as property tax and local resource tax, and allow local governments to issue revenue bonds for bridges, school dormitories, public utilities and so forth. Given the large mismatch of spending and revenue for many local governments, the central government should allocate more revenues to local governments, for example, increasing the VAT share of local governments from 25 per cent to 40 per cent. Fourth, control the scale of local government debt and prevent it from becoming explosive.

All these fiscal reforms tend to slow down China's economic growth in the short run, but will ensure equitable and sustainable growth in the long run. China's per capita income is still much lower than those of the industrialized countries, and half of China's population still lives in the rural areas. China is undergoing industrialization and urbanization, and the growth potential for China is still enormous. Several factors will significantly enhance China's future economic growth.

First, investment in local infrastructure. As urbanization proceeds, more people will move to cities. However, urban infrastructure, such as roads, subways, utility facilities, schools and hospitals, is far from well developed. China will have to continue to invest in urban infrastructure development which will promote economic growth.

Second, investment in private enterprises. Private enterprises have not fully developed in China. SOEs still play a dominant role in many essential industries in China, such as in the financial industry, natural resource industries, transportation industries and some manufacturing industries. Private enterprises in China face many obstacles on their path to development and expansion, such as market restraints and credit restraints. The government has treated the developments of private enterprises as a matter of expediency for solving the unemployment problem. In some areas private enterprises have not been treated as well as foreign-invested enterprises. China's savings rate is very high. The development of private enterprises can turn these savings into investments and sustain China's economic growth.

Third, investment in human capital. Although government spending on education is not high, Chinese families have spent an enormous amount on educating their young people. A large percentage of the Chinese youth have obtained college and graduate education. As income rises, more and more families have sent their young people abroad to study. Most of these overseas-educated students will eventually return to China. Thus China's human capital stock is increasing rapidly, which will raise the quality of the Chinese labour force and stimulate China's technological progress and economic growth.

CONCLUSION

In summary, China's future economic growth will rely less on the pro-growth tax and government spending policies of the past 20 years, and instead will increasingly rely on private investment, improvement of the skills of its labour force and technological progress. As industrialization and urbanization proceed, the Chinese economy is likely to grow at a reasonably high rate in the coming two decades.

NOTES

1. In his seminal paper, Lucas (1988) shows that human capital plays a crucial role in economic growth.
2. Zhu (2012) provided an overall discussion of China's economic growth in the past, current and future.
3. In 1985 China completed the tax-for-profit tax reforms, that is, enterprises no longer submitted profits to the government; instead they paid taxes. Before the reform, the Chinese government relied heavily on the profits from SOEs for revenue.
4. Lin (2000c) provided reasons for the decline in China's government revenue in the 1980s and the early 1990s.
5. In 2011 the US government's debt-GDP ratio reached 100 per cent causing the so-called 'fiscal cliff'. However, the US had a social security account accumulation of $2.7 trillion in 2011, accounting for 18 per cent of GDP (see http://www.ssa.gov/oact/tr/2012/tr2012.pdf).
6. See Yang (2012) for discussion of aggregate savings in China since the early 1990s.
7. Grabowski (2011) provided a comparison of the sustained growth in China and Japan and emphasized the necessity of physical and institutional infrastructures for rapid growth.

REFERENCES

Ashauer, D. (1989). Is public expenditure productive? *Journal of Monetary Economics*, *23*, 177–200.

Barro, R. (1990). Government spending in a simple model of endogenous growth. *Journal of Political Economy*, *98*(5), S103–25.

Barro, R. (1991). Economic growth in a cross section of countries. *Quarterly Journal of Economics*, *106*(2), 407–43.

Central Committee of the Chinese Communist Party and State Council of China (1993). *Outline of China's education reforms and development*. Retrieved from http://wenku.baidu.com/view/7e9e53593b3567ec102d8adf.html.

Domar, E.D. (1946). Capital expansion, rate of growth, and employment. *Econometrica*, *14*, 137–47.

Easterly, W. and Rebelo, S. (1993). Fiscal policy and economic growth: An empirical investigation. *Journal of Monetary Economics*, *32*(3), 417–58.

Fullerton, D., Shoven, J. and Whalley, J. (1983). Replacing the U.S. income tax with a progressive consumption tax: A sequenced general equilibrium approach. *Journal of Public Economics*, *20*(1), 3–23.

Grabowski, R. (2011). China's economic takeoff: A few similarities with Japan. *Chinese Economy*, *44*(2), 5–24.
Hall, R.E. (1996). The effect of tax reform on prices and asset values. In J.M. Poterba (Ed.), *Tax policy and the economy* (vol 10). Cambridge: MIT Press.
Hall, R.E. and Rabushka, A. (1985). *The Flat Tax*. California: Hoover Institution Press.
Hall, R.E. and Rabushka, A. (1996). The flat tax: A simple, progressive consumption tax. In M.J. Boskin (Ed.), *Frontiers of tax reform*. Stanford, CA: Hoover Institution Press.
Harrod, R.F. (1939). An essay in dynamic theory. *The Economic Journal*, *49*, 14–33.
IMF (2008). *Government finance statistics yearbook*. Washington: International Monetary Fund.
Joint Committee on Taxation (2011, September 22). *Testimony of the staff of the Joint Committee on Taxation before the Joint Select Committee on Deficit Reduction* (JCX-49-11). Retrieved from http://www.jct.gov/publications.html?func=startdown&id=4363
Jones, L.E. and Manueli, R. (1990). A convex model of equilibrium growth: Theory and policy implications. *Journal of Political Economy*, *98*(5), 1008–38.
King, R.G. and Rebelo, S. (1990). Public policy and economic growth: Developing neoclassical implications. *Journal of Political Economy*, *98*(October), S126–51.
Landou, D.L. (1983). Government expenditure and economic growth: A cross-country study. *Southern Economic Journal*, *49*, 783–92.
Landou, D.L. (1986). Government and economic growth in the less developed countries: An empirical study for 1960–1980. *Economic Development and Cultural Change*, *35*, 34–75.
Levine, R. and Renelt, D. (1992). A sensitivity analysis of cross-country growth regressions. *American Economic Review*, *82*, 942–63.
Li, C. and Lin, S. (2013). *China's social security debt: How large?* Unpublished paper.
Lin, S. (1997). Education and economic development in China. *Comparative Economic Studies*, *36*(3&4), 66–85.
Lin, S. (1999). Export expansion and economic growth: Evidence from Chinese provinces. *Pacific Economic Review*, *4*(1), 65–77.
Lin, S. (2000a). Foreign trade and China's economic development: A time-series analysis. *Journal of Economic Development*, *25*(1), 145–53.
Lin, S. (2000b). Resource allocation and economic growth in China. *Economic Inquiry*, *38*(3), 515–26.
Lin, S. (2000c). The decline of China's budgetary revenue: Reasons and consequences. *Contemporary Economic Policy*, *18*(4), 477–90.
Lin, S. (2001). Public infrastructure development in China. *Comparative Economic Studies*, *43*(2), 83–109.
Lin, S. and Song, S. (2002). Urban economic growth in China: Theory and evidence. *Urban Studies*, *39*(12), 2251–66.
Lin, S. and Sosin, K. (2001). Government debt and economic growth. *Economics of Transition*, *9*(3), 635–55.
Lucas, R.E. (1988). On the mechanics of economic development. *Journal of Monetary Economics*, *22*, 3–42.
Mencius (n.d.). *Teng Wen Gong*. Retrieved from http://baike.baidu.com/view/5747895.htm?pid=baike.box.

National Bureau of Statistics of China (1980–2012). *China statistical yearbook*. Beijing: China Statistical Publishing House.
National Bureau of Statistics of China (2010). China compendium of statistics 1949–2009. Beijing: China Statistical Publishing House.
National Bureau of Statistics of China (2013). *Statistical communiqué of the People's Republic of China on the 2012 national economic and social development*. Retrieved from http://www.stats.gov.cn/english/pressrelease/t20130222_402874590.htm
Perkins, D.H. (2012). Rapid growth and changing economic structure: The expenditure side story and its implications for China. *China Economic Review*, *23*(3), 501–11.
Rebelo, S. (1991). Long-run policy analysis and long-run growth. *Journal of Political Economy*, *99*(3), 500–521.
Rodrik, D. (2010). Making room for China in the world economy. *American Economic Review*, *100*(2), 89–93.
Romer, P.M. (1989). Capital accumulation in the theory of long-run growth. In R. Barro (Ed.), *Modern business cycle theory*. Cambridge, MA: Harvard University Press.
Seidman, L. (1984). Conversion to a consumption tax: The transition in a life cycle growth model. *Journal of Political Economy*, *92*(2), 247–67.
Solow, R.M. (1956). A contribution to the theory of economic growth. *The Quarterly Journal of Economics*, *70*(1), 65–94.
Smith, A. (1776). *An inquiry into the nature and causes of the wealth of nations*. (E. Cannan, 1904, 5th edn) London: Methuen and Co. Ltd.
Summers, L.H. (1981). Capital taxation and accumulation in a life cycle growth model. *American Economic Review*, *71*(4), 533–44.
The Board of Trustees, Federal Old-Age and Survivors Insurance and Federal Disability Insurance Trust Funds (2012, April 25). The 2012 annual report of the board of trustees of the federal old-age and survivors insurance and federal disability insurance trust funds. Retrieved from http://www.ssa.gov/oact/tr/2012/tr2012.pdf
Toder, E.J (1995). Comments on proposals for fundamental tax reform. Tax Notes, 2003–2015.
United Nations Development Programme (UNDP) (2010). Human development report. New York: United Nations.
World Bank (2013). Data:United States. Retrieved from http://data.worldbank.org/country/united-states
Yang, D.T. (2012). Aggregate savings and external imbalances in China. *Journal of Economic Perspectives*, *26*(4), 125–46.
Zhu, X. (2012). Understanding China's growth: Past, present, and future. *Journal of Economic Perspectives*, *26*(4), 103–24.

4. Productivity differences, technology adoption and economic growth: The case of India

Radhika Lahiri and Shyama Ratnasiri

When the acronym of 'BRIC' was coined in 2001 by Jim O'Neill of Goldman Sachs, it was expected that economic growth rates in India, Brazil and Russia would eventually catch up with that of China. However, China has continued to outperform the other economies in the group, even after it was renamed 'BRICS' to reflect the inclusion of South Africa in 2010. The focus of this chapter is on *one* of the BRICS economies, namely India. Its aim is to examine from an economic perspective, why India's performance has not lived up to expectations, and comment on the key challenges it faces in meeting them.

We begin with some descriptive statistics regarding the progress of the Indian economy since 1990. While it has been growing at a rapid rate since the reforms it introduced in the1990s, there has been a slowdown in its overall GDP growth rates since 2008. The rate of growth experienced in the period 2003–07 was an average of 10.5 per cent. However, since the recession following the Global Financial Crisis (GFC) of 2008, the growth rate has fallen. From the period 2008–12 it has only registered an average growth rate of 6.5 per cent (World Bank, 2013). This chapter suggests that one of the major factors underpinning this slowdown is the performance of India's agricultural sector.

The importance of the agricultural sector is highlighted by the following stylized facts. While the share of the agricultural sector has fallen over time from 55 per cent in 1950 to 14 per cent in 2011 (Table 4.1), the population employed in agriculture remains high at 52 per cent of the employed workforce in 2011 (RBI, 2012). A majority of this workforce consists of the rural poor. Furthermore, 70 per cent of the Indian population still lives in rural areas and consequently depends on agriculture and allied activities for its living. The agricultural sector supports the food requirements of a large urban population in addition to the rural population. The Indian population has been growing at an average rate of 2 per cent during the

Table 4.1 Agriculture, industry and services share in GDP for selected time periods (%)

Year	Agriculture	Industry	Services
1950–51	55	11	34
1960–61	51	13	36
1970–71	44	15	40
1980–81	38	17	45
1990–91	31	20	49
2000–01	24	20	56
2010–11	14	20	66

Source: Reserve Bank of India (2012).

last 50 years and India is home to more than 1.2 billion people, the second highest population in the world. The Indian agricultural sector is, therefore, an important sector in the Indian economy as it meets most of this food demand from domestic production.

To meet this demand, more than half (60.47 per cent) of India's geographical area is used for agricultural activities (World Bank, 2013). Furthermore this sector provides inputs for other industries, particularly industries such as textiles, paper and sugar which are substantially dependent on the domestic agricultural sector. In relation to agriculture's contribution to India's balance of payments, we observe that agricultural trade has increased rapidly over the recent past. Agricultural products currently account for 11 per cent of the total merchandise exports in India (WTO, 2012).

At the theoretical level, there is a large amount of literature in economics on the link between the agricultural sector and overall economic growth. The role of agricultural productivity in the structural transformation of economies, for example, has been emphasized in the literature on economic growth and development (Chenery & Syrquin, 1975; Clark, 1940; Kuznets, 1966; Timmer, 1998). Typically, classical models of economic development suggest that there is a 'stage of growth' in which an economy's agricultural productivity increases dramatically, releasing resources, particularly labour, to other sectors of the economy. This in turn facilitates further transformation through the growth of the manufacturing and services sectors of the economy. There is also a consensus in this early literature regarding the *sequence* of growth patterns with respect to these sectoral changes – agriculture expands first, followed by manufacturing and finally services. This view is based on the empirical experience of countries such as the US and UK, which reached 'modern economic growth' earlier than others, with an 'industrial revolution' following the agricultural transformation of the economy (see, for example, Mokyr, 1990, 1993; Rostow, 1956).

However, the contemporary experience of developers, although following a pattern of growth and development which involves the initial transformation of the agricultural sector, does not necessarily conform to the classical 'agriculture-manufacturing-services' sequence that was observed in industrialized economies of the US and Western Europe. In the case of India, for example, the pattern so far has involved an initial burst of agricultural transformation following the green revolution of the late 1960s and 1970s, followed by a services sector-led 'revolution' in growth and development. This is in contrast to China, another economy from the BRICS group of countries, which seems to have followed the classical pattern of development.

Our focus, however, is not the difference in these patterns per se, but an exploration of why development seems to have stalled in the case of India and not in the case of China. Particularly, it is the initial stage – that of agricultural transformation – which is of concern as it can be linked to the stalling of the growth process in India. As mentioned above, this *initial* transformation of agriculture is imperative to the growth process. The importance of this feature of development has been borne out in the empirical experience of *all* economies that have experienced modern economic growth. Basically, resources need to be released from the *agricultural* sector for growth of other sectors of the economy, which may be either manufacturing or services. In what follows, therefore, we examine, using economic-growth theory as a lens, the stalling of growth observed in the agricultural sector in India and its connection to the declines in overall GDP growth rates of that country. Underpinning this connection are factors relating to technology adoption in various sectors of the economy, and particularly in agriculture.

This brings us to the underlying sources of agricultural transformation discussed in the literature already mentioned, particularly with reference to the experience in the US, UK, and Western Europe. Underpinning the dramatic increases in agricultural productivity were technological changes in agriculture.[1] We explore this aspect in the context of the agricultural experience in India, in the growth spurt of the early 1980s and the slowdown in subsequent years. Specifically, our focus is on *technology adoption* in agriculture in the corresponding periods.

Looking at this issue from the point of view of contemporary *theoretical* literature, the mechanisms that can cause a slowdown in agricultural growth rates relate to the initial conditions governing levels and differences in the productivity of inferior and superior technologies as suggested in Lahiri and Ratnasiri, 2012, which is similar in spirit to several other models in the literature that suggest the lack of technology adoption as a barrier to sustained economic growth (see, for example, Parente & Prescott, 1994). In particular, if the productivity levels of the technologies in use are 'low' (and therefore not too disparate, that is, all technologies in use are inferior), the economy will end up in a 'poverty trap' (Lahiri & Ratnasiri, 2012). On the other hand, if the economy consists of two sets of technologies, one with low productivity levels (ie inferior technology) and another with high productivity levels (ie superior technology), it ends up in a 'dual economy' (Lahiri & Ratnasiri, 2012). Only in the case where the economy is characterized by technologies that are all of a 'high' productivity level does the economy take the 'balanced growth' path, where 'balanced growth' corresponds to the concept of sustained economic growth mentioned previously.

We examine this empirically by constructing proxies for both technology adoption and productivity for Indian state-level data corresponding to the periods that we are focusing on. These proxies help us measure the state of technological development and adoption at a given time as well as disparities in technological advancement across different states in India. We track these over time to see the trends in technology adoption and productivity, specifically with reference to the periods mentioned previously. The theoretical predictions of our model then provide us with a lens to examine the progress in India along these dimensions and to offer some policy prescriptions.

We find that India is characterized by productivity and technology adoption levels that describe a 'dual economy'. However, a transition has been taking place over time and our indices for technology adoption and productivity suggest that India is moving towards the initial conditions that characterize 'balanced growth'. Put differently, the levels of technology adoption and productivity have been growing over time and the disparities between them have been narrowing across various states of India. Nevertheless these changes have been moderate and this is reflected in the productivity slowdown mentioned earlier. Furthermore, a comparison of progress along some of these dimensions with that of other transitional economies, particularly China, is unfavourable, because these comparisons suggest that India has a long way to go before the take-off to sustained economic growth occurs.

A policy implication is that greater investment in research and development in agriculture must take place. However, this may not be enough, given that technology *adoption* and *diffusion* is the key to increasing agricultural productivity. This would entail an investment in education and infrastructure with a view to facilitating the adoption and diffusion of new technologies. A two-pronged approach of this nature, for example, has been successful in other BRICS member economies such as China and Brazil, where substantial improvements in agricultural productivity have taken place. Viewed from this perspective, the strategic cooperation in agriculture that has been mentioned in several meetings of the BRICS economies, if implemented, is a step in the right direction.

In the next section we present further details of the theoretical literature on technology adoption, with a particular focus on the model of Lahiri and Ratnasiri (2012), which then provides a framework for the analysis that follows in subsequent sections. We then discuss the empirical measurement of the levels and disparities in technology adoption and productivity, and analyse the trends along these dimensions. Finally, in the last section, we conclude by offering policy implications of the preceding analysis.

THEORETICAL LITERATURE AND A FRAMEWORK FOR ANALYSIS

The contribution of technological progress to economic growth, and the need for technology adoption to sustain it, has been theoretically explored using various approaches. Typically they stem from the neoclassical growth models due to Solow (1956) and its variants such as Cass (1965) and Koopmans (1965). These models treat technology as exogenously given, and the long-run growth rate is solely determined by the exogenous rate of technical change. For example, in the Solow model returns to capital diminish as the capital stock increases, with labour (in efficiency units) held constant. It is for this reason that the economy eventually converges to a steady state growth rate in which the capital-labour ratio is constant. Hence the only source of growth in per capita output is technological progress.

The implication of this model is that convergence in per capita incomes across countries will take place because (a) poorer countries will adopt superior technologies from richer countries at a relatively low cost, without having to reinvent them for themselves, and (b) once this has taken place, given the initially low level of capital in less developed economies, a faster rate of growth is inevitable. Capital will flow from advanced economies where there is low productivity to less advanced ones where there is high productivity, until the per capita capital-labour ratios, and consequently per capita output levels, have equalized across economies.

The nature of convergence hypothesized in the neoclassical model is of a *conditional* type. If convergence in incomes across economies has not been observed, then it must be because features (a) and (b) of the mechanism described earlier have not taken place. This explanation, however, is somewhat unsatisfactory in that it does not explain why technology adoption – the obvious solution to this problem – *does not* take place. Another critique relates to the 'exogenous' nature of technological progress; there is no explanation of the factors that underpin technological progress or the technological choices made by economic agents.

As a result of this critique, a class of models typically labelled as 'endogenous growth models' appeared in the literature on economic growth and development. These models, including Romer (1986, 1987, 1990), Rebelo (1991), Grossman and Helpman (1991), and Aghion and Howitt (1992), presume growth through the 'accumulation of knowledge', either through 'learning by doing' or through technological innovation as a result of research and development (R&D).[2] In contrast to the neoclassical growth models of Solow (1956) and Swan (1956), where the state of technology forms part of the background conditions, predetermined by the efforts of scientists and engineers but taken as given by economists, the 'new growth theory' emphasizes that there is a two-way link between technology and the economy (Howitt, 2007).

A further aspect of the 'new growth theory' involves the idea of *capital deepening* as a source of economic growth. Again, in contrast to exogenous growth models in which capital deepening refers to the accumulation of *physical* capital, and is consequently subject to diminishing returns, some endogenous growth models focus on capital as a composite good consisting of both human and physical capital, which makes the assumption of constant returns to scale a plausible one. Sustained growth is possible in this type of model as continuous capital accumulation can occur due to the fact that the returns to capital do not diminish with increases in the stock of capital.

The adoption of new technologies can further be modelled as a choice made by economic agents, and this in turn fuels the growth process – a mechanism that is central to the work of Lahiri and Ratnasiri (2012), and that of Khan and Ravikumar (2002), among others. In the discussion that follows, it is this mechanism that we focus on, using the Lahiri and Ratnasiri model (hereinafter LR model) as a benchmark for our analysis.[3]

In the LR model there are economic agents who are heterogeneous in their holdings of income and wealth and face a 'technology adoption decision'. In particular there are two technologies that can be used to produce output which, following the LR model terminology, we refer to as Technology A and Technology B respectively. Technology B is the better, more productive technology. However, unlike Technology A, it is associated with an adoption cost. The adoption cost represents the higher educational and 'learning by doing' requirements associated with Technology B.

In the LR model only some of the richer agents in the economy are able to adopt Technology B. The long run outcomes in this model can be of three types, depending on the 'initial conditions', which for a given distribution of resources and adoption cost, are determined by the productivity levels and differences between the two technologies. The descriptions of these three cases are presented:

1. **Poverty Trap**. In this case the productivity levels of the two technologies are 'low' in a sense that can be quantified using the parameters of the model. Intuitively the productivity levels are such that agents using either A or B are not able to leave sufficient resources for the next generation, drawing them into a 'poverty trap'.
2. **'Dual Economy'**. In this case the productivity levels are more disparate, with the better technology substantially superior in productivity relative to the A technology. The dynamics of this economy are such that dynasties starting with wealth levels below a critical level end up adopting Technology A forever, while the richer agents adopt B, enjoying continuous growth.
3. **Balanced Growth**. In this case the productivity levels of both technologies are high. Here all agents adopt B and enjoy continuous growth.

Our view is that the three types of initial conditions mentioned in the LR model characterize three different 'stages of growth'. As inventions and R&D take place, newer and more productive technologies come into existence, taking the economy from the initial conditions characterized by 'poverty trap' to the initial conditions characterized by 'dual economy'. In the final stage, the process of innovations and inventions has taken place and all the technologies in existence are of a high productivity level, thus characterizing the 'balanced growth stage'.

IMPLICATIONS OF THE MODEL AND DISCUSSION

While the LR model has a broader applicability in the sense that it refers to an entire economy, inclusive of the agricultural and non-agricultural sectors, we apply its predictions in the context of the agricultural sector viewed in isolation from the rest of the economy. The LR model then implies that productivity levels in *agriculture* need to increase, and that disparities between technologies in use and their productivity levels must decrease if the agricultural sector is to attain 'balanced growth'.

In the following analysis, we construct empirical measures of productivity and technology adoption to first assess which 'stage of growth', according to the LR model, characterizes India. A large body of literature (see, for example, Lewis, 1954; Harris & Todaro, 1970) suggests that India is a 'dual economy', but we are also able to support this using evidence based on our proxies of technology adoption and productivity. We then use these measures to evaluate whether the initial conditions in India are improving in the sense that over time we can see a transition from the 'dual economy' to the 'balanced growth' case. We do this by taking a snapshot view of the aforementioned dimensions – namely productivity and technology adoption and the associated disparities across regions – across four different time periods corresponding to 1962–65, 1980–83, 1990–93, and 2003–06.[4]

This is a challenging task given that we have to find an empirical yardstick to quantify what we mean by a 'high' or a 'low' productivity level, and also to find a way of measuring the disparities in these productivity levels. We also need a measure for the *extent* of technology adoption. While this concept is very stylized in the model – that is, agents have only two technologies to choose from and they either adopt the superior 'B' technology or the inferior 'A' technology – in the data there are several technologies in use, and depending on which region of India we look at, there are different 'levels' of adoption of these technologies. In the following subsection we discuss our measures for technology adoption and productivity and indices for measuring state-wide disparities in these aggregates.

Empirical Measures

We construct proxies for both technology adoption and productivity for Indian state-level data corresponding to the periods that we are focusing on. In Table 4.2 we use rupees per hectare to capture productivity levels, expressed relative to 1960 base year prices.

Next we construct an index to measure the extent of technology adoption in various states across India.[5] First, to determine the major factors underlying technology adoption that will eventually constitute our index, we conduct a factor analysis based on six technological practices. These are:

1. Percentage of cropped area sown with High Yielding Varieties (HYVs)
2. Cropping intensity
3. Number of tractors used per thousand ha
4. Fertilizer consumption (kg/ha)
5. Percentage of total cropped area irrigated
6. Number of pump sets used per thousand ha.

Table 4.2 State–wide productivity levels (Rs/ha)

State	1962–65	1980–83		1990–93		2003–06	
Andra Pradesh	4065	6276	(54.39)	8727	(39.05)	11 537	(32.20)
Assam	5727	6907	(20.60)	7998	(15.80)	8989	(12.39)
Bihar	3680	4049	(10.03)	5278	(30.35)	5670	(7.43)
Gujarat	3673	5693	(55.00)	6640	(16.63)	11 836	(78.25)
Haryana	3927	6229	(58.62)	9682	(55.43)	11569	(19.49)
Himchal Pradesh	3048	3918	(28.54)	5187	(32.39)	6176	(19.07)
Jammu Kashmir	2987	5759	(92.80)	5432	(−5.68)	5985	(10.18)
Karnataka	3208	4990	(55.55)	6342	(27.09)	6994	(10.28)
Kerala	11 376	12 334	(8.42)	14 655	(18.82)	13 858	(−5.44)
Madya Pradesh	2603	3070	(17.94)	4406	(43.52)	5640	(28.01)
Maharashtra	2899	3795	(30.91)	4490	(18.31)	5960	(32.74)
Orisssa	4114	4375	(6.34)	5740	(31.20)	6690	(16.55)
Punjab	5396	9708	(79.91)	13 215	(36.12)	15 373	(16.33)
Rajastan	1740	2335	(34.20)	3809	(63.13)	5095	(33.76)
Tamil Nadu	6690	8756	(30.88)	13 037	(48.89)	13 117	(0.61)
Uttar Pradesh	3970	5805	(46.22)	8355	(43.93)	9894	(18.42)
West Bengal	5075	5944	(17.12)	9507	(59.94)	12 142	(27.72)

Notes: Figures within parentheses are productivity growth rates.

Source: Bhalla and Singh (2010).

We conduct a Principal Components Analysis (PCA) to determine the weights that should be applied to these six components.[6] We use these weights presented in Table 4.3 to construct our technology adoption index, described as follows.

We denote each technological practice for the *jth* state by Xij, and $i = 1.6$. These indicators are standardized across the states as follows.

$$X_i = \frac{X_{ij} - X_{im}}{X_{iu} - X_{im}} \tag{4.1}$$

Here, the notations X_{ij}, X_{im} and X_{iu} respectively represent the value for the technological practice in the jth state, and the minimum and maximum values for the ith technological practice across states at a given time period. Next we use weights (denoted by αi for technological practice i) obtained from our PCA to compute the Technology Adoption Index (hereinafter TAI) at the state-level, which is given by:

$$TAI = \sum_{i=1}^{6} \alpha_i X_i. \tag{4.2}$$

Table 4.3 Weights for the variables

Variable	Normalized weights
Number of tractors used per thousand ha	0.180
Number of pump sets used per thousand ha	0.161
Fertilizer consumption	0.189
Percentage of total cropped area irrigated	0.185
Cropping intensity	0.140
Cropped area sown with HYVs	0.143

Source: Authors' calculations.

This index takes values strictly between 0 and 1, with a higher value indicating a larger extent of technology adoption.

To analyse the disparities in these aggregates we use Gini coefficients of technology and productivity levels.[7] The Gini index is a measure of inequality/dispersion in a variable, and ranges between 0 and 1, with a higher value indicating a higher level of inequality.

Discussion

As is evident from Table 4.2, productivity trends across states have been positive. However, there is some diversity in the performances of different states of India. For example, in terms of absolute levels, Punjab, Kerala and Tamil Nadu are the most productive states. Gujarat and Maharashtra are the fastest growing states. In fact the latter states are the only ones that have not experienced the productivity slowdown observed across the periods 1990–93 and 2003–06. This slowdown has been of particular concern since it has continued in addition to manifesting itself in the overall growth rate of the Indian economy (World Bank, 2004).

The disparities across states that are evident in Table 4.2 further reinforce the notion that India is a 'dual economy'. International comparisons of productivity levels also suggest that India enjoys intermediate levels of productivity that are a characteristic of transitional economies (Cagliarini & Rush, 2011). However, the Gini coefficients in Table 4.5 suggest that disparities have been falling in the last few decades, which may suggest a slow transition towards the 'balanced growth' scenario.

In terms of technology adoption, a glance at Table 4.4 suggests small improvements over time for most states in the sample. The levels of the TAI seem to correlate positively with productivity levels across states in all of the four different time periods in question. However, levels of technology adoption remain quite low with only a handful of states scoring TAI

Table 4.4 Technology adoption index

State	1962–65	1980–83	1990–93	2003–06
Andra Pradesh	0.29	0.27	0.35	0.34
Assam	0.11	0.08	0.13	0.21
Bihar	0.22	0.23	0.28	0.34
Gujarat	0.16	0.17	0.19	0.39
Haryana	0.29	0.58	0.73	0.78
Himchal Pradesh	0.20	0.19	0.18	0.39
Jammu Kashmir	0.20	0.18	0.17	0.26
Karnataka	0.10	0.14	0.18	0.24
Kerala	0.36	0.18	0.20	0.35
Madya Pradesh	0.05	0.10	0.16	0.24
Maharashtra	0.10	0.14	0.21	0.18
Orisssa	0.10	0.15	0.20	0.36
Punjab	0.71	0.94	0.97	0.83
Rajasthan	0.07	0.12	0.13	0.28
Tamilnadu	0.61	0.46	0.45	0.33
Uttara Pradesh	0.31	0.42	0.50	0.61
West Bengal	0.20	0.21	0.36	0.59

Source: Authors' calculations.

Table 4.5 Gini coefficients of technology adoption and productivity

Year	Productivity Gini	Technology adoption Gini
1962–65	0.2325	0.375
1970–73	0.2386	–
1980–83	0.2209	0.373
1990–93	0.2272	0.343
2003–06	0.2011	0.247

Source: Authors' calculations.

value above 0.5. This is further reflective of the 'dual economy' features of the Indian case, and reinforced when one examines the Gini indices for technology adoption that are presented in Table 4.5. The index in this case has a much higher value in comparison to the index based on productivity levels. It is noteworthy that the index is falling over time. However, this is subject to the caveat that our technology adoption measure does not include a 'human capital component' that is intrinsic to the 'learning by doing' associated with technology adoption and diffusion.

Nevertheless we believe that the picture presented using our TAI measure is not as bleak as the numbers suggest. There is a great scope for improvement in productivity levels, provided that agricultural reform is addressed towards removing the disparities in technology adoption. This is illustrated particularly in the case of Gujarat, which has registered a substantial increase in the TAI, making it the fastest growing state in terms of productivity levels. Ideally, a policy of agricultural reform should be targeted towards bringing about improvements in the low TAI states where there is a greater scope for productivity increases.

CONCLUDING OBSERVATIONS AND IMPLICATIONS FOR POLICY

As discussed, the Indian economy has experienced substantial growth but there has been a slowdown in this growth lately, and the slowdown in the agricultural sector is of particular concern. While the technology adoption scenario based on our analysis is not bleak, there is scope for improvement. From the perspective of the theoretical literature, there is a need for (a) an increase in the productivity levels of all technologies used in agriculture and (b) a 'complete' adoption of these technologies. In terms of the model, point (a) refers to increases in the parameters A and B, which refer to the productivity levels of the inferior and superior technology respectively. These increases, which occur through R&D financed innovations and inventions, create the initial conditions for sustained growth. Furthermore, the fact that the impact of agricultural R&D investments on productivity and poverty reduction is positive and significant, has considerable empirical support (see Thirtle, Lin & Piesse, 2003). There is indeed evidence to suggest that such R&D effort is taking place in India, particularly in relation to public *agricultural* R&D expenditures, but to a substantially lesser degree than in the case of China (Bientema & Stads, 2010).

Point (b) relates to the adoption and diffusion of technologies, and this is perhaps the more challenging aspect of the issues at hand. In terms of our model, the adoption of the superior technology occurs when a sufficient amount of capital deepening has taken place, where 'capital' consists of both human and physical capital, and 'deepening' refers to further accumulation of these components, in addition to the 'learning by doing' element that is associated with human capital. The policy implication in the context of India is that further investment in human capital development through investment in education, poverty reduction, food security and healthcare must take place, in addition to investments in physical capital and infrastructure. This would facilitate the adoption of new technologies, in addition to increasing their productivity through enhancement of the 'learning by doing' component.

The concept captured by our indicators of disparities in technology adoption and productivity is of relevance to the point made earlier. A systematic and widespread adoption of better technologies can only take place when the efforts at capital deepening have taken place across all regions of India. The preceding analysis suggests that there is in fact a greater scope of increases in overall productivity levels if such efforts are targeted towards regions that have a lower degree of technology adoption.

To that end, there is also a need to develop quantitative indicators for measuring the extent of technology adoption, of the type discussed in the previous section. Quantitative information of this type can be very useful for policymakers and other stakeholders in formulating policies and measuring and monitoring the impact of these on agricultural growth rates. We believe that our analysis here is only an exploratory step in that direction, and further refinement and development of such indicators is an important avenue of future research (Lahiri & Ratnasiri, 2013).

NOTES

1. For a detailed discussion of various technological inventions in the history of agriculture and their impact on productivity see Mokyr (1985, 1993).
2. Our aim here is to give a brief account of the literature before we discuss the model that underpins the empirical analysis of the next section, and to that end we refer only to a key selection of the literature. Interested readers can find comprehensive surveys of this vast literature in Aghion and Durlauf (2005).
3. We present an intuitive analysis here; our aim is to convey an 'in-a-nutshell' view of the model rather than its technical details. For a more rigorous presentation see Lahiri and Ratnasiri (2012).
4. We use waves of National Sample Survey Office (NSSO) data for the corresponding periods. Other sources of data used for the construction of the TAI are Zhang, Fan and Cai (2002), Chand, Raju, Garg and Pandey (2011), and Department of Agriculture and Cooperation India (2012). For the HYV variable in the TAI, we use the nearest possible estimate in the event that the data for the period in question is not available.
5. The methodology used is similar in spirit to the index constructed in United Nations Development Programme (2006) for various aggregates such as life expectancy, education, etc. See also Jain et al. (2009) who applied the same method in the context of technology adoption. Our approach differs from Jain et al. (2009) as we use a larger set of variables and a modified approach based on PCA.
6. For details regarding the method of PCA, see Rauniyar and Goode (1992).
7. The Gini coefficient is computed using the Sen (1973) version of the index.

REFERENCES

Aghion, P. and Durlauf, S. (2005). *Handbook of economic growth.* Netherlands: Elsevier.

Aghion, P. and Howitt, P. (1992). A model of growth through creative destruction. *Econometrica*, *60*(2), 323–52.

Bhalla, G.S. and Singh, G. (2010). *Growth of Indian agriculture: A district level study* (Final report of planning commission project, Centre for the Study of Regional Development). New Delhi: Jawaharlal Nehru University.

Bientema, N. and Stads, G. (2010). *Public agricultural R&D investments and capacities in developing countries: Recent evidence for 2000 and beyond.* Note prepared for GCARD 2010 and ASTI presentation at GCARD-2010, Montpellier, France.

Cagliarini, A. and Rush, A. (2011). Economic development and agriculture in India. *Bulletin, June Quarter*, 15–22.

Cass, D. (1965). Optimum growth in an aggregative model of capital accumulation. *Review of Economic Studies*, *32*(3), 233–40.

Chand, R., Raju, S., Garg, S. and Pandey, L. (2011). *Instability and regional variation in Indian agriculture* (Policy Paper). India: National Centre for Agricultural Economics and Policy Research (NCAP).

Chenery, H. and Syrquin, M. (1975). *Patterns of development 1950–1970.* New York, NY: Oxford University Press for the World Bank.

Clark, C. (1940). *The conditions of economic progress.* London, UK: MacMillan.

Department of Agriculture and Cooperation India. (2012). *Agricultural statistics at a glance.* Retrieved from http://agricoop.nic.in/Agristatistics.htm

Grossman, G. and Helpman, E. (1991). *Innovation and growth in the global economy.* Cambridge, MA: MIT Press.

Harris, J. and Todaro, M. (1970). Migration unemployment and development: A two sector analysis. *American Economic Review*, *60*(1), 126–38.

Howitt, P. (2007). Innovation, competition and growth: A Schumpeterian perspective on Canada's economy. *C.D. Howe Institute Commentary*, *246*, 1–19.

Jain R., Arora, A. and Raju, S. (2009). A novel adoption index of selected agricultural technologies: Linkages with infrastructure and productivity. *Agricultural Economics Research Review*, *22*(1),109–20.

Khan, A. and Ravikumar, B. (2002). Costly technology adoption and capital accumulation. *Review of Economic Dynamics*, *5*(2), 489–502.

Koopmans, T. (1965). On the concept of optimal economic growth. In *The econometric approach to development planning* (pp. 225–300). Amsterdam: North-Holland.

Kuznets, S. (1966). *Towards a theory of economic growth.* New Haven, CT: Yale University Press.

Lahiri, R. and Ratnasiri, S. (2012). Growth patterns and inequality in the presence of costly technology adoption. *Southern Economic Journal*, *79*(1), 203–23.

Lahiri, R. and Ratnasiri, S. (2013). *Agricultural productivity, technology adoption and economic growth in India* (manuscript). Brisbane, Qld: Queensland University of Technology.

Lewis, A. (1954). Economic development with unlimited supplies of labour. *The Manchester School*, *22*(2), 139–91.

Mokyr, J. (1985). *The economics of the industrial revolution.* London: George Allen and Unwin.

Mokyr, J. (1990). *The lever of riches: Technological creativity and economic progress*. New York: Oxford University Press.
Mokyr, J. (1993). The new economic history and the industrial revolution. In J. Mokyr (Ed.), *The British industrial revolution: An economic perspective* (pp. 1–131). Boulder, CO: Westview Press.
Parente, S. and Prescott, E. (1994). Barriers to technology adoption and development. *Journal of Political Economy*, *102*(2), 298–301.
Rauniyar, G. and Goode, F. (1992). Technology adoption on small farms. *World Development*, *20*(2), 275–82.
Rebelo, S. (1991). Long run policy analysis and long run growth. *Journal of Political Economy*, *99*(3), 500–21.
Reserve Bank of India (RBI). (2012). *Database on Indian economy, RBI's data warehouse*. Retrieved from http://dbie.rbi.org.in/DBIE/dbie.rbi?site=statistics
Romer, P. (1986). Increasing returns and long run growth. *Journal of Political Economy*, *94*(5), 1002–37.
Romer, P. (1987). Growth based on increasing returns due to specialization. *The American Economic Review*, *77*(2), 56–62.
Romer, P. (1990). Endogenous technological change. *Journal of Political Economy*, *98*(5), 71–102.
Rostow, W. (1956). The take-off into self-sustained growth. *The Economic Journal*, *66*(261), 25–48.
Sen, A. (1973). *On economic inequality*. Oxford: Clarendon Press.
Solow, R. (1956). A contribution to the theory of economic growth. *Quarterly Journal of Economics*, *70*, 65–94.
Swan, T. (1956). Economic growth and capital accumulation. *Economic Record*, *32*(63), 334–61.
Thirtle, C., Lin, L. and Piesse, J. (2003). The impact of research-led agricultural productivity growth on poverty reduction in Africa, Asia and Latin America. *World Development*, *31*(12), 1959–75.
Timmer, P. (1998). The agricultural transformation. In C. Eicher and J. Staatz (Eds), *International agricultural development* (3rd edn) (pp. 113–35). Baltimore, MD: John Hopkins University Press.
United Nations Development Programme. (2006). Technical note 1: Calculating the human development index. In *Human Development Report 2006*. New York, NY: Palgrave Macmillan.
World Bank (2004). *India: Re-energizing the agricultural sector to sustain growth and reduce poverty* (Report No. 27889). South Asia Region, Washington DC: Rural Development Unit, World Bank.
World Bank (2013). *World development indicators*. Retrieved from http://data.worldbank.org/data-catalog/world-development-indicators
WTO (2012). *International trade statistics*. Retrieved from http://www.wto.org/english/res_e/statis_e/statis_e.htm
Zhang, X., Fan, S. and Cai, X. (2002). The path technology diffusion: Which neighbours to learn from? *Contemporary Economic Policy*, *20*(4), 470–78.

5. Brazil: A soft power rising with the BRICS towards a multipolar world

Raquel Dos Santos

Over a decade ago, economist Jim O'Neil predicted that by 2050 most of the global economic growth would come from the emerging economies of Brazil, Russia, India and China, and created the acronym BRIC. What then started as an acronym has evolved into a strong brand and alliance transcending the economic role of these nations as global suppliers of goods, services and raw materials.

South Africa joined the alliance in 2010, representing the relevance of the African continent to global economic growth and extending the acronym to BRICS. In 2012 the BRICS represented approximately 56 per cent of the world's GDP growth and 20 per cent of global GDP in nominal terms.

The BRICS is increasingly becoming one of the political forces shaping the future of economic and trade policy-making, and to some extent representing the interests of developing and least developed nations in multilateral negotiations. The commitment of the BRICS nations in this regard continues to increase, and during the fifth BRICS Summit in March 2013 the BRICS announced the establishment of the BRICS Development Bank, Contingency Reserve Arrangement, BRICS Business Council and BRICS Think Tanks Council. These announcements are examples of the ability of the BRICS to develop and implement long-term economic and political strategies that will challenge the hegemony of developed nations in the world order.

The last decade has brought significant developments to economic, political and social environments in the BRICS nations. This chapter highlights some of the economic, foreign trade and policy developments that have occurred in Brazil, including:

- domestic factors that contributed to an unprecedented growth of the Brazilian economy;
- foreign trade indicators and the country's Mercosur membership as a barrier to a BRICS free trade agreement;

- some of Brazil's foreign trade policies at the WTO; and
- the country's ambition to become an active participant in global economic governance with the BRICS.

BRAZIL'S UNPRECEDENTED ECONOMIC DEVELOPMENT FROM A NATIONAL PERSPECTIVE

Brazil's economic environment in the 1980s and early 1990s was a reflection of a series of unsuccessful macroeconomic reforms designed to seek hyperinflation stabilization, including the freezing of public debt and confiscation of savings accounts under the Collor Plan, and a number of unstable currencies (*cruzeiro*, *cruzado*, *cruzado novo*, and *cruzeiro real*) until the *real* became a currency in 1994.

Since then, Brazil has experienced economic stability and growth, poverty reduction and consolidation of democracy, and has developed a self-branding ability as demonstrated by its selection to host the World Cup in 2014 and the Olympics in 2016.

Despite its relatively small share in the world economy and unimpressive military capabilities, Brazil has been consolidating its position as a global political player and becoming a soft power in the international political arena. Soft power, the ability to attract and influence others to want or accept one's values without coercion or incentives (Nye, 2004), has been Brazil's strategy to materialize its ambition of global political influence (Prusa, 2011, p. 2).

By investing in strategic diplomatic relations and leveraging its moral and material capabilities from its strong economic performance since the Global Financial Crisis (GFC), Brazil has gained a more credible and persuasive voice in global economic forums (Del Tedesco Lins & Silva, 2011, p. 22), and increased its ability to influence multilateral negotiations in important global issues, such as trade negotiations and climate change (Prusa, 2011, p. 51). On the other hand, following Brazil's GDP growth rates of 7.5 per cent in 2010, 2.7 per cent in 2011, and a sluggish 0.6 per cent in the third quarter of 2012 (OECD, 2012b), there has been some speculation as to whether the 'B' in the BRICS at the moment only stands for boring (Rapoza, 2012). Brazil faces various challenges on its path to full development, including sustaining economic growth and addressing some appalling social performance indicators. However, those who have lived or invested in Brazil would know that the 'B' in the BRICS is never boring.

According to the World Bank, Brazil's GDP growth rate is expected to be 3.4 per cent in 2013 and 4.1 per cent in 2014, and although economic growth has slowed down in developing countries, their economies are still the main drivers of global economic growth (World Bank, 2013c). In the context of the global economy, which continues to struggle following the GFC and the European Sovereign Debt Crisis, Brazil's GDP growth rate of 0.6 per cent in the third quarter of 2012 was the same as the GDP growth rate of the G20 as a whole, three times that of the EU (0.2 per cent) and just below the US rate (0.7 per cent) for the same period (OECD, 2012b).

As expected from a country rich in natural resources, Brazil's economic development has benefited from strong economic growth in industrialized and newly industrialized countries such as China, and an increase in commodity prices. However, significant domestic and 'institutional' factors have also contributed to the country's unprecedented economic development and positive business environment (Del Tedesco Lins & Silva, 2011, p. 22), including past macroeconomic reforms, the consolidation of democracy, and the introduction of socio-economic policies by the last two federal administrations directly targeting distribution of income and economic growth in the country.

The first factor dating back to the administration of former President Fernando Henrique Cardoso (1995–2003) was the introduction of successful macroeconomic reforms that served as the foundation of Brazil's current economic environment (Del Tedesco Lins & Silva, 2011, p. 21). The Plano Real, which introduced the *real* as a new currency in 1994, stabilized the country's economy after a long period of hyperinflation, at an annual rate of 2477.15 per cent in 1993 (inflation.eu, 2013), and allowed the development of credit activities and the restructuring of Brazil's financial and banking system.[1] The Cardoso administration was also responsible for a number of reforms that opened Brazil's economy and reduced the participation of the state in economic production (Del Tedesco Lins & Silva, 2011, p. 21). Subsequent presidents, Lula da Silva and Dilma Rousseff, have to some extent given continuity to a number of progressive and expansionary policies, which has contributed to a sense of political stability that has strengthened Brazil's economic and business environments (Del Tedesco Lins & Silva, 2011, p. 21).

In addition, the consolidation of democracy in Brazil should not be underestimated as a contributing factor to the country's economic development. Brazil's political history includes long periods of military dictatorship under which Brazilians advocating for political and economic freedom, including the now President and then political activist Dilma Rousseff, were reportedly arrested and tortured (Romero, 2012). A gradual transition from military dictatorship to democracy in Brazil, a period 'coloured' by President Collor de Mello's impeachment in 1992, was consolidated both in the transition from the Cardoso to the Lula administration in 2003, and from the Lula to the Rousseff administration in 2011 (Bertazzo, 2012, p. 890). As a result, confidence in the country's political environment has improved and stimulated foreign and domestic investment.

There is also a causal connection between Brazil's economic performance and the implementation of socio-economic policies by the last two federal administrations. Policies such as Family Purse and Zero Hunger have firmly targeted the reduction of poverty and inequality, whilst the Growth Acceleration Program (Programa de Aceleração do Crescimento or PAC)[2] has supported the creation of jobs, distribution of income and acceleration of economic growth through the facilitation of investment and infrastructure projects. The second edition of the PAC (PAC2 / 2012–2014), which Brazil pledged as a policy commitment in the 2012 G20 Summit, is a package for the investment of approximately US$545.7 billion for the period between 2011 and 2014 (and US$360.8 billion thereafter) in infrastructure projects, including transport, energy, water, housing and urban development (G20, 2012).

Innovative policies have also supported a decrease in unemployment rates from 13.1 per cent in 2003 to 4.6 per cent in December 2012 (IBGE, n.d.), and created approximately 17 million new formal jobs in Brazil in the last decade (DIEESE, 2012). According to the Brazilian government, the targeting of unemployment and income distribution has expanded Brazil's middle class to almost 55.05 per cent of its population and created almost 50 million new consumers in the country (Brasil, 2013a). The government's focus on eradicating unemployment is mentioned in a survey of the Rousseff administration in 2012, which highlights that:

> the true dimension of changes experienced in Brazil in recent years cannot be fully grasped without a few indicators. For instance, the fact that 798 000 new jobs were created in the first 100 days of the Rousseff administration (January–April 2011) cannot be seen in isolation, since in the same four-month period of 2010 Lula da Silva created 962 000 new jobs (Bertazzo, 2012, p. 890).

In Brazil it is said that in the last decade, millions of Brazilians have entered Brazil's public sphere, both as consumers and as citizens seeking the exercise of voting and other civil rights (Ladurner, 2011). At least in terms of inequality reduction, Brazil has outperformed the other BRICS members, with the income of Brazilian families growing at a faster pace than the Brazilian economy (on average 1.8 per cent above GDP) (Bertazzo, 2012, p. 891), while the income of illiterate workers increased by 47 per cent between 2001 and 2009 (Neri, 2010). This suggests that although Brazil's economic growth rates are unremarkable as compared to China's, the improvement of social indicators and consolidation of a democratic regime has made 'Brazil appealing as a model to be followed by developing countries' (Bertazzo, 2012, p. 891).

The test to the Brazilian government will be in continuing to address inequality, which remains relatively high for a middle-income country (World Bank, 2013a), whilst sustaining economic growth and development. In this context, one of the main challenges is to reduce education deficits to support productivity, research and development, and innovation and technology. Alarming OECD data shows that in 2009, 20 per cent of 15–29-year-old Brazilians were neither studying nor employed (OECD, 2012a).

Public spending in education increased from 10.5 per cent of Brazil's total expenditure in 2000 to 16.8 per cent in 2009 (OECD, 2012a). However, despite a clear improvement, public spending on education is still below the OECD average. Until the education deficit in Brazil is addressed, the shortage of skilled labour and productivity deficiencies will continue to hinder the development of important sectors of the economy, such as the manufacturing industry (Deloitte, 2012).

There are also some complex institutional and structural reforms that need to be undertaken in Brazil to bolster the country's economic development, including addressing infrastructure and logistic bottlenecks, simplifying a complex three-tiered tax system, reducing red tape, reforming a slow and politicized judiciary (Zimmermann, 2008, p. 41), and lowering the costs endured by companies operating in Brazil. These internal restraints continue to cause comparative disadvantages for foreign investment in Brazil, and to inhibit economic initiatives seeking international integration of Brazilian industries and businesses (Deloitte, 2012). While foreign direct investment (FDI) net inflows in Brazil increased from around US$53.3 billion for the period 2003–07 to US$71.5 billion for the period 2008–12 (World Bank, 2013b), profound institutional and structural reforms will be indispensable to the country's future, as policies targeting growth alone will not accelerate the country's economic development.

AN OUTLINE OF BRAZIL'S FOREIGN TRADE AND ITS MERCOSUR MEMBERSHIP AS A BARRIER TO A BRICS FREE TRADE AGREEMENT (FTA)

With a population of over 190 million and the expansion of its middle class, Brazil has one of the largest consumer markets in the world, and is currently the:

- largest producer of regional aircrafts and the fourth largest producer of commercial aircrafts;
- largest producer of coffee, sugar cane (along with India), oranges, guaraná and eucalyptus pulp;
- largest exporter of sugar, orange juice, poultry and beef (the largest commercial livestock in the world with over 198 million heads of cattle);
- largest exporter and second largest producer of ethanol;
- second largest exporter of soy complex (grain, meal and oil);
- second largest producer of iron ore and organic food;
- third largest producer of soft drinks, shoes, bauxite, fruits and GM food; and the third largest consumer market for cosmetics (Brasil, 2013b).

However, the largest components of Brazil's GDP in 2012 were the services (67 per cent) and industrial (27 per cent) sectors, with agribusiness accounting for only 5.5 per cent of Brazil's GPD (IBGE, n.d.).

Brazil is also expected to become an important player in the world's ongoing food and energy security crises. As one of the world's largest producers of foodstuffs, Brazil has the largest area of arable land in the world, and since 2006 has produced more oil than it consumes, having the potential to become the world's sixth largest oil producer by 2030, after the discovery of its pre-salt reserves in 2007 (IBGE, n.d.).

In terms of trade balances, although Brazil recorded a trade deficit in early 2013, the country runs regular trade surpluses. According to the Brazilian Minister for Development, Industry and Foreign Trade, since trade balance records began in the country, Brazilian export and import rates achieved the second highest value in 2012 (US$242.6 billion and US$223.1 billion, respectively), second only to the figures registered in 2011 (US$256 billion exports and US$226.2 billion imports) (MDIC, 2013).

However, in comparison to other emerging economies, Brazil's participation in international trade has been modest, despite recent growth (Del Tedesco Lins & Silva, 2011, p. 21). The main markets for Brazilian exports in 2012 were China (US$41.2 billion), the US (US$26.8 billion), Argentina (US$18 billion), the Netherlands (US$15 billion) and Japan (US$8 billion) (Keeler, 2012). Trade and investment flows between Brazil and India, Russia and South Africa have also increased in the last decade (MRE, 2012), but these countries do not even rank amongst Brazil's top ten trading partners. China, however, became for the first time in 2012 the main source of Brazilian imports (US$34.2 billion), followed by the US (US$32.6 billion), Argentina (US$16.4 billion), Germany (US$14.2 billion) and South Korea (US$9.1 billion). In fact, between 2002 and 2012,

China became the main trading partner for all the BRICS nations, with Chinese exports to Brazil increasing by 2114 per cent, to India by 1823 per cent, to Russia by 1100 per cent and to South Africa by 923 per cent during that period (Keeler, 2012).

Amongst the BRICS nations, trade increased by over 1000 per cent between 2002 and 2012 (from US$27 billion to almost US$320 billion), whilst trade between the BRICS and the US, Europe and Japan grew by 300 per cent in the same period (Keeler, 2012). The BRICS' economic leverage and increasing cohesion have therefore created a favourable environment for a BRICS FTA (Sharma & Kallummal, 2012, pp. 12–14). A simulated analysis of the impact of a full BRICS FTA on overall macroeconomic and trade indicators on several tradable commodities in different regions of the world shows that:

- in terms of absolute value, China, Brazil, India and Russia would experience high welfare gain and South Africa low welfare gain, while non-BRICS countries would experience a net welfare loss in response to a BRICS FTA;
- all members of a BRICS FTA would see all components of their GPD increase, China and Brazil being the main beneficiaries, while non-BRICS regions would see a decrease in GDP due to a BRICS FTA; and
- all BRICS countries would experience positive growth in exports and across all broad subsectors for imports, while non-BRICS nations would experience negative changes in exports and imports (Sharma & Kallummal, 2012, pp. 12–14).

Ongoing negotiations of a BRICS FTA are being closely followed by non-BRICS nations and potentially fuelling FTA negotiations between non-BRICS countries (Mead, 2013). Nonetheless from a Brazilian perspective, it will take a lot more than political will for a BRICS FTA to be agreed upon and implemented.

One of the main obstacles to Brazil agreeing to a BRICS FTA is the limit imposed by Brazil's membership to the Mercosur, the Common Market of the South established under the Treaty of Asuncion in 1991.[3] In the words of former President Cardoso, Brazil has been 'trapped and isolated' in the Mercosur in terms of FTAs (*Mercopress*, 2012). The economic and political agreement between Brazil, Argentina, Paraguay, Uruguay and subsequently Venezuela promotes free movement of capital, goods, services and people amongst these countries, but requires them to be common parties to free trade zones. A BRICS FTA would therefore require either the inclusion of other Mercosur countries, or a severe rupture of the policy of a common South American market pursued by the Brazilian government for decades, with the relinquishment of Brazil's rights as a Mercosur state party in a two-year process from the date when exit from the treaty is formalized (Mercosur, 1991, art. 22).

In the past, a political agenda prioritizing a South American common market could be justified in terms of political strategy in multilateral negotiations (including in the WTO) (Paulino, 2002, p. 91). However, in the last 20 years Brazil has only entered into three trade agreements as a member of the Mercosur (Troyjo, 2013), and hence Brazil's economic ties with other South American countries are hardly justifiable, representing a 'self-imposed low ceiling', given these countries' different stages of economic development and unimportance as buying markets in comparison to the BRICS (Troyjo, 2013).

Perhaps a comparative analysis of potential benefits to Brazil's macroeconomic and trade indicators under a BRICS FTA and Mercosur is warranted. As Brazil's foreign trade policies remain constrained by its Mercosur membership, a BRICS FTA currently seems a far-fetched step towards a more integrated BRICS. Nevertheless it may become an inevitable measure to protect Brazil's comparative advantages in global trade flows as the US–EU and other bilateral FTAs gain momentum.

TRADE POLICIES AT THE DOHA DEVELOPMENT ROUND AND THE WTO DISPUTE SETTLEMENT SYSTEM

The main objectives of the Doha Round, which covers approximately 20 areas of trade, are the reduction of tariffs and trade barriers, restrictions on subsidies and revision of trade rules to expand trade flows in developing countries (WTO, 2013b). Despite the agreed mandate to address the interests of developing nations (somewhat ignored in previous rounds), negotiations between developed and developing nations have collapsed on numerous occasions, particularly in respect of the operation of the special and differentiated treatment for developing nations, and agricultural tariffs and subsidies (WTO, 2013b).

An important point made by Cesar and Sato in respect of the Doha Round is that to some extent the mandate has been obsolete since its inception, and the disconnection between procrastinatory negotiations and dynamic global trade flows has made the role of the WTO less relevant to many economies, at least in terms of consolidating trade partnerships (Cesar & Sato, 2012, pp. 174, 180). Since the start of negotiations in 2001, the globalization of production processes through global supply chains between and within multinational corporations has transformed the global economy into a much more complex and dynamic model. Industrial, commercial and financial conglomerates have become active links within global economies responsible for the majority of global trade flows, and this calls for a revision of the concept of multilateralism and the traditional ways in which international trade negotiations are conducted (Cesar & Sato, 2012, p. 189). In this context the Doha mandate excludes consideration of important issues, including the revision of rules of origin and antidumping legislation in the context of global supply chains, and the introduction of incentives for developing and least developed countries to form new or promote existing industries in global supply chains (Cesar & Sato, 2012, p. 181).

Like many other WTO members, Brazil does not appear to have factored the role or aggregate value of global supply chains into commercial policies and multilateral negotiations in the Doha Round. Instead Brazil has clung to traditional concepts of incentive towards the export of finished products, and the protection of the domestic market against the import of parts and components, and has adopted trade policies focused on five main objectives:

1. the development of exports (which has to some extent promoted an export culture within national business);
2. the diversification of commercial partnerships, in particular through stronger cooperation with other countries in the southern hemisphere;
3. a preference for multilateral negotiations and alliances in the WTO, particularly within the Doha Round;
4. the use of WTO instruments and dispute settlement system to protect its domestic market from increases in import of particular products; and
5. a deeper regional integration prioritizing relations within the Mercosur bloc (Cesar & Sato, 2012, p. 183).

Brazil has in many cases successfully employed WTO's instruments and dispute settlement system as a protection mechanism and a means to contest the policies and positions of other WTO members, and has won strategic cases against the US and EU, particularly in relation to agricultural subsidies (Shaffer, Sanchez & Rosenberg, 2008, p. 3). The theme of Brazilian disputes in the WTO also demonstrates that the Brazilian government may potentially draw on the WTO dispute settlement system as leverage for its negotiations at the Doha Round (Arbix, 2008, p. 679). Whilst the US and EU have been the respondents in 17 out of 26 Brazilian complaints in the WTO, they have also been the main opponents to

Brazil's primary demands at the Doha Round, namely, the 'cuts on agricultural tariffs, elimination of export subsidies, and better controls on domestic subsidies' (Arbix, 2008, p. 679).

The development of Brazil's international trade policy agenda in response to the 'legalisation and judicialisation of international trade relations' in the WTO has also contributed to changes within government institutions, business and civil society, and created new networks for trade policy and dispute settlement between public and private sectors in Brazil (Arbix, 2008, p. 679). The systemic advancement of Brazil's legal capabilities in international trade has made Brazil the most active complainant in the WTO among emerging economies, including the BRICS countries, with most complaints being directed towards developed nations (ten against the US, seven against the EU, and three against Canada) (WTO, 2013a).

By contrast, Brazil's complaints in the WTO against other BRICS nations have been virtually non-existent. In fact, since the WTO dispute settlement system was created in 1995, there have been only three complaints amongst BRICS countries: one claim made by Brazil against South Africa (DS439/2012 on antidumping duties on frozen meat of fowls), one by India against Brazil (DS229/2001 on antidumping duties on jute bags from India) and one by India against South Africa (DS168/1999 on antidumping duties on pharmaceutical products from India) (WTO, 2013a). The participation of BRICS countries in the WTO dispute settlement system is summarized in Table 5.1.

Brazil's preference for alliances in the WTO was consolidated in the formation of the IBSA group (India, Brazil and South Africa), which emerged from the infamous pharmaceutical patents dispute with the US (Oliveira, 2005, p. 58). However, strategic alliances amongst these counties have since transcended the WTO system and flowed on to other significant coalitions, including the 'soft-balancing' of powers in the BRICS (Flemes, 2010, p. 145), and the BASIC group created in 2009 by agreement between

Table 5.1 The BRICS' participation in the WTO dispute settlement system, by country

Country	As complainant	As respondent	As third party
Brazil	26	14	74
India	21	22	85
China	10	30	96
South Africa	–	4	2
Russia	–	–	–

Source: WTO (2013a).

Brazil, South Africa, India and China to negotiate cohesively in climate change forums.

Coalitions such as the BRICS, IBSA and BASIC will continue to be an integral part of Brazil's and other developing countries' political agendas, and will play an important role in reconciling domestic interests in multilateral negotiations such as the Doha Round. Furthermore, in any post-Doha scenario, the stances and interests of emerging economies will be one of the forces shaping the future of trade and economic policy-making (CINDES, 2012). A systemic and deeper understanding of the role and agenda of coalitions like the BRICS is therefore essential for the development of multilateral negotiations at and beyond the WTO.

BRAZIL'S AMBITION TO BECOME AN ACTIVE PARTICIPANT IN GLOBAL ECONOMIC GOVERNANCE WITH THE BRICS

In 2012 the BRICS nations represented approximately 56 per cent of the world's GDP growth, 20 per cent of FDI flows and global GDP in nominal terms, 43 per cent of the world's reserves of foreign exchange, 40 per cent of the world's population and labour force and 25 per cent of the world's landmass (SECOM, 2012). Brazil's global governance policy agenda has immersed itself in the rhythm of the BRICS economic performance and strategically drawn on the BRICS membership to provide the Brazilian government with a more assertive voice in global decision-making processes to which it is a party. As the BRICS members' economies grow and cohesion increases, so does their potential to influence decision-making in the global economic and political arenas, particularly in light of their increasing ability to provide a 'bail-out of last resort' to the world's financial system (Kirkby, 2011, p. 31).

Evidently a change in the world's division of economic power is not in itself sufficient to reshape global governance institutions and practices, and therefore the BRICS may benefit from having a clear long-term plan for its place in global governance (Bradlow, 2010, p. 175). Despite not having articulated a clear long-term plan, the BRICS has already expressed its views on its potential to contribute to the creation of a multipolar global governance system. Former Brazilian President Lula da Silva summarized this BRICS message to the world when he highlighted the importance of renewing the Bretton Woods institutions to 'forge a more representative and transparent system of global governance that can both inspire unity of purpose and revitalise the collective will to seek consensual solutions' (Da Silva, 2010, p. 22).

The reform of the Bretton Woods institutions is an important aspect of the BRICS agenda. However, the initial reform of IMF members' quota and voting powers agreed under the 2008 Amendment on Voice and Participation was only implemented in 2011, and the 2010 IMF Governance and Quota Reform is yet to be implemented (IMF, 2012). The resistance of developed nations in recognizing the current contribution of emerging economies to the stability of the world's financial system has amplified the suspicion and frustration of the BRICS towards the Bretton Woods system.

In 2012 the BRICS expressed reservations towards making further contributions to the IMF to promote global economic stability, and stated that future contributions would be subject to the BRICS having 'confidence that the entire membership of the institution is truly committed to implement the 2010 reform faithfully' (BRICS, 2012). In this context, as well as holding informal meetings in anticipation of G20 and other global forums,[4] the BRICS has been seeking alternatives to make use of its surplus reserve. In March 2013 the BRICS went a step further when questioning the prevailing global governance landscape in the fifth BRICS Summit Declaration and stated:

> As the global economy is being reshaped, we are committed to exploring new models and approaches towards more equitable development and inclusive global growth by emphasising complementarities and building on our respective economic strengths (BRICS, 2013).

The creation of the BRICS Development Bank (BRICS, 2013) has been closely followed and supported by several economic studies, including by economists such as Nicholas Stern (London School of Economics) and Joseph Stiglitz (Columbia University) (Tautz, 2013). Stern and Stiglitz (2011) have defended the creation of a new financial institution 'to ensure a better allocation of hard-earned savings of developing and emerging economies away from risk portfolios, much of which is in rich countries, and onto sound investments in the developing and emerging world' (Stern & Stiglitz, 2011). They have also emphasized the inadequacy of existing institutions for financing such investments with appropriate arrangements, stressing that beyond facing great political challenges, in many cases their governance structure prevents them from sufficiently engaging stakeholders in the private sector, sovereign wealth funds and philanthropic entities to share their agendas and shape desired outcomes in developing countries (Stern & Stiglitz, 2011).

The feasibility report for the BRICS Development Bank received extensive input from BNDES, the Brazilian Bank for Economic and

Social Development (Tautz, 2013). The position of the Brazilian government appears to be aligned with Stern and Stiglitz's view that the bank should adopt equal quota and voting rights for main founding members, and provide other countries with access to financial resources without demanding them to adopt the public policies promoted by the bank (Stern & Stiglitz, 2011). It is not hard to imagine that the BRICS Development Bank could potentially become the lending choice in infrastructure and sustainable development projects for other non-BRICS developing and least developed nations.

The desire of the BRICS to reduce its own reliance on other countries' currencies (Del Tedesco Lins & Silva, 2011, p. 24) and its role in driving the emergence of a multipolar order should not be underestimated (Dailami & Masson, 2009). The BRICS has neither consolidated its economic and political influences, nor developed a clear vision of what a multipolar world would bring besides the fragmentation of the developed nations' hegemony. However, as 'the current process of changes in the balance of global political and economic power plays itself out' (Bradlow, 2010, p. 175), the BRICS continues to agitate global governance institutions and multilateral negotiations with the ambition of creating a more transparent and democratic global governance system.

CONCLUSIONS

The last decade has brought substantial changes to Brazil's economic, political and social environments. Brazil has experienced significant economic development, internally incentivized by continuing economic reforms, political stability, and innovative policies targeting economic growth and distribution of income. During that period Brazil has also experienced a very dynamic phase in its diplomatic history. It has developed economic, foreign trade and diplomatic policy agendas based on the formation of favourable alliances such as the BRICS, and defended its national interests with the adoption of a somewhat more critical view towards globalization (Almeida, 2004, p. 165). This view recognizes the fragility of external markets, defends policies conducive to trade surpluses without deepening the country's dependency on foreign capital, and reaffirms Brazil's traditional positions in multilateral negotiations seeking access to developed markets by insisting on mechanisms that support developing nations (Almeida, 2004, p. 165).

Between 2002 and 2012, Brazil also diversified its trading partners and increased trade with other BRICS countries, particularly with China. An increase of over 1000 per cent in trade amongst the BRICS nations, supported by progressive economic leverage and political cohesion within the BRICS countries, has created a favourable environment for a BRICS FTA (Sharma & Kallummal, 2012, pp. 12–14). Perhaps this environment requires reconsideration and potentially a shift in Brazil's foreign trade policies, from a Mercosur focus towards a BRICS free trading zone. Certainly the differences between Brazil and the other BRICS nations in terms of economic development, geopolitical interests and cultural values overshadow their commonalities. However, with elements from four different continents the BRICS' diverse political and economic power is also one of the assets of the BRICS in multilateral negotiations. The BRICS, as opposed to the fading Mercosur bloc, is increasingly becoming Brazil's main platform to promote policies and positions with a view to influencing multilateral negotiations in the G20, WTO and other global forums. It is therefore prudent for Brazil to consider how a free trading zone with the other BRICS countries could benefit its economy and interactions in multilateral negotiations.

Lastly, since the GFC Brazil has, together with other BRICS members, challenged the status quo of intergovernmental institutions. It is expected that global governance arrangements will remain the same until the economic and political powers of developed and emerging economies are rebalanced in a multipolar world order. However, once this rebalancing occurs institutional practices will eventually be reshaped to include the relative importance of emerging economies to global governance. The BRICS is set to be one of the driving forces shaping the future of global policies and practices, so a systemic appreciation of the BRICS' interests and agendas should somewhat assist in understanding the direction and future of multilateralism.

NOTES

1. A timeline of the Brazilian economy starting from the 1500s can be found at the Brazilian government's website (http://www.brasil.gov.br/).
2. Key facts on the 2012 PAC budget can be found at http://www.acceleratebrazil.com/file/2562/key-facts.html.
3. The Mercosur subsequently gained legal personality under international law under the *Protocol of Ouro Preto* of 1994 (Art. 34).
4. BRICS official documents and media declarations in the G20 can be found at http://www.g20.org/documents/.

REFERENCES

Almeida, P.R. de (2004). Uma política externa engajada: a diplomacia de governo Lula. *Revista Brasileira de Política Internacional*, *47*(1), 162–84.

Arbix, D. (2008). Brazil litigation in the WTO: Trade mix, politics and institutions. *Contexto Internacional*, *30*(3), 655–99.

Bertazzo, J. (2012). An initial survey of the Dilma Rouseff administration in Brazil. *Critical Sociology*, *38*(6), 889–92.

Bradlow, D.D. (2010, May). *Reforming global economic governance: A strategy for middle powers in the G20*. Paper presented at 'Going Global: Australia, Brazil, Indonesia, Korea and South Africa in International Affairs', Indonesia. Retrieved from http://ssrn.com/abstract=1624909

Brasil (2013a). Retrieved from http://www.brasil.gov.br/

Brasil (2013b). *Brazilian economy: Economic overview*. Retrieved from http://www.brasil.gov.br/para/invest/brazilian-economy/economic-overview/br_model1?set_language=en

BRICS (2012, March). *Fourth BRICS summit Delhi declaration*. Retrieved from http://www.brics.utoronto.ca/docs/120329-delhi-declaration.html

BRICS (2013, March). *Fifth BRICS summit declaration and action plan*. Retrieved from http://www.brics5.co.za/fifth-brics-summit-declaration-and-action-plan/

Cesar, S.E.M. and Sato, E. (2012). Doha Round, changes in the international trade regime, and the Brazilian commercial policy. *Revista Brasileira de Política Internacional*, *55*(1), 174–93.

CINDES (2012, September). *Emerging powers, national interests and the future of multilateralism* (Report by CINDES). Retrieved from http://www.wto.org/english/forums_e/public_forum12_e/session30_summ_e.doc

Dailami, M. and Masson, P.R. (2009). *The new multi-polar international monetary system* (World Bank Policy Research Working Paper 2009 No. 5147). Retrieved from http://papers.ssrn.com/sol3/papers.cfm?abstract_id=1527337

Da Silva, L. (2010). The BRICS come of global age. *New Perspectives Quarterly*, *27*(3), 21–22.

Del Tedesco Lins, M.A. and Silva, L.P. (2011). Brazil and the G20: Recent development strategy and strength among 'new' emerging economies. In W. Hofmeister and S. Vogt (Eds), *G20 – Perceptions and Perspectives for Global Governance* (pp. 21–30). Singapore: Konrad Adenauer Stiftung.

Deloitte (2012). *Competitive Brazil: Challenges and strategies for the manufacturing industry*. Retrieved from http://www.deloitte.com/assets/Dcom-Brazil/Local%20Assets/Documents/Indústrias/Manufatura/livro_ingles.pdf

Departamento Intersindical de Estatística e Estudos Socioeconômicos (DIEESE). (2012). *A Situação do trabalho no Brasil na primeira década dos anos 2000*. Retrieved from http://www.dieese.org.br/livroSituacaoTrabalhoBrasil/livroSituacaoTrabalhoBrasil.pdf

Flemes, D. (2010). Brazil in the BRIC initiative: Soft balancing in the shifting world order? *Revista Brasileira de Política Internacional*, *53*(1), 141–56.

G20 (2012, June). *Policy commitments by G20 members: Los Cabos Summit*. Retrieved from http://www.g20.utoronto.ca/2012/2012-0619-loscabos-commitments.pdf

Hounshell, B. (2011). Jim O'Neill. *Foreign Policy*, *185*. Retrieved from http://www.foreignpolicy.com/articles/2011/02/22/epiphanies_from_jim_oneill

IMF (2012). *IMF members' quotas and voting power, and IMF Board of Governors*. Retrieved from http://www.imf.org/external/np/sec/memdir/members.aspx

Inflation.eu (2013). *Historic inflation Brazil – CPI inflation*. Retrieved from http://www.inflation.eu/inflation-rates/brazil/historic-inflation/cpi-inflation-brazil.aspx
Instituto Brasileiro de Geografia e Estatística (IBGE). (n.d.). Retrieved from http://www.ibge.gov.br
Keeler, D. (2012). Shifting trade flows and the new consumer. *Global Finance, February*. Retrieved from http://www.gfmag.com/archives/147-february-2012/11604-special-report-brics.html#axzz2MRFpkc38
Kirkby, A. (2011). BRICs bailout? *Credit Management, December*, 31.
Ladurner, U. (2011, October 18). Mais poderosos do que esperado. *Die Zeit*. Retrieved from http://www.itamaraty.gov.br/sala-de-imprensa/artigos-relevantes/mais-poderoso-do-que-esperado-die-zeit-18-10-2011
Mead, W.R. (2013, January 16). US announces new trade plan, BRICS conspicuously absent. *The American Interest*. Retrieved from http://blogs.the-american-interest.com/wrm/2013/01/16/us-announces-new-trade-deal-brics-conspicuously-absent/
MercoPress (2012, December 3). Brazil 'trapped and isolated' in Mercosur, should try trade agreements with US, says former president. Retrieved from http://en.mercopress.com/2012/12/03/brazil-trapped-and-isolated-in-mercosur-should-try-trade-agreements-with-us-says-former-president
Mercosur (1991). *Mercosur Free Trade Agreement*. Retrieved from http://idatd.eclac.cl/controversias/Normativas/MERCOSUR/Ingles/Treaty_of_Asuncion.pdf
Ministério das Relações Exteriores do Brasil (MRE) (2012, August). *Comércio exterior dos BRICS*. Retrieved from http://www.brasilglobalnet.gov.br/ARQUIVOS/IndicadoresEconomicos/ComExtBRICs.pdf
Ministry of Development, Industry and Foreign Trade (MDIC). (2013, January 4). *Brazilian exports maintain high level in 2012*. Retrieved from http://www.brasil.gov.br/news/history/2013/01/04/brazilian-exports-maintain-high-level-in-2012/newsitem_view?set_language=en
Neri, M.C. (2010). *Os Emergentes dos Emergentes: Reflexões Globais e Ações Locais para a Nova Classe Média Brasileira*. FGV/CPS, Portuguese version at http://www.cps.fgv.br/cps/bd/nbrics/NBrics_Pesquisa_neri_fgv.pdf
Nye Jr, J.S. (2004). *The benefits of soft power*. Retrieved from http://hbswk.hbs.edu/archive/4290.html
OECD (2012a). *Education at a glance: OECD indicators 2012*. Retrieved from http://www.oecd.org/education/EAG2012%20-%20Country%20note%20-%20Brazil.pdf
OECD (2012b). *G20 Quarterly gross domestic product, third quarter 2012, OECD*. Retrieved from http://www.oecd.org/std/na/g20quarterlygrossdomesticproductthirdquarter2012oecd.htm#
Oliveira, M.F. de (2005). Alliances and coalitions in the Lula Administration: An analysis of Ibsa and G20. *Revista Brasileira de Política Internacional*, *8*(2), 55–69.
Paulino, L.A. (2002). O Brasil, seus sócios e seus negócio. *São Paulo em Perspective*, *16*(2), 82–93.
Prusa, A.C. (2011). *The 'soft power' power? Brazil's soft power strategy in world politics during the Lula presidency*. Masters thesis. Retrieved from Proquest Dissertations and Theses (UMI 1502441).
Rapoza, K. (2012, August 31). Brazil's B in BRICs stands for boring. *Forbes*. Retrieved from http://www.forbes.com/sites/kenrapoza/2012/08/31/b-in-brics-stands-for-boring/
Romero, S. (2012, August 4). Leader's torture in the 70's stirs ghosts in Brazil. *The*

New York Times. Retrieved from http://www.nytimes.com/2012/08/05/world/americas/president-rousseffs-decades-old-torture-detailed.html?pagewanted=all&_r=0

Secretariat for Social Communication of the Presidency of the Republic of Brazil (SECOM) (2012). *Fact sheet BRICS partnership for global stability*. Retrieved from http://www.brasil.gov.br/para/press/press-releases/march-2012/fact-sheet-brics-partnership-for-global-stability/br_model1?set_language=en

Shaffer, G., Sanchez, M.R. and Rosenberg, B. (2008, July). *Winning at the WTO: The development of a trade policy community within Brazil* (Documento de Trabajo No. 14). Argentina: Area de Relaciones Internationales FLACSO. Retrieved from http://rrii.flacso.org.ar/web/wp-content/uploads/2010/10/doc14.pdf

Sharma, S.K. and Kallummal, M. (2012, June). *A GTAP Analysis of the proposed BRICS free trade agreement*. Working draft submitted to the 15th Annual Conference on Global Economic Analysis: "New challenges for global trade and sustainable development", Geneva. Retrieved from https://www.gtap.agecon.purdue.edu/resources/download/5989.pdf

Stern, N. and Stiglitz, J. (2011, January 17). An international development bank for fostering south-south investment: Promoting the new industrial revolution, managing risk and rebalancing global savings. *Instituto Mais Democracia*. Retrieved English version from http://maisdemocracia.org.br/index.php?s=Nicholas+Stern+e+Joseph+Stiglitz+&cat=6

Tautz, C. (2013, March 12). O banco dos Brics em março. *Brasil de Fato*. Retrieved from http://www.brasildefato.com.br/node/12278

Troyjo, M. (2013, February 27). Beyond BRICS: Blocless Brazil. *Financial Times*. Retrieved from http://blogs.ft.com/beyond-brics/2013/02/27/guest-post-blocless-brazil/#ixzz2MTMB9Rwj

World Bank (2013a). *Brazil overview*. Retrieved from http://www.worldbank.org/en/country/brazil/overview

World Bank (2013b). *Data*. Retrieved from http://data.worldbank.org/indicator/BX.KLT.DINV.CD.WD

World Bank (2013c). *Global economic prospects – January 2013: Assuring growth over the medium term*. Retrieved from http://web.worldbank.org/WBSITE/EXTERNAL/EXTDEC/EXTDECPROSPECTS/EXTGBLPROSPECTS/0,,contentMDK:23319430~menuPK:612508~pagePK:2904583~piPK:2904598~theSitePK:612501,00.html

WTO (2013a). *Dispute settlement: Disputes by country/territory*. Retrieved from http://www.wto.org/english/tratop_e/dispu_e/dispu_by_country_e.htm

WTO (2013b). *The Doha round*. Retrieved from http://www.wto.org/english/tratop_e/dda_e/dda_e.htm#development

Zimmermann, A. (2008). The politics of lawlessness in Brazil: How Brazilian politics overrides the rule of law. *ELAW (Murdoch University Electronic Journal of Law)*, *15*(1), 3–42. Retrieved from https://elaw.murdoch.edu.au/0.org/documents/

6. Sino-Brazilian trade and antidumping concerns

Muruga Perumal Ramaswamy

The Sino-Brazilian trade relationship in the past decade has generally been hailed as a success story. Although the value and volume of their bilateral trade have clearly increased, there are several concerns facing both sides with the potential to derail the impressive growth thus gained.[1] While the major cause of concern for Brazilian exporters has been the concentration of trade in specific sectors, for their Chinese counterparts it has been the increasing use of trade remedies targeting Chinese imports, in spite of an unusual trade deficit with Brazil. At this juncture, when bilateral trade is experiencing an exponential growth, the tendency has been to ignore or underestimate some of these underlying concerns in the interest of maintaining cordial relations. However, in order to ensure a sustainable long-term growth in bilateral trade, and to maintain a long-lasting trade relationship, it is highly important to identify growing concerns arising from trade between the two countries and address them effectively. In this context, the role of cooperative initiatives between the two countries needs to be re-examined to determine how far they are aimed at tackling the major trade concerns. Although the cooperative initiatives between the two countries have grown beyond bilateral means, for example the cooperation among the BRICS members, their potential to effectively address the underlying concerns is unclear.

This chapter argues that any trade facilitative initiatives between the two countries should not limit themselves to conventional forms of facilitation, and should confront the reality of the underlying concerns arising from bilateral trade in order to sustain continued growth. It traces the growth and characteristics of bilateral trade between China and Brazil during the last decade. Then it identifies major concerns and challenges arising from Sino-Brazilian trade and how they could impact future trade between the two nations. Against this backdrop, it highlights how the specific Brazilian concern for the concentration of trade in sectors could lead to the potential use of antidumping measures against China. This warrants a closer examination of the Brazilian antidumping law and procedures, and the related issues and challenges facing Chinese imports. Finally the chapter concludes by examining some options that could be engaged to effectively address the underlying antidumping concerns.

SINO-BRAZILIAN BILATERAL TRADE: A SUCCESS STORY OR MARRIAGE OF CONVENIENCE?

The Sino-Brazilian trade growth can be clearly divided into two major periods, namely the pre- and post-WTO accession of China in 2001. Distinct patterns of trade are discernible in these two periods. Almost 20 years since a diplomatic relationship was established between China and Brazil, their bilateral ties received a strong impetus with the Chinese recognition of Brazil as a strategic partner in 1993. Although both countries realized the significance of each other's market, the major strides in bilateral trade happened towards the turn of the century with China's accession to the WTO. The 12-year period (2001 to 2012) since China joined the WTO was the most remarkable period in Sino-Brazilian bilateral trade history, achieving a very impressive growth. Although several leaps in bilateral trade could be pointed out in this period, two major indicators stand out as evidence of the remarkable growth. First, Brazilian exports to China witnessed a staggering 2230 per cent increase in 2011 when they soared to a peak of US$44.315 billion from the modest level of US$1.902 billion in 2001. Similarly Chinese exports to Brazil reached a peak of US$34.247 billion in 2012; a mammoth 2479 per cent increase from the level of 2001, when it stood at just US$1.328 billion (CEBC, 2012). In this impressive run, however, the overall trade was tilted more in favour of Brazil than China. In the 12-year period, except for 2007 and 2008, Brazil enjoyed a trade surplus with China. This trade surplus, which stood at a mere US$574 million in 2001, reached a record peak of US$11.524 billion in 2011, a massive 1908 per cent increase.

In spite of a rosy picture of growth in bilateral trade, a closer inspection reveals a range of underlying concerns. Despite the trade surplus Brazil's major concern stems from the concentration of its exports in primary commodities or raw materials (like soybeans and iron ore) to China at the cost of a substantial decline in the export of manufactured goods (Jenkins, 2012). For example, nearly 78 per cent of the Brazilian exports to China in 2009 consisted of basic commodities, while its exports of manufactured goods in the same year stood at a meagre 7 per cent. In 2010 this gap widened – the respective figures were 84 per cent and 4.5 per cent (SECEX & MDIC, 2011). This was in stark contrast to the imports from China, which consisted predominantly of manufactured goods. For example, manufactured goods constituted about 98 per cent and 97.5 per cent of the total imports from China in 2009 and 2010 respectively (SECEX & MDIC, 2011). Concerns over an imbalance in trade with regard to manufactured goods were further exacerbated when China overtook the US to become Brazil's largest trading partner.

This created a clear divide in Brazilian industry circles because only the producers of basic commodities benefited from Chinese trade, while most of the manufacturing industries suffered. The concerns of the Brazilian manufacturers were not limited to the minuscule share of manufactured goods in their exports to China. They were equally concerned about the increased competition from Chinese manufactured goods entering the Brazilian market and in third markets where they competed with Chinese goods (Corkin, Viana & Naidin, 2012). The declining trend of manufactured goods in Brazilian exports was also counter-intuitive to Brazilian economic policies, which were specifically conceived to increase the role of the manufacturing sector in the national economy. Such concerns called for action on the part of the government, which has found it difficult to confront China, especially when the balance of trade value has been in its favour for a long time. In such circumstances the prospect of using specific trade remedies against Chinese imports to appease the concerns of domestic manufacturers is inevitable, as there has been an increased use of antidumping actions against Chinese imports.

This discussion pertains to Brazil's concerns and its reactions. However, it is important to take cognizance of the fact that the growth of bilateral trade in the past 12 years was equally capable of creating concerns for China. Although China may have various concerns relating to trade with Brazil, this chapter focuses on one issue, namely, antidumping. Obviously the growing trade deficit with Brazil should cause a major concern for China, but such concern is set aside due to its growing appetite for commodities and raw materials to sustain its industrial growth. In as much as China may turn a blind eye towards the trade deficit, any Brazilian trade remedies that have the potential to fundamentally affect its trade in manufactured goods can trigger a serious reaction. In this context, the large number of Brazilian antidumping actions against Chinese companies should cause a serious concern for China, which calls for a closer examination in the following sections.

THE RISKS AND PITFALLS OF ANTIDUMPING ACTIONS

For Brazil, three major concerns loom from the analysis: 'export concern' (the minuscule role of manufactured goods in Brazilian exports to China);

'import concern' (the overwhelming proportion of manufactured goods in Brazilian imports from China); and 'third markets concern' (the competition from Chinese manufactured goods in foreign markets). The potential Brazilian reaction relating to the import concern should be of critical importance to China because of the specific trade remedies at the disposal of Brazil to address the imbalance. Regarding the other two areas of concern, Brazil can hardly undertake any hard measures against China and can only seek to negotiate. Among the relevant measures Brazil may use to address the 'import concern', such as antidumping, anti-subsidies and safeguards, antidumping actions should cause the most serious concern for China. This is supported by both theory and practical evidence. Before examining specific examples of potential Brazilian antidumping actions against China, it is necessary to analyse the inherent risks in antidumping actions as demonstrated in other experiences (Horlick & Vermulsti, 2005). For example, the study of Robert McGee (2000) demonstrates the shortcomings in the US antidumping experience, both philosophically and in practice. The misuse of antidumping systems and the adverse impacts of antidumping procedures help to reveal potential risks and pitfalls inherent in antidumping actions.

At the outset it is important to take note of the changing objectives of antidumping actions and how they have moved away from their original purpose of countering predatory behaviour. This is due to the increasing realization that fear of predatory behaviour is often unfounded. Different reasons undermine the possibility of a successful predatory pricing strategy. First, it is difficult to find any categorical predatory pricing in a market. Even where predatory intentions have been suspected in the past, the findings are that none of those cases has achieved its goal of driving the competitors out. This was because of the impossibility of any dominant player in an industry to reduce and maintain prices to oust all competitors, or to prevent them from re-entering the market (McGee, 2000). In spite of its irrelevance, the prevention of predatory behaviour is continuously used as a justification by states for their antidumping actions. However, such a justification is often used as a guise to tackle the competitive concerns of domestic producers. Increasingly, antidumping investigations are shown to be targeted at serving vested interests instead of aiming to prevent predatory behaviour. The practice of using antidumping actions for ulterior motives has been found in both developed and developing markets (Vandenbussche & Zanardi, 2008).

The US frequently uses antidumping actions and can be used as an example to demonstrate relevant concerns. Several cases have been put forth to show how the US antidumping laws and procedures were misused to serve the interests of domestic producers (McGee, 2000). These examples are interesting because the WTO antidumping provisions are said to have emulated the US rules. The US experience could reveal potential weaknesses in the WTO rules in preventing the misuse of antidumping actions. Often antidumping actions were found to have been aimed at protecting domestic producers at the expense of the interest of consumers (Prusa, 2005). The majority of cases were triggered by domestic producers having an aversion to foreign competition, except a few cases that were initiated by the state based on a genuine concern or evidence of dumping. Examples like the US steel industry's attempt to impose an antidumping duty against steel industries of more than 20 countries at the same time reveal the risk of misuse. Similarly the US antidumping investigations against the importation of computer chips from Asia were shown to have shielded domestic chip manufacturers from competition, thereby causing high prices and adverse effects on some allied products and related jobs. Moreover one investigation was said to have found dumping erroneously through the use of inappropriate methodology (McGee, 2000).

Studies have also shown the ill effects of investigation procedures. That is, merely initiating an investigation of dumping can adversely affect the foreign trader even if such investigation does not result in the imposition of antidumping duties. The foreign parties under investigation are generally considered to have engaged in dumping unless proved otherwise, and the process of defending involves huge expenses. The state determines the nature, format and timing of furnishing the information required for defending a dumping investigation (Czako, Human & Miranda, 2003) and several instances are cited (Gingerich, 1998) where such procedures have resulted in a huge burden for the party being investigated. Even a submission of the required information is no guarantee that the information will be relied on because the state concerned may prefer other sources of information in determining whether or not there has been dumping. Moreover failure to cooperate or produce the information sought in the required format or language or on time has been shown to result in the imposition of high antidumping duties computed by the state, often with the assistance of the domestic producers.

In spite of more harmonized rules under the WTO, divergent national methods of calculating dumping margins (Vermulst & Horlick, 2007), estimating the cost of production and comparing domestic and foreign sales have come under criticism. For example, in the past the US has found dumping in cases where the actual profit margin targeted by a foreign party was slightly less than the one calculated by the state and in cases where investigations have compared dissimilar products or qualities (McGee, 2000). Dumping investigations are also criticized for being insensitive to, amongst other things, sound accounting practices, economic theories, differences in wholesale and retail prices, volume discounts, for being inconsistent in the classification of direct or indirect costs, average prices and so forth (McGee, 2000). Although the foregoing analysis reveals some inherent risks of misuse of antidumping actions and the potential adverse impact of relevant procedures, how related issues play out in the specific context of the Sino-Brazilian bilateral trade relationship will be examined in the next two sections.

BRAZILIAN ANTIDUMPING ACTIONS AND THREATS FACING CHINA

The threat of antidumping actions facing China is generally perceived to be high. The major source of threats of contingency measures (CMs) facing China, like antidumping, is generally expected to come from developed countries. However, the source of such threats has experienced a shift in the last decade. The threat of CMs is found to emanate more from emerging rather than developed markets. For example, during the period from 2004 to 2011, the CMs facing China from emerging markets underwent a higher increase in comparison with those arising out of developed markets. By 2011, the CMs imposed by emerging economies against China had increased to 11 per cent of China's exports by value to those markets, which was found to have nearly doubled from the levels of 2004. Yet during the same period, the increase from among developed markets only stood at 4.7 per cent of China's exports by value to those markets (Bown & McCulloch, 2012). Therefore the threat of antidumping actions from emerging economies like Brazil should cause more concern to China.

Evidence pertaining to Brazil's use of antidumping actions against foreign exports reveals the reality of related trade barriers facing China. Firstly, antidumping is the most commonly utilized CM by Brazil against foreign imports. Incidentally Brazil has also been found to be the only country in Latin America whose exports have faced a large number of antidumping actions and duties in foreign markets (Feinberg, 2010). This phenomenon is important to note because studies have found that retaliatory motives could be a cause for the proliferation of antidumping laws and resulting actions (Vandenbussche & Zanardi, 2008). The fact that new users of antidumping actions like Brazil have been the target of such actions could easily prompt them to use the same as a tool to protect their domestic industry. The experience of facing such actions allowed them to appreciate the flexibility of antidumping action as a trade policy instrument and encourage them to use the same towards others (Vandenbussche & Zanardi, 2008).

From the reported data on antidumping cases and the resulting measures provided by the WTO since 1995, the extent of using antidumping measures by Brazil in general, and those specifically against China, becomes very clear. During 1995–2012, Chinese exports faced the highest number of antidumping initiations and the ultimate antidumping measures among all the countries that report dumping actions to the WTO. The antidumping initiations faced by China in this period amounted to nearly 22 per cent of the total number of initiations reported to the WTO (by 103 member territories). At the same time the levels of antidumping measures faced by China reached even higher, constituting nearly 25 per cent of all such measures reported to the WTO. The data also reveals that China has been the most frequent target of Brazilian antidumping initiations, which incidentally also stood at 22 per cent of all antidumping initiations made by Brazil during the period 1995–2012 (WTO, 2013a). The picture regarding its imposition of antidumping measures against China in the same period was no different. Antidumping measures against China stood at 27 per cent of all antidumping measures imposed by Brazil, and China happened to be the highest target again (WTO, 2013b). Among various countries that have initiated antidumping actions against China, Brazil ranks as the fifth highest after India, the US, the EU and Argentina (WTO, 2013a). Brazil also ranks as the sixth highest country imposing antidumping measures against China after India, the US, the EU, Argentina and Turkey (WTO, 2013b). The fact that two of the top five states initiating antidumping actions against China are members of the BRICS indicates the need to include antidumping concerns on the BRICS agenda.

KEY CHARACTERISTICS AND CONCERNS OF BRAZILIAN ANTIDUMPING LAW AND PRACTICE

The two bodies pertinent to antidumping actions in Brazil are the Department of Trade Remedies (DECOM) under the Secretariat of Foreign Trade (SECEX) and the Chamber of Foreign Trade (CAMEX). While the former is in charge of most of the investigations and related procedures, the latter is more powerful and endowed with final decision-making responsibilities. CAMEX may refuse to follow the decisions of SECEX arising out of an investigation on such grounds as political consideration, national interest, convenience and opportunity. The power of CAMEX to override SECEX, particularly for political reasons or for opportunity, can be utilized as leverage by China over Brazil. CAMEX enjoys key competencies to make final decisions relating to different trade remedies, including imposition of provisional and definitive antidumping; duties, their suspension, alteration or termination (upon review); and acceptance or termination of price undertakings. CAMEX is also responsible for establishing guidelines with regard to trade remedies and rules and procedures for contingency measure investigations. Antidumping investigations by SECEX are mostly initiated upon request by a domestic industry. However, it can also be initiated by SECEX ex officio, or interestingly upon a request from any affected third country. If SECEX decides to proceed with the request, it has the responsibility to determine key elements such as the margin of dumping, the threat or existence of material injury and the causal link. Although the power of SECEX to act under the auspices of a request by the third country may cause concerns to China, the same is restrained by the Brazilian law requiring permission from the WTO and has indeed never been used in practice.

One of the key challenges facing China with regard to the antidumping investigations in Brazil is the issue of Market Economy Status (MES). Although Brazil declared its intention to grant MES to China in 2004, the issue still remains murky because of the purported decision of Brazil to delay its implementation and a reported lack of such treatment in actual investigation proceedings (IBA, 2010). Due to the strong opposition from industry associations, Brazil has not formally implemented its declaration to grant MES to China through legislation. Therefore the Brazilian legislation, SECEX Act No. 59 of 28 November 2001, addressing the conduct of trade defence investigations with respect to economies that are not predominantly market-orientated, becomes more pertinent for Chinese imports to Brazil. Although individual companies from China may seek to establish that they operate under market economy conditions and receive MES treatment, they have not been successful in receiving such a treatment. In spite of the common criteria used to determine MES status such as absence of state interference and market distortions, currency convertibility, freedom to negotiate wages and so forth (Cuneo & Manuel, 1981), the broad scope of relevant MES provisions and the discretion enjoyed by investigating authorities are major reasons for the lack of success of Chinese companies (IBA, 2010). Due to the lack of MES treatment, the antidumping investigations involving Chinese companies may use the data from a third country related to the sale price or export price or a constructed value in determining the normal value of the goods under investigation. Alternatively such investigations are also allowed to use any other reasonable method of determining the normal value. The legal requirement to use a reasonable standard or method in choosing a third country for reference, or to use alternative methods, in antidumping investigations are considered to be too general and hence do not provide clear indication as to which data would be used in determining the normal value. The resulting uncertainty invariably makes it difficult for Chinese companies to defend antidumping actions by using data from China or from data from a specific third country.

The substantive laws governing antidumping in Brazil were enacted in 1995 in compliance with WTO obligations. The two major laws introduced were the Law No. 9019 of 30 March 1995, which is the substantive law regulating the application of antidumping duties, and the Decree No. 1602 of 23 August 1995, which prescribes the administrative procedures governing the application of antidumping measures. In the following year the SECEX Circular No. 21 was enacted, which prescribed the detailed procedure to make a request for an antidumping investigation. However, in 2012, the SECEX Circular No. 21 was revoked and was replaced with the new Directive No. 46 of 23 December 2011, which presently governs the procedure for making such requests. The preferred 'periods investigated for dumping and injury assessments' under Directive No. 46 of 2011 are prescribed as 12 and 60 months (divided into five intervals of 12 months each) respectively (Part II, Paras 1.1 and 1.2 of Directive No. 46 of 2011). One of the more pertinent types of information recognized in the process of establishing dumping (in cases of actual injury or threat thereof) is the information regarding the effective or potential production capacity of the exporting countries to Brazil. The recognition of this information in the Brazilian antidumping proceedings can create concerns for Chinese companies because China normally possesses a very high production capacity in a range of manufacturing goods.

In establishing the normal value in antidumping investigations, the Directive No. 46 of 2011 requires different types of pricing information from the complainant for cases involving market[2] and non-market[3] economy exporters. The complainant is also required to submit the export price of the product in the country from where the allegedly dumped goods are exported.[4] An onus is also placed on the complainant to produce relevant information needed to enable proper comparison between normal value and export price if there are any differences between products imported and the products used to determine the normal value. The Directive also prescribes additional information for complaints about threat of injury. Some of the relevant information in this context includes: production capacity in the exporting country and forecasts concerning its increase; inventories in the exporting country and its excess capacity based on production volumes and restrictive measures applied by other countries including antidumping rights capable of justifying the diversion of trade flows to Brazil. The requirement of such information would have implications for cases involving China because it often holds high production capacity and inventories, and commonly faces restrictive measures in other countries.

The dumping margin is calculated based on the differences between the normal value determined and the export price. Generally the dumping margin is calculated for each separate supplier. But if the interested party fails to provide the required information on time or if the information provided is difficult to verify, the determination could be made based on the best information available. These provisions should also cause concerns to the Chinese companies facing antidumping proceedings in Brazil because they may, as non-market economy exporters, find it difficult to produce timely and reliable information capable of being easily verified.

In determining material injury or the threat thereof, consideration is given to the volume of the imports, effects on the prices of like products and the resulting impact on domestic producers. The impact of the magnitude of the margin of dumping is assessed, based on the natural and potential declines in several critical areas related to the business, employment and wages, and the growth of the domestic industry as a whole. In the case of Chinese exports of manufactured goods to Brazil, such issues are commonly raised and are a particular challenge for individual Chinese enterprises facing the investigation. It is important to take note that in establishing the 'causal link' between the investigated imports and the injury to the domestic industry, one of the factors considered is the 'export performance and productivity of domestic producers'. In the case of Chinese manufactured goods imported into Brazil, a clear decline in the export performance of the Brazilian manufacturing industry is discernible (Gallagher & Porzecanski, 2010). Hence any potential antidumping action against Chinese companies in this sector may establish the element of causal link with relative ease.

As a result of the investigation, if dumping, injury and the causal link are established, antidumping duties could be imposed (except where CAMEX decides otherwise for the reasons stated earlier). Antidumping duties may be provisional or definitive based on the result of the respective preliminary investigation and final determination. Antidumping duties cannot exceed the margin of dumping but can be less in cases where it may be sufficient to offset the injury. However, in practice, Brazil applies a full margin of dumping on suppliers who fail to respond to the questionnaires sent to them during the investigation. Chinese companies facing the investigation should be wary of this practice in cases where they may find it difficult to respond to the questionnaires.

In 2008 Brazil amended its antidumping law of 1995 by virtue of Law No. 11 786 of 25 September 2008, to address elusive practices undermining the application of antidumping measures by extending the same to third countries, covering even parts, pieces and components of a product. Subsequently Brazil introduced relevant implementing regulations to tackle circumvention of antidumping measures in 2010 via Directive 21 of 18 October 2010, which further elaborates on the relevant provisions addressing the problem. These provisions seem to be a response to address concerns about the practices of some companies, including those from China, who have been accused of channelling products or their components using third markets to avoid antidumping measures.

Brazil has increasingly consulted its legal community to determine the improvements needed for its antidumping laws. Although satisfaction seems to be prevalent with regard to the existing laws, concerns have been expressed mainly with respect to how the laws are applied. Specific concerns over ambiguity relating to the calculation of dumping margin and consideration of the responses of exporters have been expressed. These concerns are pertinent to Chinese exporters to the Brazilian market. As a consequence their participation in antidumping proceedings is highly recommended by lawyers as it gives them greater control over the information influencing the investigation and leads to lower antidumping margins (Rowley, 2011). The new government under President Dilma Rousseff is also seen to be very supportive of antidumping remedies, as it has introduced new rules enabling possible application of antidumping duties, even retrospectively. The prospects for an aggressive use of antidumping measures by Brazil should be of particular concern to China, which may not receive a MES from Brazil until 2016.

CONCLUSIONS

This chapter reveals that what otherwise may look like a healthy trade relationship between China and Brazil is blemished by a range of underlying concerns with regard to the inherent imbalances. On the part of China, its long-running trade deficit with Brazil does not seem be a major concern. This can be attributed to the fact that Brazil is a source of raw and primary commodities, which is crucial for sustaining China's high industrial growth. In spite of the trade surplus enjoyed for the most part of the last decade, Brazil seems to be facing a lot of domestic discontent with regard to the concentration of its exports in primary materials at the cost of a considerable decline in the export of manufactured goods. This is further exacerbated by the fact that Chinese manufactured goods have constituted a mammoth part of China's exports to Brazil, creating a formidable force of competition in the domestic market. The competiveness of Brazilian manufactured goods has also been threatened in third markets, where they face equally tough competition from Chinese goods. Despite some antidumping initiations Brazil has largely tolerated this imbalance because of the fact that China has become its largest trading partner, and the resulting demand has driven up export commodity prices. Mutual tolerance can wither away when the underlying economic factors change, as experienced during the last Global Financial Crisis (GFC). Even if the likelihood of such drastic economic changes affecting bilateral trade between China and Brazil may not be immediate, this is no guarantee their trade relationship will continue to run smoothly.

The potential for trade friction between the two countries seems to have increased in light of the growing decline of the Brazilian manufacturing industry and its loss of market share, both domestically and in foreign markets. In this context the major challenge for Chinese exporters to Brazil arises from antidumping actions. Much evidence supports this conclusion. Firstly, Brazil has consistently used antidumping actions, most of them against Chinese imports during the period of 1995–2012 reviewed in this chapter. Moreover Brazil has revised its antidumping legislation and improved the scope of antidumping. In spite of declaring its intention to grant MES to China, Brazil has not extended such treatment to Chinese companies facing antidumping investigations. The increasing domestic pressure and industrial lobbying to rejuvenate the manufacturing sector does not leave the Brazilian government with much option but to resort to contingency measures such as antidumping. This is substantiated by the actions of the new Brazilian government, which has clearly expressed its intention to utilize this remedy to address domestic market concerns. Under these circumstances a more focused strategy to address the challenge of antidumping actions against Chinese exporters to Brazil is critical.

It is important to identify the implications of specific antidumping procedures and potential measures, and formulate responses through appropriate strategies. Although direct bilateral cooperation between the two countries can be a viable platform in this regard, the use of other pertinent mechanisms can be more effective in producing the desired results. In this context the role of the BRICS, the Macau Forum for Economic and Commercial Cooperation between China and the Portuguese Speaking Countries and the WTO mechanism gain more significance. Although the BRICS is yet to evolve into a stronger group, its members' common interests as emerging markets (vis-à-vis other markets and among themselves) should provide the necessary impetus for creating a specific agenda that effectively addresses antidumping concerns. China and Brazil have an additional option to utilize the Macau Forum if a BRICS agenda on antidumping concerns does not materialize. Established in Macau SAR in 2003, the Macau Forum has been focusing on promoting and facilitating business opportunities among the members. However, the Forum could be more meaningfully engaged by refocusing on the critical concerns of trade facing members and working towards effectively addressing them. Antidumping concerns between China and Brazil could be an appropriate item on the agenda of the Forum as it is well placed to cater to the needs arising out of antidumping investigations and to reduce their impact. This role would be further enhanced once China gained a MES in 2016.

Finally China can better utilize the WTO mechanism to moderate the effects of the use of antidumping actions by Brazil. Although much of the antidumping conundrum China faces are not challenged in the WTO, it may still use the mechanism for a constructive engagement with trading partners to mitigate potential antidumping actions. For example, China should utilize the WTO's Committee on Antidumping, to regularly engage with Brazil and seek clarification on its administration of antidumping procedures and investigations. While legislative changes in Brazil on antidumping have attracted questions from the US through the WTO, none were raised by China despite facing the highest number of antidumping investigations and duties from Brazil. Ranging from bilateral to multilateral forums, China has ample options to engage constructively with Brazil. China should take a more focused approach in addressing antidumping issues instead of being indifferent to the growing concerns on both sides. Although China may be hesitant to confront these concerns in the interest of maintaining a harmonious relation with Brazil, a constructive engagement to address the underlying concerns is necessary to sustain a strong long-term economic relationship.

NOTES

1. For Brazil, the major concerns arise from the adverse effects caused by the increased Chinese trade in different markets. In the export market segment, Brazilian exports of manufactured goods to China have witnessed a sharp decline. At the same time, Chinese imports of manufactured goods have increased considerably in the import market segment leading to a further decline in the domestic manufacturing sector. The adverse impact of Chinese trade is also faced in third markets, where the growing Chinese competition is causing loss of market share for Brazilian traders. Concerns for China on the other hand mainly pertain to the increase in the trade deficit and use of trade remedies in the bilateral trade with Brazil. While China enjoyed a trade surplus with most of the South American markets, it faced a deficit with Brazil during the past decade. This deficit has also witnessed a sharp increase and touched a record high in 2011. Moreover its exports to Brazil have faced a large number of challenges arising from the increased use of different trade remedies by Brazil. See Brazil-China Business Council (CEBC) (2012, February).
2. For complaints involving market economy exporters, ex-factory sale prices not subject to tax in the exporting country market are recommended. Sale prices in a form other than ex-factory sale price could be presented, but the details of necessary adjustments and related evidence for determining an ex-factory price should be presented in such cases. The Directive also recognizes a representative price based on the price of a similar

product in the exporting country, subject to certain conditions and supplementary information. Alternatively the export price to a third country could also be used, however, with relevant information and justification for the choice of that country. Finally it is also possible to use a constructed normal value in the exporting country, and the Directive recommends different categories of information that may be used for constructing the normal value. See Part II, Para 8.4.1 of Directive No. 46 of 23 December 2011.

3. For complaints involving non-market economy exporters, the Directive permits the complainant to recommend a third market economy country along with necessary justification and relevant information, which can be used in determining the normal value. As in cases involving market economy exporters, the Directive recognizes the possibility of using a representative price in the recommended third market economy country or the export price in the recommended third market economy to another country (except to Brazil), or a constructed normal value in the recommended third market economy country. See Part II, Para 8.4.2 of Directive No. 46 of 23 December 2011.
4. The export prices have to be presented under the same conditions of sale used in calculating the normal value. In case it is presented under other conditions of sale, relevant evidence and information about adjustments used to ensure an appropriate comparison between normal value and export price should be provided. See Part II, Para 8.6 of Directive No. 46 of 23 December 2011.

REFERENCES

Bown, C.P. and McCulloch, R. (2012, September). *Antidumping and market competition: Implications for emerging economies* (The World Bank Policy Research Working Paper 6197). Retrieved from http://www-wds.worldbank.org/servlet/WDSContentServer/WDSP/IB/2012/09/12/000158349_20120912085640/Rendered/PDF/wps6197.pdf

Brazil-China Business Council (CEBC). (2012, February). *China-Brazil update: Issue 4*. Retrieved from http://www.cebc.org.br/sites/default/files/chinabrasil_update_ed_4_english.pdf

Corkin, L., Viana, M.T. and Naidin, L.C. (2012, June). *Emerging economies and export promotion mechanisms: A study case of Brazil's and China's operations in Angola* (BRICS Policy Center – Policy Brief). Retrieved from http://bricspolicycenter.org/homolog/uploads/trabalhos/5420/doc/460949880.pdf

Cuneo, D.L. and Manuel, C.B. Jr. (1981). Roadblock to trade: The state-controlled economy issue in antidumping law administration. *Fordham International Law Journal*, *5*(2), 277–317.

Czako, J., Human, J. and Miranda, J. (2003). *A handbook on anti-dumping investigations*. Cambridge, UK: Cambridge University Press.

Feinberg, R.M. (2010, December). *Antidumping and the global financial crisis: The impact on Latin America and the Caribbean* (ECLAC – Studies and Perspectives series –No. 9). Washington: ECLAC, United Nations.

Gallagher, K.P. and Porzecanski, R. (2010). *The dragon in the room: China and the future of Latin American industrialization*. Stanford, California: Stanford University Press.

Gingerich, T. (1998). Why the WTO should require the application of the evidentiary threshold requirement in antidumping investigations. *American University Law Review*, *48*(1), 135–77.

Horlick, G. and Vermulsti, E. (2005).The 10 major problems with the anti-dumping instrument: An attempt at synthesis. *Journal of World Trade*, *39*(1), 67–73.

International Bar Association (IBA). (2010). *Anti-dumping investigations against China in Latin America* (Research Report). London: International Bar Association.
Jenkins, R. (2012). China and Brazil: Economic impacts of a growing relationship. *Journal of Current Chinese Affairs*, *41*(1), 21–47.
McGee, R.W. (2000). Some ethical aspects of antidumping laws. *Reason Papers*, *25*, 55–67.
Prusa, T.J. (2005). The growing problem of antidumping protection. In T. Ito and A.K. Rose (Eds), *International trade in East Asia, NBER – East seminar on economics, volume 14* (pp. 32–65). Chicago: University of Chicago Press.
Rowley, J. (2011, September 15). Brazil's antidumping review must address inefficiencies, say lawyers. *Latin Lawyer News*. Retrieved from http://www.latinlawyer.com/news/article/42416/brazil-8217s-antidumping-review-address-inefficiencies-say-lawyers/
Secretariat for Foreign Trade (SECEX) and Ministry of Development, Industry and Foreign Trade (MDIC). (2011). *Trade balance – Brazil-China* (Fact Sheet). Retrieved from http://www.brasil.gov.br/para/press/files/fact-sheet-brazil-china-trade
Vandenbussche, H. and Zanardi, M. (2008). What explains the proliferation of antidumping laws? *Economic Policy*, *23*(1), 93–138.
Vermulst, E. and Horlick, G. (2007). Problem with dumping and injury margin calculations in ten user countries. *Global Trade and Customs Journal*, *2*(1), 1–5.
WTO (2013a). *Anti-dumping initiations: Reporting member vs exporting country 01/01/1995 – 31/12/2012*. Retrieved from http://www.wto.org/english/tratop_e/adp_e/AD_InitiationsRepMemVsExpCty.pdf
WTO (2013b). *Anti-dumping measures: Reporting member vs exporting country 01/01/1995–31/12/2012*. Retrieved from http://www.wto.org/english/tratop_e/adp_e/AD_MeasuresRepMemVsExpCty.pdf

7. Joining the BRICs: The case of South Africa

Laurence Boulle and Jessie Chella

This chapter examines and evaluates the accession of the Republic of South Africa (RSA) to the BRIC group of nations in April 2011. Given the fact that South Africa was, in several respects, an unlikely candidate for membership, and it remains the junior member in terms of most relevant indicators, the usage the 'BRICs' (as opposed to the BRICS) has been adopted here to identify the group post-RSA accession. Adoption of the lower case has a symbolism beyond the convenience of providing an acronymic plural for the BRIC – it suggests that in many respects South Africa is a limited player in a grouping of emerging economies which could be a potential force in the global political economy (World Bank, 2011a).[1]

The accession of South Africa will be examined in the context of current themes in international affairs and regional relations, and with reference to some prominent issues in the global political economy. It considers factors that could have motivated the inclusion of a country which might in many respects have been overlooked as a potential BRICs member, and reflects on the roles which the new member might play in the BRICs institutional environment. It concludes with reflections on themes of inclusion and exclusion in contemporary state-to-state relations and group formations, with particular relevance to other potential inclusions in the BRICs.

The BRICs has been referred to, in a metaphor derived from the world sport of soccer, as the 'premier league' of emerging markets (Ernst & Young, 2011). While acronymic labels might seem ephemeral in the global political economy, they can sometimes matter in symbolic and iconic ways. There is an increasing use of acronyms for purposes of grouping political economies in the international arena with individual state players manoeuvring among multiple non-exclusive and overlapping 'clubs', in the search for economic and geopolitical advantages. Acronyms such as the BRICS commence life as useful heuristics for categorizing such groups and shaping the discourse around them, but they can also become reified beyond their appropriate utility and use by dates (Cooper, 2010, pp. 63–5; Sharma, 2012, p. 2).

THE BRICS AS A TRANSGOVERNMENTAL NETWORK

In this chapter the BRICs is depicted as a 'transgovernmental network', denoting an arrangement in an intermediate position between formal international institutions and mere occasional interactions. It adopts Slaughter's conceptualization of transgovernmental networks as information institutions regulating different actors from different state institutions in aspects of governance beyond the domestic level. As Slaughter and Hale describe it, these networks,

> . . . exhibit patterns of regular and purposive relations among like government units working across the borders that divide countries from one another and that demarcate the 'domestic' from the 'international' sphere, [featuring] loosely structured, peer-to-peer ties developed through frequent interaction rather than formal negotiation (Slaughter & Hale, 2010, p. 48).

The compatibility of the BRICs with this conceptualization of a transgovernmental network is reflected in the fact that it has no conventional status in international law, it deals predominantly with issues of high-level policy without specific regulatory authority, it lacks a significant infrastructure, and its meetings are interactive as opposed to negotiational in form. At the same time it involves regular, if not frequent, peer-to-peer and intergovernmental meetings, as opposed to occasional diplomatic interactions which occur in less structured settings.

Structurally the BRICs constitutes a self-selected but non-exclusive forum through which a collective of countries can act in coordination, where they would otherwise lobby and interact exclusively as a single entity, or through larger groupings such as the G20. Membership of the grouping does not preclude other associations, multiple memberships being axiomatic in transgovernmental networks.[7] It has a quixotic existence vis-à-vis the G20 group of nations, of which all the BRICs countries are also members, with the BRICs subservient to the G20 in terms of the informal 'hierarchy' of transgovernmental networks. While the pre-existing G20 assumed greater prominence in response to problems arising out of the Global Financial Crisis (GFC), the BRICs was less specific in its motivating origins, arising more casually and organically, with a diffuse mandate lacking the troubleshooting specificity of the post-GFC G20. Despite their nominal autonomy from each other, there are inevitable inter-connections between the two networks, some commentators contending that the BRICs should play agenda-setting and lobbying roles within the G20 (Boulle, 2011a).

In terms of the character of modern groupings, the BRICs is plurilateral and regional in nature, bridging the gap between multilateralism and bilateralism. While its members lack the geographical contiguity of most regional arrangements, and the community of interests associated with it, the BRICs can in some respects be portrayed as a regional grouping of states. In a contemporary world that is partly virtual in nature, there is no contradiction in entertaining the concept of a 'virtual region'. As pointed out, the BRICs is in some senses also 'a region of regions' in that each member dominates its particular geographical sector of the world. The regionalism[3] of the BRICs is incongruent with aspirational paradigms of inclusive international multilateralism, but as a self-selecting 'club of nations', it is compatible with the contemporary patterns of intergovernmental networks of many varieties.

While one may expect commonalities of interests among the BRICs members, there are in fact many disjunctions in their key attributes. These are reflected in Table 7.1.

These indicators reveal disproportionalities in many dimensions. For example the GDP of China gives it substantial potential leverage within the grouping, and South Africa presents as a relative minnow in the economic and demographic leagues. Each member has its own bag of strengths – such as Russia in the energy field, China in manufactured exports, Brazil in aerospace industries and India in the services sector. South Africa is not pre-eminent in any field but it has a strong services sector, referred to further on, and surprising export resilience in the automotive industry. The differences provide the occasion for both complementarity and competition among individual members. However, there are also other important differences among the members at the constitutional and institutional levels where there are vastly different levels of statism, of participatory government, of rule of law enforcement and of private sector involvement in the economy.

The functionality of the BRICs is linked to its structural features and the attributes of its members. Given the institutional looseness of the group it has no direct political functions, nor even common political positions – particularly in international relations; members' heterogeneity is preserved in respect of foreign policy and on matters such as nuclear weapons, disarmament and reform of the UN Security Council.[4] As a collective its main focus is economic in nature, with particular reference to reform of the international financial architecture, changed governance arrangements in the IMF and World Bank (or alternatives to the latter), and a shift towards trade agreements and credit facilities being denominated in member states' own currencies as opposed to US dollars. Even in economic matters it has none of the formal authority associated with some

Table 7.1 Key indicators for the BRICS members

Indicator	Brazil	Russia	India	China	South Africa
Population (million)	194	142	1155	1331	49
Gross domestic product (GDP) in purchasing power parity (PPP) terms	2017	2690	3778	9091	507
GDP per capita, PPP (current international $)	10412	18963	3270	6828	10278
Land area (million km2)	8.5	16.4	3	9.3	1.2
Urban population (% of total)	86	73	30	44	61
Under-five mortality rate (per 1000)	21	12	66	19	62
Gross savings rate (% of GDP)	14.6	22.7	33.6	53.6	15.4
Ores and metal ores exports (% of GDP)	1.7	5.7	6.2	1.2	29.3
Ores and metal ores imports (% of GDP)	2.9	1.6	5.6	13.5	1.3
Portfolio inflows, net ($ billion)	37.1	3.4	21.1	28.2	9.4
Agriculture (% of GDP)	6.1	4.7	17.1	10.3	3
Manufacturing (% of GDP)	14.8	15	15.9	33.9	15.1
Carbon dioxide emissions (kg per PPP $ of GDP)	0.2	0.6	0.5	0.9	0.9
Energy use (kg of oil equivalent per capita)	1239	4730	529	1484	2784
GDP per unit of energy use (PPP $ per kg of oil equivalent)	7.9	3.6	5.4	3.7	3.6

Source: World Bank (2009).

international institutions and only the soft power of an intergovernmental network.

The loose structure of the BRICs and the indeterminacy of its functionality make it difficult to identify how it might respond to some of the key questions relating to its meta-objectives. For example there is debate over whether the BRICs is seeking greater inclusion within the existing institutions and processes of global governance, or pushing to change or replace the institutions. While the G20 operates predominantly within a Bretton Woods framework and policy agenda, the BRICs, despite overlapping membership with the Bretton Woods institutions, constitutes a potential rival to Washington Consensus thinking and to institutions such as the World Bank and IMF. Whereas developing countries have historically established interdependent relations with the EU and the US (and other G7 countries), the BRICs grouping provides a potentially alternative point of interconnectedness for such economies. There is, conspicuously, no overlap of membership between the G7 and the BRICs, reinforcing the axis of prospective rivalry.

Whatever the structural and functional indeterminacies of the BRICs, it allows a small emerging power in the form of South Africa to interact in supranational governance at a level of prominence not formally offered by many other international organizations (Slaughter & Hale, 2010, p.48). Its non-exclusive nature also allows the RSA to retain membership of other groupings with similar organizational arrangements and some overlap of membership and objectives.[5]

SOUTH AFRICA'S ACCESSION TO THE BRIC

In terms of economic ranking or population size, countries such as Indonesia, Turkey, Mexico or South Korea might have been more likely additions to the original BRIC foursome – each significantly outranks South Africa on both dimensions, a factor referred to again in the final section. Moreover, as previously alluded to, South Africa as a 'candidate' member was relatively insignificant vis-à-vis the existing members, in relation to many economic indicators. This can be illustrated by reference to one such dimension, namely inward and outward foreign direct investment (FDI) flows, as indicated in Tables 7.2 and 7.3.

These figures reveal the limited status of the RSA in the field of cross-border investment. Given the mode of accession it is not possible to identify precise motivating factors leading to its acceptance in the BRICs, and the self-selecting nature of membership entailed that there was no official record of the decision to admit the new country.[6] The RSA was first invited to attend a summit by then host country China in what some commentators see as a reward for the country's political support for China (Khan, 2011). Nonetheless South Africa had in other respects, relevant and even unique attributes, which could have motivated its accession, not only to the BRICs but also to bodies such as the G20.[7] These include the following factors.

The Regional Power Argument

South Africa is a regional power in its own right, as is the case with each of the other BRICs countries, and it has contributed to the reconfiguration of the global order through its part in the rise of regional powers (Nolte, 2010; Carmody, 2012). A regional power has economic, political

Table 7.2 Inward FDI flows, 2000–11

Year	Brazil	Russia	India	China	South Africa
2000	32779	2714	3588	40715	887
2001	22457	2748	5478	46878	6784
2002	16590	3461	5630	52743	1569
2003	10144	7958	4321	53505	734
2004	18146	15444	5778	60630	798
2005	15066	12886	7622	72406	6647
2006	18822	29701	20328	72715	−527
2007	34585	55073	25506	83521	5695
2008	45058	75002	43406	108312	9006
2009	25949	36500	35596	95000	5365
2010	48506	43288	24159	114734	1228
2011	66660	52878	31554	123985	5807

Notes: US dollars at current prices and current exchange rates.

Source: UNCTAD (2012b).

Table 7.3 Outward FDI flows, 2000–2011 (US$ million)

Year	Brazil	Russia	India	China	South Africa
2000	2282	3177	514	916	271
2001	−2258	2533	1397	6885	−3178
2002	2482	3533	1678	2518	−398
2003	249	9727	1876	2855	565
2004	9807	13782	2175	5498	1350
2005	2517	12767	2985	12261	930
2006	28202	23151	14285	21160	6063
2007	7067	45916	19594	22469	2966
2008	20457	55594	19257	52150	−3134
2009	−10084	43665	15927	56530	1151
2010	11588	52523	13151	68811	−76
2011	−1029	67283	14752	65117	−635

Notes: US dollars at current prices and current exchange rates.

Source: UNCTAD (2012b).

and strategic significance over and above its own immediate attributes, acting as a centre of gravity in respect of contiguous and other accessible countries. In this context the region, in respect of which South Africa is a centripetal force, extends through much of Sub-Saharan Africa, a vast expanse with extensive natural resources, population growth, investment attraction and economic potential.[8] Needless to say, however, not all African countries view South Africa as the regional hegemon, and some do so with considerable reluctance (Shaw, Cooper & Chin, 2009), but this does not detract from the de facto reality.

In its combination of existing regional powers into a super-regional entity, the BRICs suggests a new conceptualization of regionalism as involving associations extending beyond geographical boundaries – what might be termed 'intentional regionalism'. Here there is strategic significance in the 'regional' BRICs grouping having regional members in Europe, Asia, South America (the sub-continent) and now Africa. This phenomenon is consistent with the shift to regional trade agreements and the continuing stalemate in multilateralism as epitomized by the WTO. While regionalism runs counter to idealized notions of multilateralism, it has together with bilateralism, become prominent in the global political economy. Deadlocks in the multilateral trade regime and the challenges of the GFC have also contributed to the regionalist trend.

Apart from being a regional power, South Africa is also the largest and most sophisticated economy in the African continent. It not only dominates the economy of the region and the continent, but also has significant diplomatic and political leverage, allowing it to expand its own economy into many parts of Africa through FDI, trade and finance. While South Africa's regional economic integration is currently focused primarily on the Southern African Development Community (SADC) and Common Market for Eastern and Southern Africa (COMESA),[9] this is not incompatible with its further integration into the BRICs' intentional regionalism (Castel, Mejia & Kolster, 2011).[10]

The African Gateway Hypothesis

South Africa is often depicted as a 'gateway' to the rest of Africa.[11] While it is in overall terms an emerging economy, the RSA has a highly developed 'sub-economy' within the economic whole and is seen as one of the most attractive African countries from which to conduct business into other jurisdictions (Ernst & Young, 2011). South Africa's extensive economic interests in countries to its north contribute to the 'gateway' into Africa theme.[12] At least three, and potentially four, BRICs members have interests in Africa's resources and other potential benefits, and the gateway hypothesis is to the effect that they could utilize the competencies the RSA has developed over the past century (Kahn, 2011, p. 37). It might be contended, under the hypothesis, that Brazil would be attracted to using the RSA as a gateway into Lusophone Africa.[13]

Apart from its pervasive economic presence in Africa, South Africa has comparative advantages in many aspects of the services sector, which at 67 per cent dominates the domestic economy, with particular strengths in banking, finance and insurance, telecommunications, education and construction. Comparative advantage can also be identified in South Africa's existing memberships of, and economic influence within, the SADC, the Southern African Customs Union (SACU), the African Union (AU) and the New Partnership for Africa's Development (NEPAD). The comparative advantage attraction is exemplified by a pre-BRICs investment into a major South African bank with extensive existing interests in other African countries,[14] and although not relating to a BRICs member, by the transnational Walmart Corporation's takeover of a major South African retailer with subsidiaries in more than ten African economies (*Walmart Stores v Massmart Holdings Ltd*, 2011). Needless to say this does not suggest any intra-BRICs exclusivity – China's largest ever investment bid occurred in another resource-rich country, namely, Canada (Kelly, 2012).

In reality the idea of South Africa being a gateway to Africa is an imprecise and diffuse notion, and is not incompatible with investors using other gateways or investing directly in relevant African economies.[15] This is evidenced by the ever increasing diplomatic outreach initiatives in Africa.[16] Moreover the very success of South African countries in their expansion into Africa, for example in brewing and telecommunications, suggests that some corporate interests in the RSA would vigorously oppose any facilitation of new competition. Nonetheless the gateway theme is prevalent in business and diplomatic circles, as well as in the literature.

South Africa as Representative Agent

Allied to the 'gateway' theme is the proclaimed 'representative' nature of South Africa in respect of its geopolitical neighbours. This is reflected in South Africa's self-defined 'African voice' mission, particularly evident in relation to the G20 group of countries where the RSA has conspicuously claimed to speak on behalf of African interests. It is also reinforced by the expectations, and sometimes explicit endorsements, of other countries and institutions of South Africa playing this role. For example in relation to the G20, South Africa engages in consultative discussions with other African countries before summit meetings, and undertakes to convey African views to the summit. Conversely other African countries have indicated that they regard South Africa as their voice in this grouping which has only one African member.

Whatever South Africa's self-depiction of its representative role, or the perceptions of other African countries, the BRICs, like the G20, has not developed on a constituency basis. This is in keeping with other transgovernmental networks where leaders and other elites do not operate with direct mandates from their own political constituents, let alone from other countries. Importantly the BRICs overlooks the fact that Africa comprises over 50 countries with deep variations in culture, history, politics and economic policy. Different African countries and regions are responding to the forces of globalization and neo-liberalism in different and contrasting ways, and there can be no concerted representation of these interests. Nonetheless the African voice syndrome persists.

South Africa and the African Renaissance

The regional, gateway and representative factors which may have influenced South Africa's accession to the BRICs are located within the umbrella context of an 'African renaissance' in the twenty-first century. A decade ago the *Economist* magazine referred to Africa as the 'hopeless' continent ('The hopeless continent', 2000), whereas a 2012 KPMG survey portrayed the continent as a major source of economic growth, investment and opportunity for 'exploitation' (KPMG, 2012). This is substantiated in other reports on the continent, indicating it to be one of the fastest growing regions of the world with projected economic growth of 4.8 per cent in 2013 (OECD, 2012).[17] The reports also indicate surprising resilience in the continent with respect to financial and other global crises, subject to the normal vicissitudes of a global economy; this is partly a function of the appetite of Asian and Latin American countries, including those represented in the BRICs, for natural resources. In this sense the BRIC countries might have seen South Africa's inclusion as facilitating their involvement in the latest 'scramble for Africa'.

The African Renaissance project was in fact conceived by the then South African President Mbeki, and was followed institutionally by the creation of the African Union (AU) (Kahn, 2011, p.40). While there is some analytical content underlying the renaissance theme there are also limits to the concept. It has become a popular theme for journalists and editors who emphasize the continent's high economic growth, the world's interest in its abundant commodities, relatively high levels of foreign direct investment and a population fast reaching 1 billion in number (Holman, 2011). These factors attract captains of industry to seminars and summits but tend to overlook current problems of authoritarian government, managerial shortcomings and undeveloped infrastructure. Moreover there is a surprising lack of regional economic integration in the continent, and human development remains low in comparison with other global regions. As in other economic regions of the world there are also immense discrepancies in the distribution of economic strengths among and within African states.

Among the founding BRIC countries it was China, South Africa's largest trading partner, which was the strongest supporter of the Republic's accession (Noury, 2011). On the investment front China had previously made one of its largest ever investments in a South African bank, and on the trade front China is the main purchaser of South African commodities and the main exporter of manufactured goods to the Republic.[18] While Chinese support for South African membership was a necessary condition for inclusion, it was not a sufficient condition and as with other optional groupings, acquiescence from all members would have been necessary. However, India was already an established investor in the country, and the African economic renaissance had awoken interest in all members as reflected in the fact that prior to South Africa's accession each had conducted a 'cooperation forum' with African states.

South Africa's Membership Benefits

The motivations for South Africa's accession to the BRICs have been depicted in terms of the individual and collective interests of the original four members. There were also significant economic, political and strategic motivations for South Africa to join the grouping.

In pure economic terms there are potential short-term benefits for the smallest and latest member of the BRICs, but it is hard to ascribe causatively specific economic benefits in regard to trade, investment or finance to BRICs membership. As the South African-Brazil trade dispute referred to further on suggests, the BRICs countries stand in a dialectical relationship with one another in relation to economic issues. At present they are in many respects economic competitors, contesting not only within their intra-group economic relations, which is the case with all membership organizations, but also with one another for trade and investment opportunities with other countries, including those in Africa (Castel, Mejia & Kolster, 2011). In this context it is likely that the benefits to South Africa will accrue more in terms of political leverage at the diplomatic level than material advantage at the economic level. As discussed earlier, labels do matter, hence membership of the club has symbolic significance and symbols are relevant in the world of international relations. Nonetheless South Africa's services industry, which contributes over 60 per cent of GDP, is dependent for growth on market access and global value chains, accentuated by current economic constraints in the country (CIA, 2013); the RSA has a particular need for outlets for its resources and commodities and for its rare manufacturing successes in the automotive exports.[19]

Table 7.4 Global competitiveness of the BRICS members

Category	Brazil	Russia	India	China	South Africa
Overall country ranking /142	53	66	56	26	50
12 Pillars of Global Competitiveness					
Basic requirements	*83*	*63*	*91*	*30*	*85*
Institutions	77	128	69	48	46
Infrastructure	64	48	89	44	62
Macroeconomic environment	115	44	105	10	55
Health and primary education	87	68	101	32	131
Efficiency enhancers	*41*	*55*	*37*	*26*	*38*
Higher education and training	57	52	87	58	73
Goods market efficiency	113	128	70	45	32
Labour market efficiency	83	65	81	36	95
Financial market development	43	127	21	48	4
Technological readiness	54	68	93	77	76
Market size	10	8	3	2	25
Innovation & sophistication factors	*35*	*97*	*40*	*31*	*39*
Business sophistication	31	114	43	37	38
Innovation	44	71	38	29	41

Source: *The global competitiveness report*, World Economic Forum, Switzerland 2011 (p. 39).

The fact that only two BRIC countries were in the country's top ten trading partners in 2011, [20] suggests that trade diversification could be an intermediate-term benefit of South Africa's accession.

With respect to global competitiveness, South Africa is the most competitive economy in Sub-Saharan Africa. More significantly its competitiveness ranks second among the BRICs countries. As Table 7.4 indicates, South Africa scores well on the quality of its institutions and the efficiency of its goods market (World Economic Forum, 2011, p. 39).[21] In addition, the country's financial market development measurements are extremely high, denoting confidence in the country's financial markets. South Africa's competitive measures in business sophistication and innovation are also of note (World Economic Forum, 2011, p. 39).

In terms of tangible economic benefits for South Africa, much depends on the grouping's future activities. For example if the BRICs does provide infrastructure and incentives for intra-group trade and investment, South Africa might well be a beneficiary. As regards foreign investment South Africa could find new access to the large pool of capital provided by the other four members. This opportunity would come at a sensitive time in terms of South Africa's FDI policy as there are currently proposals for the development of a new foreign investment framework comprising an Investment Act, a new Model Bilateral Investment Treaty (BIT), an Investment Agency and possibly a dedicated tribunal for investment disputes (Boulle, 2012). However, regardless of the BRICs connection, South Africa faces a dilemma in regard to the way it balances inconsistent interests in its evolving investment policy. Besides maintaining constitutional values and regulatory policy space, any changes need to ensure continued attractiveness to overseas capital, to comply with international trade and investment obligations, and to avoid unfair treatment of investors from treaty parties (Boulle, 2012).

As regards trade, China is South Africa's main trading partner, but the other BRICs economies do not feature in its next five most important import or export partners, suggesting that any impetus for trade among BRICs members would be an improvement over existing patterns. Here a practical example concerns mineral beneficiation within the RSA to add value prior to export. This would prospectively break the pattern exporting raw materials and importing manufactures. However, despite some apparent Chinese support for such a programme, there is no institutional basis for its implementation.

The BRICs' Declarations and Reports

Before commenting on South Africa's potential role within the BRICs it is appropriate to refer to the organization's self-perceived roles and functions, as reflected in its declarations and reports.

Collectively the BRICs could operate as a lobby group and be influential in the global arena, but this is yet to manifest. It might for instance have acted concertedly during the selection of a new IMF chief in 2011, but it missed the opportunity. When the head of the IMF resigned, the prospect arose of breaking the convention that the position be held by a European, to balance traditional US leadership of the World Bank.[22] South Africa in fact had a highly regarded candidate who was a long-serving Treasurer and leader of reform initiatives in the Fund itself.[23] Not only was there no collaboration in this regard but Brazil allegedly engaged in quiet negotiations with the favoured G8 candidate for the position (Lukyanov, 2011, p. 113). In the end the old convention was preserved and the BRICs did not assert its influence.

Another possible function for the BRICs as a whole is to legitimize international institutions which might otherwise be seen to lack legitimacy from the perspective of emerging states. Thus the grouping has been informally recognized by the G20 in terms of its ability to feed agenda items into the larger group,[24] and it does formulate its collective positions in advance of G20 meetings. In this way it can serve as a counterbalance to the exclusive G7 which has always had a strong influence over G20 agendas and outcomes. The recognition and participation of the BRICs as an emerging power entity affords greater legitimacy to the workings of the G20.

South African Functions in the BRICs

South Africa's role in the BRICs will clearly be circumscribed by the grouping's own limitations, as a loose alliance of states with minimal infrastructure, and by the fact that the grouping will only be motivated to act where it is in the common interests of member states to do so. For the rest, a 'proportionality' principle can be expected to operate in respect of South Africa, as it would in relation to its involvement in the G20 group of nations (Boulle, 2011a, p. 135) – it will only have an influence more or less commensurate with its economic and strategic powers. For a relatively small member of an intergovernmental network it would be inappropriate to expect more than modest roles within the group. These include the following.

Contributing to the agenda

Danny Bradlow has contended that one of the roles for developing countries in new intergovernmental frameworks is to attempt to influence their work agenda and to 'focus on long term goals which are infused with short term objectives' (Bradlow, 2010). Agency is recognized as a significant factor in the development of agendas for meetings and summits (Boulle, 2011a, p. 139). Agendas include and exclude, they prioritize some items and marginalize others, and they frame agenda issues by using language which reflects the interests of agenda-setting agents. Work agendas provide the normative framework for meetings and, as referred to further on, they also control the discourse for political debates.

There are numerous agenda items falling within the remit of the BRICs, which could serve South African needs and the wider interests of the developing world. They include sustainable economic development, reform of international financial institutions, introduction of a financial transactions tax, reciprocal investment and credit arrangements, the rebalancing of international economic principles to accommodate domestic policy space, and explicit systems for currency management.[25] The financial transactions tax (FTT), for example, has been on the agendas of various countries and international institutions for some years, but also faces immense political opposition.[26] In this area, as well as in relation to currency balancing where the country's exports suffer from a strong currency, South Africa has direct interests in global intervention, possibly brokered through the BRICs. Another agenda item at the meta-level of global policy would be the promotion of multilateralism in key areas of trade, investment and finance, despite the BRICs providing in part a contradiction of this principle.

As to how smaller countries could influence agenda-setting, this would be facilitated by the leadership level of BRICs summits and the small size of the grouping vis-à-vis bodies such as the G20, though in reality officials and technocrats on all sides are the real drivers of agenda items. There is some precedent for agenda influence in the G20 where the topic of financial inclusion, not a high priority for developed nations, became part of the agenda through pressure from emerging and developing countries. Over 30 per cent of the world's population is excluded, wholly or in part, from financial services and products. The matter was taken up by the G20 in conjunction with other institutions, with the promulgation of a Financial Inclusion Plan.[27] In fact South Africa is, by developing country standards, relatively well off in terms of financial inclusion, particularly in relation to mobile phone banking. However, this is not the case throughout the continent and it is an area in which South Africa could give voice in the BRICs to the needs of African and other developing countries.

Framing the discourse

While the empowerment of new actors such as South Africa on the international stage might allow the introduction of agenda items, it can at a more general level contribute to changes in the discourse of the global political economy. This is based on the notion that language provides part of the normative framework for social and economic issues and influences judgements, attitudes and behaviours. Thus while many international institutions and policies give lip service to economic growth and development, developing countries would benefit by a stronger definitional focus on sustainable development in the discourse of international economic law.

A topical illustration relates to the coupling of FDI more closely with sustainable economic development. This is pertinently reflected in the UNCTAD *World Investment Report* (2012b) which incorporates an Investment Policy Framework for Sustainable Development (IPFSD). While this is by no means the first report to bring economic growth and sustainability to the forefront of FDI policy and law, it does so on a systematic and comprehensive basis and provides detailed policy options for incorporation of relevant provisions into International Investment Agreements (IIAs). Some of the suggested institutional arrangements are compatible with the predominant language of globalization, but others provide different degrees of challenge to the prevailing discourse.[28]

This is an area in which South Africa could, through the BRICs and its own devices, use the 'objective' criteria set out by the UNCTAD in the IPFSD to modify the discourse of FDI. One issue to introduce into the discourse is the development of Investment Protection Agencies in developing countries to perform pre-establishment scrutiny of proposed FDI in terms of relevant criteria; another, relating to the renegotiation of IIAs, involves the greater use of treaty exceptions for domestic regulatory measures pursuing legitimate public policy objectives (UNCTAD, 2012b, Art. 5.1.4). The Seoul Development Consensus, deriving from a G20 Summit in South Korea, provides another source of reference for changing the discourse;[29] it can serve to legitimize specific applications of generalized policies, for example, job creation through national budgetary allocations, local industry policies or regional agricultural projects designed to improve food security. Another example involves reframing highly generalized issues, for instance strengthening global financial regulation in terms of more specific factors relevant to member countries, such as ensuring the viability and transparency of domestic banks.

A significant segment of contemporary discourse relates to measuring the successes and failures in economic globalization. Despite globalization entailing in large measure a reduction in national boundaries for purposes of borderless trade and investment and finance (but not in the movement of people), global measurements tend to be made in terms of traditional state identities (such as various countries' growth rates) and in aggregate terms (such as increases in national GDP or FDI). Even where reduced to per capita figures, the conventional measurements tend to exclude statistics on distributions within nation states, on regional and local variations within countries, or on specific economic sectors or enterprises within a national economy. A consistent emphasis on measurements such as these would modify the globalization discourse and therefore how the phenomenon is perceived and acted upon. Other parts of the dominant discourse such as 'free trade', 'removal of trade barriers' and 'market choices' impose a particular ideology on globalization discourse, and the terms limit the scope for challenging prevailing practices and trends.[30] Here there is potential scope for a country such as South Africa to use the vehicle of the BRICs to modify the discourse of trade, investment and finance.

Monitoring and compliance

International diplomacy is littered with ambitious multilateral statements on various matters, such as the Millennium Development Goals, G8 aid commitments and climate change mitigation, which never achieve implementation and fall quietly from global political agendas. This raises the question of compliance surveillance and measurement in respect of the BRICs' declarations and policies.

At present there is no treaty basis to the BRICs, nor are there dedicated infrastructural systems for performing monitoring and compliance functions. These realities entail intrinsic limitations within the group itself in regard to the enforceability of the BRICs' policy decisions, and to compliance measures requiring the positive actions of individual member states. The larger members in particular will respond to policy pronouncements and directives in accordance with their domestic strategic interests. Here South Africa, less able to assert its own strategic interests, could play a monitoring function in relation to member compliance.[31]

Monitoring and compliance constitute more defensive than activist roles in any organization. In the BRICs context they could not be undertaken unilaterally by a country such as South Africa. However, they could be agitated for as part of the network's work programme and the monitoring itself could be 'monitored'. This initiative would contribute a 'governance' element to the operation and functioning of the BRICs.

Governance issues

Despite being the smallest brick in the edifice, South Africa could, as indicated in the previous section, raise governance issues relating to the operation of the BRICs. The democratic dispensation of 1996 provided South Africa with a modern and progressive constitution resplendent with arrangements for representation, transparency, inclusivity, checks and balances, accountability, reasoned decision-making, court access and other accoutrements of good constitutional governance. These factors operate in widely differing degrees among the country's BRICs partners.

The transgovernmental framework nature of the grouping precludes any simplistic prognosis of significant constitutional governance within the BRICs. However, there are several areas in which South Africa could attempt to influence issues of governance. One possibility relates to organization and leadership in the grouping. Here the G20 provides a model of rotating chairs with accompanying responsibilities to develop agendas. It would be salutary to find that the same transparency and meritocracy which developing countries claim for international financial institutions, such as in selecting the head of the IMF, could operate in relation to the BRICs itself.

The BRICs' proposal for a new international development bank, which has been supported by South Africa (Zuma, 2012), could be seen as providing a new agency of transnational governance. The BRICs envisages that the bank could play an instrumental role in 'fostering investment among emerging markets and developing countries' (BRICS, 2012b). Here South Africa could both contribute its financial expertise and be a beneficiary of investment finance on conditions favourable to it (World Economic Forum, 2011, p. 323).[32] More significantly it is the potential for the RSA to draw on its own constitutional and banking experiences in good governance, to promote the structures and procedures which the developing world claims are absent from institutions such as the World Bank.

Other Issues

In the absence of a significant administrative infrastructure and of sufficient common interests in the BRICs, South Africa might also involve itself in single issue topics arising within the forum. These have already been foreshadowed by the establishment of groups on, inter alia, urbanization and local government, both pressing issues in the RSA. A focus on such 'overt' but no less significant issues could lead to drafting policy declarations on the single issue topics, and eventually to model laws. Here South Africa would be both a recipient and a donor of expertise and experience. A more remote possibility is the development of dedicated dispute resolution processes for dealing with intra-BRICs disputes.

RESOLVING INTRA-BRICS DISPUTES

It is trite to observe that common membership in a grouping such as the BRICs does not obviate the need for dispute resolution procedures. At present there is no provision for dedicated dispute resolution procedures in the BRICs, as is the case with other G-groups. This is, however, unlike the situation with other regional groupings such as the EU, the SADC and the NAFTA.

As regards investment disputes among member states, only China is a member of the predominant dispute resolution services provided by the International Centre for the Settlement of Investment Disputes (ICSID, n.d.),[33] and there is no reliable indicator of the extent to which other members are involved in such disputes. As to trade conflicts, some indication of the propensity for involvement in these disputes by and among the five member states is provided by the figures in Table 7.5, with respect to matters brought before the WTO.[34]

These statistics confirm the truism that BRICs membership is not incompatible with the invocation of external dispute resolution systems among members. Each member state has a history of involvement as

Table 7.5 The BRICS and the WTO (December 2012)

Member as a complainant	Member as a respondent					
	Brazil	Russia	India	China	South Africa	Any country
Brazil	–		–	–	1	26
Russia	–	–	–	–	–	–
India	1	–	–	–	1	21
China	–	–	–	–	–	11
South Africa	–	–	–	–	–	–
Any country	14	–	21	29	4	–
Member as a complainant	**Member as a third party**					
	Brazil	Russia	India	China	South Africa	Any country
Brazil	–	–	4	3	1	26
Russia	–	–	–	–	–	–
India	2	–	–	3	–	21
China	6	1	3	–	–	11
South Africa	–	–	–	–	–	–
Any country	73	6	80	92	2	–

Source: WTO (2013).

complainant, respondent or third party in the WTO's dispute resolution system, although, as indicated in Table 7.5, in only three instances have the BRICs members faced off against each other.[35] While the grouping as yet has no significant infrastructure, it might be conjectured that at some stage in the future consideration will be given to an internal mechanism for dealing with intra-member trade, and especially investment disputes of the nature referred to in the next section.

The BRICs and Chicks

On 21 June 2012, Brazil notified the WTO of a dispute relating to the export of its frozen chickens to South Africa (WTO, 2012). Prior to this, in February 2012, South Africa had imposed provisional antidumping duties on frozen chickens and chicken pieces which originated or were imported from Brazil. At the time South Africa contended that these imports created unfair competition within its domestic markets (see preliminary findings of the International Trade Administration Commission of South Africa, ITAC, 2012). Brazil, the complainant in the matter pending before the WTO, argues that in imposing duties on the imports, South Africa is acting in contravention of its obligations under the General Agreement on Tariffs and Trade (GATT) (1994) and the Agreement on Implementation of Article VI of GATT 1994 (WTO, 2012).

Brazil and South Africa are both members of the WTO. In the absence of a BRICs-based dispute resolution mechanism, or even of an informal infrastructure for dealing with the chicken dumping dispute, it was perhaps predictable that once diplomacy failed, a WTO complaint would begin. In this regard one may query whether the BRICs will develop systems for facilitating the future resolution of inevitable trade and investment disputes among member states, as have occurred in other regional groupings. The WTO matter is yet to be determined.

CONCLUSION

As an intergovernmental network the BRICs constitutes a small reconfiguration of the global order which currently provides largely indeterminate benefits for all its members, including its latest and smallest. Conversely South Africa's influence and benefits within the grouping cannot be identified in definitive terms and will depend on future political and economic developments.

This chapter contends that the BRICs association provides some institutional and political space for a voice otherwise relatively muted in international relations. More particularly South Africa could, through its BRICs membership, attempt to strengthen its political and diplomatic relations and promote its policies of sustainable economic development, to contribute to the agenda of global governance, to reframe the prevailing discourse in parts of the international political economy, to promote a degree of surveillance and accountability in relation to policy decisions, and to promote principles of good governance in the BRICs. Moreover for the RSA its BRICs membership provides not only international diplomatic leverage but an opportunity to exploit its comparative advantages in the services sector through its 'gateway' into Africa role. This occurs at a time of immense geopolitical and economic change, partly as a consequence of the GFC.

As regards the future of the BRICs there has been extensive speculation over additional memberships. Inclusion and exclusion are sensitive themes in contemporary intergovernmental networks, whether in the G7, the G20 or the BRICs. Inclusion in the BRICs might assist relevant member countries economically, and could have negative implications for developing economies continuing to be excluded. South Africa's inclusion suggests some degree of idiosyncrasy in relation to membership, with the sponsorship of a dominant existing member and an eclectic range of attributes providing limited predictability for the future. The self-selecting nature of groupings such as the BRICs precludes any political or legal challenge from those excluded.

Inclusion has significance for the extent to which it allows different states and groupings to operate within traditional international institutions in the global political economy, or to challenge existing principles and paradigms. For these reasons countries such as South Korea, Mexico, Indonesia and Turkey, already members of the G20, might have an interest in inclusion in the BRICs. Further afield, countries such as Malaysia, Poland and African contenders such as Nigeria – which could, over the next two decades, challenge South Africa's economic dominance on the continent – might also seek inclusion. Here a noticeable point of difference is that the US will have less direct influence over membership directions in the BRICs than it had in the G20.[36] In this context South Africa may have an influence over the addition of new bricks to the BRICs.

NOTES

1. In economic terms, the Republic ranks as the twenty-seventh largest economy in the world. All other BRICs members rank in the top ten. In terms of population, it is considerably smaller than the other four. While India and China are its major trading partners, South Africa has more limited trade with Russia and Brazil. In relation to the G20, South Africa's membership was justified in terms of its developed financial system and expertise and not its overall economic size.
2. South Africa has become a member not only of the BRICs but also of the G20 (seen domestically as a more politically important membership) and has long been a member of the Southern African Development Community (SADC), the African Union (AU), the Southern African Customs Union (SACU), the WTO, the IMF and the World Bank.
3. There is a vast body of literature on regionalism, see for example Shaw, Grant and Cornelissen, 2012, p. 3.
4. Brazil, India, and to a lesser extent South Africa have lobbied for permanent representation on the UN Security Council, alongside Russia and China. This was not supported by China.
5. For example the IBSA group of countries, comprising Brazil, India, and South Africa, was established in 2003 to provide a combined voice on international issues and to enhance relationships among member economies. The IBSA also has various projects with smaller developing countries. However the future of the IBSA has become less certain now that all its members are in the BRICs.
6. It is not unusual in the state clubs for the rotating chair to have a prerogative to invite other states, and for this attendance to lead to membership. China invited South Africa when it was the chair, and was the major 'sponsor' of South African membership.
7. South Africa had previously been appointed to the G20 in 'preference' to larger economies but this was based on its financial status when the G20 comprised mainly finance ministers during its pre-GFC stage.
8. As of 2009, Africa's population exceeded 1 billion, much of which is located south of the Sahara (World Population Review, 2012).

9. It is also involved in the tripartite discussions among the Southern African Development Community (SADC), the Common Market for Eastern and Southern Africa (COMESA) and the Eastern African Community (EAC) for the creation of a super-regional body.
10. For instance the African Development Bank has reported the BRICs' increasing interest in trading and investing with North African countries (Castel, Mejia & Kolster, 2011). Geographical proximity to the EU and the Middle Eastern markets is one of the region's many attractive features.
11. This concept has been articulated by high-ranking South African officials.
12. It is sometimes overlooked that the biggest investor in Africa is not China but South Africa, with over 1200 companies currently operating in most parts of the continent.
13. The main countries in Lusophone Africa are Mozambique and Angola, both with booming resource-based economies.
14. The Bank of China and Standard Bank of South Africa.
15. Mauritius has also developed the gateway pathway for investors, and has been relatively successful in acting as a conduit for investment from India – including that directed to South Africa.
16. For example outreach initiatives by some of the BRICs members include the Forum on China-Africa Cooperation, India-Africa Forum Summit, African-South American Summit, while non-BRICs countries such as Japan have also responded to African economies with initiatives such as the Tokyo International Conference on African Development.
17. There are strong regional differences in this pan-African indicator, with countries in North Africa, and ironically South Africa itself, growing well below the continental average.
18. While China is South Africa's largest single trading partner, the EU is collectively a larger trading partner.
19. Base metals accounted for over 35 per cent of South Africa's exports in 2011 (World Bank, 2011b).
20. That is China and India. In the same year the other four BRICs members accounted for less than 20 per cent of South Africa's trade (World Bank, 2011b).
21. According to the World Economic Forum, the 'goods market efficiency' pillar is denoted by indicators such as intensity of local competition, extent of market dominance, effectiveness of market antimonopoly policy, extent and effect of taxation, etc.
22. With respect to the nominations for the World Bank Presidency, South Africa's President Jacob Zuma, in his official address at the BRICS Delhi Summit 2012, made the point that the BRICS should work together to support a candidate, particularly one nominated from the developing world (Zuma, 2012).
23. Trevor Manuel was South Africa's Treasurer and wrote a reform paper for the IMF (Manuel, 2011).
24. The BRICS Delhi Declaration (2012a) applauds Russia's Presidency of the G20 in 2013 and provides its commitment to support the institution.
25. In his presentation to the 2012 BRICs forum, President Zuma emphasized the following factors: multilateralism, conformity with the rule of law and comprehensive reform of the UN and international financial institutions (Zuma, 2012).
26. An FTT, even if levied at a very small rate, could generate extensive revenue for economic development or for mitigating climate change's effects, and serve to impose a check on financial volatility.
27. The G20 has a financial inclusion expert group and various sub-groups.
28. Thus the UNCTAD report referred to in the text (2012) emphasizes economic development and the reservation of policy space for host states, both of which are important priorities for developing and emerging economies in IIAs.
29. The Seoul Consensus has nine focus areas, including infrastructural development, human resources development, trade, private investment, job creation, food security and growth with resilience (G20 Seoul Summit, 2010).

30. A term which has acquired a solely negative connotation that is difficult to challenge is 'protectionism'; a term such as 'safety measure', used in respect of the same phenomenon, has a more positive connotation.
31. This is not to overlook the role of domestic and international NGOs in monitoring and reporting on countries' compliance with their international commitments.
32. With respect to global competitiveness, South Africa scored extremely high (fourth out of 142 countries) in relation to financial market development. Of particular interest regarding this pillar of competitiveness is the availability of financial services, financing through local equity market, soundness of banks, and regulation of securities exchanges.
33. With respect to ICSID membership, China signed and ratified the Convention in 1993. Russia has signed the Convention, but is yet to ratify it. Brazil, India and South Africa are not signatories of the Convention.
34. WTO membership has for some time included Brazil, India, China and South Africa. Russia was an observer government until formally approved for an Accession Package in December 2011. Russia ratified its accession in July 2012.
35. South has been a respondent to complaints brought by both Brazil and India, while Brazil has been a respondent to a complaint brought by India. A contributing factor to the infrequency is that Russian's WTO accession occurred only in 2012.
36. It is suggested that Indonesia's inclusion in the G20, over the claims of neighbouring Malaysia, was a result of US preferences.

REFERENCES

Boulle, L. (2011a, May). *The Republic of South Africa and the G20*. Paper presented at the Konrad-Adenauer-Stiftung International Symposium: The G20 process–perceptions and perspectives for global governance, Seoul, Korea.

Boulle, L. (2011b). *The Republic of South Africa and the G20: Its political, national interests and priorities as members of the process*. In W. Hofmeister (Ed.), *G 20 – Perceptions and perspectives for global change* (pp. 135–46). Singapore: Konrad-Adenauer-Stiftung.

Boulle, L. (2012, July). *Balancing investment: South Africa*. Paper presented at the third biannual conference of the Society for International Economic Law, Singapore.

Bradlow, D. (2010, May). *Reforming global economic governance: A strategy for middle powers in the G20*. Paper presented at the workshop on Going Global: Australia, Brazil, Indonesia, Korea and South Africa in International Affairs, Jakarta, Indonesia.

BRICS (2012a, March 29). *Fourth BRICS summit: Delhi declaration*. Retrieved from http://www.bricsindia.in/delhi-declaration.html

BRICS (2012b). *The BRICS report: A study of Brazil, Russia, India, China, and South Africa with special focus on synergies and complementarities*. India: Oxford University Press.

Carmody, P. (2012). Another BRIC in the wall? South Africa's developmental impact and contradictory rise in Africa and beyond. *European Journal of Development Research*, *24*(2), 223–41.

Castel, V., Mejia, P.X. and Kolster, J. (2011). The BRICs in North Africa: Changing the name of the game? *North Africa Quarterly Analytical, First Annual Quarter*, 1–20. Retrieved from http://www.afdb.org/fileadmin/uploads/afdb/Documents/Publications/the%20BRICs%20in%20North%20Africa%20First%20annual%20ok_Mise%20en%20page%201.pdf

Central Intelligence Agency (CIA) (2013). *The world fact book*. Retrieved from https://www.cia.gov/library/publications/the-world-factbook/index.html
Cooper, A.F. (2010). Labels matter: Interpreting rising states through acronyms. In A.S. Alexandroff and A.F. Cooper (Eds), *Rising states, rising institutions: Challenges for global governance* (pp. 63–82). Washington: Brookings Institution Press.
Ernst & Young (2011, June 24). It's time for Africa. *Africa attractiveness survey*. Retrieved from http://www.ey.com/AU/en/SearchResults?SRT_F=&SRT_O=&ACT=&Page=&CF=&LF=&FILTER=&DF=&IF=&SF=&FF=&query=It%27stime+for+Africa&search_options=country_name
G20 Seoul Summit (2010). *Seoul development consensus for shared growth*. Retrieved from www.g20.utoronto.ca/2010/g20seoul-consensus.pdf
Holman, M. (2011, March 22). The African renaissance is under way. *The Times*. Retrieved from http://www.thetimes.co.uk/tto/public/article2955163.ece
International Centre for Settlement of Investment Disputes (ICSID). (n.d.). Retrieved from https://icsid.worldbank.org/ICSID/FrontServlet
International Trade Administration Commission of South Africa (ITAC). (2012, February 10). Report No. 389, Notice No. R 105, *Government Gazette* No. 35030.
Kahn, M. (2011). The fall of the wall, the rise of the BRICs and the new scramble for Africa. *Foresight*, *13*(3), 38–49.
Kelly, P. (2012, July 28). Future financial lifeblood, China, needs safe hands. *The Australian*. Retrieved from http://www.theaustralian.com.au/opinion/columnists/future-financial-lifeblood-china-needs-safe-hands/story-e6frg74x-1226437121573
KPMG (2012). *African emergence – The rise of the phoenix*. Retrieved from http://www.kpmg.com/africa/en/issuesandinsights/articles-publications/pages/african-emergence-the-rise-of-the-phoenix.aspx
Lukyanov, F. (2011). Global governance: Challenges of unpredictable era. In W. Hofmeister (Ed.), *G 20 – Perceptions and perspectives for global change* (pp. 109–16). Singapore: Konrad-Adenauer-Stiftung.
Manuel, T. (2011). Global economic governance: The search for economic justice in a globalised world. In L. Boulle (Ed.), *Globalisation and governance* (pp. 33–42). Cape Town: Siber Ink.
Nolte, D. (2010). How to compare regional powers: Analytical concepts and research topics. *Review of International Studies*, *36*(4), 881–901.
Noury, V. (2011). What BRICS membership means to Africa. *African Business*, *38*(376), 37–9.
OECD (2012). *African economic outlook 2012*. Retrieved from http://www.oecd.org/general/searchresults/?q=African Economic Outlook 2012&cx=012432601748511391518:xzeadub0b0a&cof=FORID:11&ie=UTF-8
Sharma, R. (2012). Broken BRICs – Why the rest stopped rising. *Foreign Affairs*, *91*(6), 2–7.
Shaw, T., Cooper, A. and Chin, G. (2009). Emerging powers and Africa: Implications for/from global governance? *Politikon: South African Journal of Political Studies*, *36*(1), 27–44.
Shaw, T.M., Grant, J.A. and Cornelissen, S. (2012). Introduction and overview: The study of new regionalism(s) at the start of the second decade of the twenty-first century. In T.M. Shaw, J.A. Grant and S. Cornelissen (Eds), *The Ashgate research companion to regionalisms* (pp. 3–28). Farnham, UK: Ashgate.
Slaughter, A. and Hale, T. (2010). Transgovernmental networks and emerging

powers. In A.S. Alexandroff and A.F. Cooper (Eds), *Rising states, rising institutions: Challenges for global governance* (pp. 48–62). Washington: Brookings Institution Press.

The hopeless continent (2000, May 13). *Economist*. Retrieved from http://www.economist.com/printedition/2000–05–13

UNCTAD (2012). *World investment report 2012: Towards a new generation of investment policies*. Retrieved from http://unctad.org/en/Pages/DIAE/World%20Investment%20Report/WIR2012_WebFlyer.aspxhttp://unctadstat.unctad.org/TableViewer/tableView.aspx?ReportId=88

Walmart Stores v Massmart Holdings Ltd, Case No. 73/LM/Dec 10 (May 31, 2011).

World Bank (2009). *Data: Indicators*. Retrieved from http://data.worldbank.org/indicator

World Bank (2011a). *Gross domestic product 2011*.Retrieved from www.databank.worldbank.org/databank/download/GDP.pdf

World Bank (2011b). *South Africa economic update: Focusing on savings, investment and inclusion growth*. Retrieved from http://www.worldbank.org/

World Economic Forum (2011). *The global competitiveness report 2011–2012*. Switzerland: World Economic Forum. Retrieved from http://www.weforum.org/

World Population Review (2012). *Population of Africa 2012*. Retrieved from http://worldpopulationreview.com/population-of-africa-2012/

WTO (2012). *Dispute DS439: South Africa – Anti-dumping duties on frozen meat of fowls from Brazil*. Retrieved from http://www.wto.org/english/tratop_e/dispu_e/cases_e/ds439_e.htm

WTO (2013). *Dispute settlement: The disputes*. Retrieved from http://www.wto.org/english/tratop_e/dispu_e/find_dispu_cases_e.htm#results

Zuma, J.G. (2012, March 29). *Address by President of the Republic of South Africa at the fourth BRICS summit*. Retrieved from http://www.thepresidency.gov.za/pebble.asp?relid=5872

8. Implications of the rise of the BRIC countries for Africa

Emmanuel T. Laryea

This chapter discusses the possible implications for Africa[1] of the emerging change in the global politico-economic paradigm epitomized in the rise of the BRIC countries, namely Brazil, Russia, India and China. South Africa joined the BRIC in 2010 to form the BRICS. Thus South Africa can be seen from two perspectives: (1) as an African country dealing with the BRIC countries and (2) as a BRICS country dealing with the rest of Africa. In this chapter, South Africa is discussed more as the former for three reasons. First, it is arguable that South Africa is an appendage to the BRIC, due to its strategic location as a gateway to the rest of Africa. Thus it is seen as an African country with and through which the BRIC countries deal. Second, a lot of the BRIC-Africa trade and investment occurs between South Africa and the BRIC countries. Consequently if South Africa is construed as a BRICS country dealing with the rest of Africa, the value of the BRICS–Africa economic inter-data would be heavily diminished. Third, there is evidence that the performance of the South African economy has correlative implications for the rest of Africa (Arora & Vamvakidis, 2005).[2] Thus inherent in a discussion of the implications of the BRIC–Africa economic relations is the BRIC–South Africa relationship.

Though resource rich, Africa lags behind all other continents in terms of economic development. The continent is home to 33 of the 48 countries currently classified as the least developed by the UN and the World Bank (UNCTAD, 2011; World Bank, 2011). It is therefore arguable that Africa occupies a unique place in the current global geo-political and socio-economic developments. The BRIC countries, particularly China, India and Brazil, have increased their economic relations with African economies in recent times. Some have surmised that these increased engagements represent a 'new scramble for Africa' (Carmody, 2011; Kimenyi & Lewis, 2011).

This chapter argues that the rise of the BRIC countries, and their increasing engagement with Africa, present both opportunities and challenges for the continent and its people. The outcome for Africa, whether positive or negative, depends on how economies on the continent deal with these opportunities and challenges. Africa has had both opportunities and challenges in the past, and seems to have crumbled under the challenges rather than take advantage of the opportunities. For instance, in the early 1960s Africa seemed to be a more promising and prosperous continent than Asia, which was then 'mired in seemingly irredeemable poverty and ravaged by wars' (UNECA, 2010, p. 60). As 'Africa emerged from colonialism, East Asia was the region in trouble and turmoil' (Noman, Botchwey, Stein & Stiglitz, 2012, p. 3). Yet Africa stagnated, or even retrogressed, while Asia emerged from its troubles to achieve remarkable economic successes that are widely acknowledged today.

While there are some signs that the emerging new international economic order is impacting Africa positively, such as in investment inflows, infrastructure development and general economic performance (see Global Finance, 2012),[3] real challenges – pitfalls in fact – remain. In this chapter, the relationships between each of the BRIC countries and Africa are considered individually, for a number of reasons. First, while the BRIC might be emerging as a bloc in the international political and economic order, the individual countries pursue their own economic and geo-political interests, often in direct competition with each other (Ancharaz, 2011). Second, beyond the broad statements common to the BRIC countries, each has its own model of engagement. Third, some BRIC countries are more involved in Africa than others; the value of the economic interrelation of each BRIC country and Africa varies greatly. As will be seen further on, China has by far the highest value of trade and investment annually, followed by India. Brazil and Russia are a distant third and fourth.[4] This chapter is divided into five parts, including this introduction. Part two briefly outlines the rise of the BRIC nations and their engagement with Africa. Part three discusses the beneficial prospects for Africa of the rise of the BRIC countries. Part four discusses the pitfalls for Africa of the rise of the BRIC countries and their modes of engagement with the continent. Part five concludes this chapter.

THE RISE OF THE BRIC COUNTRIES AND THEIR ENGAGEMENT WITH AFRICA

The Rise of the BRIC

The BRIC countries include the two most populous countries on the planet – China and India. The average economic growth rates of these countries have outpaced those of advanced economies over the last two decades. The growth of China in particular has been led by exports, which has resulted in its accumulation of huge foreign reserves (CIA, 2013).[5] With this financial power, China is able to invest and acquire assets overseas, as well as wielding political influence (Miller, 2010, pp. 96–7). Russia, India and Brazil have less in foreign reserves, though enough to be able to invest abroad, including in Africa. Russia's estimated foreign exchange reserve of $561.1 billion (as of 31 December 2012) is the fourth largest in the world (CIA, 2013). Brazil's estimated $371 billion and India's $287 billion rank them sixth and tenth in the world respectively (CIA, 2013).[6]

The economic growth of the BRIC economies has been fuelled by, and has further precipitated demand for, and consumption of, natural resources. For some years now, China has been the world's number one consumer of copper, steel, iron ore and scrap steel, and one of the largest consumers of oil (Botchway, 2011, pp. 377–8). While these countries are also major depositories and producers of some commodities, the rapid growth of their economies has helped create global commodity booms that have improved the terms of trade of developing countries, many of them in Africa (IMF, 2011). The BRIC economies are also major exporters of various products consumed by African economies. China has also developed its construction technologies, which it is increasingly exporting.

The BRIC's Engagement with Africa

Africa abounds in most of the resources that BRIC countries, particularly China, consume and need (Economist Intelligence Unit, 2010). With an estimated population of 1 billion (Kobo, 2009, p. 100), Africa also potentially offers a vast market for both capital and consumer products from the BRIC countries. Further, Africa is the continent with the least infrastructure development (Botchway, 2011, pp. 378–80). Despite decades of policy prescriptions by the world's main multilateral financial institutions (IMF and the World Bank), foreign aid and debt write-offs, the level of infrastructural development remains deplorable in most African economies (Moyo, 2009, p. 100). Africa needs substantial investment in infrastructure development (Foster & Briceño-Garmendia, 2010, p. 43). Africa also needs substantial investments for the development of its resources, and economies in general. In short, Africa has resources, but it is in need of investment for development.

The conditions in Africa – availability of resources (for which China thirsts), a need for infrastructure and resource development, as well as its market potential for products manufactured by the BRIC countries, particularly China – make it ideal for trade and investment partnerships between the BRIC and African countries. The BRIC countries have recognized this potential and have been pursuing stronger economic relations with the continent. African countries seem to see the new interests from the BRIC countries as potentially beneficial and have responded positively. The respective circumstances and approaches by the BRIC countries are outlined.

China

China initiated a new Sino-African relationship that has resulted in exponential growth in its trade and investment flows with the continent.[7] To put this in perspective, China has engaged Africa in different periods and at different levels over the centuries, going as far back as 202 BC, when merchants from China traded with parts of East Africa (Taylor, 2006, pp. 16–18). There are reports of relationships during the Sung dynasty (960–1279), Yuan dynasty (1279–1368) and the Ming dynasty (1368–1644) (Alden & Alves, 2008, pp. 46–7). But large-scale encounters between Chinese and the peoples on the continent did not occur until the colonial era, with the colonial powers using Chinese labour in their colonies in Africa (Adem, 2010; Grant, 2005, pp. 94–100).

Nonetheless 1955 is hailed as the genesis of the modern phase of Sino-African relations (Botchway, 2011). But the greater part of the interaction occurred between 1960 and 1965, a period during which most of colonized Africa gained independence, China having supported the independence effort (Yu, 1977, pp. 97–102). China retreated as political instability ensued in African in the mid-1960s (Yu, 1977, p. 98). It returned slowly in the 1970s, helping fund and construct the Tanzania–Zambia railway (TANZAM).

China intensified its engagement with the African continent at the beginning of this century. For instance, trade between Sub-Saharan Africa and China rose from just $10 billion in 2001 to $35 billion in 2005, and from $106.8 billion in 2009 to $160 billion in 2011 (Schneidman & Lewis, 2012, p. 24). China has been Africa's largest trading partner since 2009 (Schneidman & Lewis, 2012). It named 2006 as the 'Year of Africa', and quadrupled its investment commitments to infrastructure in Sub-Saharan Africa to $8.4 billion, adding a further $4.5 billion in 2007 (Shasha, 2009). Since then trade between China and Africa, and Chinese foreign direct investment (FDI) outflows to Africa, have been increasing. It is estimated that China's Exim Bank lent about $67.2 billion to Sub-Saharan Africa between 2001 and 2010, $12.6 billion more than the World Bank lent to the region in this period (Cohen, 2011). The engagement is quite spread out through many countries on the continent.[8] China funded the building of a new African Union (AU) headquarters worth some $200 million in

Addis Ababa, the Ethiopian capital (Bayoumy, 2012). Inevitably the value of the relationship varies, particularly investment flows into individual African countries.

The purpose and mode of China's engagement with Africa has differed over the different periods of encounter. The dominant purpose of the earliest contact was trade. Though couched in terms of economic and political cooperation, the motivation for China's re-engagement with Africa from the 1950s to the 1970s seemed to be predominantly political and ideological. A major goal of China was to win new friends and seek new allies to break out of the American encirclement (China saw America as its primary adversary). Following its 'open break with the Soviet Union in the early 1960s, China sought to challenge Soviet diplomatic influence' on the continent and elsewhere (Yu, 1977, p. 97). China called on the peoples of Africa who were not yet independent to engage in liberation struggles, supporting some materially (Yu, 1977, p. 99).

China's latest, most aggressive engagement with Africa was predominantly for economic reasons. Investment and acquisition of natural resources are central to the engagement. Its strategy is based on solidarity, mutual respect, mutual interest and benefit, non-interference in internal affairs and cooperation (Adem, 2010, pp. 341–2).[9] The spread of ideology, high principles or the achievement of hegemonic status does not seem to be a purpose of the engagement (Botchway, 2011).

To this extent China has sought to distinguish itself in its relationship with Africa from that of the West, which typically reflects a relationship of unequals; the West being the superior party offering help to the African countries that is often discretionary and conditioned on the recipients committing to a string of principles. These include observance of human rights, rule of law, gender rights, pluralistic and democratic governance, transparency, anti-corruption, commitment to market economy and competition rules (Botchway, 2011).

China has adopted the mode of 'resources for infrastructure', sometimes referred to as the 'Angola model', in its new Sino-African relationship (Zongwe, 2009). The model allows China to build critical infrastructure, which is in a deplorable state in most African states, in return for natural resources (Adem, 2010, p. 339). Through this model the Chinese have funded several infrastructure projects in African countries, with several more in the pipeline (Moyo, 2009, pp. 103–6; Gadzala & Hanusch, 2010, p. 4). China has also been pursuing policies to open its market to some African goods, affording a higher number of African products duty-free entry to China (Botchway, 2011). It is therefore not surprising that China is now Africa's largest trading partner (Schneidman & Lewis, 2012, p. 24).

India

India has followed China's lead. Like China, India has had historical links to Africa, but it only intensified its engagement with Africa after China's new push into the continent (Naidu, 2008). In April 2008, India launched its own African strategy at the India-Africa Summit hosted in New Delhi and attended by 14 African heads of state and leaders of eight African regional groups (India-Africa Summit, 2008; Kragelund, 2010). India promised, among other things, increased credit lines and the opening of its market to African products.

Trade between India and Africa has been growing rapidly. While the value of trade was $3 billion in 2002, it was $62 billion in 2011 (still far behind China's $160 billion), and it is expected to reach $90 billion by 2015 (PTI, 2012). India intends to set up an 'integrated textiles cluster' in Africa that is expected to create tens of thousands of jobs (Schneidman & Lewis, 2012, p. 26). Indian companies, such as Bharti Airtel, Tata Motors, the Mahindra Group, Cipla and Ashok Leyland, have been active in Africa, particularly South Africa (Schneidman & Lewis, 2012, p. 26). India has announced plans to invest $70 billion in Africa by 2015 (Baldauf, 2011).

Brazil

Brazil has also intensified its engagement with Africa in the last decade. While in power, Lula da Silva visited 25 African countries and doubled the number of Brazilian embassies in the region (Grudgings, 2011). To build on this, Dilma Rousseff visited Africa soon after ascending the Brazilian presidency in 2011. She then created an Africa Group in her administration, led by her Trade and Industry Minister, Fernando Pimentel, to deepen Brazil's commercial engagement in Africa (Schneidman & Lewis, 2012, p. 26; Grudgings, 2011). Brazil has been focusing on Africa as a prospective trading and investment partner alternative to the slower growing economies of Europe and the US (Grudgings, 2011). Nonetheless Brazil's trade with Africa is small compared to China and India; it was $20 billion in 2010 (Barka, 2011a, p. 2).

Russia

Russia has had historical ties with Africa going back to the Cold War years. However, in the aftermath of the collapse of the Soviet Union, the Russian Federation disengaged from Africa and other developing regions. The new independent states began to focus on building their economies and relationships with the West.

Russia has begun to renew its relationship with Africa. Russia's trade relations with Africa are still small ($3.7 billion in 2008) when compared to the other BRIC countries (Barka, 2011b, p. 1). It seems unlikely to improve much due to the nature of Russia's own major exports (being oil and gas), resources which are available in Africa. Not surprisingly, Russian investments in Africa are dominated by the resources sector (Barka, 2011b, pp. 3–5). But Russia's renewed interest in Africa is not driven by economic interest alone; it is as much political. The Russian Federation, which was an ideological friend and ally of many African countries during the Cold War period, started to disengage from Africa and other developing countries, and to develop closer relations with the Western countries in the aftermath of the collapse of the Soviet Union in 1991 (Barka, 2011b, p. 1). It started to re-establish its geo-political connections when its economic standing began to strengthen at the beginning of the century. It has already written off over $20 billion of Africa debt and like other G8 members, has pledged to double its overseas development assistance to African countries (Barka, 2011b, p. 7).

In summary, the BRIC countries have differing profiles of interests and engagements with Africa. For Africa, the more important issues are the prospects and challenges posed by the interest from the BRIC countries, and how to ensure that the continent obtains the best outcomes possible. These issues are explored in the next two sections.

BENEFICIAL PROSPECTS FOR AFRICA

There are divergent opinions as to whether the relationships are beneficial for Africa. There are the optimists, who maintain that the relationships are beneficial and should be celebrated (Adem, 2010, p. 335). There are the sceptics, who view the renewed interests of the BRIC countries and their greater engagement in Africa as neo-colonial both in intent and consequence. They see the BRIC countries as being in Africa for their own self-interest (Adem, 2010, p. 335). Then there are the pessimists who claim that the renewed relationship will not only perpetuate the existing structure of dependency and underdevelopment in Africa, it will also block Africa's efforts to overcome them (Adem, 2010, p. 335). This author does not claim to belong to any of these strands of thought. The following discussion may suggest that the author's thoughts have shades of all three, but probably more of the first two than the third.

Higher Commodity Prices

There are various ways in which the BRIC–Africa relationship may be beneficial for African countries. As noted earlier, the economic rise of the BRIC countries and the consequent demand for resources have resulted in a commodity boom that has improved the terms of trade of many resource-rich African countries. To give just two examples, oil prices rose from $30 a barrel in 2004 to over $147 a barrel in 2008, due to speculation on increasing global demand, attributed mainly to China. Although the Global Financial Crisis (GFC) that hit the global economy in mid-2008 resulted in a sharp fall in the price of crude oil, the current price of around $90 a barrel is still much higher than the long-term global average. The price of gold went from less than $400 an ounce in 1999 to over $1500 currently. As Africa is a major commodity exporter, the higher prices hold benefits for the countries with those resources.

It must be conceded that the extent of the share of increases in commodity prices on the world markets, which translates into higher revenues for a nation, depends on the fiscal and contractual arrangements between the companies exploiting the resources and the government. Where the producing entities are multinationals, government take – in tax revenues, royalties and share of profits – may not grow in line with prices if the fiscal regime is lopsided in favour of the investor, which is often the case in many African situations (Laryea, 2011a, p. 107).

It should also be noted that the commodity booms and associated higher stream of revenues to government (where that happens) can cause volatility, instability and dislocation within an economy. However, such effects can be managed with the implementation of appropriate policies. Many African economies seem to have benefited from the commodity booms, particularly in the form of increased investments in their resources.

Gains in Competition for African Resources

The renewed interest from the BRIC in Africa has ushered in steep competition to the traditional Western dominance in the exploitation of Africa's resources. This opens up options for resource-rich African economies. It means the competing entities are likely to offer more attractive terms. Ordinarily it means African economies may be able to extract better fiscal terms and prices for their resources. Evidence for this already exists. Moyo gives an example of a deal between Nigeria and the World Bank in 2007 to revitalize Nigeria's railway system. China offered almost double the amount of the offer from the World Bank just before Nigeria was to sign the deal with the World Bank. Nigeria went with the Chinese (Moyo, 2009, pp. 107–8). Similarly the Chinese have outbid their Western counterparts for the development of aspects of Ghana's oil ('Ghana: Lining up for Jubilee', 2010).

Appropriate Investments and Launch Platforms for Entrepreneurship and Economic Growth

China's strategy and mode of investment seem to respond to Africa's most critical need – development of physical infrastructure, industry and agriculture (Moyo, 2009, p. 111). The projects cover transportation (road and rail), telecommunications, health and education (Schmitt, 2007). These may serve as launch platforms that can unleash African entrepreneurship, spur further investments on the continent, create jobs and economic growth, and alleviate poverty. It may be natural to look at the failures of the previous (Western-led) models and doubt the possibilities, but initial signs of the BRIC, particularly the Chinese model, seem positive.

Prompting Others to Rethink Their Engagement with Africa

The new aggressive engagement with Africa by the BRIC countries in the face of ever increasing demand for natural resources has prompted others to rethink their engagement with the continent. Turkey signed a regional trade agreement with 35 African countries in May 2008, and Japan hosted the Fourth Tokyo International Conference on African Development in the same month (Moyo, 2009, p. 112). Crucially, there are calls on Western governments and institutions to rethink their approach to aid and investment in Africa (Lyman, 2005). These result in or lead to increased competition for economic relations with Africa, giving the continent advantages.

Improved International Economic System

There are arguments that the design of the international economic system disadvantages developing countries (Stiglitz & Carlton, 2005, p. v; Joseph, 2011). Developed economies, mainly Western European and North American countries, have dominated the development of international economic law (IEL) (Laryea & Sucker, 2012, p. 1). In the process, they have designed the system to their advantage and, conversely, to the disadvantage of developing countries. Developing countries have tried unsuccessfully in the past to redesign the system. In particular, following the mass decolonization of Africa in the 1960s the newly independent countries, together with developing countries in other regions, agitated, mainly through the UN system, for reformulation of the rules and principles in IEL in order to afford them better ownership and control over their natural resources. This led to various UN General Assembly Resolutions, including the Permanent Sovereignty of States Over their Natural Resources (PSNR)[10] and the New International Economic Order

(NIEO)[11] (Duruigbo, 2006; Schrijver, 1997, pp. 57–119). Though these resolutions favoured developing countries, they had little positive impact on their economies (Waelde, 1995). They resulted in a lack of investment capital flow from developed (capital exporting) countries to developing countries, leading to economic stagnation or retrogression in many of those countries in the 1970s and 1980s. Many developing countries changed their approach, opting to operate with the Western designed system rather than fighting it. For instance, they started signing Bilateral Investment Treaties (BITs), the terms of which were counter to what they had been fighting for (Laryea, 2011b).

With the rise of economic power of the BRIC countries, there are renewed calls for reform of the international economic system (Huang, 2011, pp. 31–2). If the BRIC countries act in concert as a bloc, they would have real prospects of succeeding in their reform objectives. Unlike in previous periods when they were not only large importers of capital but also economically weaker, their improved economic power may enable them to achieve real positive changes, which may benefit Africa. However as the BRIC countries are now exporters of capital, technology and goods, the changes they might want are likely to be punctuated by their own economic interests. They are likely to agitate for changes that benefit them, which might not necessarily be beneficial to Africa.

PITFALLS FOR AFRICA

The beneficial prospects of the BRIC's engagement with Africa have been extolled, but naturally there are downsides. Some of the pitfalls for the African continent are now discussed.

Reversal of Governance Gains

A principal cause of Africa's underdevelopment, debt and poverty amidst heavy resource endowments is poor governance (Laryea, 2011c; Siegle, 2009, p. 45). Arguably, strong political will and institutions underpinning sound governance can ensure that the economies of resource-rich countries are efficiently and effectively managed for the betterment of those countries and their peoples (Harford & Klein, 2005, p. 1).

The concept of 'good governance' (or even 'governance') is itself difficult to define succinctly (Botchway, 2001, pp. 160–61; Weiss, 2000). Nonetheless it is generally accepted to include transparency and accountability, low corruption, efficient and equitable management of resource revenues, democracy, and rule of law (Iimi, 2007, pp. 672–3). Democracy and rule of law has the capacity to engender the others – transparency and accountability, low corruption and efficient economic management.[12]

Following pressure by Western governments and institutions, through conditions attached to development aid and finance, African countries have gradually moved from dictatorships to democratic regimes. Today there are more democracies (even if they are not robust) in Africa than at any time since the mass decolonization in the 1960s. Rule of law, transparency and accountability, freedom of speech and human rights have been improving in many states.

The mode of engagement by the BRIC countries with Africa, and elsewhere, has been to separate business from politics, at least theoretically (Meiden, 2006). It is based on the policy of mutual respect, equality, solidarity and non-interference in domestic affairs. This approach is not only understandable; it seems sensible. However, it has the danger of emboldening African governments to reverse gains towards good governance, and entrench governments in countries that are yet to make progress. It can blunt economic and diplomatic sanctions against bad governments in Africa. For instance, it is common knowledge that Mugabe, the long-reigning Zimbabwean President, retained support from China at the height of international sanctions against his brutal regime.

It is arguable, however, that a case like the Mugabe example is extreme and uncommon. Also, Western governments do support long reigning dictators (such as Mobutu of the Democratic Republic of Congo (which Mobuto named Zaire) and Mubarak of Egypt) when it suits them. However, the West seems to do more for the promotion of good governance. Efforts such as the Extractive Industry Transparency Initiative (EITI), which is aimed at strengthening governance by improving transparency and accountability in the extractives sectors of resource-rich developing countries, can improve the management of resources in Africa (EITI, n.d.). Typically there is little transparency in commercial and investment contracts between African governments and governments and companies from the BRIC countries. This can undermine the objectives of the EITI, as payments and revenues from such arrangements can be misappropriated without the opportunity for public scrutiny. Improved governance is critical to long-term development of African economies.

Environmental, Labour and Safety Standards

Companies from the BRIC countries, particularly China, are often accused of violating sound safety, social and environmental standards. For instance, a mining accident in Zambia in 2006 resulted in 51 fatalities (Chellaney, 2010) and led to protests and demonstrations against Chinese companies and their government (Schmitt, 2007, p. 8). It is often reported that workers in Chinese mines and factories suffer from systematic violations of workers' rights. For instance, in May 2008, there were demonstrations by miners in a Chinese-run mine in Zambia ('Exploited workers protest', 2008). In 2010 there was another demonstration in Zambia against a Chinese-run mine that resulted in the Chinese operators shooting and wounding 12 demonstrators ('Chinese bosses shoot', 2010).

Many African countries do not have adequate laws to protect the environment, or the citizens who work for foreign investors. Those that have laws often lack the capacity to enforce them with rigour, or they omit to enforce the laws due to corruption of those who are supposed to enforce them. Without adequate laws or enforcement, the expected benefits for the citizens from Africa's engagement with the BRIC would be undermined.

Not that it is unknown for Western owned companies to use substandard environmental and safety standards in developing countries, or abuse workers' rights there; they do. Criticisms against the operation of Royal Dutch Shell in Nigeria are quite common. The difference, however, is that civil society is able to exert pressure on Western companies who are more sensitive to their public standing. Moreover the Western companies may be liable to legal action, in some cases both civil and criminal, under the laws of their home countries. For instance, Royal Dutch Shell was held by a Dutch court to be liable for environmental damage in Nigeria ('Dutch court finds Shell liable', 2013). These may compel Western companies to make an effort to avoid breaches or to remedy breaches when they occur.

While there may be consequences in the BRIC countries for breaches of standards in Africa (and elsewhere) by their companies (Chellaney, 2010),[13] civil society may have little or no effect on them. Their legal systems may not be accessible to victims of their breaches. For instance, the Chinese legal system is opaque (Economist Intelligence Unit, 2007, p. 128), so the rights of overseas victims of breaches by Chinese companies might be difficult to ascertain. African governments hosting investments should therefore endeavour to implement appropriate laws, enforcement mechanisms and institutional capabilities that can ensure responsible economic activities by entities from the BRIC countries, to safeguard interests of their citizens and the environment.

Mortgaging of the Future

Considering the model under which the BRIC countries operate, particularly China's Angola model of 'resources for infrastructure', there is the danger that African governments would commit too much of their resources too soon and too far into the future. In their desperation to clinch deals to build that long-eluded highway, railway or hospital, they may overcommit. Overcommitment of resources upfront will deprive African countries of optimal returns from their resources.

A strategy of systematic development of the resources informed by detailed public discussion and consideration of all the economic, social and environmental impacts is to be preferred. Admittedly, however, that may be difficult to achieve in the particular circumstances of Africa, considering that a lot of the resources have remained undeveloped for so long.

Selling Short the Natural Resources

There is a danger that corrupt public officials may, in return for private benefits, commit their countries to contracts that grant to their counterparts from the BRIC countries lopsided gains, thereby depriving their countries of the expected benefits (Laryea, 2011a). Lopsided contracts in favour of foreign investors may also stem from incompetence, bad advice, poor judgement or ignorance on the part of African officials (Laryea, 2011c).

It should not be ignored that investors from the BRIC countries are there for their own interest – to win markets and procure resources and profits. They have been investing elsewhere; in Asia, Latin America, Australia and North America, among other places. They have the capacity, capability and expertise to negotiate corporate deals with global giants at the highest levels. They are in business and seek to obtain the maximum possible risk-adjusted return on their investments over the life of the investment.

Normally the broad primary objective of the host state is the general public interest of economic development, translating into expectations of maximum revenue from the exploited resources, job creation (direct and indirect), provision of training and skills upgrade, transfer of technology to the host state, increased capital stock, and spin-offs of new and allied industries. However, history has shown that the interest of most governments of host African countries is often private benefit, not the public interest of economic development. Those in political office often deprive the rest of the population of benefits from the resources with which their countries have been abundantly endowed (Duruigbo, 2006, p. 34). This is why there is little to show for the past 50 years of African resource exploitation.

Some African governments may want to continue as before. If African governments do not change their approach and attitudes, their economies will experience little progress from the ensuing international economic reordering. The opportunities presented by the emergence of the BRIC would pass them by. If they do not find appropriate linkages and synergies between sectors of incoming investments and other sectors of their economies, the potential benefits of the investments would be lost.

CONCLUSION

This chapter has discussed the prospects and pitfalls of the rise of the engagement by the BRIC countries in Africa, particularly China, India and Brazil. It finds that there are benefits to Africa, particularly in higher commodity prices and leverage from competition for resources in Africa. The investments may also serve as a launching pad that unleashes African entrepreneurship, spurs further investments on the continent, creates jobs and economic growth and alleviates poverty. Further, the rapid investment by the BRIC in Africa has prompted others to rethink their own relationships with Africa and to increase their investments on the continent. These are to be celebrated.

However, there are identifiable pitfalls that must be recognized. First, there is the danger that improvements in governance in African economies may slip where governments become content with the no-conditions investments from the BRIC countries. Second, companies from the BRIC economies may not uphold high environmental, labour and safety standards in their African operations. As many African countries have inadequate laws and enforcement capabilities, violations may be rampant and deprive the citizenry of expected benefits from the investments. It is therefore imperative that African governments implement appropriate laws, and strengthen their monitoring and enforcement capabilities in order to protect their citizens and the environment. Third, in their enthusiasm to clinch deals to build the critical infrastructure that has long eluded them, African governments may commit too much, too soon, and too far ahead. That will deprive African countries of optimal returns from their resources. A strategy of systematic development of the resources informed by detailed discussion and consideration of all the economic, social and environmental impacts should be adopted. Fourth, African officials may sell their economies cheaply due to corruption, incompetence, bad advice, poor judgement or ignorance on their part. Investments in capacity building are therefore important.

NOTES

1. Africa is a huge and diverse continent, so any attempt to refer to the continent in the singular or refer to it in the collective is problematic. It must be noted that: (1) Africa consists of several countries and regions with different levels of economic development; (2) the various countries have distinct economic policies, and engage in external relations (political, economic and legal) differently, including their relations with the BRIC countries; and (3) the BRIC countries engage with the various African countries differently, due to varying interests. However, this chapter will not look at the specificities of each country or region, except for giving examples. 'Africa' is used mainly in the collective, to refer to countries on the continent generally – both those lying south of the Sahara, often referred to as 'Sub-Saharan Africa', and those north of the Sahara, often referred to as 'Arab North-Africa'.
2. The South African economy is more intertwined with the rest of Africa than with the BRIC countries. Thus the discussion in this chapter will predominantly refer to the BRIC countries (i.e. excluding South Africa).
3. For instance, many economies on the African continent are now growing faster than their developed counterparts, albeit from a very low base. The average economic growth of Sub-Saharan Africa in the last ten years (2002–12) is estimated as 5.7 per cent (5 per cent for the Middle East and North Africa), while that of advanced economies for the same period is 1.6 per cent (and 3.8 per cent for the global economy as a whole).
4. See Section: *The BRIC's engagement with Africa.*
5. According to the US Central Intelligence Agency (CIA) fact book, China's foreign reserves were estimated to be $3.213 trillion at the end of 2011 ($2.876 trillion in 2010).
6. All $ references are to US$.
7. See following discussion for details.
8. Countries include Angola, Botswana, Chad, Congo, Democratic Republic of Congo, Central African Republic, Liberia, Madagascar, Niger, Egypt, Ethiopia, Gabon, Ghana, Guinea, Kenya, Mauritania, Nigeria, South Africa, Sudan, Tanzania, Zambia and Zimbabwe.
9. Some critics have argued that China applies its non-interference policy selectively (i.e. when it suits China), citing incidents constituting interference in the domestic affairs of other countries.
10. UN General Assembly Resolution 1803 (XVII) 14 December 1962.
11. Declaration on the Establishment of a New International Economic Order, UN General Assembly Resolution 3201 (S-VI) 1 May 1974; and Program of Action on the Implementation of the Declaration on the Establishment of a New International Economic Order, UN General Assembly Resolution 3202 (S-VI) 1 May 1974.
12. There are seemingly democratic countries which have a high incidence of corruption and mismanagement. Some examples are India, Indonesia, Ghana, Nigeria, and Kenya to name a few.
13. For instance, following the mine disaster in Zambia, the Chinese State Council issued in 2006 nine good-conduct directives to Chinese companies engaged in overseas operations.

REFERENCES

Adem, S. (2010). The paradox of China's policy in Africa. *African and Asian Studies*, *9*(3), 334–55.

Alden, C. and Alves, A.C. (2008). History and identity in the construction of China's Africa policy. *Review of African Political Economy*, *35*(115), 43–58.

Ancharaz, V.D. (2011). China's challenge to India's economic hegemony over Mauritius: A tale of two giants and a pigmy. *Journal of African Development, 13*(2), 197–222.

Arora, V. and Vamvakidis, A. (2005). *The implications of South African economic growth for the rest of Africa* (IMF Working Paper 05/58). Retrieved from http://www.imf.org/external/pubs/ft/wp/2005/wp0558.pdf

Baldauf, S. (2011, May 25). India boosts bid to rival China in Africa. *Christian Science Monitor*. Retrieved from http://www.csmonitor.com/World/Africa/Africa-Monitor/2011/0525/India-boosts-bid-to-rival-China-in-Africa

Barka, H.B. (2011a). Brazil's economic engagement with Africa. *Africa Economic Brief, 2*(5), 1–11.

Barka, H.B. (2011b). Russia's economic engagement with Africa. *Africa Economic Brief, 2*(7), 1–7.

Bayoumy, Y. (2012, January 29). Glitzy new AU headquarters a symbol of China-Africa ties. *Reuters*. Retrieved from http://www.reuters.com/article/2012/01/29/ozatp-africa-china-idAFJOE80S00K20120129

Botchway, F.N. (2001). Good governance: The old, the new, the principle, and the elements. *Florida Journal of International Law, 13*, 159–210.

Botchway, F.N. (2011). Regime theory and China-Africa economic relations: New ideas in old paradigms? In F.N. Botchway (Ed.), *Natural resource investment and Africa's development* (pp. 368–94). Cheltenham, UK: Edward Elgar.

Carmody, P. (2011). *The new scramble for Africa*. Cambridge, UK: Polity Press.

Central Intelligence Agency (CIA) (2013). *The world fact book*. Retrieved from https://www.cia.gov/library/publications/the-world-factbook/index.html

Chellaney (2010, July 5). China now exports its convicts. *The Japan Times*. Retrieved from http://search.japantimes.co.jp/print/eo20100705bc.html

Chinese bosses shoot protesting Zambian miners: Police. (2010, October 16). *Terra Daily*. Retrieved from http://www.terradaily.com/reports/Chinese_bosses_shoot_protesting_Zambian_miners_police_999.html

Cohen, M. (2011, December 29). China's EXIM lend more to Sub-Sahara Africa than World Bank, Fitch says. *Bloomberg*. Retrieved from http://www.bloomberg.com/news/2011-12-28/china-exim-loans-to-sub-sahara-africa-exceed-world-bank-funds-fitch-says.html

Duruigbo, E. (2006). Permanent sovereignty and peoples' ownership of natural resources in international law. *George Washington International Law Review, 38*(1), 33–100.

Dutch court finds Shell liable for Nigeria oil damages (2013, January 30). *Environment News Service*. Retrieved from http://ens-newswire.com/2013/01/30/dutch-court-finds-shell-liable-for-nigeria-oil-damages/

Economist Intelligence Unit (2007). *World investment prospects to 2011: Foreign direct investment and the challenge of political risk*. Retrieved from http://www.vcc.columbia.edu/pubs/documents/WorldInvestmentProspectsto2011.pdf

Economist Intelligence Unit (2010, July 13). Sub-Saharan Africa economy: Strategic rise. *The Economist Intelligence Unit*. Retrieved from http://viewswire.eiu.com/index.asp

Exploited workers protest against Chinese company (2008, May 3). *AsiaNews.it*. Retrieved from http://www.asianews.it/news-en/Exploited-workers-protest-against-Chinese-company-11685.html

Extractive Industries Transparency Initiative (EITI) (n.d.). *EITI*. Retrieved from http://www.eiti.org

Forster, F. and Briceño-Garmendia, C. (2010). *Africa's infrastructure: A time for transformation*. Washington DC, US: The World Bank.
Gadzala, A. and Hanusch, M. (2010). African perspectives on China-Africa: Gauging popular perceptions and their economic and political determinants. *Afrobarometer Working Papers No. 117 (January)*, 1–25.
Ghana: Lining up for Jubilee (2010, September 27). *Ghana Oil*. Retrieved from http://ghanaoilonline.org/2010/09/asias-big-oil-companies-backed-by-their-governments-are-outbidding-their-western-rivals/
Global Finance (2012). *World's GDP growth by region*. Retrieved from http://www.gfmag.com/tools/global-database/economic-data/11854-worlds-gdp-growth-by-region.html#axzz2BQqqmrQs
Grant, K. (2005). *A civilised savagery: Britain and the new slaveries in Africa, 1884–1926*. London: Routledge.
Grudgings, S. (2011, November 17). Analysis: As rich world sputters, Brazil looks to Africa. *Reuters*. Retrieved from http://us.mobile.reuters.com/article/businessNews/idUSTRE7AG1EQ20111117?irpc=932
Harford, T. and Klein, M. (2005). Aid and the resource curse: How can aid be designed to preserve institutions? *Public Policy for the Private Sector*, *291*, 1–4. Retrieved from http://www.eldis.org/vfile/upload/1/document/0708/DOC20032.pdf
Huang, Y. (2011). What does China want in international economic reforms? *East Asia Forum Quarterly*, *3*(3), 31–2.
Iimi, A. (2007). Escaping from the resource curse: Evidence from Botswana and the rest of the world. *IMF Staff Papers*, *54*(4), 663–99.
IMF (2011). *New growth drivers for low income countries: The role of BRICs*. Retrieved from http://www.imf.org/external/np/pp/eng/2011/011211.pdf
India-Africa Summit (2008). *Africa Quarterly: Indian Journal of African Affairs*, *48*(2), 1–80.
Joseph, S. (2011). *Blame it on the WTO? A human rights critique*. Oxford: Oxford University Press.
Kimenyi, M.S. and Lewis, Z. (2011). The BRICS and the new scramble for Africa. In E. Aryeetey et al. (Eds), *Foresight Africa: The continent's greatest challenges and opportunities for 2011* (pp. 19–21). Washington, DC: Brookings Institute.
Kobo, K. (2009, August 25). Africa's population now 1 billion. *AfricaNews.com*. Retrieved from http://www.africanews.com/site/Africas_population_now_1_billion/list_messages/26588
Kragelund, P. (2010). *India's African engagement* (ARI). Retrieved from http://www.realinstitutoelcano.org/wps/wcm/connect/460919004118f560af3fef6d616c2160/ARI10-2010_Kragelund_India_Africa_Engagement.pdf?MOD=AJPERES&CACHEID=460919004118f560af3fef6d616c2160
Laryea, E. (2011a). Contractual arrangements for resource investment. In F.N. Botchway (Ed.), *Natural resource investment and Africa's development* (pp. 107–33). Cheltenham, UK: Edward Elgar.
Laryea, E. (2011b). Evolution of international investment law and implications for Africa. In F.N. Botchway (Ed.), *Natural resource investment and Africa's development* (pp. 293–327). Cheltenham, UK: Edward Elgar.
Laryea, E. (2011c). Promoting good governance through ICT systems: Improving transparency and reducing corruption. In R. Buckley (Ed.), *Debt-for-development exchanges: History and new applications* (pp. 260–95). New York: Cambridge University Press.

Laryea, E. and Sucker, F. (2012). Introduction: The importance of an Africa voice in, and understanding and use of, international economic law. In E. Laryea, N. Madolo and F. Sucker (eds), *International economic law: The voices of Africa* (pp. 1–13). Cape Town, South Africa: Siber Ink.

Lyman, P.N. (2005, July 21). *China's role in Africa*. Testimony before the US-China Commission. Retrieved from http://www.cfr.org/publication/8436/chinas_rising_role_in_africa.html

Meiden, M. (2006). China's Africa policy: Business now, politics later. *Asian Perspective*, *30*(4), 69–93.

Miller, K. (2010). Coping with China's financial power: Beijing's financial foreign policy. *Foreign Affairs*, *89*, 96–109.

Moyo, D. (2009). *Dead aid: Why aid is not working and how there is another way for Africa*. Place: Penguin.

Naidu, S. (2008). India's growing African strategy. *Review of African Political Economy*, *35*(115), 116–28.

Noman, A., Botchwey, K., Stein, H. and Stiglitz, J.E. (2012). *Good growth and governance in Africa: Rethinking development strategies*. USA: Oxford University Press.

Press Trust of India (PTI) (2012, March 17). India, Africa set trade target of $90 billion by 2015. *Economic Times*. Retrieved from http://articles.economictimes.indiatimes.com/2012-03-17/news/31204825_1_sacu-trade-target-india-africa-business-council

Schmitt, G. (2007, October). Is Africa turning east? China's new engagement in Africa and its implications on the macro-economic situation, the business environment and the private sector in Africa. Paper presented to the Donor Committee for Enterprise Development Africa Regional Consultative Conference. Retrieved from http://www.businessenvironment.org/dyn/be/docs/160/Schmitt.pdf

Schneidman, W. and Lewis, Z.A. (2012). *The African growth and opportunity Act: Looking back, looking forward*. Retrieved from http://www.brookings.edu/~/media/research/files/reports/2012/6/agoa/agoa_full_report

Schrijver, N. (1997). *Sovereignty over natural resources: Balancing rights and duties*. Cambridge: Cambridge University Press.

Shasha, D. (2009,January 19). Chinese-African trade volume hits all time high to reach $106.8 bln. *China News*. Retrieved from http://news.xinhuanet.com/english/2009-01/19/content_10684845.htm

Siegle, J. (2009). Governance strategies to remedy the natural resource curse. *International Social Science Journal*, *57*, 45–55.

Stiglitz, J.E. and Carlton, A. (2005). *Fair trade for all*: *How trade can promote development*. Oxford: Oxford University Press.

Taylor, I. (2006). *China and Africa: Engagement and compromise*. Oxfordshire, UK: Routledge.

UNCTAD (2011). *The least developed countries report 2011: The potential role of South-South cooperation for inclusive and sustainable development*. Retrieved from http://unctad.org/en/docs/ldc2011_en.pdf

United Nations Economic Commission for Africa (UNECA). (2010). *Economic report on Africa 2012: Unleashing Africa's potential as a pole of global growth*. Retrieved from http://new.uneca.org/era/era2012.aspx

Waelde, T.W. (1995). A requiem for the 'new international economic order': The rise and fall of paradigms in international economic law. *CEPMLP Internet*

Journal, 1–2. Retrieved from http://www.dundee.ac.uk/cepmlp/journal/html/Vol1/article1-2.html

Weiss, T. (2000). Governance, good governance and global governance: Conceptual and actual challenges. *Third World Quarterly*, *21*(5), 795–814.

World Bank (2011). *Least Developed Countries: UN Classification*. Retrieved from http://data.worldbank.org/region/LDC

Yu, G.T. (1977). China's role in Africa. *Annals of the American Academy of Political and Social Science*, *432*, 96–109.

Zongwe, D.P. (2009). Ore for infrastructure: The contractual form of economic complementarities between China and Africa. *The China Monitor*, *42*, 7–11.

9. The BRICS: Experiments with state capitalism and institutional investment

John Farrar and Mohamed Ariff

The BRICS is a loose international political association of leading emerging economies which were grouped together by Jim O'Neill of Goldman Sachs in a paper in 2001 (O'Neill, 2001; see also O'Neill, 2011). This term has entered the lexicon of meetings and mass media debate on public policy, especially after the common concern to promote economic growth as a result of the Global Financial Crisis (GFC). It originally was the BRIC – the Federative Republic of Brazil, the Russian Federation, the Republic of India and the People's Republic of China – but now the Republic of South Africa has been added ('New era', 2011).

Russia in some respects is the odd one out as the others are all developing countries. South Africa under Apartheid was not necessarily regarded as a developing country, but since the political reforms it has been going through difficult adjustments. All of the BRICS countries are regarded as growing economies, representing 43 per cent of the world's population, although recently they have slowed down. All are having significant influence on regional and global affairs. Hu Jintao claims that the group is a defender and promoter of developing countries ('BRICS is the defender', 2012) and increasingly seems to be seeking to balance the weight of US hegemony for a greater role in international organizations. Next year Russia has the presidency of the G20. The BRICS is pressing for reform of the IMF, World Bank and the Security Council of the United Nations. The two models suggested for the association to follow are the G8 and the OECD (Guihai, 2011). Some of the members of the BRICS have entered into joint ventures,[1] and there is talk of a bank to rival the World Bank (BRICS, 2012, para. 13).

A common characteristic of the original BRIC countries is that all have followed a socialist path with policies characterized by state capitalism, but are now experimenting with aspects of market capitalism. State capitalism is a term with many meanings, but it normally connotes one in which the state acts as the dominant economic player and uses markets for political as well as economic gains (Binns, 1986).[2] All the BRICS countries experience difficulties in managing a public/private interface (Lin, 2012).[3] Of the five countries, South Africa has had the longest history of a successful private sector.

EXPERIMENTS WITH STATE CAPITALISM

Brazil

Brazil has the largest economy in Latin America; by GDP size it ranks sixth in the world and it has now overtaken the UK (CIA, 2012). For nearly 50 years Brazil followed a form of nationalist mercantilism through state control of commerce and credit once it came out of the militaristic tradition some four decades ago (Cardoso, 2006). It was capitalist in principle, but with extensive state controls (de Onis, 2000). The emphasis was on internal development, but by 1980 it suffered from high inflation and corruption. Since the 1990s, steps have been taken to liberalize and open up the economy (Cardoso, 2006, pp. 179–202). It has a population of over 190 million and rich natural resources, which is its basis for economic growth.

Brazil's economy is divided as follows: service sector 67 per cent of GDP, industrial sector 27.5 per cent, agriculture 5.5 per cent. The service sector includes a developing banking sector and stock market. The industrial sector ranges from automobiles and petrochemicals through to computers and aircraft. Agricultural goods include coffee, sugar, orange juice and beef; sugar has been useful to extract ethanol as a substitute for petrol (Cardoso, 2006).

Brazil was one of the first emerging markets to begin recovery after the GFC of 2007–09. However, it was ranked 130th out of 183 countries by the World Bank, in terms of ease of doing business in 2012 (World Bank, 2012).

Russia

Russia possesses the world's largest territory and enormous resources. It has, however, had a complicated past with the breakup of the USSR in 1994 and a drastic attempt with little success to switch to a true market economy (Hedetoft & Blum, 2008). This produced considerable social hardship and a reaction to the oligarchs still in power (Hedetoft & Blum, 2008, p. 15). Russia has rebuilt some of its state-owned enterprise system but has also had some further limited privatization. At the same time, it has had a declining birth rate (Hedetoft & Blum, 2008, p. 25). In 2012 it joined the WTO (BRICS, 2012). Russia was badly affected by the GFC but cushioned the effect by dipping into its oil stabilization fund and investment funds (Sharma, 2012, p. 88; Lynch, 2011, pp. 70–74).

Russia's major exports are oil and gas, so its wealth is affected by the price of energy. Russia has a large industrial sector and has a large defence sector which accounts for 20 per cent of manufacturing jobs. Other important sectors are automobiles, aircraft, telecommunications and agriculture (Wikipedia, 2012; Lynch, 2011, pp. 72–3); however, attempts to diversify the economy have not been successful. The World Bank ranked Russia 112th out of 183 countries for ease of doing business (World Bank, 2012).

India

India has socialism and social objectives in its constitution, and has a mixed economy of state-owned enterprises and a family-controlled private sector (Sarkar & Sarkar, 2012, p. 11). At the time of independence in 1947, the corporate landscape was dominated by the managing agency system (Sarkar & Sarkar, 2012). This was abolished in 1969. On independence, there was a switch to an industrial policy which emphasized state regulation of the private sector and accorded commanding heights to the public sector (Sarkar & Sarkar, 2012). This led to an over-elaborate and inefficient bureaucratic system known as 'permit raj', which is still a major impediment to progress. India's share of world trade halved during Nehru's premiership, in spite of his good intentions. Added to this was the fragmentation of politics with the result that there was no consensus in favour of change. This led to weaker economic growth.

India has engaged in liberal reforms since 1991 (Sarkar & Sarkar, 2012). Since then there has been increasing globalization of the economy through cross-border mergers and acquisition, cross listing, foreign direct investment (FDI) and international trade. Its exports rose from US$1.3 billion in 1950 to US$177.2 billion in 2010 (Bhat, 2011). It bought 200 metric tonnes of gold from the IMF in 2009 to diversify its assets and ease reliance on the US dollar (Gangopadhyay & Behrmann, 2009). However, there has been slower growth and a failure to realize potential, for reasons which are complex.

India's main sectors are industry (28 per cent), services (23 per cent), agriculture (15.7 per cent) and energy, although it is a big importer of oil. Until the 1990s the main institutional investors were government-owned development financial institutions, commercial banks, insurance companies and mutual funds (Sarkar & Sarkar, 2012, p. 172). Mutual funds were publicly controlled until the 1990s. India ranked 132nd out of 183 countries in terms of ease of doing business in 2012 (World Bank, 2012). In this respect, India scored the lowest of the BRICS countries.

China

China benefited greatly from joining the WTO, as well as being accorded most favoured nation status by the US, and its economy has grown from an industrial backwater to rivalling the US. Its total manufacturing output is the largest in the world. This has been largely due to cheap labour costs. Much of the economy is still in state-owned enterprise and restrictions are placed on the private sector.

The state sector consists of three parts (Chiu & Lewis, 2006; Szamosszegi & Kyle, 2011, p. 1; Lin & Milhaupt, 2011):

1. SOEs which are wholly state-owned through the State-Owned Assets Supervision and Administration Commission (SASAC) or similar commissions at the local level;
2. SOEs which are majority owned or controlled by the state; and
3. entities owned or controlled indirectly.

There is a lack of clarity in ownership structures, which makes external monitoring of the Chinese position difficult: central government and provincial governments own majority stakes (Szamosszegi & Kyle, 2011). This is particularly relevant for WTO purposes.

An attempt has been made to create an intermediate institutional investment structure through the SASAC and similar bodies at the local or regional level (Szamosszegi & Kyle, 2011). The SASAC has the responsibility of exercising ownership rights on behalf of the state. Since 2004 it has initiated structural adjustment of central enterprises. It has moved to reduce the involvement of a number of enterprises in property development where it is not listed as their core business. At the end of the day, however, key governance roles of hiring and firing senior management still remain with the Communist Party. Indeed a report for the US-China Economic and Security Review Commission states that most Chinese SOE boards fall within four types (Frederick, as cited in Szamosszegi & Kyle, 2011, p. 74): 1) the operational board which runs the SOE as an extension of a government department; 2) the conduit board which simply relays directions given by ministers; 3) the symbolic board which is circumvented; and 4) the subjugated board which is dominated by a powerful CEO.

One is left with the impression that China appears to have adopted some Western ideas on corporate governance and some of the Washington

Consensus ideas, but deep down not a lot has changed and the Communist Party has increased its control since the GFC. China ranked 91st out of 183 countries in terms of ease of doing business in 2012 (World Bank, 2012).

South Africa

South Africa was not originally a BRIC member, but was added as much for its role in Africa and its increasing relationship to China as for its economy. It has the largest economy in Africa and a First World infrastructure. In the Apartheid era it practised a form of state capitalism and mercantilism in spite of its protestations to the contrary. It had extensive state ownership and interference with the labour market. This led to allocative inefficiency and distributional inequity (Lowenberg & Kaempfer, 1998, p. 31). The African National Congress (ANC) has been reconsidering state capitalism because of the apparent success of the Chinese model.

South Africa's main sectors are mining, manufacturing, agriculture and a significant service sector, particularly in financial services, which makes it important to Africa (SouthAfrica.info, 2013).

Although South Africa has been important politically and financially, it is falling behind because of its size, low savings rate, and capital and brain drain. It has an inadequately educated workforce, restrictive labour regulations and inefficient government bureaucracy. It has also suffered from power shortages and strikes. It is difficult for the government to meet the expectations of the black majority and there has been increased corruption (Johnson, 2010). South Africa is a difficult country to govern because it is a developed market wrapped inside an emerging market. Economic justice remains a distant hope (Sharma, 2012, p. 173; Johnson, 2010). South Africa ranked 39th out of 183 countries in terms of ease of doing business in 2012 (World Bank, 2012) and 52nd out of 144 in the Global Competitiveness Report 2012–2013 of the World Economic Forum.

COMPARISON WITH THE EUROPEAN UNION AND THE US

In this section, we make a comparison of the BRICS with the European Union and the US. To understand the comparative strengths, it is worthwhile to do a comparison of two key facts, namely the share of world income by the BRICS and the share of world trade by the BRICS countries (IMF, 2013; World Bank, 2012). As is widely known, these two factors are the key to understanding the challenge coming from the BRICS. In the

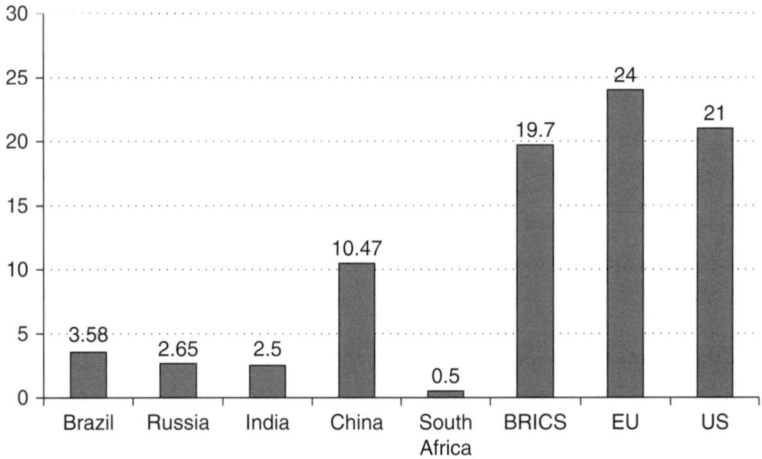

Source: Authors' computation from their data set.

Figure 9.1 BRICS vs EU vs US: Percentage of world GDP, 2012

last century, challenges to the US and EU came from groupings of the developing countries aimed at securing concessions on several issues in the 1970s to 1980s in the bipolar world of the West-with-Japan and the Soviet bloc.

Figure 9.1 is a chart of the world share of the five BRICS nations against the EU and US. As can be seen, the five BRICS countries accounted individually for about 4 per cent on average of the world's GDP in 2012. That is, each of the BRICS countries accounts for about 1/25th of the world's GDP. Together the BRICS' share is 19.7 per cent, which means as a group they almost reach the US share of world GDP, although individually they would not count as a powerful entity. Compare that with the average of 22 per cent for either the EU or the US. It appears that the BRICS nations, despite their substantial cumulative growth rates over the last 20 years, are lower than the current position of the EU and the US purely in terms of GDP share of the world economy. If we translate these statistics to per capita income instead of the total GDP, then the statistics reveal an even worse position for the BRICS compared to either that of the EU or the US. Per capita income of the BRICS countries would place them squarely as low-income countries, far below countries like Korea, Malaysia or even Thailand.

Another well-publicized aspect of the BRICS is the domination of China in respect of world trade. Figure 9.2 provides comparative statistics on the world trade (import plus export).

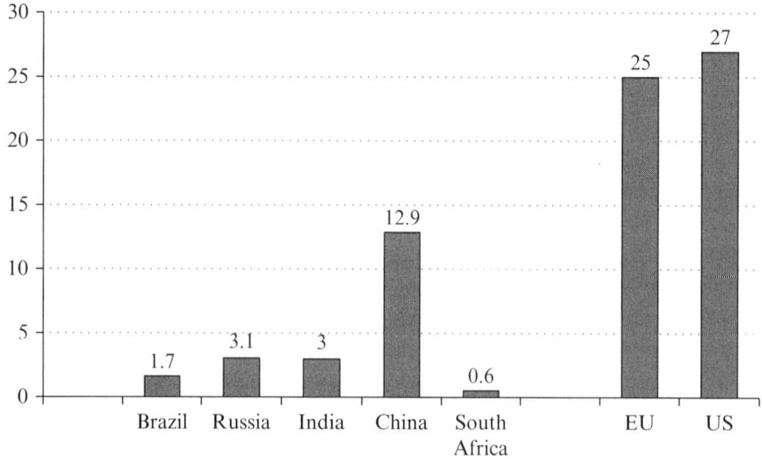

Source: Authors' computation from their data set.

Figure 9.2 BRICS vs EU vs US: Percentage of world trade, 2012 (% GDP)

The average trade share of each of the BRICS country is 4.25 per cent of world trade and that can be valued at US$1117 billion. China, with 12.9 per cent, dominates world trade since it was, in 2011, the largest manufacturing country. Her trade value is US$3600 billion (or on a monthly basis, US$300 billion of trade). The BRICS' total trade value is US$5850 billion of the world's total trade of US$27 600 billion. The EU and US share of the world trade are: 25 per cent (US$6890 billion) and 27 per cent (US$7440 billion) respectively. In terms of trade the BRICS countries together account for 85 per cent of the US share and 78 per cent of the EU share of trade.

Again, we address the issue of trade by the BRICS, which is about half of the joint trade share of the two of the non-BRICS major economies. It appears that there is a considerable gap to close for the BRICS to reach parity with either of the two major private-sector led economies in terms of world trade. Non-BRICS countries would still find a greater degree of trade linkages with the two largest groups more appealing to develop private-sector led trade arrangements. In this connection, one is reminded of the failure of the communist blocs' barter trade model that was partly based on the state-owned firms serving as the front runners under the state capitalism model that prevailed in the world for several decades till the 1980s.

A closer examination of the trade statistics in the public domain – for example on the website of the World Bank –shows that with the exception of China and Russia, all other BRICS countries have substantial trade deficits, which weakens their currencies. Russia and China conversely had trade surpluses in recent years. The EU and US also have trade deficits. The deficits have been narrowing in the last two years on the back of declining US and EU currencies, which is giving a boost to exports and curtailing imports in those two areas. Consequently, in terms of the trade share of the BRICS, there is a lot of room to gain before the BRICS can truly be a challenge to the two established major economies. There are also a few star performing countries that are emerging to challenge the dominion of the others in trade. These nimble economies such as Turkey, Taiwan, South Korea, Malaysia and Singapore are making trade their priority for growth, and these countries are not in the BRICS.

INSTITUTIONAL INVESTMENT

Each of the BRICS countries has some form of domestic institutional investment which has a close relationship with the state. These include sovereign wealth funds, foreign exchange reserves, pension funds, mutual funds, banks and insurance companies. Currently, India and South Africa do not have sovereign wealth funds, but are considering introducing them.

Sovereign Wealth Funds (SWFs)

Sovereign wealth funds (Ariff & Farrar, 2013) are a mixture of funds and entities which are set up for various purposes by states. Hence, it is difficult to prescribe similar goals or generalize about the operational processes of all funds. Operating within market capitalism, they represent examples of state ownership of savings, set aside for future consumption from current incomes of resource-rich nations such as Saudi Arabia since 1978 or set aside by small economies such as Singapore and Hong Kong, which have less expenses than larger countries and so are able to invest the surplus.

The US Government Accountability Office defines SWFs by four criteria (US GAO, 2008, pp. 7–8):

- They are government-chartered or government-sponsored investment vehicles.
- They invest some or all of their funds in assets other than sovereign debt outside the country that established them.
- They are funded through government transfers arising primarily

from sovereign budget surpluses, trade surpluses, central bank currency reserves or revenues from the commodity wealth of a country.
- They are not actively functioning as a pension fund.

The International Working Group (IWG) on SWFs defines them as follows in the Generally Accepted Principles and Practices (GAPP) (IWG, 2008):

> SWFs are special-purpose investment funds or arrangements that are owned by the general government. Created by the general government for macroeconomic purposes, SWFs hold, manage, or administer assets to achieve financial objectives, and employ a set of investment strategies that include investing in foreign financial assets (IWG, 2008).

Certain types are excluded from SWFs – foreign exchange reserves, state-owned enterprises and public servant pension funds.

According to the IMF, SWFs can be grouped into five categories (IMF, 2007):

1. Stabilization funds;
2. Savings funds;
3. Reserve investment funds;
4. Development funds; and
5. Pension reserve funds.

The impact of SWFs has entered public discussion (Truman, 2010; Avendano & Santiso, 2009). In the West there has been increasing concern about the governance of SWFs, which led to an initiative in 2010 cumulating in an agreement adopting the Santiago Principles to provide some governance guidelines for these entities. The latest wave of SWFs is arguably a product of the financial instability caused by Western financialization and Eastern neo-mercantilism. At the same time, they are funds which are recycling global financial flows rather than acting as a source of new funds. Apart from the need to adopt some degree of disclosure on how such large sums of money are deployed, there is also public debate on whether some countries with large SWFs could use these assets for political purposes. An OECD document raises this latter issue, and concludes that that is a matter of grave concern (OECD, 2008).

Figure 9.3 is a summary of the largest SWF countries around the world. These statistics show that there are some seven nations that dominate the SWF scene. China is the only country in the BRICS among the top seven

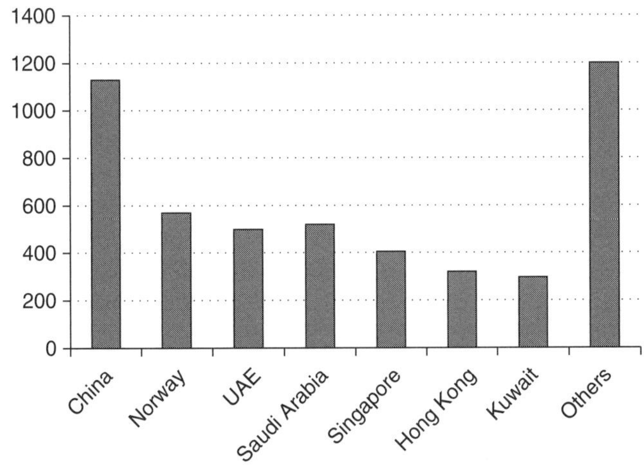

Source: Authors' computation from their data set.

Figure 9.3 The top sovereign wealth fund countries, 2011 (US$ billion)

SWF nations. It accounts for the largest accumulation of state revenues placed as SWFs. Much of this is the result of state-owned firms owned mostly by the central and provincial governments having profits and dividends, which are now being channelled as SWFs.

This is the result of the state capitalist model of development rather than private sector-led growth. Under the private sector model, countries with depleting assets (such as Norway, Canada and Saudi Arabia) create economically justifiable accumulation of wealth for the days when the assets will all be depleted. Brazil and Russia have smaller SWFs. India and South Africa do not currently have SWFs.

Data available from reliable sources suggest that 44 nations hold about US$4800 billion or 7.5 per cent of the world GDP in the form of SWFs (SWFI, 2013).

Foreign Exchange Reserves

SWFs are distinguished from foreign exchange reserves (Ariff & Farrar, 2013). The purposes of the latter are described by the Centre for Central Banking Studies of the Bank of England as follows (Nugee, 2012):

1. Formal backing for the domestic currency.
2. A tool of exchange rate or monetary policy.

3. Funds for servicing foreign exchange liabilities and debt obligations.
4. A source of funds for payment for government expenditure overseas.
5. A defence against emergencies or disaster.
6. An investment fund for financial gains.

Clearly (6) overlaps with SWFs. Foreign exchange reserves in the post-War era were the result of two great movements in economic ideology – the promotion of development and world trade. The idea of providing support for underdeveloped economies through state-supported plans, such as most favoured nation status and assisted WTO membership, led to some states pursuing a self-interested policy of (i) open free trade with the developed nations while (ii) restricting entry to the home markets and (iii) use of managed currency as the tool to make domestic production continually cheaper than would be the case with freer trade and investment.

Figure 9.4 depicts the major hoarders of foreign exchange reserves. Under the IMF model, reserves are meant to service the trade financing. The idea was that a nation would need about eight months of trade value as foreign reserves to service the smooth payments of imports and exports when payments are due. If one takes the total trade value of China (which is US$300 billion per month), that would require a foreign reserve of about US$2400 billion. The actual reserve of China is above US$3000 billion, which means that the extra cash being held provides a safety net

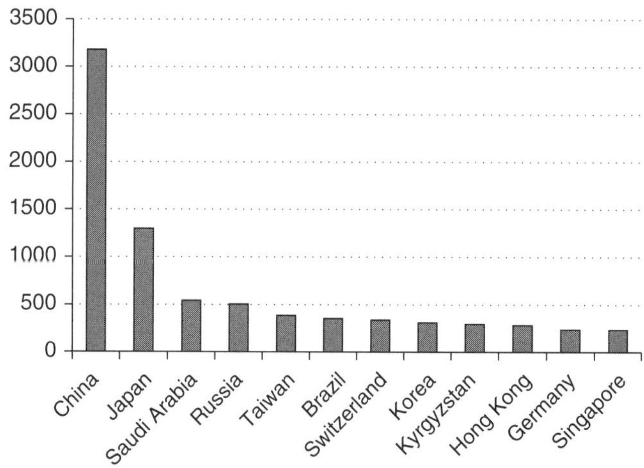

Source: Authors' computation from their data set.

Figure 9.4 The top foreign reserve holdings by countries, 2011 (US$ billion)

above the market wisdom of holding eight months' worth of finance in foreign currencies. The actual amount caters for about 12 months of trade.

We find 12 nations account for two-thirds of the total reserves: China, Japan, Saudi Arabia, Russia, Taiwan, Brazil, Switzerland, South Korea, Kyrgyzstan, Hong Kong, Germany and Singapore. Note that BRICS nations China, Russia and Brazil, with about US$370 billion, are among the largest accumulators of foreign reserves. India with US$300 billion in reserves and South Africa with negligible reserves are not in the figure.

The 12 countries have foreign reserves totalling US$8000 billion while the rest of the world has nearly 35 per cent of the reserves of the world; the world's total foreign reserves are about US$23 000 billion (IMF, 2013).

Summarizing the position of the BRICS from the point of view of (i) income, (ii) world trade, (iii) SWF value and (iv) foreign reserves as discussed in the previous pages suggests that the BRICS group is not as dominating a group as it is made out to be by the policy-makers and the popular media. Our analysis of the aggregate statistics suggests that the BRICS is a pressure group seeking to gain a negotiating position in the world's forums, such as the World Bank, IMF, WTO and G20 on financial reforms. This suggests that the BRICS serves the same role as the North–South dialogue in the second half of the last century. The Non-Aligned Group also served the same platform to obtain concessions in world body negotiations. This has to be recognized in dealing with the BRICS.

Pension Funds

Pension funds are either public or private. Brazil has a public fund and a number of private funds. Russia has a Retirement Fund, a fund for social security, a fund for compulsory medical insurance and private funds. It also has a Reserve Fund and a National Wealth Fund. The latter are sovereign wealth funds. Russia moved funds around to cope with a recession in 2009. India has an Employees Provident Fund and a number of private funds. China has, in addition to its four sovereign wealth funds, a National Social Security Fund and some private funds. South Africa has a public fund and some private funds.

Mutual Funds

All the BRICS countries have mutual funds. The first mutual fund in Brazil was created in 1957. Now it has the largest mutual fund assets in Latin America and had about half of the assets of the BRIC countries in 2007. It has grown due to basic economic factors that include diversification, liquidity, professional management and low transaction costs.

Russia has developed mutual funds since 1991. As at 1 January 2007, it had 641. Russia suffers from oligarchical behaviour and state intervention which can be unpredictable. Until 1993 Indian mutual funds were 80 per cent under the control of the government's Unit Trust of India, the remainder in funds floated by public sector banks. Since then, private sector mutual funds have been allowed.

China's mutual funds industry has grown since its entry into the WTO. As at 2011, it was managing assets with US$30.2 billion. There are also a number of foreign and Hong Kong-based funds, some of which are entering into joint ventures with Mainland funds. South Africa has had mutual funds for many years.

Banks and Insurance Companies

All the BRICS countries have banks and insurance companies. Brazil has a sound banking system, which has performed well in the GFC. About 50 per cent is domestic and 35 per cent domestic with foreign ownership. Public banks account for less than 8 per cent of the total assets. There is significant public financing of business.

Russia inherited a few large banks from the USSR. The role of the banks was to finance the central government's economic plans. An attempt to introduce a market system has been hazardous. Russia suffered in the 1998 crisis, but has been less affected by the GFC. The market system is 60 per cent state-controlled. It lacks a modern financial system.

India was subject to five-year plans and banks had to serve state policy. There was also nationalization, and the whole system tended to be inward-looking. About 90 per cent is still under state control. In fact, India is like China in these respects. Its main difference is the extent of the family-controlled private sector.

Before the reforms China had only one bank, the People's Bank of China, which was a bureau under the Ministry of Finance. It operates in an accounting and cashier's role for the SOEs (Lin, 2012, p. 184). China now has a state-controlled banking sector, still with problems of politicized loans which represent considerable bad debts (Walter & Howie, 2011). South Africa inherited a thriving banking sector which is well regulated, but it is affected by the state of the economy and political tensions.

Brazil has a developed insurance sector. Russia developed an insurance sector mainly after the collapse of communism, and the industry has been going through difficulties in the motor industries and banking sectors. India has had extensive state ownership, and the largest life insurance company is still state-owned. There is now increased foreign investment.

China has developed an insurance industry which has become profitable, but the industry is still in its infancy. Ownership is in the hands of the state, local shareholders or joint ventures. South Africa has a well-established insurance industry.

REGULATORY ISSUES

Regulation is a means whereby a state fosters and controls economic development and the structure in which it operates (Baldwin, Cave & Lodge, 2012, p. 409). Institutional investment falls under a multiplicity of systems of regulation in the West. In the past the BRICS countries have not been key players in the development of international regulation. Membership of the WTO has put pressure on them to adopt international standards, which results in more focused regulatory oversight, but where many of the key operators are state-owned, regulatory supervision is sometimes not easy or independent. Adoption of international standards is of limited use without enforcement (Braithwaite & Drahos, 2000, p. 10). However, that is not to say that they have no use whatsoever. At the very least they contribute to development where previously there was no equivalent infrastructure. China is a classic case of such development.

Sovereign wealth funds are only governed by the Santiago Principles which are a form of self-regulation, but they can attract domestic attention in countries in which they seek to invest. Foreign exchange reserves are subject to article IV of the Articles of Agreement of the IMF (IMF, 2011).

Pension funds are primarily regulated by their home state, although in the OECD there are some guidelines for its members which some non-members follow. Much depends on the legal structure adopted. Some fall under financial services regulation. Mutual funds are governed by financial services regulation and fall under the supervision of the International Organisation of Securities Commission (IOSCO). Brazil, India, China and South Africa are members of the IOSCO Board and the Emerging Markets Advisory Board.

Insurance is covered by domestic regulation and is subject to ineffective international regulation by the International Association of Insurance Supervisors. All the BRICS countries are members of the association. Banking is covered by domestic regulation and the Basel Accords, and is subject to the supervision of the Financial Stability Board. All the BRICS members are on the Basel Committee on Banking Supervision and the Financial Stability Board.

The GFC exposed the weaknesses in both domestic and international regulation to the near destruction of the Western financial system. The GFC has led to a greater role being asserted by the BRICS countries, particularly China, which now has the largest number of sovereign wealth funds and foreign exchange reserves. China is experimenting with other forms of institutional investment, although its banking system has hidden weaknesses.

The key weaknesses of the BRICS' systems are corruption and a lack of adequate regulation of competition. All the BRICS countries suffer from corruption in spite of campaigns to deal with it. Corruption is not just a product of one-party systems. The BRICS' systems tend towards state monopoly or oligarchy. Indeed this is encouraged under the guise of promotion of state champions. On Transparency International's Corruption Perceptions Index 2011 (Transparency International, 2011), Brazil registered 3.8, Russia 2.4, India 3.1, China 3.6 and South Africa 4.1. New Zealand had the highest score at 9.5, Australia 8.8, the US 7.1, the UK 7.8, Germany 8 and Greece 3.4. As the numbers indicate, the lower the score the higher the corruption.

CONCLUSION

The BRICS countries show diversity in systems of government. Brazil, India and South Africa operate as democracies. China is essentially a one-party state. Russia was a one-party state and now falters as a democracy.

China has shown increasing impatience with the workings of market capitalism. In 2006 Wen Jiabao sought to have iron ore contract negotiation taken out of the hands of the private sector (Uren, 2012). Since then the role of the state in the activities of SOEs has been more manifest. China operates like a corporate state, although the extent of cohesion in decision-making can be exaggerated. The BRICS countries are experimenting with different forms of capitalism, but are still making extensive use of state-owned enterprises. The format ranges from state capitalism and regulatory capitalism to market capitalism.

The BRICS countries, despite their growth rates, still have a long way to go to challenge the US and the EU in terms of world trade. For example, the BRICS countries, particularly Russia and China, seem to show greater flexibility in transfers of funds between different categories of institutional investment, often with politically inspired loans from banks which are not subject to effective international regulation.

A fourth point of difference is the question of the stakeholders that corporations serve. Doug Guthrie in his interesting book, *China and Globalisation*, states (2009, p. 308):

> In the US system, multi-national corporations often operate beyond reach of US law and they rarely serve any national interests beyond the narrowly-defined interests of their shareholders. But China's hybrid-form corporations are a different breed. They are increasingly efficient in ways that other MNCs are, but they are also directed toward a much broader set of stakeholders. They are also constrained in a way that might just be healthy from an economic perspective. In the decade that has given us the economic debacles of Enron and Bear Sterns, it seems increasingly difficult to make the case that the unfettered capitalist model is truly superior. As China's influence grows over the course of this century, it will be interesting to see just how powerful and prominent Chinese corporations become.

Each of the other BRICS countries has to a greater or lesser extent espoused a social use of capital and the principle of the public good. Indeed this is expressly stated in clause 39(b) of the Indian Constitution, which refers to socialism in its Preamble. There has been disillusionment with the Washington Consensus ideas. They restrict national sovereignty, reflect the domination by Western ideology (Ye, 2011, pp. 61–3) and are thought to be a system which has failed. They have not been conspicuously successful in the developing world and are under question even in the West where there is increasing talk of enlightened shareholder value and sustainability. In terms of institutional investment, the new emphasis is on stewardship values (Financial Reporting Council, 2011).

The BRICS countries have high rates of inflation, and this affects their attempts to achieve price stability. As they were less affected by the GFC, they have not fully adjusted to the new goal of financial stability which is becoming a key objective of Western central banks.

Concern has been expressed in the West at the New Mercantilism being demonstrated by countries like China at the expense of Western and developing countries (Nolan, 2012). An example of the latter is Indonesia ('Challenges abound', 2012), whose economic performance looks good but when examined closely can be seen to rely on global commodity prices driven by China's appetite for raw materials. Indonesia's manufacturing sector has suffered as a result of China's cut-price competition and this affects employment. This perception somewhat undermines the international leadership role being sought by China and the other BRICS members. Lack of cohesion due to some discord on specific issues also inhibits this development. China and India have a border problem. Russia and China have had a complicated history. Brazil, Russia and South Africa export resources to China but import manufactured goods to the detriment of their domestic markets. This leads to unemployment in the manufacturing sector. While China has developed trade and financial links with the other four BRICS members, those four do not do much business with each other (Sharma, 2012, p. 253). All except South Africa make it difficult for others to do business with them, India ranking the lowest of the BRICS members in the World Bank rankings for ease of doing business in 2011. Leadership claims, purporting to be made on behalf of the developing world but increasingly representing self-interest, risk increased friction with the US and EU and within the international organisations. This is not to deny the need for reform of those organizations to reflect changing realities.

Where does this leave us? The BRICS is an artificial construct which is an experiment in an international organization still finding its way. It does not represent a region. It is not an economic union. It is a loose association of members with some common interests, which needs to deal with sources of discord as well as its relationship with non-BRICS countries. Prominent amongst the latter are Indonesia, South Korea, Mexico and Turkey, which all represent growth markets. The acronym N11 has been given to these countries, but they represent a less cohesive grouping, which involves differing degrees of risk for those seeking to do business with them. It is always a mistake to confuse investment banking with statesmanship; a mistake which has been made with disastrous consequences in the past.

NOTES

1. For example, China and India's joint venture on wind turbines. There is talk of a joint venture to develop Russian mineral resources.
2. Marx thought of capitalism as a process (1973, p. 258). It is interesting to note that Mao Tse-tung wrote on 9 July 1953: 'the present-day capitalist economy in China is a capitalist economy which for the most part is under the control of the People's Government and which is backed with the state-owned socialist economy in various forms and supervised by the workers' (comment on a document of the National Conference on Financial and Economic Work).
3. Some reports on country risk analysis take the view that the BRICS nations are in violation of some basic human rights. Such advisory firms rank these countries as having high sovereign risk (Maplecroft, 2012). Another dimension is that the BRICS countries are rated as being higher in risk than major economies for bond issuing purposes. These dimensions of social policy and financing risk of the BRICS countries are relevant for international investors but are not pursued in this version of the paper.

REFERENCES

Ariff, M. and Farrar, J.H. (2013). The governance and regulation of sovereign wealth funds and foreign exchange reserves in a post-GFC world. In J.H. Farrar and D.G. Mayes (Eds), *Globalisation, the global financial crisis and the state* (pp. 272–94). Cheltenham: Edward Elgar.

Avendano, R. and Santiso, J. (2009). *Are sovereign wealth funds' investments politically biased? A comparison with mutual funds* (OECD Development Centre

Working Paper No. 283). Retrieved from http://www.oecd.org/dev/44301172.pdf

Baldwin, R., Cave, M. and Lodge, M. (2012). *Understanding regulation: Theory, strategy and practice* (2nd edn). USA: Oxford University Press.

Bhat, T.P. (2011). *Structural changes in India's foreign trade*. New Delhi: Institute for Studies in Industrial Development.

Binns, P. (1986). *State capitalism*. Retrieved from http://www.marxists.de/statecap/binns/statecap.htm

Braithwaite, J. and Drahos, P. (2000). *Global business regulation*. Cambridge: Cambridge University Press.

BRICS (2012, March 29). Fourth BRICS summit – Delhi declaration. Retrieved from http://mea.gov.in/bilateral-documents.htm?dtl/19158/Fourth+BRICS+Summit++Delhi+Declaration

BRICS is the defender of the developing world (2012, March 28). *The Hindu*. Retrieved from http://www.thehindu.com/opinion/interview/brics-is-the-defender-of-the-developing-world/article3251562.ece

Cardoso, F.H. (2006). *The accidental President of Brazil – A memoir*. New York: Public Affairs.

Central Intelligence Agency (CIA) (2012). *The world factbook: South America- Brazil*. Retrieved from https://www.cia.gov/library/publications/the-world-factbook/geos/br.html

'Challenges abound for Indonesia's economy' (2012, June 28) *Leading company*. Retrieved from http://leadingcompany.smartcompany.com.au/execution/challenges-abound-for-indonesia-s-economy/201206281578

Chiu, B. and Lewis, M.K. (2006). *Reforming China's state-owned enterprises and banks*. Cheltenham: Edward Elgar.

de Onis, J. (2000). Brazil's new capitalism. *Foreign Affairs*. Retrieved from http://www.foreignaffairs.com/articles/56050/juan-de-onis/brazils-new-capitalism

Financial Reporting Council (2011, December). *Developments in corporate governance 2011: The impact and implementation of the UK corporate governance and stewardship codes*. Retrieved from https://www.frc.org.uk/Our-Work/Publications/Corporate-Governance/Developments-in-Corporate-Governance-2011-The-impa.aspx

Gangopadhyay, A. and Behrmann, E. (2009, November 4). India buys 200 tons of IMF's gold allotment. *Wall Street Journal*. Retrieved from http://online.wsj.com/article/SB125722876971624729.html

Guihai, G. (2011, April 14). Orientation of the BRICS mechanism. *China US Focus*. Retrieved from http://www.chinausfocus.com/slider/orientation-of-the-brics-mechanism-2/

Guthrie, D. (2009). *China and globalisation* (revised edn). New York: Routledge.

Hedetoft, U. and Blum, D. (2008). Introduction. In D.W. Blum (Ed.), *Russia and globalization: Identity, security and society in an era of change* (pp. 1–36). Baltimore: John Hopkins University Press.

IMF (2007). *Global financial stability report: Market developments and issues*. Retrieved from http://www.imf.org/External/Pubs/FT/GFSR/2007/01/

IMF (2011). *Articles of agreement of the International Monetary Fund*. Retrieved from http://www.imf.org/external/pubs/ft/aa/index.htm

IMF (2013). *Data and statistics*. Retrieved from http://www.imf.org/external/data.htm

International Working Group of Sovereign Wealth Funds (IWG). (2008). *Generally*

accepted principles and practices (GAPP) – Santiago principles. Retrieved from http://www.iwg-swf.org/pubs/gapplist.htm
Johnson, R.W. (2010). *South Africa's brave new world: The beloved country since the end of Apartheid*. London: Penguin Books.
Lin, J.Y. (2012). *Demystifying the Chinese economy*. Cambridge: Cambridge University Press.
Lin, L.-W. and Milhaupt. C.J. (2011). *We are the (national) champions: Understanding the mechanisms of state capitalism in China* (Columbia Law and Economics Working Paper No.409). New York: Columbia University.
Lowenberg. A. and Kaempfer, W. (1998). *The origins and demise of South Africa apartheid: A public choice analysis*. Ann Arbor, MI: The University of Michigan Press.
Lynch, A.C. (2011). *Vladimir Putin and Russian statecraft*. Washington DC: Potomac Books.
Maplecroft (2012, January 23). *Human rights complicity is principal ESG investment risk in the BRICs*. Retrieved from http://maplecroft.com/about/news/esg_risk_atlas_calculator.html
Marx, K. (1973). *The Grundrisse*. Harmondsworth: Penguin.
'New era as South Africa joins BRICS' (2011, April 11). *SouthAfrica.info*. Retrieved from http://www.southafrica.info/global/brics/brics-080411.htm
Nolan, P. (2012). *Is China buying the world?* Cambridge: Polity Press.
Nugee, J. (2012). CCBS handbook – Foreign exchange reserves management. *Bank of England*. Retrieved from http://www.bankofengland.co.uk/education/Pages/ccbs/handbooks/ccbshb19.aspx
OECD (2008). *OECD guidance on sovereign wealth funds*. Retrieved from http://www.oecd.org/daf/inv/investment-policy/oecdguidanceonsovereignwealthfunds.htm
O'Neill, J. (2001, November 30). *Building better global economic BRICs* (Goldman Sachs Global Economics Paper No. 66). London: Goldman, Sachs & Co.
O'Neill, J. (2011). *The growth map: Economic opportunity in the BRICS and beyond*. London: Portfolio.
Sarkar, J. and Sarkar, S. (2012). *Corporate governance in India*. New Delhi: Sage Publications.
Sharma, R. (2012). *Breakout nations: In pursuit of the next economic miracles*. London: Allen Lane.
SouthAfrica.info (2013, May 7). Retrieved from http://www.SouthAfrica.info
Sovereign Wealth Fund Institute (SWFI) (2013). Retrieved from http://www.swfinstitute.org/
Szamosszegi, A. and Kyle, C. (2011, October 26). An analysis of state-owned enterprises and state capitalism in China. *US-China Economic and Security Review Commission*. Retrieved from http://origin.www.uscc.gov/sites/default/files/Research/10_26_11_CapitalTradeSOEStudy.pdf
Transparency International (2011). *Corruption perceptions index 2011*. Retrieved from http://www.transparency.org/cpi2011/in_detail/
Truman, E. (2010). *Sovereign wealth funds: Threat or salvation*. Washington DC: Peterson Institute for International Economics.
Tse-tung, M. (1953). *On state capitalism*. Retrieved from http://www.marxists.org/reference/archive/mao/selected-works/volume-5/mswv5_30.htm
Uren, D. (2012). *The kingdom and the quarry*. Collingwood: Black Inc.

US Government Accountability Office (US GAO). (2008). *Sovereign wealth funds: Publicly available data on sizes and investments for some funds are limited* (Report to the Committee on Banking, Housing, and Urban Affairs, US Senate). Retrieved from http://www.gao.gov/assets/290/280267.pdf

Walter, C. and Howie, F. (2011). *Red capitalism*. Singapore: John Wiley & Sons.

Wikipedia (2012). *Economy of Russia*. Retrieved from http://en.wikipedia.org/wiki/Economy_of_Russia

World Bank (2012). *Ease of doing business index*. Retrieved from http://data.worldbank.org/indicator/IC.BUS.EASE.XQ

World Bank (2013). *Data*. Retrieved from http://data.worldbank.org/

Ye, Z. (2011). *Inside China's grand strategy – The perspective from the People's Republic*. Lexington, USA: University Press of Kentucky.

10. The power of the BRICS in world trade and growth, analysing the macroeconomic impacts within and across the bloc

Ahmed Khalid

The BRICS is a composition of five emerging economies: Brazil, Russia, India, China and South Africa. The five countries together represent about 42 per cent of the world's population, over 24 per cent of all land, and about 20 per cent of the world's total GDP, contributing a combined nominal GDP of more than US$14.9 trillion. Over the past decade trade between the BRICS and other regions such as North America, the EU and Japan has surpassed the US$2 trillion mark. Trade within the BRICS countries is growing at an average of 28 per cent per annum, reaching more than US$300 billion in 2012 and is expected to achieve US$500 billion by 2015. Obviously these numbers suggest that the BRICS has emerged as a major power bloc. However, given the size of its population and the economy as well as other socio-economic indicators, China seems to be the power pillar of this bloc.

The term was first introduced as the BRIC (without South Africa) through a report by Goldman Sachs in 2001, claiming the emergence of four countries as a major trade bloc (O'Neill, 2001). However, the idea received more attention with another Goldman Sachs report, which provided projection of the BRIC's growth by 2050 (Wilson & Purushothaman, 2003). Later another Goldman Sachs report further extended the analysis of the BRIC with other emerging economies (O'Neil, Wilson, Purushothaman & Stupnytska, 2005). These reports, using plots depicting the movements of variables, such as the BRIC countries' share in global trade, capital flows, intra-trade, foreign exchange reserves, and so forth, attempted to present the BRIC as an important trade bloc with the potential to play a significant role in future policy-making in the world. Later South Africa was included to make it what is now known as the BRICS, and its scope increased from a trade bloc to include broad economic integration and cooperation. Since then the bloc has received significant attention from both journalists and academic circles.

The aforementioned Goldman Sachs reports seem to have over-exaggerated the importance and operational capacity of the BRICS and of countries within the group. This led to a series of comments by journalists emphasizing the importance of the BRICS as an emerging power and economic and trade bloc. These expectations predicted that the BRICS would have a major impact on the future structure of global trade and finance, including 'the BRICS to have its own currency', 'the BRICS Bank as a possible replacement of IMF and the World Bank', 'the BRICS trade to reach US$6 trillion by 2015'.[1]

However, these claims, and the so-called 'power of the BRICS', are questioned by some other journalists.[2] The academic research shows concerns regarding the 'power' of the BRICS and questions its composition. Macfarlane (2006) and Cooper (2006) believe that Russia should not be part of the group as it is not even an emerging power. Using basically political arguments, Macfarlane (2006) remarked that Russia's first priority was its foreign policy which was to consolidate regional power and increase its influence within the former Soviet bloc. Cooper (2006) showed concerns regarding the lack of common features between Russia and the other BRIC countries. Russia does have a GDP (in US dollar terms) similar to Brazil and India, and a better growth rate than Brazil, while its export trade is due to oil exports. On social indicators, life expectancy in Russia is inferior to the levels found in Brazil and China, and the Human Development Index shows a declining trend even though educational standards are much higher than those of Brazil and India. Xiao (2006) believed that although China faced the problem of an aging population (perhaps mainly due to its one-child policy), it would not impact the projected growth trend, and that China would soon achieve the status of a developed country. Sotero and Armijo (2007) see a positive future outlook for Brazil and suggest that Brazil's future status in the international system (such as the BRICS) depends on its better economic management. Kregel (2009) has a positive outlook for Brazil but asserts that in the post-Global Financial Crisis (GFC) period the positive impact of export-led growth may not continue. The BRICS needs to build on domestic demand, and Brazil is in the best position to do so. Sinha and Dorschner (2010) suggest that India should focus on capacity building through political will and institutional reforms to keep pace with Brazil and China within the bloc. Muller (2011) remarked that there were many differences within the BRIC. For instance, India is part of the BRICS due to its large size but scores poorly regarding adequate nutrition, basic education and poverty. Russia has a bad record on governance, corruption, legal justice and human well-being. Roubini (2009) also observed that 'there are many differences between the BRICs members in terms of their growth outlook, the channels through which they were affected by the global recession and their future growth possibilities'. In brief, these academic studies are not very optimistic regarding the BRICS' potential to make a significant difference in the future global economic and financial set-up.

The purpose of this chapter is to further investigate the significance of the BRICS as a trade bloc[3] and its potential to be an important economic bloc[4] in the global world. It extends the aforementioned debate and provides a careful assessment of the scope and operational capacity of the BRICS. Through a careful analysis and an inside look at the basic economic and social indicators it shows that: (a) the BRICS is no more than a trade bloc; (b) the BRICS is basically China, as others are too small (and too different) in comparison; and (c) in scope and operational capacity the BRICS falls short of being a basic economic cooperation (as a group) as compared to the achievements of other major blocs such as the EU and Association of South East Asian Nations (ASEAN) in the mid-1980s.

This chapter is organized in the following manner. Section two provides an overview of the BRICS countries. Section three investigates the potential for an integrated currency arrangement for the BRICS countries, with a special focus on China and India, followed by section four, which looks into the BRICS intra-trade integration and its impact on other regions. Section five provides some empirical evidence on the impact of trade and financial openness on growth in the BRICS and the causal relationship of growth and trade within the BRICS countries. Finally some concluding remarks are provided in section six.

AN OVERVIEW OF THE BRICS COUNTRIES

The foreign ministers of Brazil, Russia, India and China met in New York in 2006 to initiate a series of high-level meetings for cooperation in certain areas, followed by a full diplomatic meeting in May 2008 in the Russian city of Yekaterinburg. A year later, the BRIC (without South Africa) was formed and the BRIC countries had their first Summit on 16 June 2009 in Yekaterinburg, with the heads of Brazil, Russia, India, and China attending the Summit. The focus of the first Summit was to discuss the possible reforms of the financial institutions given the global economic conditions and prospects of cooperation among the member.

In 2010 South Africa was included as a new member, thus changing the name to the BRICS. The group is an independent, international organization with a focus on commercial, political and cultural cooperation among member countries. Since its inception the group has held five summits, the last held in March 2013 in Durban (South Africa). As of 2012 the five BRICS countries represent almost 3 billion people, with a combined nominal GDP of US$14.9 trillion, and an estimated US$4 trillion in combined foreign reserves (Wikipedia, 2013a). It is important to note that most of the economic development in all of the BRICS countries dates back merely two decades. It is also important to provide account of the developmental process experienced by each of the member countries in the last few decades before we analyse and compare the economic performance of the group as a whole.

Brazil

Brazil is the richest and fastest growing economy in the South American region. The Brazilian economy weathered the GFC better than most of the world's largest economies, bolstered predominantly by the huge domestic demand that pushed Brazil rapidly into a recovery position. Goldman Sachs predicted Brazil to be one of the five largest economies in the world in the decades to come (Wilson & Stupnytska, 2007).

The current growth performance of Brazil dates back just over a decade, as a result of some bold reforms changing the economy's path from basically an agriculture-driven nation and an import-driven economy into a rapidly expanding and highly diverse economy. The liberalization policies were initiated in the 1990s when the then government put into place a number of measures to open up the market, for instance by facilitating free market access to the IT sector or abandoning the statutory monopoly in the energy and telecommunications sectors. Measures were also taken to boost investment and trade. The positive economic prospects and stable economic environment helped to attract foreign investment, expanding such sectors as the services and heavy industries. A capital inflow of more than US$400 billion was recorded in 2009 (World Bank, 2012).

The Brazilian economy now ranks eighth, in terms of GDP, in the world. Only 6.1 per cent of its economic activity is attributed to agriculture, whereas industrial production amounts to 25.4 per cent and services account for 68.5 per cent. Inflationary pressures have also eased due to strict monetary policy reducing inflation to less than 5 per cent on average. Bovespa, the Sao Paulo Stock Exchange, is the largest in South America and accounts for more than 70 per cent of the entire region's trade volume (Datamonitor, 2010).

Despite this high profile, Brazil still suffers from some major problems, such as corruption, ranking 69th out of 174 countries (Transparency International, 2012) and an inadequate infrastructure. Similarly not much attention was paid to the education sector during the period of economic reforms. Corrupt practices act as a deterrent for both domestic and foreign investment, and hamper long-run economic growth. High crime rates and piracy are other major obstacles in Brazil's long-term and stable growth path (IIPA, 2012).

It is obvious that Brazil's current economic environment is the result of significant reform policies and good macroeconomic management. However, Brazil does not score well on some social indicators. The true effect of these economic policies is contingent upon investing in education, combating corruption, and controlling crime to provide a secure investment environment for both domestic residents and foreigners. The future outlook seems promising but a lot needs to be done to achieve sustainable economic growth.

Russia

In terms of GDP, Russia is the ninth largest economy in the world while it is considered the sixth largest based on purchasing power parity (PPP). Russia has rich natural resources, including oil, natural gas, coal and precious metals, which makes a significant contribution towards Russia's current account surplus. Russia was affected by the 2008 GFC and suffered with a recession in late 2008 and early 2009, after ten years of upward growth. However, this recession was short-lived and the stable growth resumed in late 2009 and 2010. Economic growth was predicted to be around 3.4 per cent of GDP during 2012 (Rose & Tanas, 2013).

Since the collapse of the Soviet Union in the late 1980s, Russia has gradually moved from a centrally planned economy to a market one and has integrated itself with the world through trade. Russia only initiated economic reforms in the 1990s by privatizing the agricultural and industrial sectors, with notable exceptions in the energy and defence-related sectors. The first set of reforms was announced by President Yeltsin in October 1991; however, they did not work, resulting in economic collapse creating hyperinflation, a huge debt burden and eventually threatening the country's solvency, the so-called 1998 Russian Financial Crisis. The deteriorating economic conditions increased the level of poverty, corruption in the public and private sectors and violent crimes, leading to massive capital outflows and making economic conditions even more difficult.

When Vladimir Putin became President, Russia was effectively bankrupt as it owed more money to the IMF than it had in foreign currency reserves. Putin's government brought in a series of sweeping reforms, resulting in a sixfold increase in nominal GDP.[5] By 2013 Russia's GDP is expected to cross the $2 trillion level. Unprecedented economic growth and political stability also helped Russia to attract huge foreign investment, increasing foreign exchange reserves to above $600 billion. The outlook for Russia is good. However, Russia needs to implement policies to have a more global perspective rather than simply exerting influence within the former Soviet Union (Wikipedia, 2013d).

India

India embarked on policies of major economic reforms and openness (from import substitution to export promotion) in the early 1990s. Until 1955 the Indian economy depended heavily on the agricultural sector, whilst the industrial sector made a minimal contribution. Since then the structure of the Indian economy has changed significantly, with a remarkable decline in the share of the agricultural sector to only 20 per cent from a huge 60 per cent in the earlier period. The series of reforms implemented in the 1990s provided a much needed boost to saving and investment, by increasing investment to GDP ratio to above 23 per cent (Ariff & Khalid, 2000). Although the reforms in India are linked to the major policy initiatives introduced in 1991, there were some steps taken as early as the 1980s. Unlike other emerging economies, Indian reforms are characterized as 'gradualism'. These reforms have completely transformed the Indian economy, including the elimination of quantitative controls on imports of industrial machinery, a reduction in the number of industries subject to government licensing, an expansion of the role of the private sector, the dismantling of import controls, a lowering of customs duties, a reduction in tariffs on imports of capital goods, a modest tax system rationalization, an increase in foreign direct investment, a flexible exchange rate, and a restructuring of the government's role in the Indian economy. The obvious result was the increase in India's GDP growth from 5.7 per cent during 1980–90 to 9.6 per cent during 2005–07 (Wikipedia, 2013c).

By early 2000 India was completely integrated into the global economy and at present is an important player in the global world. Although India scores well in terms of economic performance (growth), its record is not so good based on social indicators, including education, basic health and poverty. Without allocating sufficient resources to improve the standard of living and providing essential social services, India may not be considered a developed country.

China

The main difference between pre-reform economic models of India and China is that China was a completely closed economy, whereas India had an open financial sector and private enterprises but with trade controls and a policy of import substitution. Historically China followed a similar path to the former Soviet model of economic structures and development strategies, resulting in numerous but inefficient state-owned enterprises. A closed economy was to grow from internal demand with minimal external openness. The only visible change that occurred during a short period between 1971 and 1975 was a slight increase of state investment in agricultural inputs such as machinery and fertilizers, with heavy industry still being the major recipient of state investment. The transition from the planned economy to a market economy in China started in the 1980s, with the introduction of wide-ranging reforms, including the introduction of a contract system, wider enterprise autonomy and privatization, trade facilitation and openness, and financial sector reforms. These policies resulted in China's integration into the global world and eventually becoming a member of the WTO.

During the last three decades China has attained extraordinary levels of economic progress by any standard. China's GDP growth increased from 10.3 per cent during 1980–90, to 11.7 per cent during 2005–07. As of 2012 China has emerged as a major economic power accounting for about 10 per cent of world GDP. China showed a significant improvement in reducing inflation from above 500 per cent during the 1980s, to single digits in most of the second half of 2000, sustaining a growth rate of above 10 per cent on average, attracting huge foreign capital, accumulating about US$3 trillion of foreign exchange reserves and having a total trade volume of over US$2.8 trillion. China has also improved its social indicators, although it still has to further restructure its industrial sector, combat corruption, enforce laws to reduce piracy, and improve upon private property rights (Wikipedia, 2013b).

South Africa

Until 1994 South Africa suffered with a long period of colonization by different countries and nationals including the Dutch, French, Germans and British. In the post-World War period, this resulted in a strictly race-based policy (Apartheid) which prevailed until the 1990s. The first independent election was held in 1994 giving power to the African National Congress (ANC) party. The newly elected government inherited long years of internal conflicts and external sanctions. As a result the main task of the new government of the ANC was to restore law and order and design economic policies. The tasks were difficult but the performance achieved in less than two decades was unprecedented. In 2000, the government of President Thabo Mbeki implemented policies to promote growth, attract foreign investment, launch privatization, reduce government spending and introduce trade and financial liberalization and labour reforms.

South Africa was indirectly affected by the 2008 GFC but showed a gradual recovery, mainly due to its prudent fiscal and monetary policies. The far-reaching reforms of the late 1990s and early 2000 helped South Africa to establish a stable political environment, a well-capitalized banking system, a good regulatory system and a focus on research and development. Compared with Brazil and Russia, South Africa has managed to significantly improve its governance structure and copyright and patent policies.

At present, the South African economy is the largest in Africa accounting for 24 per cent of the region's GDP (PPP-based). Its GDP grew at 3.2 per cent in 2012. Prices were steady due to the policy of 'inflation targeting' by the South African Reserve Bank, reducing inflation to 5.6 per cent in 2012 ('South Africa: Economy Overview', 2013). The 2012–13 Global Competitiveness report (World Economic Forum, 2013) ranked South Africa second in the world for the accountability of its private institutions, and third for its financial market development. The country's securities exchange, the JSE, is ranked among the top 20 in the world in terms of size.

South Africa also has some major issues. Unemployment is extremely high (about 25 per cent) and a quarter of South Africans live on less than US$1.25 a day. Such high levels of unemployment and income inequality are considered to be the main cause of economic and social problems (such as the high crime rate), making it difficult to attract foreign investment. South Africa has also not invested much in education (spending under 4 per cent of GDP) and is ranked poorly in this category (India ranks the worst among the BRICS countries). South Africa ranked 11th out of 14 countries when it comes to the country's use of technology and innovation, putting the African country behind Korea as well as the other BRICS countries.

The BRICS as a Bloc – a Comparison

Although the BRICS countries have formally formed a group and are committed to the policies of trade integration as well as cooperation in other areas, it is evident from the earlier discussion that there are major differences in terms of the economic and social environments of each member country. Goldman Sachs (O'Neill et al., 2005) reported Growth Environment Scores (GES) for the BRIC, looking at a number of micro and macroeconomic and social indicators such as political stability, openness to trade, fiscal position, inflation, external debt position, investment,

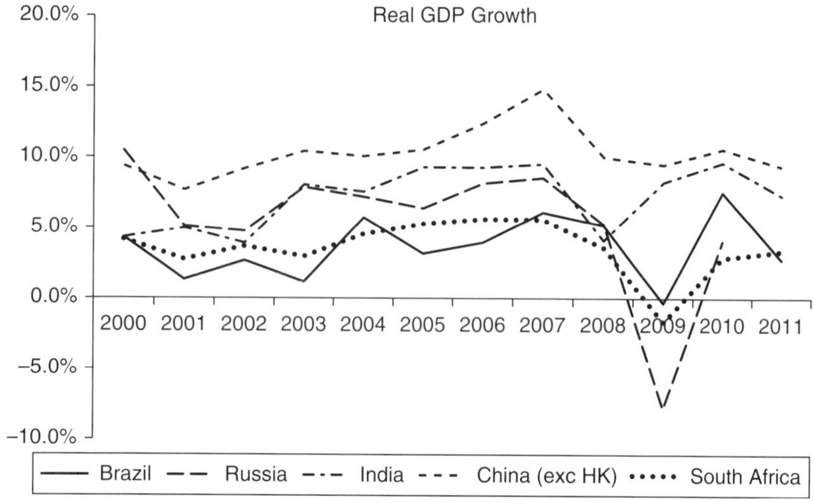

Source: IMF (2012b).

Figure 10.1 The BRICS – Real GDP growth, 2000–11

adoption of technology, life expectancy, education, corruption and so forth. In general, the BRIC countries were placed in the top half of the rankings for developing countries and above the developing country mean. In a total of 133 countries, China scored the highest ranking (16th), followed by Russia (44th), then Brazil (58th) and finally India (60th). Just as a comparison, the same report ranked Luxemburg at the top, Canada eighth, the US tenth, and Korea in 17th place, thus showing China scoring the best in Asia. The performance of the BRICS countries on the basis of some of these listed macroeconomic indicators suggest that the positions of these countries have not changed significantly since then and China is still the single major player in the group.

With respect to the performance of the BRICS countries since 2000 using a few economic and social indicators, Figure 10.1 shows real GDP growth in the BRICS countries over the period 2000–11. Growth in general faced many cycles but the main downturn was felt in the 2008–09 period in the aftermath of the GFC. Russia suffered the most with a recession during 2009, followed by Brazil and South Africa dipping into the negative for a short period before showing some signs of recovery. China's GDP growth was around 10 per cent during the period, while India experienced an average growth rate of above 6 per cent. Figure 10.2 shows that all member countries managed to reduce inflation within single digits, with China experiencing a disinflation, first in 2002 and then again in 2009.

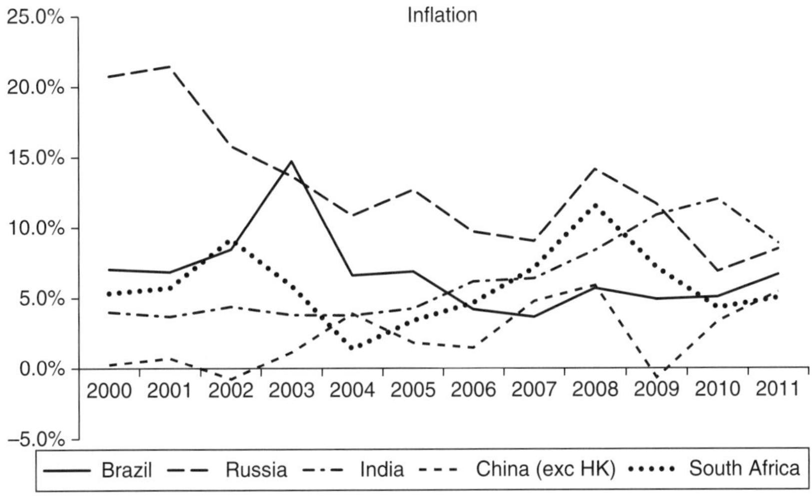

Source: IMF (2012b).

Figure 10.2 The BRICS – Inflation, 2000–11

In terms of domestic and external balances (see Figure 10.3 and 10.4), Brazil is the only country enjoying twin surpluses, maintaining an average of above 3 per cent of budget surplus/GDP ratio and an average of about 4 per cent of current account surplus/GDP ratio, with the exception of 2010 and 2011 when it recorded a marginal deficit (less than 1 per cent of GDP) in external balances. Russia enjoyed a budget surplus/GDP ratio of above 10 per cent, including a peak of 20 per cent in 2005, but then recorded a deficit of about 10 per cent in 2009 (due to the GFC) and 5 per cent in 2010. The domestic account then recovered and showed a surplus of around 5 per cent of GDP in 2011. The external account for Russia showed a surplus of above 10 per cent on average, as a ratio to GDP. The remaining three countries (India, China and South Africa) recorded a budget deficit during the entire sample period. The statistics for China showed a consistent current account surplus, maintaining an average of about 5 per cent of GDP, whereas South Africa had a surplus external account until 2003 and then recorded a deficit. India was the only country facing a twin deficit, reaching a maximum of budget deficit of over 6.6 per cent of GDP in 2009 and over 6 per cent of current account deficit to GDP ratio in 2008.

Table 10.1 shows another set of macroeconomic indicators for 2011. The size of population is a major difference among the group, ranging from over 1 billion for China and India, to 197 million for Brazil and 142

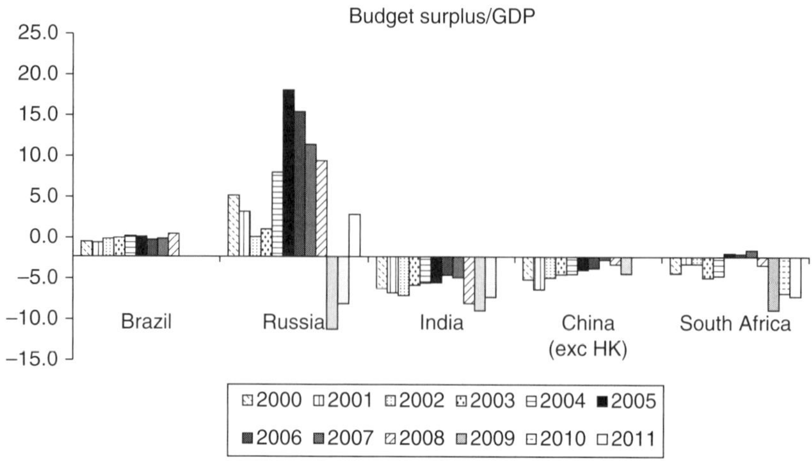

Source: IMF (2012b).

Figure 10.3 The BRICS – Domestic (fiscal) balances, 2000–11

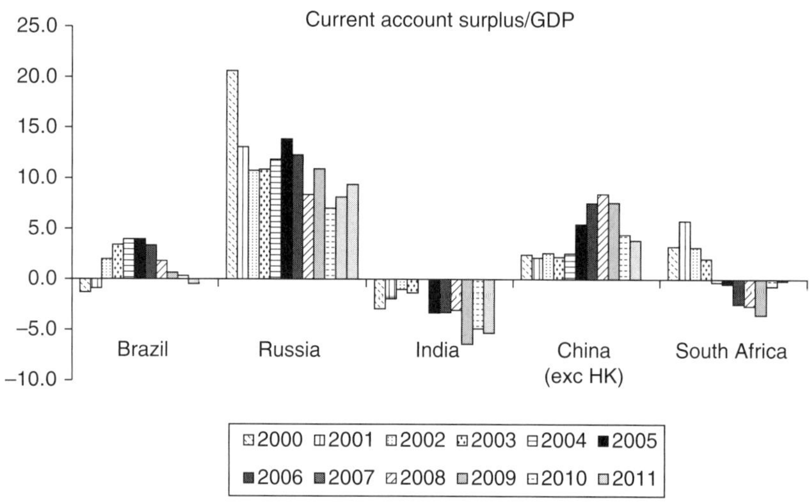

Source: IMF (2012b).

Figure 10.4 The BRICS – External (current account) balances, 2000–11

Table 10.1 Macroeconomic performance and growth (through trade)

Categories/countries	Brazil	Russia	India	China	South Africa
Population (million)	197	142	1241	1344	51
GDP (2011; current US$ billion)	2476	1857	1848	7298	408
GDP Goldman Sachs proj. (2025)	2280	2873	3617	11677	–
Per capita GDP (US$)	12594	13089	1489	5430	8070
Poverty ($1.25/day)	6.1	0	32.7	13.1	13.8
Exp. of G&S (% of GDP)	12%	28 %	25%	29%	2%
Imp.of G&S (% of GDP)	13%	21%	30%	27%	28%
Ease of doing business (2012)	126	120	132	91	35

Notes: G&S = goods and services.

Sources: Author's own calculations and World Bank (2012).

million for Russia, to just 51 million in the case of South Africa. The size of the economy is inconsistent with the population size, with China having a GDP of more than US$7 trillion, followed by Brazil with a GDP of US$2.476 trillion, Russia and India with a GDP of US$1.857 trillion and US$1.848 trillion respectively, and South Africa at the bottom with a GDP of US$408 billion. Combining the two figures gives us per capital GDP (or wealth of individuals), with Brazil at the top with US$12 594, and India at the bottom with US$1489. Obviously India has the highest poverty level, with 32.7 per cent of the population living on less than US$1.25 a day. Trade concentration is the same in all countries (except Brazil), registering export/GDP and import/GDP ratios of above 25 per cent. The same ratios for Brazil are reported around 12 per cent. Finally the 'doing business' indicator shows South Africa is the most business-friendly country while India is the least.

Regarding the financial market indicators for the BRICS countries for 2011, Table 10.2 shows a diverse reserve position for the group. China has accumulated a massive US$3.3 trillion of reserves, accounting for 44.6 per cent of GDP, followed by Russia with 26.8 per cent, India 16.2 per cent, Brazil 14.2 per cent and South Africa only 12 per cent. China is also the recipient of more than US$185 billion of foreign direct investment (FDI) during the same year, while the remaining four collectively attract FDI of US$117.2 billion, with South Africa registering only US$1.2 billion. India and China are the largest recipients of remittances, accounting for over US$50 billion, while Brazil, Russia and South Africa receive US$10.4 billion in total (South Africa at the bottom with US$1.1 billion). Finally the numbers for

Table 10.2 The BRICS' finances – A comparison (2011)

	Reserves incl. gold (US$ million)	FDI net flows (US$ billion), 2010	Remittances (US$ billion)	Market capitalisation (% of GDP)
Brazil	352 (14.2%)	48.5 (1.94%)	4.0 (0.16%)	49.6
Russia	497 (26.8%)	43.3 (2.33%)	5.3 (0.29%)	42.9
India	299 (16.2%)	24.2 (1.31%)	54.0 (2.92%)	54.9
China	3255 (44.6%)	185.1 (2.54%)	53.0 (0.73%)	46.4
South Africa	49 (12%)	1.2 (0.29%)	1.1 (0.27%)	209.6

Source: Author's own calculations.

market capitalization indicate that South Africa is at the top with a market capitalization/GDP ratio of 209 per cent. The remaining four countries record a market capitalization/GDP ratio of around 50 per cent each.

It is evident from the preceding discussion and the supporting statistics in this section that the BRICS countries have diverse economic, social and political environments, making it difficult to consider the group as an emerging economic bloc similar to the EU or ASEAN. The next sections will further investigate the potential for the BRICS to become a bloc and test the conjectures presented in the media reports.

CURRENCY ARRANGEMENTS IN THE BRICS COUNTRIES: CURRENT SCENARIO AND FUTURE OUTLOOK

The issue of having an optimal currency arrangement has been discussed in detail in the context of emerging economies. In the BRICS context there are three questions that may be of interest for further elaboration and discussion in view of the claims made by journalists. These claims include: (a) the BRICS countries to have their own currency, the BRICS dollar and/or (b) the BRICS to have its own financial manager similar to those of the World Bank and the IMF. Obviously these claims have an extreme, and to a large extent, unrealistic approach. These claims, however, deserve a thorough assessment based on academic and economic principles. With respect to the first claim, that the BRICS countries are set to have their own currency, in order for any region to have its own currency, it MUST satisfy the requirements of the optimum currency area (OCA). The requirements to satisfy OCA have been widely discussed in the literature in the contexts of the EU and ASEAN. The research overwhelmingly agrees that the EU did satisfy the requirements of the OCA. On the contrary, a rich debate for ASEAN does not conform to this conjecture. As these issues have been widely discussed and published papers are available, there is no added value to replicate this literature and report country/region specific findings. It should be noted though that intra-ASEAN trade amounts to about 40 per cent of total ASEAN trade. Intra-BRICS trade is well below this figure.[6] Further, the composition of the BRICS countries is spread over Asia (China, India and Russia), Europe (Russia), Africa (South Africa) and the Americas (Brazil). As such, the BRICS does not represent a region (against a well-known gravity model). Additionally there are the political differences between China and India, and China and Russia.[7] It is then obvious to deduce that if the ASEAN does not qualify as an OCA, then the BRICS definitely has no chance of satisfying such requirements. Hence the possibility of a BRICS currency is almost impossible.

As an alternative to a BRICS currency, can the BRICS adopt a single major currency as an anchor currency? An obvious choice is to look at the US dollar, euro and yen as potential anchors. The yen gained importance in the post-East Asian crisis period but later lost its strength. The euro was expected to be a stable and strong currency when it was launched in 1999 and was predicted to replace the US dollar as an anchor in many countries. However, that did not happen either, and the current problems regarding the euro do not show a positive outlook for it. During the last few years China has emerged as an important player and economically a superpower in the world. Given the huge trade volume and massive currency reserves of China, some anticipated the Chinese currency, the renminbi, to be an anchor for East Asia (the same argument could hold for the BRICS). Figure 10.5 shows how strongly China keeps its currency to the US dollar. Using monthly exchange rates, the plot shows the changes in exchange rates for both currencies. Although China claims to have adopted a free-float currency regime since 2006, the plot does not show any significant difference between the two currencies.

Although the empirical evidence on this issue is mixed, it points to the dominance of the US dollar as a transaction currency in many East Asian countries including China. In a study by Khalid and Rajaguru (2011) sufficient evidence was found that the US dollar is still a dominant currency in East Asia. One can argue that if East Asia has the US dollar as the main currency and that China has a pseudo-pegged arrangement with the US dollar, then the chances of any other currency within the BRICS, other than the US dollar as an anchor, is almost impossible.

A third and final alternative is the possibility of a currency basket for the BRICS. Table 10.3 shows the reserves position of each country within the BRICS, from 2000 to 2011. It is interesting to observe that the reserve

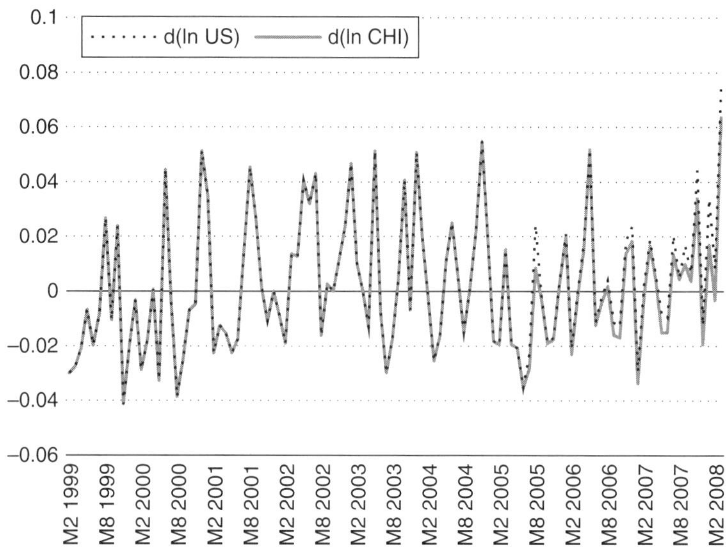

Source: Author's own calculations.

Figure 10.5 Changes in US dollar and Chinese yuan (1999–2008)

Table 10.3 Reserves (excluding gold) as a per cent of GDP

Year	2000	2005	2011
Brazil	5.37	5.80	15.72
Russia	9.35	23.29	26.25
India	8.43	16.10	16.10
China	14.04	35.85	42.79
South Africa	4.99	7.48	11.70

Source: IMF (2012b).

position of Brazil tripled during the period but was about 16 per cent of its GDP. Russia's reserve also tripled (perhaps due to oil price hikes) but constituted about 26 per cent of GDP. South Africa's reserves more than doubled and accounted for about 12 per cent of GDP. India's reserves just doubled with 16 per cent of GDP. China's reserves during the same period also tripled, accounting for about 43 per cent of GDP.

Given the size of China and India, this study focuses on these two countries to investigate a currency basket for the two which may also be used for the remaining three countries. The empirical evidence is provided in

Table 10.4 Bilateral currency weights

Country	Own basket			Trade weight based common basket			Currency based common basket[a]	
	Currencies	2004	2010	Currencies	2004	2010	2004	2010
China	Euro	18.6	25.1	Euro	26.54	30.47	0.0	3.13
	Yen	22.1	19.9	Yen	34.50	32.26	0.0	0.0
	USD	22.4	25.8	USD	38.96	37.27	100.0	96.87
	HK dollar	14.9	15.3					
	Won	11.8	13.9					
	NTD	10.3						
India	Euro	33.814	28.328	Euro	14.135	11.463	43.87	46.64
	Yen			Yen	34.50	32.26	19.49	21.43
	USD	25.698	18.413	USD	10.741	7.451	36.64	31.93
	RMB	13.997	25.350	China	5.451	10.158		
	NTD							

Notes: [a] indicates a currency based common basket is determined using a VAR model.

Source: Khalid and Rajaguru (2011).

Table 10.4. For this analysis two different methods are used, endogenous and exogenous weights. For this basket the currencies of all countries with which China and India have a trade volume of more than 5 per cent are used. From there the basket weight is computed. A comparison between 2004 and 2010 suggests that for China, the US dollar has maintained its strength with above 25 per cent weight in the basket. The euro has gained about 10 per cent but at the cost of the yen and other currencies. In India, the US dollar lost its weight from 25.7 per cent in 2004 to about 18.4 per cent in 2010. The euro has lost its weight but the renminbi has emerged with above 25 per cent weight in the Indian rupee. For a common basket the focus is on three major currencies: the US dollar, the yen and the euro. In the case of a trade-based common basket (exogenous weights), the US dollar has the highest weight in renminbi, whereas the yen is stronger than the Indian rupee. For the currency-based common basket (endogenous weights), the US dollar is again dominant for renminbi whereas the euro has the highest weight in the Indian rupee.

The discussion in this section suggests that the BRICS countries in general are not ready to have their own currency. Given China's undeclared foreign exchange policy of keeping the renminbi pegged to the US dollar, any discussion of own currency arrangements is purely hypothetical. If so, the remaining observations by journalists on the establishment of a BRICS Bank are far from reality.

A TRADE BLOC NOT AN ECONOMIC BLOC

The preceding discussion suggests that the BRICS cannot be treated as an economic bloc. The natural question is whether it is a trade bloc. The BRICS is usually referred to as a 'Three Trillion Dollar Trade' Club. In fact the total trade of the BRICS is recorded as US$3.41 trillion. Although it may be a convincing argument to consider the BRICS as a major trading bloc, a more careful analysis shows that China is the main contributor to this three trillion dollar trade for the bloc.

Table 10.5 shows that China alone accounted for $2.28 trillion (about 67 per cent of total trade) of this $3.41 trillion during 2011. The share of the remaining countries in the BRICS was 33 per cent in total (Russia: 11.6 per cent; India: 11.1 per cent; Brazil: 7.4 per cent; and South Africa: 3.4 per cent), and less than half what China contributed. These numbers are consistent with Figure 10.6 where a time-series plot from 2001 to 2011 presents the share of each country's total trade.

Another important indicator of a trade bloc is intra-bloc trade. Again the numbers presented in Table 10.5 do not suggest the BRICS to be a trade bloc. Table 10.5 looks at the five major trading partners (both for exports and imports) for each of the BRICS countries. For China, none of the other BRICS countries appears as the five largest export destinations or importing sources. It is evident that Chinese exports to or imports from any country within the bloc is less than 5 per cent. Of the remaining BRICS countries, does any one of those appear as one of the five largest trading partners? China is the only country that appears as a trading partner for the rest of the bloc. For Russia, China is the fourth largest export destination whereas China is at the second place for Russian imports. In the case of India, China is the third most important country for exports while Indian imports from China are placed at number one. For Brazil, China is the largest export destination and is the second largest for its imports. For South Africa, again China turns out to be the most important trading partner for both exports and imports. India is the only other BRICS country that appears as the fifth largest export destination for South Africa but it is still less than 5 per cent of total exports.

Finally trade balance statistics for the year 2011 show that China enjoyed a record $233 billion trade surplus, higher than the total exports of India, Brazil and South Africa. Russia is the only other country with a trade surplus (due to oil) accounting for $188 billion. India, Brazil and South Africa reported a deficit of $153 billion, $30 billion and $6.9 billion respectively. Figure 10.7 also confirms that China and South Africa were the only two countries in the bloc with trade/GDP ratios of above 50 per

Table 10.5 Three trillion dollar trade club (2011)

	Total trade in dollar (US$, million)	Exp. of G&S (% of GDP)	Major exports	Major export partners	Imp. of G&S (% of GDP)	Major imports	Major import partners	Trade deficit
China	2278056	12	Electrical and other machinery, including data processing equipment, apparel, textiles, iron and steel, optical and medical equipment	US 20.03%, Hong Kong 12.03%, Japan 8.32%, South Korea 4.55%, Germany 4.27% (2009)	13	Electrical and other machinery, oil and mineral fuels, optical and medical equipment, metal ores, plastics, organic chemicals	Japan 12.27%, Hong Kong 10.06%, South Korea 9.04%, US 7.66%, Taiwan 6.84%, Germany 5.54% (2009)	Exports: $1897bn Imports: $1664bn
Russia	395643	28	Petroleum and petroleum products, natural gas, metals, wood and wood products, chemicals, and a wide variety of civilian and military manufactures	Netherlands 10.62%, Italy 6.46%, Germany 6.24%, China 5.69%, Turkey 4.3%, Ukraine 4.01% (2009)	21	machinery, vehicles, pharmaceutical products, plastic, semi-finished metal products, meat fruits and nuts, optical and medical instruments, iron, steel	Germany 14.39%, China 13.98%, Ukraine 5.48%, Italy 4.84%, US 4.46% (2009)	Exports: $498.6bn Imports: $310bn
India	377225	25	Petroleum products, precious stones, machinery, iron and steel, chemicals, vehicles, apparel	US 12.6%, UAE 12.2%, China 8.1%, Hong Kong 4.1% (2009)	30	Crude oil, precious stones, machinery, fertilizer, iron and steel, chemicals.	China 12.4%, UAE 6.5%, Saudi Arabia 5.8%, US 5.7%, Australia 4.5% (2009)	Exports: $298bn Imports: $451bn

Table 10.5 (continued)

	Total trade in dollar (US$, million)	Exp. of G&S (% of GDP)	Major exports	Major export partners	Imp.of G&S (% of GDP)	Major imports	Major import partners	Trade deficit
Brazil	252 440	29	Transport equipment, machinery, steel, airplanes, paper, electric machinery, iron, ore, soybeans, footwear, coffee, autos, automotive parts, machinery	China 17.3%, United States 10.1%, Argentina 8.9%, Netherlands 5.3%, Japan 3.7% (2011)	27	Machinery, electrical and transport equipment, chemical products, oil, automotive parts, electronics	United States 15.0%, China 14.5%, Argentina 7.5%, Germany 6.7%, South Korea 4.5% (2011)	Exports: $256bn Imports: $226.2bn
South Africa	103 500	26	Gold, diamonds, platinum, other metals and minerals, machinery and equipment	China 13.7%, U.S. 10.1%, Japan 8.7%, Germany 7.3%, UK 7.1%, India 4.3% (2010)	28	Machinery and equipment, chemicals, petroleum products, scientific instruments, foodstuffs	China 13.4%, Germany 11.2%, U.S. 7%, Saudi Arabia 5.3%, Japan 4.7%, Iran 4.3%, UK 4.3% (2010)	Exports: $92.4bn Imports: $98.9bn
Total	3 406 864							

Sources: Author's own calculations and Wikipedia (2013a).

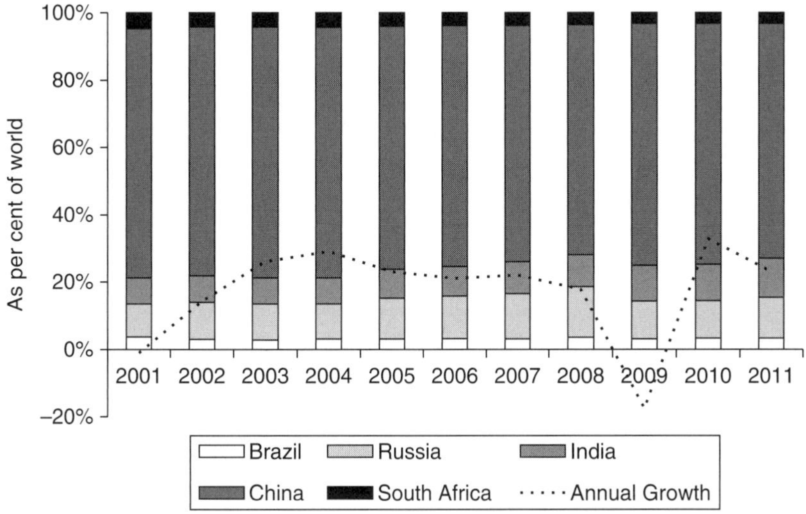

Source: IMF (2012a).

Figure 10.6 Trade share within the BRICS, 2001–11

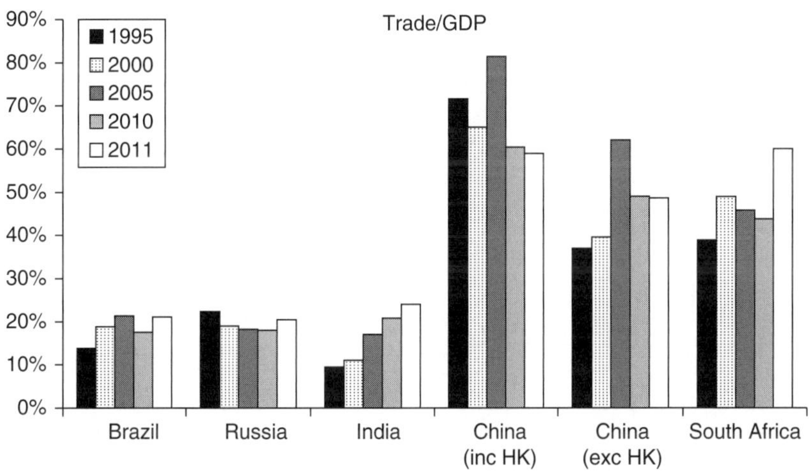

Source: IMF (2012a).

Figure 10.7 The BRICS' trade balances

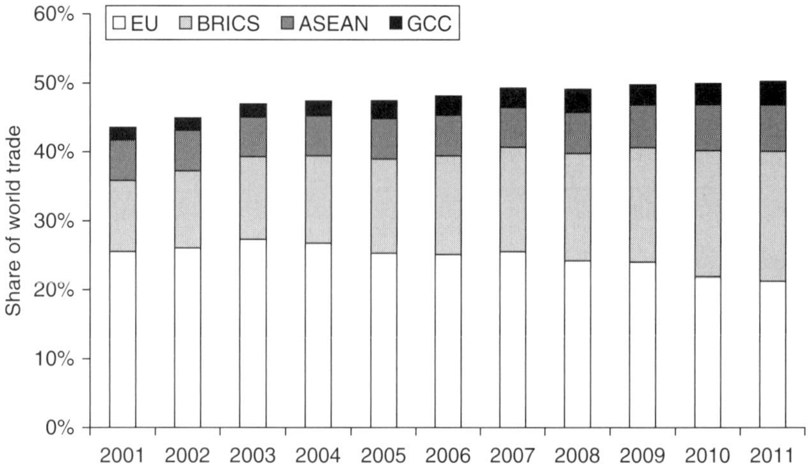

Source: IMF (2012a).

Figure 10.8 The BRICS' share of world trade, 2001–11

cent. Since 1995 the remaining three countries maintained a trade/GDP ratio of around 20 per cent. These numbers strongly contradict the claim that the BRICS is even a trade bloc.

However, Figure 10.8 looks at the BRICS in comparison with other trade and economic blocs such as the EU, ASEAN and Gulf Cooperating Council (GCC). It shows that as a percentage of world share in total trade, the BRICS has increased significantly since 2001 and overtaken the EU reflecting the importance of the BRICS as an emerging trade bloc. The published statistics thus support the view that the BRICS is indeed a trade bloc, with China being the major player.

GROWTH-TRADE LINKAGES WITHIN THE BRICS – EMPIRICAL EVIDENCE

Most of the discussion in earlier sections of this chapter focuses on providing evidence on whether the BRICS can be considered an important economic bloc. It is obvious from the preceding discussion that the BRICS is just a trade bloc, with China in the driving seat. Although there are some common factors within the BRICS countries, it can also be asserted from the data analysis that there are also a wide range of differences, making it difficult to have any significant impact as a group, at least in the near future.

A final segment of this issue is to use some empirical evidence using data from the BRICS countries to investigate linkages between trade and economic growth. This question has not been directly investigated in the existing research, but studies have been conducted exploring the determinants of growth, using data from the BRICS countries with a focus on India and China. It may be useful to briefly review this literature before moving to formal statistical tests. Haddad (2007) finds that 'production networks centred on China have significantly contributed to growth in East Asia'. The paper also argues that any conflicts between two countries or among countries in the bloc could be a threat to the competitiveness of firms within the region. Kowalski (2008) shows that Chinese reforms, especially in the manufacturing sector, have contributed to China's better growth performance compared to India. Kowalski finds that while China has implemented important policies in trade liberalization and attracting FDI, India made a significant effort to reduce tariffs on non-agricultural products and selected non-tariff barriers while still keeping some moderate protection within the manufacturing sector. This is one area where India may need to focus its future policies. Kuboniwa (2011), however, observes that half of Russia's growth can be explained by trading gains, while such trading gains contributed to about 20 per cent of Brazilian growth. The impact of trading gains for Indian and Chinese growth was found to be almost negligible. Looking at the impact of trade integration, Kose, Prasad and Terrones (2006) find that countries with more openness (open to trade) have a relatively higher capacity to tolerate volatility without affecting growth. Using a gravity model, the IMF (2011) looks at the positive spillovers of the BRICS on low-income countries and found that (a) the emergence of the BRICS has a positive impact on low-income countries' exports and terms of trade, and (b) closer economic ties between the BRICS and low-income countries are expected to sustain economic growth in the future. Similarly Samake and Yang (2011) using a Global Vector Auto-Regression (GVAR) model find that rapid growth in the BRIC (without South Africa) has increased their trade and financial integration with low-income countries. The empirical findings of this study suggest that the direct (and positive) spillovers from the BRIC to low-income countries are 'significant and persistent' with a positive impact on low-income countries' growth. This study also finds a significant impact of indirect spillovers from the BRIC to low-income countries through global demand and price channels.

Another interesting question, and perhaps a testable hypothesis, is to empirically verify how closely economic growth and trade linkages work within the BRICS. More specifically, this section is devoted to empirically explore this hypothesis. The following hypotheses are tested:

1. Are there any growth linkages among the BRICS countries (does economic growth represent a causal relationship)?
2. Are there any trade linkages among the BRICS countries (does trade represent a causal relationship)?
3. Does growth cause trade or vice versa among the BRICS countries (is there any direct or reverse causality between economic growth and trade)?

To test these hypotheses, causality tests on time-series data from four countries in the group are performed. Russia is not included in this analysis due to the non-availability of complete data. For empirical analysis we used two variables, a growth variable and openness variable. Growth (GDPPC) is measured as the annual per capita economic growth based on GDP. Openness is measured as a ratio of total trade (imports plus exports) to GDP. Depending on data availability, data for Brazil spans from 1985–2011, India from 1985 to 2010, China from 1985 to 2011 and South Africa from 1985 to 2011. Both variables are used in log-form.

The paper first performs a unit root test as a diagnostic test to determine the order of integration of the variables included in the empirical analysis. Augmented Dickey-Fuller (ADF) and Phillip-Peron (PP) are the most commonly used tests of stationarity. The results of ADF and PP tests as reported in Table 10.6 suggest that both growth (LRGDPPC) and

Table 10.6 Unit root test

Country/variables	Levels		First difference	
	ADF	PP	ADF	PP
Brazil				
LRGDPPC (growth)	−0.799576	−0.052239	−2.298724	−2.430484
LTOGGDP (openness)	−2.921187	−0.164435	N/A	−8.435741
India				
LRGDPPC (growth)	3.015249	3.015249	7.885035	−7.920898
LTOGGDP (openness)	−0.084901	0.294490	−10.27283	−10.24398
China				
LRGDPPC (growth)	−0.610672	−0.010674	−3.752463	−2.515804
LTOGGDP (openness)	−0.965329	−1.415879	−4.427713	−4.321144
South Africa				
LRGDPPC (growth)	1.230622	1.706610	−3.874734	−3.803880
LTOGGDP (openness)	−1.618201	−1.667864	−7.042109	−8.536470

Notes: According to MacKinnon (1996) one-sided p-values: –3.542097 (1%); –2.910019 (55); and –2.592645 (1%).

Source: Author's own calculations.

Table 10.7 Causality tests

A: Cause/Effect(GDP)	Brazil	India	China	South Africa
Brazil		3.38334*	1.67768	0.07263
India	2.82472***		9.33266*	2.78759**
China	0.18932	1.01094		2.05212
South Africa	4.00386*	1.25746	5.64982*	
B: Cause/Effect (Trade)				
Brazil		2.57502***	1.02856	0.37599
India	1.32243		3.85107**	6.88972*
China	0.65582	2.29764		1.34628
South Africa	8.49224*	0.36559	3.98787**	
C: Cause/Effect (GDP/ Trade)				
Brazil		4.44619*	1.63546	7.43892*
India	1.95081		0.53502	7.50553*
China	4.77792**	2.60388***		1.74301
South Africa	0.25576	5.12869*	0.11789	
D: Cause/Effect (Trade/ GDP)				
Brazil		3.54026*	1.65559	0.84304
India	0.20922		0.25740	1.46446
China	0.04113	1.84898		1.19149
South Africa	0.56387	1.03495	6.66735*	

Notes: Based on F-statistics, ***, ** and * denote statistical significance at 1%, 5% and 10% level.

Source: Author's own calculations.

openness variables (LTOGGDP) are first-difference stationary, I (1), for all four countries. Openness variable is also found to be first-difference stationary for all variables.[8]

Table 10.7 presents the result of the causality tests. The tests are subdivided into four panels. Panel A shows the causal relationship of economic growth among sample countries. The results suggest a bidirectional causal relation in economic growth between India and Brazil. Economic growth in India causes economic growth in China and South Africa, while growth in South Africa causes GDP growth in Brazil. Economic growth in China does not influence GDP in any other country in this group. The evidence on trade relationship (see Panel B) shows a unidirectional causal relationship in trade from Brazil to India; India to China and South Africa; and South Africa to Brazil and China. There is no evidence of Chinese trade influencing trade in any of the remaining three countries. These results are consistent with Kuboniwa (2011) and Table 10.5, and confirm that no BRICS country is a major trading partner with China. Trade balance between China and India shows a trade surplus for China, indicating that India imports more from China than it exports to China. Hence India's trade does not affect trade in China.

Finally the trade/growth relationship is tested among the sample countries. The results are reported in Panels C and D of Table 10.7. It shows that economic growth in Brazil causes trade in India and South Africa. Indian growth only influences trade in South Africa, while growth in China influences trade in Brazil and India. Growth in South Africa only impacts trade in India. As for the trade/growth relationship (see Panel D), trade changes in Brazil have a positive impact on economic growth in India, while South Africa has the same effect on China. There is no empirical support from any other BRICS country where trade impacts on economic growth. This is a further confirmation of our conjecture in the beginning of this chapter, suggesting that the BRICS countries are no more than a trade bloc.

CONCLUSIONS

Since the publication of the Goldman Sachs' report in 2003 (Wilson & Purushothaman), prospects for the BRICS countries as an emerging economic bloc are on the forefront of regional debate. The existing published research (from both a journalistic viewpoint and a more comprehensive academic research viewpoint) gives mixed signals, some supporting claims that the BRICS has the potential to be a major trading and economic bloc in years to come, while others remain unconvinced of its potential. This chapter attempts to provide current analysis on this debate investigating both sides of the argument. Different approaches are used in this study, including the basic structure of the BRICS as a bloc, statistical facts as well as empirical analysis. The detailed analysis presented in this chapter does not support the claim that the BRICS countries are, or have a potential to be, an important economic bloc in the near future. No doubt the bloc accounts for 20 per cent of the world's GDP, but this is due to the advantage of having China as part of the bloc, China being a large economy with over US$7 trillion of GDP (2011). The BRICS' impact has grown over time but it is mainly due to trade. As O'Neill et al. (2005) observed, the BRIC countries were generally doing a reasonable job, but there were clear weaknesses in each case. The BRICS is a trade bloc and will remain as a trade bloc, again China being the major contributor to its US$3 trillion trade. The findings of this chapter are consistent with Kuboniwa (2011), who observed that the BRICS countries were affected by trading gains, especially growth in Russia and Brazil, but not much impact was observed for India and China. The reported statistics and the empirical analysis did not find any intra-trade among the BRICS countries. This scenario is expected to remain as is until the BRICS countries embark on policies of intra-trade and more economic integration within the bloc. The BRICS countries, especially Russia and India, should also change their attitude towards neighbouring countries. ASEAN is a good example, with a clear distinction between ASEAN early-five and later-five[9] but all working as a group, with the more developed countries helping the relatively less developed countries through dissemination of information, cooperation in education and research and development. The BRICS could adopt a similar approach by engaging countries in central Asia (rich in natural resources) as well as South Asia (rich in human capital). This could bring a significant impact on the effectiveness of the BRICS as a major player in the global economy.

NOTES

1. See Suryamurthy (2012), Hawksworth and Cookson (2008), Goyal (2012), 'BRICS bank replacement for IMF and World Bank' (2012), 'BRICS to trade in local currency' (2012), 'Dynamic BRICS is good news even to developed world' (2012), 'BRICS may agree to trade in local currencies' (2012).
2. See also 'The trillion-dollar club: The BRICs' (2010) and Escobar (2011).
3. A **trade bloc** is a type of intergovernmental agreement, often part of a regional intergovernmental organization, where regional barriers to trade (tariffs and non-tariff barriers) are reduced or eliminated among the participating states (Wikipedia, 2013d).
4. An **economic bloc** is more than a trade bloc where countries cooperate in various aspects of economic activities, including trade, finances, education and so forth. Examples of economic blocs are the EU, ASEAN and NAFTA.
5. During his first eight years of office, Vladimir Putin put Russia through a series of sweeping economic reforms. These focused on a number of economic sectors, including industry and agriculture, energy and defence-related areas, privatization of state-owned enterprises as well as liberalization of the financial sector. As a result of these reforms, industry and investment grew by 75 per cent and 125 per cent respectively. The agricultural and construction sectors also enjoyed sizeable increases, while real income more than doubled. In the period 2000–06, consumer credit increased 45 times. The poverty level reduced from 30 per cent in 2000, to 14 per cent in 2008.
6. Table 10.5 shows that apart from China, none of the BRICS countries rank among the top five major exporting destinations or importing partners for the bloc.
7. Apparently there are no political issues between Brazil and South Africa. However, the point emphasized here is about the group as a whole.
8. The only exception is Brazil where openness is I (0) on the basis of ADF.
9. ASEAN was established in August 1967 by five East Asian countries (called the 'early five') namely, Indonesia, Malaysia, Philippines, Singapore and Thailand. During 1990 another five East Asian countries (called the 'later five') joined the group making it a group of 10 East Asian countries. The later five are namely, Brunei, Cambodia, Laos,

Myanmar and Vietnam. The main objective of ASEAN was to enhance economic and socio-economic cooperation among member countries.

REFERENCES

Ariff, M. and Khalid, A. (2000). *Liberalisation, growth and the Asian financial crisis: Lessons for developing and transitional economies in Asia*. Cheltenham, UK: Edward Elgar.

BRICS bank replacement for IMF and World Bank (2012, April 9). *AsiaNow*. Retrieved from http://asianowblog.com/2012/04/09/brics-bank-replacement-for-imf-and-world-bank/

BRICS may agree to trade in local currencies (2012, March 28). *The Indian Express*. Retrieved from http://www.indianexpress.com/news/brics-may-agree-to-trade-in-local-currencies/929226

BRICS to trade in local currency (2012, March 29). *Business World*. Retrieved from http://www.businessworld.in/en/storypage/-/bw/brics-to-trade-in-local-currency/397429.0/page/0

Cooper, J.M. (2006). *Russia as a BRIC: Only a dream?* (European Research Working Paper Series No. 13). Birmingham, UK: Centre for Russian and East European Studies, University of Birmingham.

Datamonitor (2010). *Datamonitor: Brazil*. Retrieved from http://connection.ebscohost.com/c/articles/55715460/datamonitor-brazil

Dynamic BRICS is good news even to developed world (2012, March 29). *CCTV*. Retrieved from http://english.cntv.cn/20120329/110107.shtml

Escobar, P. (2011, September 23). BRICS plan to revive the global economy. *Al-Jazeera*. Retrieved from http://www.aljazeera.com/indepth/opinion/2011/09/201192292011236419.html

Goyal, K. (2012, May 16). India sets $2 billion currency swap deal for South Asian Nations. *Bloomberg*. Retrieved from http://www.bloomberg.com/news/2012-05-16/india-sets-2-billion-currency-swap-deal-for-south-asian-nations.html

Haddad, M. (2007). *Trade integration in East Asia: The role of China and production networks* (World Bank Policy Research Paper No. 4160). Washington DC: World Bank EASPR.

Hawksworth, J. and Cookson, G. (2008). *The world in 2050: Beyond the BRICs – a broader look at emerging market growth prospects*. UK: PricewaterhouseCoopers LLP.

IMF (2011). *New growth drivers for low-income countries: The role of BRICs*. Washington DC: World Bank.

IMF (2012a). *Direction of Trade Statistics*. CD-ROM.

IMF (2012b). *International Financial Statistics*. Accessed through e-library.

International Intellectual Property Alliance (IIPA). (2012). *Brazil*. Retrieved from http://www.iipa.com/rbc/2012/2012SPEC301BRAZIL.PDF

Khalid, A. and Rajaguru, G. (2011, September). *Currency arrangements for East Asia: Anchor or a basket*. Paper presented at the joint GDC, Bond and EGC, NTU workshop, Bond University, Qld, Australia.

Kose, M.A., Prasad, E.S. and Terrones, M.E. (2006). *How do trade and financial integration affect the relationship between growth and volatility?* (IZA Discussion Paper No. 2252). Bonn, Germany: Institute for the Study of Labor.

Kowalski, P. (2008). *China and India: A tale of two trade integration approaches* (Working Paper No. 221). New Delhi, India: Indian Council for Research on International Economic Relations.
Kregel, J. (2009). The global crisis and the implications for developing countries and the BRICs: Is the "B" really justified? *Brazilian Journal of Political Economy*, *29*(4), 341–56.
Kuboniwa, M. (2011). *Impact of trading gains on economic growth in BRICs for 1995–2010: Some lessons from BRICs* (RRC Working Paper Series No. 31). Tokyo, Japan: Russian Research Center, Institute of Economic Research, Hitotsubashi University.
Macfarlane, N.S. (2006). The "R" in BRICs: Is Russia an emerging power? *International Affairs*, *82*(1), 41–57.
Muller, M. (2011). New kids on the block: The rise of the BRIC and the reconfiguration of global economic ties. *European Researcher*, *12*(15), 1615–25.
O'Neill, J. (2001, November 30). *Building better global economic BRICs* (Goldman Sachs Global Economics Paper No. 66). London: Goldman, Sachs & Co.
O'Neill, J., Wilson. D., Purushothaman, R. and Stupnytska, A. (2005, December 1). *How solid are the BRICs?* (Goldman Sachs Global Economic Paper No. 134). London: Goldman, Sachs & Co.
Rose, S. and Tanas, O. (2013, February 1). Russian GDP growth slowest since 2009 as investment wanes. *Bloomberg*. Retrieved from http://www.bloomberg.com/news/2013-01-31/russian-economy-expanded-3-4-last-year-slower-than-estimated.html
Roubini, N. (2009, June 18). The BRICs: An analysis. *Forbes*. Retrieved from http://www.forbes.com/2009/06/17/bric-brazil-russia-india-china-renminbi-yekaterinberg-opinions-columnists-roubini.html
Samake, I. and Yang, Y. (2011). *Low-income countries' BRIC linkage: Are there growth spillovers?* (IMF Working Paper 11/267). Retrieved from http://www.imf.org/external/pubs/ft/wp/2011/wp11267.pdf
Sinha, A. and Dorschner, J. (2010). India: Rising power or a mere revolution of rising expectations? *Polity*, *42*(1), 74–99.
Sotero, P. and Armijo, L.E. (2007). Brazil: To be or not to be a BRIC? *Asian Perspective*, *31*(4), 43–70.
South Africa: Economy Overview (2013, February 28). *SouthAfrica.info*. Retrieved from http://www.southafrica.info/business/economy/econoverview.htm#ixzz2K9bzXOTF
Suryamurthy, R. (2012, March 29). Brics trade to double in 3 years. *The Telegraph*. Retrieved from http://www.telegraphindia.com/1120329/jsp/business/story_15308520.jsp
The trillion-dollar club: The BRICs (2010, April 15). *The Economist*. Retrieved from http://www.economist.com/node/15912964
Transparency International (2012). *Corruption perceptions index 2012*. Retrieved from http://www.transparency.org/cpi2012/results
Wikipedia (2013a). *BRICS*. Retrieved from http://en.wikipedia.org/wiki/BRICS
Wikipedia (2013b). *Chinese economic reforms*. Retrieved from http://en.wikipedia.org/wiki/Chinese_economic_reform
Wikipedia (2013c). *Economic liberalisation in India*. Retrieved from http://en.wikipedia.org/wiki/Economic_liberalisation_in_India

Wikipedia (2013d). *The Economy of Russia*. Retrieved from http://en.wikipedia.org/wiki/Economy_of_Russia

Wikipedia (2013e). *What is a trade bloc?* Retrieved from http://en.wikipedia.org/wiki/Trade_bloc

Wilson, D. and Purushothaman, R. (2003, October 1). *Dreaming with BRICs: The path to 2050* (Goldman Sachs Global Economics Paper No. 99). London: Goldman, Sachs & Co.

Wilson, D. and Stupnytska, A. (2007, March 28). *The N-11: More Than an Acronym* (Goldman Sachs Global Economics Paper No. 153) London: Goldman, Sachs & Co.

World Bank (2012). *World development indicators*. Retrieved from http://data.worldbank.org/data-catalog/world-development-indicators

World Economic Forum (2012). *The Global Competitiveness Report 2012–2013*. Retrieved from http://www3.weforum.org/docs/WEF_GlobalCompetitivenessReport_2012-12.pdf

Xiao, Q. (2006). *Observation and perception of China's economy in the post-crisis period – Policy options and recovery management*. Retrieved from http://www.slideshare.net/NCUSCR/qin-xiao-nyse-post-crisis-chinese-economy

11. The BRICS+: Fault lines and opportunities

Umair Ghori

Brazil, Russia, India, China and South Africa (collectively referred to as the BRICS countries) are some of the world's fastest emerging economies. They occupy a central position in their respective regions and often act as a trade and investment hub for other less-developed satellite countries. Lately, the BRICS countries have increasingly sought to enhance their politico-economic profiles and are now mulling over the idea of greater mutual cooperation. But the question remains what form would this cooperation take?

The BRICS countries have little in common, and in many respects these countries may be considered as political rivals. The genesis of the BRICS of course lies in economic cooperation but the group itself has yet to become an economic bloc. It also demonstrates some signs of a quasi-political alliance. This chapter, however, focuses on trade and investment issues only.

This chapter discusses issues pertaining to greater cooperation amongst the BRICS countries in terms of trade and investment. It is divided into three parts. Part one sets out a brief background and overview of the investment inflows and outflows, and trade in goods and services from the BRICS countries. Part two concentrates on the inclusion and the exclusion aspects of the BRICS. It raises the question whether a Free Trade Agreement (FTA) or any other integration model offers a possible solution. It discusses possible forms any future FTA structure would take if the BRICS policymakers decide to proceed down that path. The author puts forth the inclusive FTA as the best possible option that can serve the long-term needs of the BRICS as it expands its manufacturing base and enhances its investment portfolios. Part three then discusses fault lines that act as barriers to enhanced intra-BRICS cooperation. Amongst the many challenges faced by the BRICS countries, this chapter briefly raises the issues regarding China and its place within the BRICS, the internal divergences in establishing the BRICS Bank (an initiative born out of necessity due to the economic downturn), risk of expropriation, the BRICS' specific dispute settlement and the impact of the BRICS' poor track record in upholding intellectual property (IP) rights. Part four concludes.

THE BRICS SCORESHEET

Investment Profile

Amongst the ranks of emerging economies, the BRICS countries occupy a central position. These diverse countries collectively comprise more than 40 per cent of the world's population, and each faces its own challenges. China and India are highly populous regional rivals with distinct political systems. Russia grapples with a large geographical expanse endowed with unexploited mineral wealth. Brazil represents a hybrid of the three – a large country with densely populated urban centres juxtaposed with uninhabited regions. The newest member of the BRICS, South Africa, is the only developed economy in the African continent and hence represents the nucleus of Southern African commerce. Yet despite all the differences and their individuality, in the last few years the BRICS countries have become increasingly linked to each other, mainly because of common economic interests.

According to Goldman Sachs' estimates for 2012, the BRICS countries would continue to post strong economic growth rates in the post-Global Financial Crisis (GFC) period (Wilson, Burgi & Carlson, 2011, p. 4).[1] This growth comes on the heels of quicker recovery by the BRICS from global economic slowdown compared to the developed economies. While it is not yet clear whether the BRICS countries would continue their current trajectory, their consistent growth figures and solid economic performance have transformed each of them into central economies of their respective regions. This is attested to by the large shares of foreign direct investment (FDI) inflows and outflows held by the BRICS countries in their respective regions. For example, according to UNCTAD's World Investment Report 2012, Brazil accounts for 50.3 per cent of all investment attracted into South American countries from 2006 to 2011 (see Figure 11.1). The FDI outflow figures for Russia and India are even more impressive. Both countries are virtually the only foreign investor in their regions, accounting for 91.94 per cent and 97.08 per cent outward FDI from 2006 to 2011 respectively. South Africa exhibits similar characteristics amongst the Southern African countries, controlling 61.86 per cent of investment inflow and 41.16 per cent of investment outflow from 2006 to 2011.

It is also important to track the recipients of the investment by the BRICS investors. Table 11.1 summarizes some of the major investment

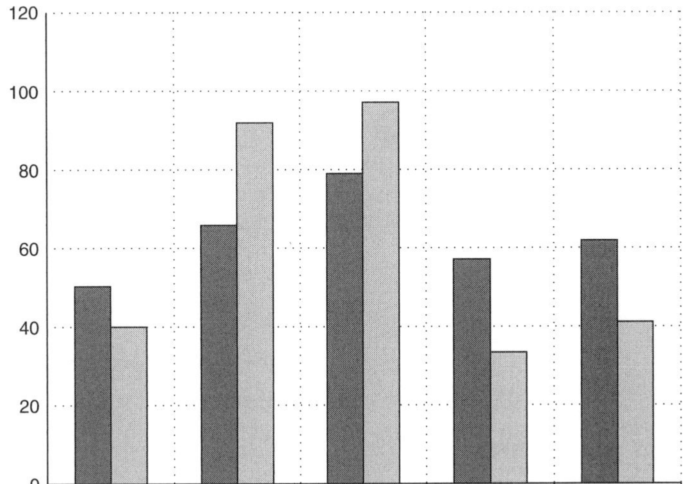

	Brazil (South America)	Russia (CIS)	India (South Asia)	China (East Asia)	S Africa (Southern Africa)
Y06-Y11 Inflow	50.3	65.9	79	57.1	61.86
Y06-Y11 Outflow	40	91.94	97.08	33.46	41.16

Source: Calculated from UNCTAD (2012, Annex Table 1.1).

Figure 11.1 FDI inflows & outflows as percentage in regions for the BRICS (2006–11)

transactions in 2010. It is clearly noticeable that the investment mostly came in the natural resources, telecommunications and infrastructure sectors. However, note that these multi-billion dollar deals were conducted by large transnational corporations. This investment trend represents a leap forward from the traditional tendencies of transnational corporations to invest closer to home (Gammeltoft, 2008, p. 9). The rationale behind investing closer to home was based on acquired familiarity through trade and/or cultural ties (Gammeltoft, 2008, p. 9). Peter Gammeltoft notes that the BRICS-based transnational corporations are becoming increasingly confident in acquiring assets beyond their proximate markets (2008, p. 9).

Major investment acquisitions for 2011 summarized in Table 11.2 confirm the continuation of this trend with the BRICS-based transnational corporations conducting large investment in developing economies. Investment from the BRICS countries in other developing and emerging markets continued throughout the GFC period. UNCTAD's data shows a decline from 41 per cent (pre-GFC period) to 34 per cent (2011) in FDI in developed countries from the BRICS-based investors. At the same time 65

Table 11.1 Major foreign investment transactions in 2010 involving the BRICS

Value (in US$ billion)	Acquired company	Host economy	Acquiring Company	Home economy	Sector
10.7	Zain Africa BV	Nigeria	Bharti Airtel	India	Telecom
9.1	EDF Energy	UK	Investor Group	HK China	Electric Services
7.1	Repsol YPF	Brazil	Sinopec Group	China	Fuels and gas
5.5	ZAO Kyivstar GSM	Ukraine	Vimpelkom	Russia	Telecom
4.8	Carabobo Block	Venezuela	Investor Group	India	Fuels and gas
4.1	Denway Motors	HK China	CLI Ltd	HK China	Automotive
3.8	Bunge Participacoes	Brazil	Vale SA	Brazil	Minerals
3.1	Bridas Corp	Argentina	CNOOC Ltd	China	Fuels and gas

Source: UNCTAD (2012).

per cent of FDI by value from the BRICS countries was invested in developing economies, compared with 59 per cent in the pre-GFC period (note that UNCTAD figures cited here do not include figures for South Africa) (UNCTAD, 2012, p. 6). It is also noticeable that the BRICS countries are not just investors but are recipients of foreign investment as well. The predominant investment interests are in the minerals, fuels and gas sectors. This is evidenced through data presented in Tables 11.1 and 11.2, which summarize findings from the latest World Investment Reports published by UNCTAD.

The BRICS-based investors have also begun to target developed countries, although their modus operandi seems to be evolving after attempts to acquire high value/sensitive assets in the developed countries failed following high profile media attention.[2] One such mode of entering an investment market is through 'indirect FDI'. The indirect FDI flows are dependent on factors such as routing investment through tax havens or conducting transactions through special purpose entities (UNCTAD, 2012, p. 7). FDI through these methods is considered indirect because the economy from which the investment originates is not the actual home economy of the ultimate investors (UNCTAD, 2012, pp. 7–8). BRICS-based investors are

Table 11.2 Major foreign investment transactions in 2011 involving the BRICS

Value (in US$ billion)	Acquired company	Host economy	Acquiring company	Home economy	Sector
9.0	Reliance Industries Ltd	India	BP PLC	UK	Fuels and gas
6.3	OAO Polyus Zoloto	Russia	KazakhGold Group	Kazakhstan	Minerals (gold ores)
5.5	Vivo Participacoes	Russia	Tele-communica-tions de Sao Paulo SA	Brazil	Telecom
5.5	OAO Polimetall	Russia	PMTL Holdings	Jersey	Minerals (gold ores)
4.9	Vale SA	Brazil	Norsk Hydro ASA	Norway	Fuels and gas
4.9	Shell International	Brazil	Cosan SA Industria e Comercio	Brazil	Fuels
4.5	Cairn India Ltd	India	Vedanta Resources PLC	UK	Minerals
4.2	OAO Pervaya Gruzovaya Kompaniya	Russia	OOO Nezavisinaya Transportnaya Kompaniya	Russia	Courier services
4.0	OAO Novatek	Russia	Total SA	France	Fuels and gas
3.8	OAO Vimm Bill	Russia	Pepsi Cola Bermuda Ltd	Bermuda	Carbonated beverages
3.3	Hutchinson Essar Ltd	India	Vodafone Group	UK	Telecom
3.3	GDF Suez SA	France	China Investment Corp	China	Investment management
3.1	Peregrino Project	Brazil	Sinochem Group	China	Fuels and gas

Source: UNCTAD (2012).

increasingly using this method to penetrate the US market. For example, Brazil's investment in the US stock for 2010 stood at US$1.093 billion. However, when considered through ultimate beneficial ownership, the investment figure swells to US$15.476 billion (UNCTAD, 2012, p. 8).

Trade in Services

Trade in services is another segment where the BRICS countries are gradually increasing their market penetration, although their performance over the last five years (2005–10) appears patchy. China, India and Russia feature more prominently in trade in services than South Africa and Brazil. India especially stands out amongst the BRICS countries with its service-led growth model (BRICS, 2012b, p. 163).

Tracking services data is a complicated task and this is perhaps best reflected in varied data availability. Table 11.3 summarizes the main services sectors and the performance by the BRICS. China appears to be leading the pack in terms of diversity and presence in almost all of the services categories. Russia and India are gradually developing their services capabilities, whilst Brazil has yet to make its mark in this area of world trade. Data for South Africa was not available at the time of writing this chapter.

Note that transport is a major services sector where China, India and Russia have lodged 15 per cent, 20 per cent and 11 per cent growth in their exports of transportation services over the years 2005–11 respectively (WTO, 2012, p. 148). Taken collectively these three BRICS members hold 8.1 per cent of the world's transport services exports for the year 2011 (Table 11.3).

One major services category is that of commercial services, where healthy growth rates were recorded for the years 2005–11. The highest growth rate for commercial services was recorded by China at 22 per cent, followed by Brazil at 21 per cent, while Russia and India both recorded 17 per cent (Table 11.3). Overall, the BRICS share of world trade in commercial services in 2011 stood at 11.1 per cent (excluding South Africa). Table 11.3 also reveals varied strengths and fields of activity in services trade. For example, China's strength in construction services stood out with a market share of 17.2 per cent in 2010 and a growth rate of 41 per cent from 2005 to 2010. The only other competitor in this segment was Russia with a 3.1 per cent market share in 2010 and a growth rate of 4 per cent from 2005 to 2010. Another example of the varied strengths and weaknesses of the BRICS in services trade is the computer services sector where India held a 23.7 per cent market share in 2010. Conversely India's performance in the telecommunications services declined by 2 per cent from 2005 to 2010.

The BRICS countries are also major importers of services in addition to being exporters. Currently the EU is the largest and the most prolific supplier of services across various services categories to the BRICS countries. Table 11.4 summarizes major exporters of services to the BRICS coun-

Table 11.3 The BRICS in the services trade (by major export categories)

BRICS	Main services sectors	Market share (2011) or (2010) where marked as *	Annual percentage change (2005–11) or (2005–10) where marked as *
Brazil	Commercial services	1.1%	21%
	Personal, cultural & recreational	0.9%*	15%*
Russia	Transport	2.0%	11%
	Commercial services	1.1%	17%
	Telecommunications	2.1%*	15%*
	Construction	3.1%*	4%*
	Computer services	0.7%*	28%*
	Personal, cultural & recreational	1.2%*	20%*
	Audio-visual services	1.3%*	23%*
India	Transport	2.0%	20%
	Travel	1.6%	15%
	Commercial services	4.5%	17%
	Telecommunications	1.2%*	−2%*
	Insurance	2.4%*	14%*
	Financial services	2.3%	39%*
	Computer services	23.7%*	Data not available
	Other business services	5.3%	Data not available
China	Transport	4.1%	15%
	Travel	4.5%	9%
	Commercial services	4.4%	22%
	Communications	1.7%*	20%*
	Construction	17.2%*	41%*
	Insurance	2.4%*	14%*
	Computer & information	4.7%*	38%*
	Royalties & licence fees	0.4%*	39%*
	Other business services	7.3%*	21%*
	Audio-visual services	0.4%	−2%
S Africa	Data not available	Data not available	Data not available

Source: Summarized from WTO (2012).

tries and their annual percentage changes from 2005 to 2010. However, due to some gaps in available data, Table 11.4 provides the 2010 market share of the exporter in the BRICS importer in lieu of annual percentage share figures. Also note that a complete picture of South African services imports is not available due to a lack of available data. According to

Table 11.4 Annual percentage change of exports in main services sectors by selected countries to the BRICS countries (2005–2010)

BRICS (Importer)	Main services sectors	Major exporters (Annual percentage change 2005–10)
Brazil	Transport	EU (10%), US (18%), S Korea (28%), Norway (4%)
	Travel	EU (21%), US (21%)
	Other commercial services	EU (22%), US (27%), Japan (30%), Norway (20%)
	Telecommunication	EU (42%), US (19.5%)*
	Construction	EU (28%)
	Insurance	EU (47%), US (36%)
	Financial	EU (25%), US (2.3%)*
	Computer & information	EU (28%), US (1.8%)*
	Royalties & licence fees	EU (44%), US (29%)
	Other business services	Japan (39%)
Russia	Transport	EU (8%), S Korea (19%), Norway (−5%)
	Travel	EU (17%), Turkey (7.7%)*, S Korea (16%)
	Other commercial services	EU (17%), Norway (8%), Korea (42%)
	Telecommunication	EU (29%)
	Construction	EU (15%)
	Insurance	EU (7%), S Korea (199%)
	Financial	EU (29%)
	Computer & information	EU (21%)
	Royalties & licence fees	EU (23%)
	Other business services	EU (12%), Japan (14%) HK China (1.3%)*
India	Transport	EU (12%), US (37%), Japan (16%), S Korea (21%), HK China (10%), Norway (−10%)
	Travel	EU (13%), US (12%), Australia (28%), HK China (14%), Japan (0.7%)*, S Korea (10%)
	Other commercial services	EU (22%), US (16%), Japan (31%), HK China (32%), S Korea (39%), Russia (4%), Norway (6%)
	Telecommunication	EU (25%)
	Construction	EU (15%), Japan (23%), Singapore (12.3%)*
	Insurance	–
	Financial	US (0.8%)*

Table 11.4 (continued)

BRICS (Importer)	Main services sectors	Major exporters (Annual percentage change 2005–10)
	Computer & information	EU (60%), US (1.9%)*, HK China (74%)
	Royalties & licence fees	US (25%), S Korea (29%)
	Other business services	EU (15%), Japan (36%)
China	Transport	EU (12%), US (17%), Japan (10%), S Korea (16%), HK China (9%), Norway (−20%), Russia (2%)
	Travel	EU (12%), US (23%), Australia (19%), Japan (25.3%)*, S Korea (23%), Russia (14%)
	Other commercial services	EU (16%), US (19%), Japan (−5%), HK China (51%), S Korea (23%), Russia (13%), Norway (16%)
	Telecommunication	US (0.7%)*
	Construction	EU (10%), Singapore (5.3%)*, Japan (−23%)
	Insurance	EU (36%), Japan (8%), S Korea (28%), HK China (17%)
	Financial	EU (8%), HK China (40%), US (3%)
	Computer & information	EU (52%), HK China (21%), Japan (9%), US (1.8%)*
	Royalties & licence fees	US (23%), Japan (25%), EU (17%), S Korea (17%)
	Other business services	EU (13%)
S Africa	Transport	–
	Travel	–
	Other commercial services	EU (11%)
	Telecommunication	EU (29%)
	Construction	–
	Insurance	EU (−7%)
	Financial	EU (10%)
	Computer & information	EU (18%), US (1.2%)*
	Royalties & licence fees	EU (6%), US (13%)
	Other business services	EU (11%), Japan (0.2%)*

Notes: * shows market share for year 2010 rather than annual percentage change. This is due to lack of available data.

Source: Summarized from WTO (2012).

WTO figures, the EU is the dominant supplier of services such as telecommunications, financial, computer and information, commercial and other business services.

Similar to Table 11.3, Table 11.4 also highlights the varied stages of economic emphasis of each of the BRICS economies (although some similarities are still noticeable). Table 11.4 also reveals the subtle impact of international politics on services trade. For example, there is a noticeable absence of the US and China in Russia's services market, with the EU clearly being the preferred supplier of services in all services categories. South Korea's explosive growth by 199 per cent from 2005 to 2010 in Russia's insurance services market demonstrates that EU suppliers may be facing competition from New Industrialized Countries (NICs) based suppliers, although it may take some time for the non-EU based suppliers to fully supplant the EU in the Russian services market.

Reading the data presented in Table 11.3 with Table 11.4 reveals that Brazil is an importer of services and has yet to establish itself as a services exporter. The EU and the US are the major providers of nearly all services categories to the Brazilian services consumer. Brazilian services importers continue to source telecommunications, insurance and other commercial services from the EU, US and other suppliers such as Japan and Norway, even when most of these developed economies had slipped into recession. The EU and the US also appear to be the primary suppliers of licensed products and technologies as is evidenced by their growth by 44 per cent and 29 per cent respectively in the royalties and technical fee category (Table 11.4).

India represents the more diverse services recipient in terms of diversity in suppliers. The annual growth of major exporters of services such as transport, travel and other commercial services is spread across several suppliers when compared to Russia and Brazil. Note the healthy 37 per cent growth by US-based providers of transport services to India. The other major provider is South Korea, with 21 per cent growth from 2005 to 2010 in the same segment. South Korea, Japan and Hong Kong China also feature as growing suppliers of commercial services to India, with 39 per cent, 31 per cent and 32 per cent growth respectively from 2005 to 2010. However, the EU-based services suppliers continue to record strong growth in computer and information services, telecommunications and other business services, with 60 per cent, 25 per cent and 15 per cent growth respectively in the years under consideration (Table 11.4). The growth in the Indian economy (even during the recession years) continues to attract services providers from developed economies and the NICs (Bajpai, 2011, p. 2).

China represents a picture that more closely resembles India than

Brazil and Russia. The transport sector again stands out for its diversity in service suppliers, with the EU, the US, Japan, South Korea and Hong Kong China all recording growth over the years 2005–10. Travel and other commercial services are also categories where there are several suppliers vying for a greater share of the Chinese services market. In travel services, the EU, the US, Australia and South Korea have recorded increases of 12 per cent, 23 per cent, 19 per cent and 23 per cent respectively in the period under consideration. We can also see some intra-BRICS services trade with Russia posting a 14 per cent growth in the Chinese travel services market (Table 11.4). The EU remains the leading supplier of services across various categories, recording 36 per cent and 52 per cent growth in the lucrative insurance and computer and information sectors respectively. Another noticeable non-EU/US provider that experiences increased activity was South Korea in the insurance market with 28 per cent growth over the 2005–10 period. Similar to India, the Chinese economy also grew, albeit less slowly, during the GFC. But even accounting for the economic slowdown, figures in Table 11.4 show solid growth in services exports to the Chinese economy.

Trade in Goods

In addition to their investment and services profiles, the BRICS countries appear to be increasing their share of global trade, although their overall share in global merchandise trade is still below other industrialized countries. Figure 11.2 tracks the exports from the BRICS countries for the years 2000, 2010 and 2011. Strong performance in telecom equipment stands out amongst the value added sectors of global trade, that is, from 7.53 per cent share in world exports for 2000, the share of telecom equipment increased to 31.87 per cent in 2010. This share further grew to 34.27 per cent in 2011. Note that this growth also coincides with increased investment activity in the telecom sector (see Tables 11.1 and 11.2).

Figure 11.2 also shows a steady increase in fuel exports (increasing from 9.89 per cent in 2000 to 14.71 per cent in 2011), the agricultural sector (8.82 per cent in 2000 to 13.48 per cent in 2011) and integrated circuits (increasing from a mere 1.88 per cent in 2000 to a respectable 14.3 per cent in 2011). Slow growth was witnessed in the automotive sector (only increasing from 1.68 per cent in 2000 to 5.62 per cent in 2011). The figures for textiles and clothing are deceptively impressive; however, these figures must be considered in light of China and India's large-scale manufacturing capabilities and export potential. For example, for global textiles exports in year 2011, China accounts for 32.16 per cent out of the cited exports figure of 37.97 per cent (Figure 11.2). Similarly,

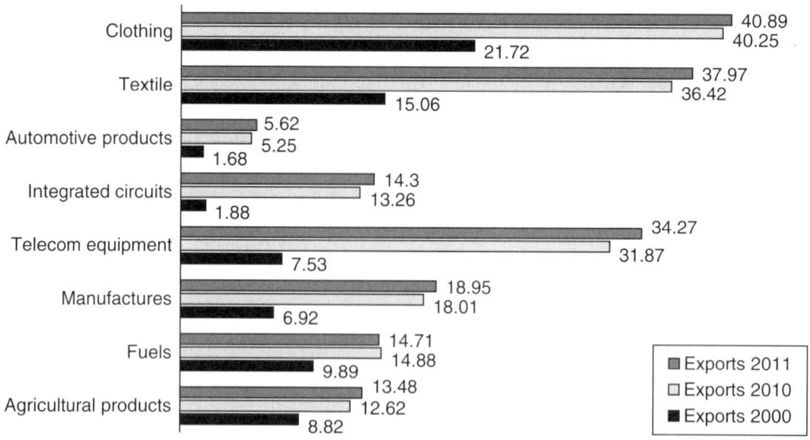

Source: WTO (2012, Tables 11, 16, 26, 32, 51, 55, 60, 65 and 70).

Figure 11.2 Percentage share of exports from the BRICS countries in major sectors of world trade (2000, 2010 and 2011)

out of 40.89 per cent share cited in Figure 11.2 for clothing exports in 2011, China's share stood at 37.28 per cent. Table 11.5 provides a more specific picture with a breakdown of major sectors of world merchandise trade in 2011 and the performance of the BRICS countries as exporters and importers. Data for the EU and the US for the same year has been included by way of comparison. The data presented again confirms the varied positions of the BRICS countries as traders in merchandise (Table 11.5).

China stands out amongst the ranks of the BRICS countries as the most active exporter and importer. Although still behind the EU and the US in many sectors, China has significantly increased its market share of world exports in the office and telecom sector for the year 2011 to 29.6 per cent, overtaking the EU and the US with 22.5 per cent and 8.4 per cent respectively. As a result, the EU and the US have both become net importers of office and telecom equipment as is evidenced from their increased share in world imports in 2011 (Table 11.5). For other BRICS countries, Table 11.5 paints a mixed picture. India appears as an exporter of textiles and clothing but in other sectors still occupies a lesser position. India's export performance is almost balanced with it imports. South Africa only occupies a minimal share in the export of automotive products as a top 15 producer while not featuring as a leading importer in any sector. This is perhaps indicative of the smaller size of its economy amongst the ranks of

Table 11.5 Performance of the BRICS as leading exporters and importers in world merchandise trade (2011, percentage of world share in exports and imports) compared with the EU and the US

Countries	Export sectors (% share in world exports in 2011 as a Top 15 exporter)	Import sectors (% share in world imports in 2011 as a Top 15 importer)
Brazil	Agriculture (5.2%)	Manufactures (1.4%)
	Automotive products (1.1%)	Chemicals (2.1%)
		Automotive products (1.7%)
		Textiles (1.4%)
Russia	Agriculture (1.8%)	Agriculture (2.3%)
	Chemicals (1.6%)	Manufactures (1.9%)
		Chemicals (0.6%)
		Office & telecom (1.2%)
		Automotive products (3.0%)
		Textiles (1.2%)
		Clothing (1.8%)
India	Agriculture (2.1%)	Agriculture (1.3%)
	Manufactures (1.6%)	Manufactures (1.6%)
	Chemicals (1.6%)	Chemicals (2.1%)
	Automotive products (0.7%)	Office & telecom (1.4%)
	Textiles (5.1%)	Textiles (1.1%)
	Clothing (3.5%)	
China	Agriculture (3.9%)	Agriculture (8.3%)
	Manufactures (15.4%)	Manufactures (8.7%)
	Chemicals (5.7%)	Chemicals (8.9%)
	Office & telecom (29.6%)	Office & telecom (16.6%)
	Automotive products (2.9%)	Automotive products (5.3%)
	Textiles (32.2%)	Textiles (6.1%)
	Clothing (37.3%)	Clothing (0.9%)
South Africa	Automotive products (0.6%)	
EU	Agriculture (37.7%)	Agriculture (37.5%)
	Manufactures (40.2%)	Manufactures (35.5%)
	Chemicals (48.7%)	Chemicals (41.3%)
	Office & telecom (22.5%)	Office & telecom (28.1%)
	Automotive products (51.2%)	Automotive products (38.2%)
	Textiles (26.1%)	Textiles (27.0%)
	Clothing (28.2%)	Clothing (43.8%)
US	Agriculture (10.1%)	Agriculture (7.9%)
	Manufactures (8.4%)	Manufactures (12.8%)
	Chemicals (10.4%)	Chemicals (10.0%)
	Office & telecom (8.4%)	Office & telecom (16.2%)
	Automotive products (9.3%)	Automotive products (16.2%)
	Textiles (4.7%)	Textiles (8.2%)
	Clothing (1.3%)	Clothing (20.5%)

Source: WTO (2012, Tables II.15, II.31, II.38, II.42, II.59, II.64, II.69).

the BRICS countries. Brazil and Russia also appear as leading importers rather than exporters of merchandise.

Distilling the data cited in the earlier figures and tables, it is observable that the BRICS countries do not follow a uniform pattern in their trade and economic activities. Their current emphasis is more on investment in both a regional and international context rather than merchandise production and export. Russia and China demonstrate a particular appetite in acquiring assets in natural resources and the extractive sectors. The outgoing investment by these two countries in such acquisitions is mostly by large state-owned enterprises (SOEs) (Gammeltoft, 2008, pp. 11–12). Brazil and India's investment portfolios are more diverse, with an added interest in telecommunications (both as investor and recipient of investments) along with the ubiquitous natural resources sector. The services sector is another area where the BRICS countries are gradually increasing their share in global trade. Data for trade in services is patchy but available figures (see Table 11.3) show that the BRICS is not only increasing its market share but is increasingly becoming attractive to other services exporters, particularly based in the EU (see Table 11.4).

FAULT LINES AND OPPORTUNITIES

Exclusive or Inclusive?

The BRICS is currently in the exploration phase of its relationship (see BRICS, 2012b, pp. 169–70).[3] If the relationship is pursued energetically, the BRICS countries are uniquely positioned to coordinate their politico-economic policies to enhance their own international standing. The numerous benefits of mutual cooperation would not just be limited to the BRICS but are likely to spread regionally, given the investment 'hub' roles played by the BRICS countries in their respective regions (UNCTAD, 2012, pp. 4, 7–8, 26; see also Figure 11.1 and the accompanying discussions). However, as attractive as it may sound, the decisions taken by leaders of the BRICS are more political in character than economic. In other words, the BRICS countries have to carefully balance domestic political considerations with their economic interests. More than domestic political considerations, the policymakers are mindful of the underlying tensions and conflicts within the BRICS countries themselves. These tensions stem from the fact that, in addition to being eager business partners and traders, some of the BRICS members are also regional rivals competing for international influence and control over resources to fuel their growing economies.

The combination of politics, business and rivalry has meant that the

BRICS currently exhibits characteristics of an interest/pressure group rather than a formalized, treaty-based bloc of nations. The question for discussion is this; should the BRICS countries continue operating on the current basis for the foreseeable future or should these countries work towards a more formalized trade relationship? There are numerous dimensions to this question. This chapter does not look at the politico-economic issues underpinning such a decision but rather answers the query strictly from a trade and investment policy perspective.

Flexibility and adaptability are the indubitable advantages of the interest/pressure group option. This alternative may also be a safer course of action in the short term especially when viewed from the lens of domestic realpolitik, where some interest groups may not be amenable to closer cooperation with perceived regional rivals. Another advantage offered by this flexible approach is that the BRICS countries would be better able to juggle any conflicting commitments in other international groups such as the Shanghai Cooperation Organisation (SCO), Commonwealth of Independent States (CIS), OECD, G20, etc. For example, one indication of the BRICS countries utilizing their current affiliation is found in the 2012 Delhi Declaration:

> . . . the primary role of the G20 as premier forum for international economic cooperation at this juncture is to facilitate enhanced macroeconomic policy coordination, to enable global economic recovery and secure financial stability, including through an improved international monetary and financial architecture (BRICS, 2012a, para. 7; Bagchi, 2012).

Although this statement is purely on the issue of monetary stability following the recovery from the GFC, it does betray the reluctance of the BRICS leaders to commit to a more BRICS-exclusive relationship at this stage. The BRICS leaders continue to express hope for the successful conclusion of the beleaguered Doha Round and also endorse multilateralism as the best option to achieve this end. The BRICS leaders declared:

> We do not support plurilateral initiatives that go against the fundamental principles of transparency, inclusiveness and multilateralism. We believe that such initiatives not only distract members from striving for a collective outcome but also fail to address the development deficit inherited from previous negotiating rounds (BRICS, 2012a).

The upshot of these 'feel good' statements is that the BRICS leaders do not seek to unsettle the delicate monetary environment in the post-GFC recovery phase and are happy to continue their developmental trajectories in the current economic ordering. This strategy is safer but is not

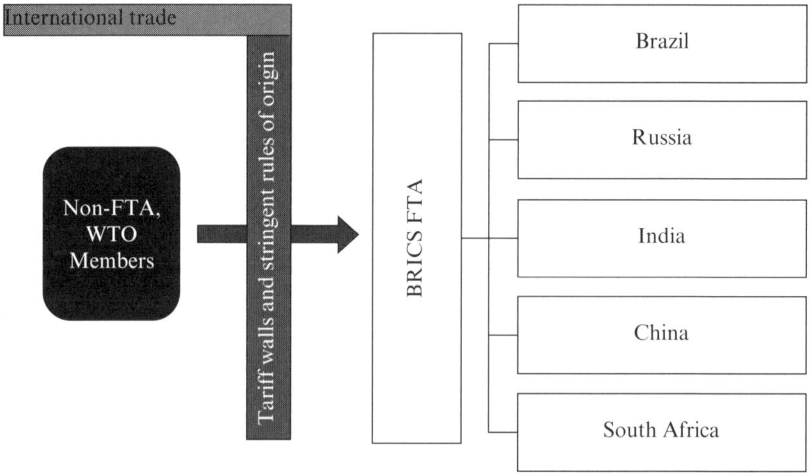

Source: Author's own calculation.

Figure 11.3 The BRICS FTA (exclusive)

necessarily the most appropriate in helping the BRICS countries achieve their true potential as regional investment and trade hubs. This means that the BRICS policymakers must eventually grapple with the question of their future direction as either exclusive or inclusive. This question, in turn, hinges on whether the BRICS decides to integrate its trade and investment flows under the aegis of a possible BRICS FTA.

In considering the FTA option, the BRICS policymakers must determine (amongst other things) its central character, that is, is the proposed FTA exclusive (a traditional, rigidly defined framework that excludes benefits to non-members), or inclusive (an innovative solution that takes into account the central role played by the BRICS countries in their respective regions)? Figure 11.3 summarizes the exclusive FTA option.

The underlying rationale for following the exclusive model is to promote maximization of public welfare through intra-BRICS trade and investment. The exclusive model envisions the BRICS members shielded behind high tariff barriers while simultaneously lowering tariffs for fellow BRICS members. Non-member countries or FTA partners of individual BRICS countries may continue trade according to the WTO's most-favoured-nation (MFN) status or according to their individual agreements respectively. The exclusive BRICS FTA structure aims to promote flow of intra-BRICS trade in goods, services and investment on a more preferential basis as compared to the individual FTA or investment treaties that any of the BRICS members enter into with other non-BRICS countries.

Purely from the perspective of intra-BRICS trade in goods, this structure may not be suitable for intra-BRICS trade in goods. This is due to the effects of general cuts in applied tariffs under the WTO commitments by member states (of which the BRICS countries are members). Therefore, the advantages offered by this model for conducting intra-BRICS trade in goods through a BRICS FTA are minimal. Any advantage that BRICS countries extend to each other under the exclusive model must go beyond mere cuts in tariffs, and must also encompass reduction/elimination of non-tariff barriers. The real gain under the exclusive model comes in the services trade and to a lesser extent in intra-BRICS investment.

In the services sector, China and India enjoy relatively more developed capacities than South Africa, Russia and Brazil. By incentivizing intra-BRICS services trade, BRICS-based service providers stand a better chance of competing against the EU-based suppliers (which are currently the largest supplier of services to the BRICS countries). However, if the BRICS policymakers opt for the exclusive model, then the risk is ignoring the advantages associated with the regional investment hub characteristic of the BRICS countries. This problem can be resolved by altering the structure of the BRICS FTA in more inclusive rather than exclusive terms (the alternative model is explained in Figure 11.4).

Under the alternative model ('inclusive FTA'), the BRICS countries conclude a FTA but deliberately maintain low tariffs and relaxed rules of

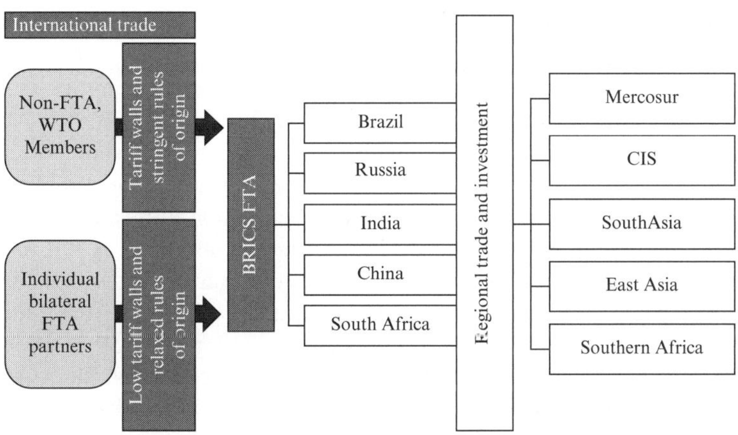

Source: Author's own calculation.

Figure 11.4 The BRICS FTA (inclusive)

origin towards a set of pre-identified countries, that is, countries that are already in a bilateral or regional FTA-type arrangement with one of the BRICS countries. To illustrate, Brazil is a member of the Latin American trading bloc known as Mercosur, and India is a party to the South Asian FTA (SAFTA) (a regional trade agreement covering seven other proximate South Asian countries). Brazil and India both identify trading partners in their respective regional FTAs at the time of conclusion of the BRICS FTA. The rationale behind maintaining low tariffs is to encourage inclusive trade with countries that are either in proximity to each of the BRICS members or are the usual investment venues for the BRICS-based small and medium enterprises (SMEs).

The inclusive model enables regional cumulation, which is particularly relevant to manufacturing. Regional cumulation allows for localized sourcing of inputs. Therefore as the BRICS members enhance their manufacturing capabilities and transition towards higher value added sectors, the need to source cheaper inputs increases. By maintaining low tariff barriers and relaxed rules of origin, the BRICS-based manufacturers are able to source necessary inputs at competitive prices. The actual manufacturing, value addition and quality control processes can be performed by the BRICS-based manufacturers themselves or, as needed, outsourced to cheaper venues. Figure 11.5 explains the effect of the inclusive approach on manufacturing of goods by BRICS countries. This model proceeds from the premise that the BRICS-based SMEs tend to invest closer to home whereas large SOEs invest in natural resources and infrastructure projects overseas.

Under the inclusive model, the BRICS-based SMEs invest in sectors in proximate countries or bilateral FTA partners that can provide cheaper inputs compared to indigenous sources. The producers in the recipient country are then incentivized to export these inputs to the investing country (the BRICS country), which maintains low tariffs and extends preferential treatment to such exports. These inputs are then used in manufacturing value added goods which are then exported at a competitive price (capitalizing on low wage levels and cheaper input costs).

The effect of structuring an inclusive FTA is that proximate countries are transformed into ready suppliers of inputs for eventual value added manufacturing within the BRICS countries (Figure 11.5). Therefore following the inclusive route can have a flow-on effect for the satellite economies in both regional and bilateral terms. China and India stand to gain the most from this model due to their more developed manufacturing bases and abundance of labour resources along with established investment profiles in their respective regions. Furthermore China already has an FTA with Pakistan and is also an active investor in South East Asian

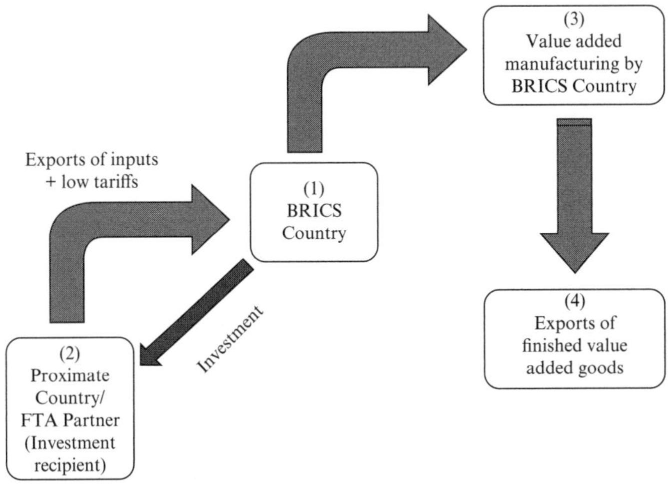

Source: Author's own calculation.

Figure 11.5 *Export manufacturing by the BRICS under the inclusive model*

countries. Similarly India is a member of the SAFTA and has undergone relaxation in trade and investment restrictions on Pakistan. The inclusive model affords these two countries with an immense opportunity to further enhance their manufacturing profiles by harnessing the potential of the proximate countries/bilateral FTA partners to furnish their input needs.

Other BRICS countries can follow a similar model to enhance their manufacturing competitiveness. The complementarities already exist. For example, Russia, South Africa and Brazil can consider outsourcing the labour intensive part of manufacturing in the form of SME investments to CIS, Southern African and Mercosur countries respectively, while retaining control over the value addition, quality assurance and eventual export processes.

Another aspect in favour of the inclusive model as the future blueprint for the BRICS is that it takes into account the eventual regional transmission that occurs with rising manufacturing costs. Briefly this transmission occurs when industries facing high operational costs and import competition evolve into investors. These manufacturers transfer their manufacturing capabilities through FDI in other developing countries in the same region. This regional transmission is referred to as the 'flying geese' model[4] where a country ('lead goose') transplants its manufacturing expertise in proximate countries ('follower goose') where wage levels are lower than those of the transmitting country (Kojima, 2001, p.377; Dowling & Cheang, 2000, pp.443–6). Japan followed the same pattern in the late 1960s when it gradually began the process of transmitting the textiles and clothing sector to South Korea, Taiwan and China. There are strong indications that Chinese textiles and clothing manufacturers are following a similar path by outsourcing their operations to countries such as Vietnam, Laos and Indonesia due to rising wages in the coastal manufacturing belts (Ghori, 2012, pp.169–74, 220–25). In doing so, Chinese manufacturers are essentially jettisoning the now less lucrative sectors in favour of higher value added sectors, but at the same time these manufacturers retain control over their business interests through investment transactions (Ghori, 2012, pp.169–74, 220–25).

Therefore by structuring their future trading activities under the inclusive model, the BRICS policymakers ensure that their manufacturers can easily transition to becoming investors in ready-to-access, outsourcing venues proximate to their countries. However, it must be kept in mind that the future structures described earlier are no more than possibilities and that in order to reap the immense opportunities afforded through the FTA path, the BRICS must first contend with significant fault lines that hinder closer economic cooperation.

Fault Lines

Controlling China and resolving disputes

The first of such fault lines stems from within; the fear of total dominance by China. With its massive manufacturing capability coupled with the advantages flowing from its monetary policies, China is a cause of worry not just to the developed economies but also to fellow BRICS members. The biggest potential winners emerging from any BRICS FTA (regardless of the structure adopted) would undoubtedly be China followed by India due to their relatively better developed manufacturing bases compared to South Africa, Brazil and Russia. Any FTA incorporating tariff reductions would immediately increase competitive pressures on BRICS-based domestic manufacturers. This contention becomes all the more plausible when the adverse effects of imports from China on Brazilian footwear and South Africa's textiles industries are considered (Naidu, 2011). Thus there is understandable apprehension amongst some of the BRICS countries over the desirability of extending any more trade benefits to China beyond the WTO MFN standard.

One response to such concerns may be that since China is now a member of the WTO, other BRICS countries can easily employ trade remedy measures such as safeguards to protect their economies from an influx of damaging imports. This response may partially answer the problem but could lead to an increase in referrals to the WTO dispute settlement system. This system itself is a much criticized, time-consuming process often accused of providing relief long after damage has been done to the importing economy.[5] The other alternative is that a BRICS-specific dispute settlement system be integrated into any future BRICS FTA. In simpler terms, any new system devised by the BRICS countries must be more efficient and less time-consuming than the existing WTO system.

A further challenge is that the intra-BRICS dispute settlement system must also cover investment disputes between the BRICS-based investors and the host countries. Nowadays investment disputes are increasingly being resolved through institutional dispute settlement mechanisms under the International Centre for Settlement of Investment Disputes (ICSID) Convention, the ICSID Additional Facility and the UNCITRAL Arbitration Rules (ICSID, 2006; UNCITRAL, 2010). The ICSID system is the most commonly adopted investment dispute mechanism and establishes arbitration as the primary method for resolving state–investor disputes. Countries can directly incorporate the ICSID mechanism within their FTAs/investment treaties and thus reduce reliance on domestic courts for dispute resolution. The ICSID Additional Facility is a variant of the ICSID system which covers the situation where one party to the investment dispute is a signatory to the ICSID and the other is not. Arbitration under the UNCITRAL Arbitration Rules is yet another alternative that states, investors or even private parties can use as a dispute settlement mechanism.

It is interesting to note that Brazil, India and South Africa are not signatories to the ICSID Convention, whilst Russia is a signatory but has not ratified the ICSID Convention. Therefore for all practical purposes Russia does not apply the ICSID Convention to state–investor disputes. The general effect of not being privy to the ICSID convention means that if any of the non-party countries is involved in an investment dispute with foreign investors, an ICSID arbitration process cannot be undertaken unless they agree to resolve their dispute through the ICSID Additional Facility.

If the BRICS decides to form an inclusive FTA and envisions greater intra-BRICS investment, then this increases the importance of a uniform system of investment arbitration, especially when the investment trends by BRICS-based transnational corporations (TNCs) are considered. Tables 11.1 and 11.2 show that the main investment focus by the BRICS-based transnational corporations is in the natural resources sector, which is the sector most prone to expropriation by the host state. A further complication comes through the fact that the majority of investment in the natural resources sector from the BRICS-based TNCs is actually made by large SOEs. This is especially true in the case of China and Russia. In other words, the outward investment is in reality coming from a state organ. This creates immense problems if the host state expropriates the investment. Without a uniform investment arbitration regime, either in the form of accession to the ICSID Convention or a BRICS-specific dispute settlement system, the BRICS-based SOEs may become reluctant to make their investments.

Adopting a BRICS-specific dispute settlement route means that special attention needs to be given to the enforceability of awards. The importance of this issue comes from the fact that some of the BRICS countries such as Russia and China apply the doctrine of absolute state immunity, which greatly hinders enforceability of arbitral awards. A well-known arbitration matter demonstrating the hardship of parties which have secured an arbitral award but struggle at the enforcement stage is *Sedelmayer v The Russian Federation* (7 July 1998, Stockholm, Sweden). In this case between Russia and a German national, Russia's claim for sovereign immunity was rejected because it was party to the Bilateral Investment Treaty (BIT) with Germany. This fact was considered as the basis of the waiver of sovereign immunity as far as arbitration proceedings were concerned. However, the waiver was not extended to the enforcement proceedings following an award in favour of Sedelmayer in July 1998. It took Sedelmayer ten years and multiple enforcement actions in various European jurisdictions against Russian commercial interests to finally start the recovery process.

Sedelmayer's difficulties in enforcing the arbitral award show the hardship that foreign investors may face when dealing with countries applying the doctrine of absolute state immunity. In the enforcement stage, the private party must prove that assets of the state located within the enforcement jurisdiction are commercial in nature and not for the use of the sovereign. The opposing state may resist these proceedings by adopting the defence of non-disclosure of state information. In short, as the BRICS enhances its mutual investment activities it must adequately prepare for the inevitable investment disputes that arise when large volumes of investments are made in the natural resources, infrastructure and other sensitive sectors. Adopting an intra-BRICS dispute settlement regime for both trade and investment certainly carries its own challenges, particularly when reconciling competing interests within the BRICS. The complications associated with such an idea may well lead the BRICS policymakers to automatically consign the idea to the 'not possible' basket. However, if the BRICS contemplates closer trade and investment relations, then sooner or later its policymakers must grapple with issues pertaining to dispute settlement and the enforcement of settlement awards.

Payments in domestic currencies and establishment of the BRICS Bank

As part of promoting intra-BRICS commerce, the BRICS leaders in their 2012 meeting in New Delhi declared their support for the establishment of the BRICS Bank in order to mobilize 'resources for infrastructure and sustainable development projects **in BRICS and other emerging economies and developing countries** [emphasis added]'(BRICS, 2012a, para. 13). The proposed BRICS Bank accomplishes several aims. The first is the facilitation of payment in own currencies in order to lessen the effects of currency volatility while enhancing intra-BRICS trade flow by allowing settlement in own currencies (BRICS, 2012b, p. 171; Auboin, 2012, pp. 3–8). This idea assumes greater importance in the wake of the GFC and the demonstrated volatility of major global currencies markets. Clearing invoices in domestic currencies is an attempt by the BRICS policymakers to break free of the risks associated with invoicing in major international currencies. In this regard, China has made significant progress by invoicing bilateral trade in the renminbi and promoting the Hong Kong-based offshore bond market since 2009 (BRICS, 2012b, p. 171; Auboin, 2012, p. 14). Another attempt of settlement through local currencies in bilateral trade was made by Brazil and Argentina in 2008. This scheme was managed by the central banks of these Latin American countries and covered trade in goods and other costs such as insurance and freight (BRICS, 2012b, p. 171; Parks & McCarthy, 2012).

The second aim of the BRICS Bank is to cater for the ever increasing developmental needs of the BRICS countries. However, the language used in the New Delhi Declaration gives a sure hint that the BRICS recognizes the benefits of inclusivity for the future. The immediate focus of the BRICS Bank would be on infrastructure development since this is the key determining factor in economic growth (Wilson, Burgi & Carlson, 2011, p. 2). As the BRICS economies expand, the need to establish new projects while upgrading the existing infrastructure greatly increases. Infrastructure will also assume greater importance if the inclusive FTA option is looked at with a wider scope. The aim of the inclusive FTA route is to become regional trading hubs where the proximate non-BRICS countries act as investment recipients and producers of raw materials/inputs for value added processing in the BRICS countries. A well-established infrastructure obviously aids this aim.

The BRICS has global political ambitions as well. The BRICS Bank is one manifestation of this ambition. The existing developmental institutions such as the World Bank and the IMF are dominated by the developed countries, and the latest appointment of the World Bank leadership is the continuation of the same trend. The New Delhi Summit saw the BRICS members criticizing the West for financial mismanagement, and now with the proposed BRICS Bank, these rising economies seek to demonstrate their growing power, influence and independence in order to spearhead much needed reform of the international financial system (Xu, 2012; Bagchi, 2012).

The idea of the BRICS Bank remains in the early stages of development. Essential issues such as funding, mandate and governance still need to be ironed out. However, the greatest challenge comes from the divergences within the BRICS. These countries have distinct politico-economic systems and harbour mutual suspicion of each other's ambitions. One indication of this suspicion and rivalry is the view of Indian finance officials on the BRICS Bank being an attempt to legitimize the use of the renminbi in international trade (Bagchi, 2012). Another view is that the BRICS Bank would be under the heavy influence of China because other BRICS countries currently lack the financial capacity to fund such an institution (Bagchi, 2012). These opinions show that internal division among the BRICS countries hinders closer economic cooperation. It will take the BRICS countries some time to overcome their suspicion and rivalry in order to forge mutual trust.

Intellectual property issues

Another fault line concerns the chequered reputation of the BRICS in protecting intellectual property (IP) rights. This fault line has two dimensions. The first is the external dimension which represents the concerns of developed countries. The second is the internal dimension which concerns the trade and investment dynamics of the BRICS countries.

As far as the external dimension is concerned, the BRICS faces continuous criticism from the US and other developed countries on its deficient IP protection. The most recent criticism came in December 2012 in the form of low rankings awarded by the US Chamber of Commerce in a new index for protecting copyrights, patents and other types of intellectual property (Palmer, 2012). This index is intended as a policy instrument by the US to seek protection for US copyrights, patents and trade secrets in FTAs and other international negotiations (Palmer, 2012). The index rates 11 countries on a point scale from zero to 25. The US receives the highest score of 23.73, followed by the UK at 22.40 (Palmer, 2012). Amongst the BRICS countries, India ranks last with 6.24 points, whilst China, Brazil and Russia score 9.13, 9.57 and 11.17 respectively (Palmer, 2012). The major points of concern expressed in this index are software and music piracy, patent violations (in particular the licensing of generic drug manufacturers that undercut the patent holding US pharmaceuticals), and lack of protection of trade secrets (Palmer, 2012; Bird & Cahoy, 2007, pp. 402–10). This is damaging criticism indeed. If the BRICS aims to enhance its trade and investment relations with the developed countries, then allaying these concerns assumes central importance (Bird & Cahoy, 2007, pp. 410–11).

In addition, the BRICS countries must grapple with the internal dimension of IP protection. This becomes important as the BRICS enhances its mutual investment and trade activities, especially in sectors involving innovation such as India's IT industries and Brazil's aeronautical sectors. The BRICS policymakers must cater for the eventual transformation of the BRICS countries from manufacturers to innovators. Therefore it is in the longer-term interests of the BRICS to improve its IP protection regime. The BRICS-specific IP protection regime is also essential if the BRICS decides to pursue an FTA based on the inclusive model since this would involve dealings with non-BRICS FTA countries. Without a strong IP protection regime and an internal dispute settlement system that resolves disputes expeditiously, closer economic cooperation (especially in the technology-intensive industries) would remain but a dream.

THE ROAD AHEAD

The BRICS is not a treaty-based entity and only exists because the countries involved believe it is in their immediate interests. Longer-term engagement can only be assured if the BRICS countries solidify their relations in the form of a treaty. This is by no means an easy task. Concluding treaties means undergoing a difficult process of give and take where countries do not always get their own way. As a result, countries carefully examine the effects of treaty implementation in their domestic sphere. In the event of incompatibility, countries often express dissatisfaction with the entire process and aim to renegotiate their obligations to better suit their interests.

We can see that the BRICS countries are trying to find common grounds for enhanced partnerships. We can see joint statements following 'successful' summits. However, there is not much that can be achieved collectively by these countries if the current loose interest/pressure group type arrangement continues. It appears that because of politico-economic and geostrategic factors, some of the BRICS countries are reluctant to move beyond the current malleable state of the BRICS. Flexibility and adaptability are indeed desirable attributes that are offered by the present approach, but the benefits of such an approach will stagnate in the future as the BRICS economies expand.

If the expansion of the BRICS economies along the current trade and investment trends continues, then in the next few years the BRICS members would assume leading positions in the global economy. These economies have already demonstrated their resilience to the GFC by recording growth even when developed economies were in recession. Data cited in part one of this chapter shows the varied performances in investment, trade and services sectors by the BRICS economies. This is a clear indication of the relative strengths and weakness of the BRICS economies. A closer and more coordinated approach would allow the BRICS countries to capitalize on each other's strengths. This aim can only be accomplished if a formal treaty-based structure is adopted as opposed to the current pressure group structure. Notwithstanding the challenges and the fault lines that hinder closer economic cooperation, the benefits of formalizing financial, trade and investment relations surpass those of the loose interest/pressure group type arrangement in the long run.

The BRICS policymakers must also keep in mind the lack of diversity exhibited in the trade and investment behaviour of the BRICS countries. For example, Brazil, Russia and South Africa are heavily reliant on exports of natural resources and commodities (BRICS, 2012b, p. 166). Lack of diversity can be cured by following through with the FTA option because this structure allows maximum exploitation of potential complementarities that exist in countries exhibiting a lack of diversification in their export baskets. In other words, the BRICS members have the potential to feed off each other's strengths to become leading suppliers of commodities, manufacturers of goods and exporters of services.

Closer cooperation in the form of the BRICS Bank would also assist in meeting the growing infrastructure demands of the BRICS economies. But this endeavour (difficult to initiate and establish) cannot succeed in isolation without complementary support from an FTA. The FTA itself requires far-reaching reforms and a change in attitudes in order for it to go ahead. Also, any FTA must involve greater public-private partnership and inputs from the industries to achieve success. In the post-GFC recovery phase the BRICS countries have the opportunity to become a stabilizing factor for the global economy. A closely coordinated position in the form of an inclusive FTA carries immense rewards not just for the BRICS economies but for other developing countries as well.

NOTES

1. For example, the estimated growth rate in the fourth quarter (2012) for both China and India was 9.3 per cent and 7.7 per cent respectively.

2. See for example China's oil giant CNOOC Ltd's failed attempt in 2005 to acquire US oil company Unocal Corporation because of intense political pressure from the US Congress, or the Chinese telecom Huawei's attempt to partner with US-based Bain Capital Partners to secure 16.5 per cent of shares in 3Com Corp, a US company that manufactured systems designed to protect against computer hackers (see UCLA, n.d.).
3. The BRICS Report identifies 13 focus areas for closer cooperation. These include cooperation in intra-BRICS trade and investment, infrastructure financing, industrial development, transport, food security, technical education, financial markets, research, tourism, energy security and a development bank for promoting South–South investment.
4. This theory was pioneered by Japanese economist Kaname Akamatsu in the 1930s and further developed by Kiyoshi Kojima. According to Akamatsu, the 'wild-geese flying pattern of industrial development denotes the development after the less-advanced country's economy enters into an international economic relationship with the advanced countries'.
5. The best illustration is Ecuador's experience with the EU in the wake of *EC – Bananas III* (WT/DS27/AB/R) decision despite having obtained WTO-Dispute Settlement Body (DSB) authorization to cross-retaliate in the intellectual property sector.

REFERENCES

Auboin, M. (2012, May). *Use of currencies in international trade: Any changes in the picture?* (WTO Staff Working Paper ERSD-2012-10). Retrieved from http://www.wto.org/english/res_e/reser_e/ersd201210_e.pdf

Bagchi, I. (2012, March 30). BRICS summit: Member nations criticizes [sic] the West for financial mismanagement. *The Times of India*. Retrieved from http://articles.timesofindia.indiatimes.com/2012-03-30/india/31260243_1_brics-summit-brics-economies-brics-development-bank

Bajpai, N. (2011, July). *Global financial crisis, its impact on India and the policy response* (Working Paper No. 5). New York: Columbia Global Centers, Columbia University. Retrieved from http://globalcenters.columbia.edu/content/global-financial-crisis-its-impact-india-and-policy-response

Bird, R.C. and Cahoy, D.R. (2007). The emerging BRIC economies: Lessons from intellectual property negotiation and enforcement. *Northwestern Journal of Technology and Intellectual Property*, *5*(3), 398–425.

BRICS (2012a, March 29). *Fourth BRICS summit: Delhi declaration*. Retrieved from http://www.bricsindia.in/delhi-declaration.html

BRICS (2012b). *The BRICS report: A study of Brazil, Russia, India, China, and South Africa with special focus on synergies and complementarities*. India: Oxford University Press.

Commission on International Trade Law (UNCITRAL) (2010). *UNCITRAL arbitration rules (as revised in 2010)*. Retrieved from http://www.uncitral.org/pdf/english/texts/arbitration/arb-rules-revised/arb-rules-revised-2010-e.pdf

Dowling, M. and Cheang, C.T. (2000). Shifting comparative advantage in Asia: New tests of the 'flying geese' model. *Journal of Asian Economics*, *11*(4), 443–63.

Gammeltoft, P. (2008, September). *Emerging multinationals: Outward FDI from the BRICS countries*. Paper presented at the IV Globelics Conference, Mexico City.

Ghori, U.H. (2012). *Global textiles and clothing trade – Trade policy perspectives*. The Hague: Kluwer Law International.

International Convention for Settlement of Investment Disputes (ICSID) (2006,

April 10). *Rules*. Retrieved from https://icsid.worldbank.org/ICSID/ICSID/RulesMain.jsp

Kojima, K. (2000). The 'flying geese' model of Asian economic development: Origin, theoretical extensions, and regional policy implications. *Journal of Asian Economics*, *11*(4), 375–401.

Naidu, S. (2011, April 19). What influence does China have in BRICS? *China US Focus*. Retrieved from http://www.chinausfocus.com/slider/what-influence-does-china-have-in-brics/

Palmer, D. (2012, December 11). BRICs score lowest on intellectual property protection index. *Reuters*. Retrieved from http://www.reuters.com/article/2012/12/11/trade-copyright-countries-idUSL1E8NA77920121211

Parks, K. and McCarthy, E. (2012, May 17). Argentina, Brazil local-currency trade makes slow headway. *The Wall Street Journal*. Retrieved from http://online.wsj.com/article/SB10001424052702303448404577410520154520612.html

Sedelmayer v The Russian Federation (1998, July 7). *Arbitration Award*. Stockholm, Sweden. Retrieved from http://italaw.com/documents/investment_sedelmayer_v_ru.pdf

UCLA (n.d.) *Asian American Studies Center*. Retrieved from http://www.aasc.ucla.edu/uschina/trade_investment.shtml

UNCTAD (2012). *World investment report 2012: Towards a new generation of investment policies*. Retrieved from http://unctad.org/en/Pages/DIAE/World%20Investment%20Report/WIR2012_WebFlyer.aspx

Wilson, D., Burgi, C. and Carlson, S. (2011). A progress report on the building of the BRICs. *BRICS Monthly*, *11*(7). Retrieved from http://www.goldmansachs.com/our-thinking/topics/brics/brics-reports-pdfs/progress-on-building-the-brics.pdf

WTO (2012). *International trade statistics 2012: Trade in commercial services*. Retrieved from http://www.wto.org/english/res_e/statis_e/its2012_e/its12_trade_category_e.htm

Xu, M. (2012, April 28). Will a common development bank benefit the BRICS? *China US Focus*. Retrieved from http://www.chinausfocus.com/finance-economy/will-a-common-development-bank-benefit-the-brics/

12. The BRICS: A model for living on the earth

Dilyara B. Karimova

Official economic reality is steadily forming among the BRICS members in terms of both political and economic participation. In fact the five BRICS countries together encompass:

- 50 per cent in terms of adjusted global GDP in the 2000–08 period;
- the highest economic growth (over the past decade their economies have grown by 4.2 times compared with 61 per cent growth in developed countries);
- 42 per cent of the world's population;
- 26 per cent of the Earth's territory;
- 20 per cent of the global economy; and
- 14.6 per cent of the world's trade (BRICS, 2012c).

The fast growing 'modus operandi of the twenty-first century', free from bureaucratic paraphernalia, is representative of a new kind of institution; the BRICS is such an institution, with its own political ambitions in terms of the changing global balance (Azambuja, 2010). All the BRICS countries are prominent members of the UN, G8 and G20 at both a global and regional scale. As 'the key pieces on the global chessboard' (Pereyra, 2012), the BRICS group 'could become a much more significant force in the world economy' and 'would dramatically change the list of the world's 10 largest economies' (BRICS, 2012b). Within the last ten years this informal union of the fastest growing economies has achieved an intensive agenda:

- 2006 September (NY), UN Session, Summit of Prime Ministers of Brazil, China, India and Russia;
- 2008 July (Japan), meeting of Brazil, China, India and Russia following on from the G8 meeting;
- 2009 March (Brazil), Summit of Ministers of Finance of the BRIC members;

- 2009 June (Russia), the first BRIC Summit;
- April 2010 (Brasilia), the second BRIC Summit (discussing how to overcome the world financial crisis, creation of a new financial structure and enhancement of the BRIC members' influence in the World Bank and the IMF);
- November 2010 (Korea), South Africa expressed a will to enter the BRIC group at the G20 Summit;
- April 2011 (China), the third BRIC Summit (South Africa became the fifth BRICS member and accepted the Declaration in relation to the fast accession of Russia to the WTO, reorganization of the UN and peaceful resolution of the Lebanon situation); and
- March 2012 (India), the fourth BRICS Summit (planning to create a new mutual bank, mechanisms for the development and rapprochement of the national markets and also strengthening of national currencies).

COMMUNITY OF INTERESTS AS THE FOUNDATION FOR NEW POSSIBILITIES AND NEW ANSWERS TO THE 'OLD' RESOURCE QUESTIONS

Real economic power resulting from fast growing economies, demographics, natural resource potential and historically maintained national values have proven to be good ingredients for a new kind of unstructured global rearrangement which characterizes the BRICS.

In the BRICS context the model of its sustainable development has led to a real and profound growth. However, economic models simulated in terms of the sustainable development approach do not take into account the influence of both political and technological developments (Peccei, 1980; Forrester 1971, 1978). This point is well-known and has been discussed at length by both Western and former Soviet political economists, including ecological economists (Jahoda, Pavitt, Cole & Freeman, 1973; Ryumina, 2000; Makhov, 2005).[1] Such an approach seems to continue the traditions of colonialism, where the political system governing the world economic relations between a mother country, its colonies and other countries is replaced by a system governing the availability of natural resources. But is it even possible for the introduction and development of new technologies to be under the same strong prohibition and control? Historical experience and the current economic realities of the BRICS members contribute to the creation of long-shared interests for the group that bring them together to face a multitude of common challenges related to both economic and social modernization. These shared interests include:

1. The group's commitment to international law and rejection of power politics and infringement on others' sovereignty.
2. The reform of the outdated global financial architecture, characterized by the long existing South–North kind of relations, which does not reflect the increased economic weight of the BRICS and other emerging economies. The group's initiatives to launch a new kind of development bank are an important step.
3. Mutual complementarity among many sectors of the BRICS economies, which have been clearly identified by researchers, can lead to a new kind of synergistic cooperation, and also contribute to the strategic rapprochement in terms of the emerging multipolar system.

According to the Delhi Declaration, adopted by the fourth BRICS Summit, 'BRICS is a platform for dialogue and cooperation in transcontinental dimension, where Asia, Africa, Europe, Latin America take part', and 'the expected future is to be characterized by global peace, economic and social development, and also comprehensive scientific approach' (BRICS, 2012a). These formulations differ from a traditional approach where social and technological developments are not considered. In this context, ideas concerning the BRICS vision of the future strike a new note:

1. Establishment of a more representative international financial architecture.
2. Creation and improvement of the international monetary system that will promote sustainable development of emerging economies.
3. Elimination of opium trafficking.
4. Maintenance of peace and stability in Afghanistan, East and Northern African regions (BRICS, 2012b, art. 4).

According to the Minister of Foreign Affairs of Russia, Sergei Lavrov, the priorities of Russia in the context of the BRICS, are as follows:

1. Cooperation within the BRICS is a key long-term foreign policy priority for the Russian Federation. Russia welcomes a step-by-step transformation from this cooperation into a multilateral strategic partnership, embracing far-ranging issues of global economy and politics.
2. Russia supports the positioning of the BRICS as a new model of global relations overriding the old East–West or North–South barriers. The association of states populated by almost 3 billion people is not likely to limit itself to the role of bridge or mediator between the

North and the South, or to operating only within the South–South political space, because such an approach would definitely restrict the opportunities for the BRICS to pursue independent policies in international affairs.

3. Russia calls upon its BRICS partners to adopt priorities for international security. First, the BRICS must coordinate its position and formulate joint proposals for strategic stability, international and regional security, non-proliferation of weapons of mass destruction, as well as resolution of regional conflicts and maintaining regional stability. Second, the BRICS should engage in joint efforts to strengthen the UN's role in the fight against terrorism, ensuring the implementation of its Global Counter-Terrorism Strategy and universal anti-terrorism conventions, as well as strict compliance with relevant UN Security Council resolutions. Third, the BRICS should coordinate its approach to combat illicit drug trafficking and take joint steps to regulate this issue in the UN and related regional organizations. Fourth, the BRICS' interaction should support international information security, with greater cooperation in combating cyberterrorism and cybercrime. Fifth, the BRICS should enhance its cooperation with stakeholders in fighting maritime piracy, and increase efforts to create an international mechanism for prosecuting and punishing pirates (BRICS, 2012c).

As the Russian President, Dmitrii Medvedev, mentioned in 2012, reforming the international monetary and financial system will remain a key long-term priority of the BRICS cooperation (Official Site of the President of Russia, 2012). These tasks can be achieved mainly through the existing international institutions, including the G20. Every effort should be made to strengthen the G20's central role in responding to global financial shocks and in reforming the global financial and economic architecture.

Russia attaches great importance to using the established structures of cooperation within the BRICS to accelerate the modernization of each member's economy to its fullest potential, ensure food and energy security, and address social issues. It is essential to raise mutual awareness of each member's culture and traditions in order to expand public support for the objectives of the members as a group. A shared information network for the BRICS members could help to accomplish this objective. In fact by 2014, the BRICS will be able to engage in Internet communication through a unique cable system, which is 34000 km long and 12.8 TBt/s capacity.

WHAT IS IN ALL THAT FOR ECOLOGY?

An unsustainable model of natural and human resources exploitation will cause the ultimate depletion of those resources, which in resource-dependent economies will lead to increasing ecological damage. Being resource-dependent, the BRICS members are all faced with similar ecological problems that are both the result of and the price of rapid economic growth. And what is more important, these problems must be solved *in situ*, without impacting on financial, natural or human resources, by the BRICS members themselves as the largest owners, largest consumers and the largest operators. In such a new economic context, the BRICS obviously has a vested interest in working out new solutions to environmental problems. A comprehensive approach to solving environmental problems is fundamental to truly sustainable development, an approach based on the introduction and development of new technologies and management skills in national systems and not only through formal rearrangement of the tax system or for the account of internal markets of national economies. Such new technologies and management skills are becoming vital, and that is why the label of 'externalities' is hardly effective (Karimova, 2012a–g).

A new understanding of the principles regarding the transformation of mineral matter can be used to create more resource and energy efficient management decisions. For example, regarding the 'old' problem of coal ash utilization, ash material has been investigated by different complex physical-chemical methods, including transmission electron microscopy. The results prove that because of its structural transformation, the coal ash's properties have changed dramatically. The key role of water in the physical-structural rearrangements of coal ash has also been explained. At the first stage coal ash is an extremely useful material, which can be used as it is in the production of clinker and chamotte. Fifty years after being deposited, it is transformed into sand-like material that is ecologically safe, and can be used as a filler material for land levelling if its pH characteristic is close to that of country rocks (see Figure 12.1). These physical-structural results have been used as the basic arguments for adopting legal regulations to organize the secondary usage of coal ash wastes instead of its land deposition.

Figure 12.2 shows the results for the mechanism of gold concentration and deposition in vein material which has been demonstrated. This data proves that vein quartz material is a rich source of Au^0 (from 'invisible' gold) and can help to improve traditional technologies of gold ore exploration and extraction (Stenina et al., 1995; Gubareva & Vaskov, 1997; Gubareva & Stenina, 1997, 1998a, 1998b; Stenina & Gubareva, 1996, 1997).

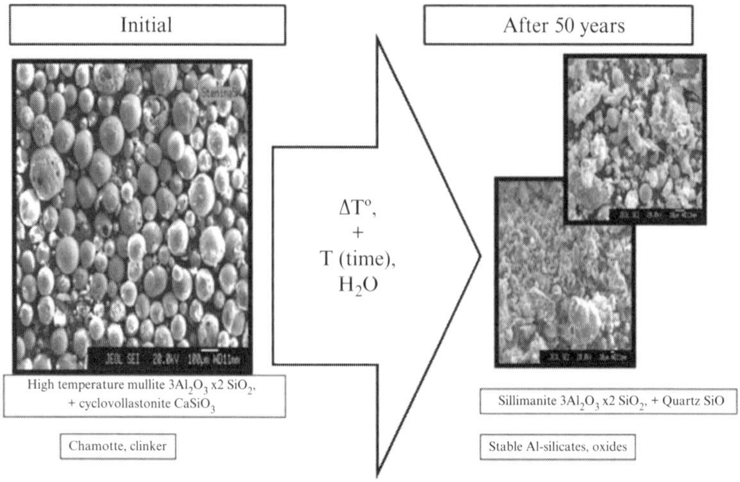

Source: Karimova (2012g).

Figure 12.1 New knowledge about the structural and physical-chemical properties of ash (coal energy waste)

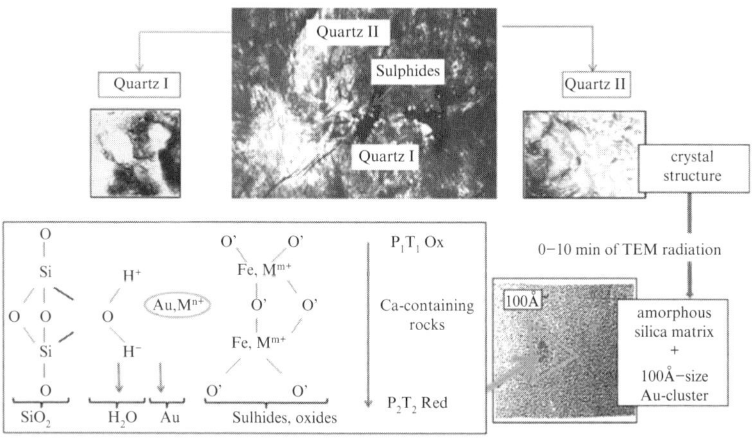

Sources: Stenina et al. (1995, 1996, 1997); Gubareva (1997, 1998a, 1998b).

Figure 12.2 The nature of the 'invisible' gold in quartz: Visual stories of clean quartz (I) and Au-pregnant quartz (II) from the gold-bearing vein quartz from the Sarala ore field (Kuznetskii Alatau)

New knowledge about the physical properties of mineral matter and new technological solutions based on that new knowledge become reliable foundations for new management solutions, which not only utilize new knowledge and technological solutions, but can also change the direction of economic and political developments of the national economy. Such an approach should not be formal because it requires a new kind of comprehensive thinking, aimed at finding environmental solutions *in situ*, which takes into consideration the national interests of the BRICS economies.

CONCLUSIONS

Being resource-dependent, the BRICS nations are faced with similar environmental problems – as a result of, and the price the pay for, their rapid economic growth. These problems must be solved *in situ* without depletion of their national wealth (World Bank, 2006) This is why environmental externalities in the BRICS context make it necessary to develop and introduce new technologies and management skills to produce rapid economic and political growth. This task can be achieved through a comprehensive approach based on new knowledge about the physical properties of mineral matter, which leads to the development of new technological solutions, resulting in new management solutions.

This chapter has demonstrated how an understanding of the mechanisms of physical-chemical structural transformation over time can provide solutions for secondary usage of coal ash waste instead of its deposition, and how revealing the mechanism of gold concentration and deposition in vein material yields solutions for rich new sources of Au^0 (from 'invisible' gold) and an improvement on traditional technologies of gold ore exploration and extraction.

NOTE

1. This discussion entails a detailed critique of the 'Limits to Growth' approach, addressing assumptions, methodologies and results. The authors believe that the 'Limits to Growth' approach is negative in outlook and simply 'computerizes' inappropriate theories. A brief response by the authors of the 'Limits to Growth' approach is included, focusing on the five major areas of disagreement: 1) short-term vs long-term models, using the results of a single model vs large scale considerations; 2) stability vs dynamic characteristics of specific variables; 3) use of 'perfect' models vs 'imperfect' models for policy making; 4) the role of mankind relative to the Earth; and 5) 'modeling of socio-ecological systems, based on the technical approach of modeling analysis without assumptions of the main patterns of economic development, means cancellation from its decision at the very beginning'. It should be noted that the Rome Club was created as an informal union of science, business and politics.

REFERENCES

Azambuja, M. (2010). Making the BRIC project work: Institutional aspects. In N. Unnikrishnan and S. Saran (Eds), *BRIC in the new world order: Perspectives from Brazil, China, India and Russia*. New Delhi: Macmillan India.

BRICS (2012a, March 29). *Fourth BRICS summit: Delhi declaration*. Retrieved from http://www.mid.ru/brics.nsf/WEBdocBric/1DB82FF3745BA8FE442579D5004778E6

BRICS (2012b). *The BRICS report: A study of Brazil, Russia, India, China, and South Africa with special focus on synergies and complementarities*. India: Oxford University Press.

BRICS (2012c). *Wikipedia: BRICS*. Retrieved from http://ru.wikipedia.org/wiki/%D0%91%D0%A0%D0%98%D0%9A%D0%A1

Forrester, J.W. (1971). *Urban dynamics*. Moscow: Progress.

Forrester, J.W. (1978). *World dynamics*. Moscow: Progress.

Gubareva (Karimova), D.B. and Stenina, N.G. (1997). Energy of connection of water in matrix of silica as the indicator its ore-bearing. In *The basic problems in the doctrine about magmatogenic ore deposits* (pp. 217–8). Moscow: IGEM.

Gubareva (Karimova), D.B. and Stenina, N.G. (1998a). Crystallochemical features of water and impurities incorporation in natural vein quartz. *Materials Structure*, special issue A, pp. 250–56.

Gubareva (Karimova), D.B. and Stenina N.G. (1998b, August). *Microstrucutural features of natural vein quartz*. 18th European Crystallographical Meeting, Prague, Czech Republic.

Gubareva (Karimova), D.B. and Vaskov, A.S. (1997, December). *Features of ore-bearing of quartz from gold-bearing veins of Sarala ore field under the data of analysis of its crystallochemical features*. Abstract presented at the Youth and problems of geology XXI centuries international workshop, Tomsk, Russia.

Jahoda, M., Pavitt, K.L.R., Cole, H.S.D. and Freeman, C. (1973). *Models of doom: A critique of the limits to growth*. England: Universe Books.

Karimova, D. (2012a). Eco-effectiveness for the governing solutions under low carbon economy. *Ecological Review of Russia*, *8*, 22–7.

Karimova, D. (2012b). Eco-effectiveness of the environmental activity in Russia in 2005–2010. *Ecological Review of Russia*, *6*, 20–27.

Karimova, D. (2012c). Ecology can become objective. *Fuel Energy Complex*, *2*, 50 51.

Karimova. D. (2012d). New environmental demands give rise new solutions. *Environmental Review of Russia*, *8*, 1.

Karimova, D. (2012e, April). *New solutions for eco-effectiveness in current economic situation of Russia*. Paper presented at the fourth Political Economy of Energy in Europe and Russia (PEEER) conference, Perm, Russia.

Karimova, D. (2012f, December). *Sustainable resource development*. UNESCO International Training Course, Moscow, Russia.

Karimova, D. (2012g, August). *The holistic approach for the solution of the current environmental problems of the energetic industry*. Paper presented at the Global Ecological Problems Conference, Moscow, Russia.

Lavrov, S. (2012). *BRICS – Global forum of new generation*. Retrieved from http://www.mid.ru/brics.nsf/WEBforumBric/F8C251DB09032059442579C000531B68

Makhov, S.A. (2005). *Mathematical simulation of world dynamics and sustainable development by the example of Forrester's model.* Retrieved from http://www.keldysh.ru/papers/2005/prep06/prep2005_06.html

Official Site of the President of Russia (2012, March). *Russian President's address at the BRICS summit.* Retrieved from http://eng.news.kremlin.ru/transcripts/3608/print

Peccei, A. (1980). *The human quality.* Moscow: Progress.

Pereyra, C. (2012, February 3). Sudamérica y el Caribe, donde el BRICS desafía al viejo orden mundial. *Rebelion.* Retrieved from http://www.aporrea.org/internacionales/a137838.html

Ryumina, L. (2000). *The analyses of the ecological-social interactions.* Moscow: Nauka.

Stenina, N.G., Berezin, Yu. A., Gutakovskii, A.K., Distanova, A.N. and Gubareva (Karimova), D.B. (1995). Transport and mechanisms of concentration of metals under transformation of mineral substance. *RFFR in the Siberian area (Earth crust and mantle). Theses of the reports, Irkutsk, ò.2, Petrology, geochemistry, metallogenia* (pp. 120–21).

Stenina, N.G. and Gubareva (Karimova), D.B. (1996, August). *Water speciation in quartz: TEM combined with IRS.* Abstract of the 30th International Congress, Beijing, China.

Stenina, N.G. and Gubareva (Karimova), D.B. (1997). Crystallochemical features of vein quartz as a guide for gold concentration mechanism. In H. Pappunen (Ed.), *Mineral deposits* (pp. 323–6). Rotterdam: Balkema.

World Bank (2006). *Where is the wealth of nations? Measuring capital for the 21st century.* Retrieved from http://siteresources.worldbank.org/INTEEI/214578-1110886258964/20748034/All.pdf

13. The BRICS and Russia

Stephen Fortescue

The focus of this chapter is Russia's participation in the BRICS grouping. Russia claims to be a keen participant, indeed a driving force. The grouping is seen by most commentators, to a greater or lesser extent, as a challenge to the 'hegemonic' Western-oriented world order. This chapter examines how Russia sees that challenge and the BRICS' relevance to it. This is done in terms of two possible broad approaches which are called 'great power diplomacy' and 'new diplomacy'. 'Great power diplomacy' means an aggressive challenge to the established order by a small group of states with great power claims, who see themselves as at least the equals of, if not ultimately in a position to replace, the existing hegemonic order. 'New diplomacy' refers to a more 'democratic' approach to modifying or replacing the existing order, in which any or all nation states – and non-state actors – are able to participate in the shaping of the international order, including through membership of a multitude of multilateral bodies, with various and often overlapping memberships and diverse agendas. The analysis includes consideration of both international security and economic aspects of the BRICS agenda.

RUSSIA'S INVOLVEMENT IN THE BRICS

Russia claims not only to be serious about its participation in the BRICS, but indeed to be an initiating and driving force within the organization. The first time the countries involved were treated as a self-conscious grouping by the Russians was in April 2006 at the 10th St Petersburg Economic Forum. The general theme of the forum was emerging markets, and a round table was held on the topic 'The new Big Four – BRIC'. Participants included: Dmitrii Medvedev, then Russian First Deputy Prime Minister; German Gref, then Russian Minister of Economic Development; the Brazilian Minister for Development, Trade and Industry; the Indian Minister for Trade and Industry; and the Deputy Chair of the Chinese Committee for Development and Reform (Istomina,

2006). Although it has not been possible to find an account of the proceedings of the round table, the portfolios of the participants, and the fact that it was organized by the Russian Ministry of Economic Development at an economic investment forum, suggest that its focus was on the economic and investment prospects of the four countries, in the spirit of the original Goldman Sachs concept. Nevertheless it brought together senior officials of the four countries at an event specifically recognizing their collective identity.

The first formal meeting of the BRIC representatives took place in September 2006, when Foreign Ministers met in New York during the UN General Assembly. The meeting is said by official Russian sources to have been on the initiative of President Putin. The first meeting at a heads of state level, on the sidelines of the G8 meeting in Japan in July 2008, is also said to have been on the initiative of Russia. At that meeting it was agreed, also at the behest of the Russian side, to meet next at a dedicated Heads of State Summit, which took place at Ekaterinburg in June 2009 ('O razvitii', 2012). Russia claims that it would welcome further formal institutionalization of the grouping, while recognizing the preference of its partners to keep things relatively informal for the moment, and the benefits of such an approach (Ryabkov, 2012).

Given this enthusiasm, what does Russia hope to gain from its engagement? Two possibilities are offered. Firstly, that Russia sees the BRICS as an instrument to challenge and ultimately replace the existing 'hegemonic', US-dominated world order with a world order dominated by itself and a small group of 'rising powers'. In the Russian view, this would be a matter of restoring it to its rightful place in the world, the place it had enjoyed in the guise of the Soviet Union. Alternatively, Russia has accepted that it no longer has the capacity to be a world-dominating great power, and indeed that this is no longer a feasible or desirable role for any state in the modern world. The BRICS is therefore one of the many multilateral institutions of which Russia is a member, pursuing a limited agenda of adjustment of the international order, particularly financial, in recognition of the need for a more democratic world order. The pros and cons for each view will now be discussed.

'GREAT POWER DIPLOMACY'

'Great power diplomacy' is a traditional realpolitik approach in which nation states aggressively pursue their national interests by all means at their disposal, including security, economic and ideological capacity, both independently and in alliances with others. It being largely a zero-sum game, the international order comes to be dominated by one or a small number of great powers, who set the rules of behaviour not just for themselves but for everyone else as well.

In these terms, the BRICS is a small grouping of 'rising powers' with great power pretensions, combining in order to occupy a collective place in the world which at the very least becomes another pole in what has been a unipolar world, and at the most displaces the representative of that unipolar world with a new, albeit collective, single pole.

Security Aspects

What are the arguments for a 'great power diplomacy' view of Russia's involvement in the BRICS? The core evidence is the clear commitment of Vladimir Putin, the dominant figure in Russian politics since the beginning of the current century, to restore Russia to its rightful place in the world. His view of the collapse of the Soviet Union as 'the greatest geopolitical catastrophe of the twentieth century', expressed in a state of the union address to Parliament in April 2005 ('Putin deplores collapse', 2005), conveys more than adequately what he believes Russia's rightful place in the world to be.

Russia's enthusiasm for the BRICS as a more or less formal grouping coincides with the hardening of Russia's position in its relations with the West. Putin's notorious Munich speech on 10 February 2007, in which he savagely criticized the unipolar world claimed by the US, came at the same time as the BRIC concept was taking shape. In that speech he referred specifically to the BRIC, noting that the economies of the BRIC countries were on track rapidly to overtake those of the West, and that 'there is no doubt that the economic potential of these new centres of global growth will inevitably be converted into political influence and will strengthen multipolarity'. He concluded by stating; 'Russia is a country with more than 1000 years of history, and virtually throughout it has enjoyed the privilege of conducting an independent foreign policy. We do not intend changing that tradition now.' The speech immediately produced claims of a new Cold War, indeed one of Putin's questioners made that very point immediately after he had finished speaking ('Vystuplenie', 2007).

A 'great power diplomacy' view of the BRICS would see its membership as reflecting Putin's aggressive geostrategic goals, which match those of the other members. China's global ambitions need no revealing here, with India being perhaps no less ambitious. The other members might limit their great power pretensions to the recognition on the global stage that comes with regional dominance. Yet they, like the others, cannot be described as limiting their ambitions to a 'democratic' place in the world, equal to any other state actor.

The BRICS has long had a structured security dimension. A meeting of ministerial-level officials responsible for security matters was held, on the initiative of the Russian side, in Moscow in May 2009. The official report of the meeting was brief and vague, but referred to discussion of the security implications of the Global Financial Crisis (GFC), cooperation in dealing with 'challenges and threats', 'as well as broader cooperation in other areas' ('O vstreche', 2009).

Another meeting was held the following year at the Heads of State Summit in Brazil in April. It was reported that at that meeting a Russian proposal that a further meeting be held in Moscow in October of the same year was accepted ('Sekretar', 2010). The author has found no evidence that that meeting went ahead, or that there has been a ministerial-level meeting since. However, the BRICS continue to feature in Russian security statements, for example, the desire for deeper security cooperation expressed by the head of the Russian Security Council, Nikolai Patrushev, in a newspaper interview in January 2012 ('Real'nye', 2012), and an October 2012 meeting of the Russian Governmental Commission for Foreign Military-Technical Cooperation specifically dedicated to such cooperation with the BRICS countries ('Sekretar', 2012).

Economic Aspects

Can the economic issues that dominate the BRICS agenda be described in 'great power diplomacy' terms? If the BRICS was primarily about asserting Russia's right to a dominant role in the world, one would expect energy issues to be a major item on the agenda, given the extent to which hydrocarbon exports are the foundation of Russia's economic status. Matthew Hulbert (2012) has provided a detailed argument as to how the BRICS should be all about energy. There is a clear division between Russia and Brazil on the one hand, as raw material suppliers (including energy in the Russian case), and China and India as buyers on the other hand. If Russia became a major supplier to China, there would be advantages to all members; China would be able to drive a better bargain with other energy suppliers, Russia's hand would be strengthened in its dealings with European customers, and India would be free to seek supplies without feeling that it was in competition with China. 'Putin's BRIC power play is therefore pretty simple. Place Russia at the heart of BRIC ascendancy by turning it into a serious energy club' (Hulbert, 2012).

But as Hulbert himself notes, that is not the way things have happened. Early on the Russians suggested that they could play the role of core energy supplier for Russia's BRIC partners, and had some success in pushing the idea of a combined approach to an alternative to Western Europe's Energy Charter, which they saw as being too oriented towards consumers (Abzalov, n.d.). The joint communiqué of the first meeting of the BRIC Foreign Ministers in May 2008 included a statement on the need to balance the interests of suppliers, consumers and transit nations (the transit nations are not a group whose rights Russia is keen on promoting; its inclusion is an indication that the statement was a negotiated one) ('Sovmestnoe kommiunike', 2008). Similar wording appeared in the joint statement of the first Heads of State Summit the following year ('Sovmestnoe zaiavlenie', 2009). By 2010 the wording had disappeared, and the emphasis was on renewable energy and global warming, surely not prominent in Putin's global energy plans ('Sovmestnoe zaiavlenie', 2010).

In the absence of energy issues the most consequential economic component of the BRICS' deliberations has been international financial architecture and processes. After an early focus on how to deal with the GFC, the main interest shifted to reserve currencies and IMF procedures. In the eyes of some, these agenda items are clear examples of an aggressive attempt to change the international financial order in favour of the rising powers that make up the BRICS (Luzianin, 2010).

Russia has long spoken of its desire to strengthen the international role of the ruble, as part of Moscow becoming an international financial centre. However, within the BRICS, new reserve currencies have received unenthusiastic attention. Even when treated by the Russians as a security issue – in November 2010 a meeting of the economic and social security section of the research committee of Russia's Security Council discussed it – the talk is limited to the use of national currencies in dealings within the group and there is no great sense of enthusiasm ('Zasedanie', 2010). Official statements of the group speak in the same terms, while recognizing the importance of the stability of the existing major reserve currencies ('Sovmestnoe zaiavlenie', 2010).

The story regarding the IMF is a mixed one. It is claimed that BRIC coordination helped achieve a positive outcome regarding IMF quotas and representation in international financial organisations at the G20 Summits in London and Pittsburgh in 2009 ('BRIK', 2010, pp. 2, 5). But the surrender to Western pressure of individual members of the grouping over the appointments of Christine Lagarde to the IMF and Jim Yong Kim to the World Bank is seen as indicating a lack of genuine commitment to the issue (Lukyanov, 2012).

With reserve currencies and IMF structures slipping off the agenda, the most topical economic agenda item has been a BRICS Development Bank and bailout fund. A BRICS think-tank group, set up in June 2012

(Kuzmin, 2012), has been working on both proposals. The bailout fund is described as being similar to the Chiang Mai initiative (China, Japan, South Korea and ASEAN). On the development fund, which among at least some of its proponents is seen as a serious challenge to the IMF, it was reported that the working group reached a consensus on the desirability of such a fund at the 2012 BRICS Think-Tanks Forum in Chongqing (Ivanov, 2012). Moscow went to the Heads of State Summit in South Africa in March 2013 with a reasonably detailed proposal. However, agreement could not be reached. Although some commentators see a commitment in principle to the concept as a major step (Dabagian, 2013), the more widespread view – including from Russian officials – is that any such institution is a long way off (Strokan', 2013).

Is it Really 'Great Power Diplomacy'?

Generally the Summit is seen by Russian commentators as having achieved very little in moving the BRICS beyond 'talking shop' status (the Russian bureaucratic phrase being 'dialogovoi format' – 'dialogue format'). There are reasons to doubt, however, that Russia's real motivation for involvement in the BRICS is in fact a great power one. Although there is no doubting Putin's obsession with Russia's place in the world, his own views – and those of Russian society more generally – are a lot more complex than might have been suggested in his Munich speech.

Since the collapse of the Soviet Union, Russia has had a confused and ambiguous view of its place in the world. Even under Putin there have been ebbs and flows – sometimes both at the same time – in the relationship with the West. Russia sees itself as a great power, 'one of the few truly sovereign countries in the world together with the USA, India and China, each with the ability (and right) to sustain an independent civilisational world view' (Sakwa, 2011, p. 971).

And yet Russia has no real interest in a 'civilizational' challenge to the West, of the sort that communism – at least up to a point in time – was. The hegemonic Western global order, as much as it might have taken a beating, is still a powerful force, geostrategically, commercially and even, in complicated but important ways, civilizationally. Indeed, when turbulence in the world takes on a civilizational tone, Russia is likely to come down on the side of the West, as seen after the 9/11 attacks in New York. Even if it wanted to, Russia clearly does not have the capacity – economic, political or cultural – to mount a true civilizational challenge. To do so on a global scale would require wholehearted adoption of radical Islamic or Venezualan-style critiques of Western values and their place in the world

(Sakwa, 2011, pp. 964, 968). That would be both too dangerous and too demeaning an approach to the problem.

Another approach is essentially the one adopted by the Soviet Union at some point in its existence, to limit its great power pretensions (including their civilizational component) to the immediate region – in post-World War II terms, the 'Soviet bloc'. Putinist Russia has given up the non-USSR component of the bloc and arguably some of the USSR. But most, if not all, of the former USSR is firmly considered as part of Russia's rightful sphere of influence. Putin tries increasingly to give a 'civilizational' tone to these claims, strongly evident in his December 2012 state of the union speech to the Parliament ('Poslanie', 2012). The speech reveals, with its intensely inward-looking and even autarchical elements, how limiting the approach is.

In these terms, the BRICS is an attempt to square the circle of challenging 'Western hegemony' without rejecting it, and doing so in a way that does not require either demeaning or dangerous alignments with more radically critical states, or limiting its ambitions to dominating its own part of the world. The BRICS is made up of countries which, to varying degrees, have their own great power and civilizational claims, both at global and regional levels, and are thereby seen as worthy partners in a limited challenge to the West.

But while the attraction of these countries is that they are serious rising powers, the geographical location of the most ambitious of them, China, and to a lesser extent India, means their increasing geostrategic clout creates problems for Russia. While it is unlikely that China sees Russia as a global geostrategic competitor, regionally the situation is somewhat different. One Russian academic, Nikita Astashin, notes that while China might be prepared to tolerate or even welcome a multipolar world, it sees Asia in unipolar terms ('BRIK', 2010, p. 9). The Chinese challenge is currently most evident in practical terms in Central Asia (Lo, 2008, chap. 6). But Russia feels the challenge also in its own Far East, albeit a challenge which well-informed observers believe to be entirely imaginary (Larin, 2011, p. 64). Certainly if Russia's much vaunted 'turn to the East' means anything at all, it entails a troublesome account of the role of China, which cannot be dealt with within the confines of the BRICS.

India is less of a challenge, not just because it is a lesser power, but also because its geographical location is less challenging. However, India's – and the world's – expectations of its proto-great power status make it a country with whom Russia has to be careful in its dealings, not least because of its difficult relationship with China.

The BRICS might be a forum in which the competitive tensions between the various would-be great powers that make up its membership can be smoothed over and worked out. However, some sceptical commentators see the reverse as a danger. In noting the very different understandings of multipolarity of the BRICS members, including his reading of China's understanding mentioned earlier, Astashin says: 'For Russia Chinese-Indian tensions in the final analysis might turn out unfruitful, if the need arose to make an unneeded but unavoidable foreign policy choice' ('BRIK', 2010, p. 25). Nikita Zagladin states that it is a complete illusion to think that the BRIC could be a counterweight to NATO and the EU, not least because of the Indian-Chinese tensions just mentioned and the unwillingness of China to give serious military or foreign policy commitments to anyone. He considers that, while on the one hand the BRICS countries will not support Russia in any serious dispute with the West, on the other hand Russia needs to carefully avoid the risk of either thinking that because of the BRICS it can be more confrontational with the West, or of allowing the other BRICS countries to drive Russia into a conflict with the West ('BRIK', 2010, pp. 10–11).

The evidence for the 'great power diplomacy' motivation is not strong. It is not what Putin really wants, it is unlikely to be what his BRICS partners want, and even if he and they do want it, the BRICS is not a good framework to achieve such a goal. There are other bodies with more explicit security agendas, including RIC (BRIC without Brazil) and the Shanghai Cooperation Organisation (Lo, 2008, pp. 104–13; Khramchikhin, 2008).

'NEW DIPLOMACY'

Many BRICS supporters and spokespeople would claim that any talk of geostrategic competition and great power games is beside the point, since the BRICS has never claimed – indeed the reverse – to be an instrument of great power games, either with regard to the rest of the world or within itself. The talk has been all in 'new diplomacy' terms.

'New diplomacy' is an ever broadening concept that has been around since at least the end of World War I. It has always in its various forms contained a sense of challenge to 'great power diplomacy' and has always had a 'democratic' element; whether that be in the form of a greater role for domestic public opinion in foreign policy making, greater openness in diplomatic processes, or the direct involvement of a whole range of non-state organizations, formal and informal, or individual private citizens in shaping how the world is governed (Sofer, 1988).

The 'democratic' element of 'new diplomacy' is in the BRICS rhetoric, with the grouping presented as an example of the opening of global governance to a wider range of actors than just the traditional hegemonic powers. A Russian Ministry of Foreign Affairs official describes BRICS members as being united by 'a commonality of approaches to the creation of a fairer, more democratic and safer world, with a world order reflecting a culture of civilisational diversity' ('BRIK', 2010, p. 4).

A particular element of the 'democratic' dimension of the 'new diplomacy' is its multilateral nature, a response to the enormous increase in the number of state and non-state actors over the last half century, all trying to get involved and be relevant. International processes are seen as highly fluid combinations of actors coming together in multiple combinations to deal with specific issues, without being tied to traditional obligating alliances, with their hierarchical and hegemonic characteristics. The Ministry of Foreign Affairs official just quoted refers to the BRICS as an example of 'networking multidirectional diplomacy' ('BRIK', 2010, p. 5). Its strength comes from the diversity of its members and their interests, with the informality of its institutional arrangements making it possible for participants to pick and choose issues of mutual interest without any attempt to bind them to a broader range of collective positions as would have been expected of 'great power diplomacy' alliances and partnerships (Luzianin, 2010). It is noted that such arrangements increase the combined weight of the members on those issues in which they have identified a common interest ('BRIK', 2010, p. 5).

The 'new diplomacy's' multilateralism is much loved by middle powers searching for a way to engage themselves and make themselves relevant or – as Australians, a classic example of the phenomenon, like to put it – 'punch above their weight' (Sussex, 2011). It is worth considering that it is this aspect of the 'new diplomacy' that has attracted Russia to the BRICS. Even in his Munich speech Putin, after declaring Russia's determination to continue its centuries-long tradition of having an autonomous foreign policy, concluded with the words:

> At the same time we clearly see that the world has changed, and realistically calculate our own capacities and our own potential. And of course we would like to deal with responsible and also independent partners, with whom we would be able to work together to build a fair and democratic world order, providing security and development for all, not just the chosen ('Vystuplenie', 2007).

One of the symptoms of the 'middle power' condition is the desire to join multiple multilateral organizations, a feature of Russian foreign policy nowadays. Indeed it has become somewhat notorious for its desperation to join anything and everything that is going. Sakwa refers to Russia's general approach to international affairs under Putin as 'bandwagoning and joining' (2011, p. 963).

It is true that the BRICS is a slightly awkward example of the 'new diplomacy' since it brings together countries with serious global and regional 'great power' pretensions. One suspects that for Russia, the fact that they all have such pretensions reduces some of the reputational costs of its 'new diplomacy' behaviour, of appearing as the somewhat desperate manoeuvrings of a middle power. Nevertheless while leaving it to others to explain why China, and to a lesser extent India, might want to be involved in such a game, one cannot help feeling that there is an element in Russia's membership of what is now a middle power trying to 'punch above its weight'. It is worth noting in this regard that it is the two 'junior' members of the BRICS, Russia and Brazil, that have been apparently the most pushy in advancing it as an active multinational body.

CONCLUSION

The BRICS is a reflection of what could be called an existential issue for Russia. Russia wants to challenge the post-Soviet global order to the extent of ensuring that it has a respected and autonomous place within that order, most particularly in its regional sphere of influence. But it does not want to replace the existing order, and certainly not by aligning itself with radical movements and states.

The BRICS members are all in a similar position, believing that they have the right and capacity to demand a greater say in how the world is run. But they are too highly integrated into the world order, and too frightened of unpredictable alternatives, to push their agenda too hard. The BRICS also has the advantage for Russia of taking it outside its regional comfort zone and maintaining a global outlook.

The problem is that Russia's prickliness about its place in the world, which drives it to seek similar partners in a similar situation, means that those very partners have the same prickliness. In broad symbolic terms the BRICS agenda is clear, and one that Russia can very readily sign up to. But in practical terms it is far more limited. Perhaps the Chinese representative in a 2009 Moscow-Beijing video discussion of the BRICS was right; the most important thing for the grouping is to declare that it exists (Kukol & Vasenin, 2009). The clearest sign of its lack of a truly serious agenda as far as Russia is concerned is the minor role of energy.

A twist to describing Russia's participation in the BRICS as joining a multipolar, would-be 'great powers' club is to see it more broadly as a symptom of Russia's post-Soviet bandwagoning and joining syndrome. Typical of a middle power wanting to punch above its weight, it wants to join as many organizations as possible, with the BRICS just one of many. If true, that view of Russia's involvement in the BRICS is a telling statement of Russia's real place in the world.

If we take the 2012 programmatic statement on Russia's future foreign and domestic policy orientations, Putin's message to the Parliament ('Poslanie', 2012), we see evidence of such a turning in on itself and retreat to its traditional sphere of influence, presented in strong civilizational terms, that one wonders whether the BRICS and other multilateral involvements might decline into further irrelevance. One should not be overdetermined by Putin's rhetoric. It changes regularly depending on specific circumstances and the audience. But it is not hard to argue that his psychological and policy response to various challenges, from social forces he sees as not having Russia's proper place in the world at heart – whether it be Russia's protesting middle class and its liberal soulmates in the ruling elite, or corrupt and illiberal bureaucrats – is to retreat more and more into the fortress, in terms of both domestic and foreign policy. The 'C' in the BRICS is too important a direct neighbour of the fortress to be ignored. The rest of the initials, and therefore the organization itself, could well become increasingly irrelevant.

REFERENCES

Abzalov, D. (n.d.). Rossiia mozhet igrat' rol' garanta energobezopasnosti stran gruppy BRIK. *Ministerstvo energetiki Rossiiskoi Federatsii*. Retrieved from http://minenergo.gov.ru/press/experts/1476.html?sphrase_id=273057

BRIK kak novaia kontseptsiia mnogovektornoi diplomatii. (2010). *Vestnik MGIMO*, *1*, 1–27. Retrieved from http://www.vestnik.mgimo.ru/fileserver/10/vestnik_10-06_krug-stol.pdf

Dabagian, E. (2013, March 28). BRICS – estafetu peredaet Afrika. *Politcom.ru*. Retrieved from http://www.policom.ru/15552.html

Hulbert, M. (2012, May 6). Putin's BRIC power play. *Forbes*. Retrieved from http://www.forbes.com/sites/matthewhulbert/2012/05/06/putins-bric-power-play-2/

Istomina, K. (2006). Desiatyi iubileinyi. *Boss*, *8*. Retrieved from http://www.bossmag.ru/archiv/2006/boss-08-2006-g/desyatyiy-yubileynyiy.html

Ivanov, S. (2012, October 3). BRICS think-tanks mull alternative to World Bank. *Russia & India Report*. Retrieved from http://indrus.in/articles/2012/10/03/brics_think-tanks_mull_alternative_to_world_bank_18081.html

Khramchikhin, A. (2008, January 12). Chto-to tikho briknulo. *Chastnyi Korrespondent*. Retrieved from http://www.chaskor.ru/article/brik__16787

Kukol, E. and Vasenin, V. (2009, June 2). BRIK nachinaet pervym. *Rossiiskaia gazeta*. Retrieved from http://www.rg.ru/2009/06/02/brik.html

Kuzmin, V. (2012, November 21). BRICS create their own financial instuitions. *Russia Beyond the Headlines*. Retrieved from http://rbth.ru/articles/2012/11/21/brics_create_their_own_financial_institutions_20285.html

Larin, V.L. (2011). Tikhookeanskaia Rossiia v kontekste natsional'noi i regional'noi bezopasnosti ATR: element stabil'nosti ili slaboe zveno? In V.L. Larin (Ed.), *Tikhookeanskaia Rossiia v kontekste vneshnei politiki i mezhdunarodnykh otnoshenii v ATR v nachale XXI veka* (pp. 62–66). Vladivostok: Institut istorii, arkheologii i etnografii narodov Dal'nego Vostoka.

Lo, B. (2008). *Axis of convenience. Moscow, Beijing, and the new geopolitics.* London: Chatham House.

Lukyanov, F. (2012, March 29). Uncertain world: Sovereignty as the foundation of BRICS unity. *RIANovosti.* Retrieved from http://en.rian.ru/columnists/20120329/172466498.html

Luzianin, S. (2010, April 11–17). Kto i kuda vedet BRIK? *Rossiiskie vesti.* Retrieved from http://rosvesty.ru/2004/expert/?id=1000001890&i=1

O razvitii vzaimodeistviia v formate BRIKS. (2012, March 23). *Ministerstvo ekonomicheskogo razvitiia Rossiiskoi Federatsii.* Retrieved from http://www.economy.gov.ru/minec/activity/sections/foreignEconomicActivity/economic_organization/doc20120323_013

O vstreche vysokikh predstavitelei stran BRIK otvechaiushchikh za voprosy bezopasnosti (2009, May 29). *Sovet Bezopasnosti Rossiiskoi Federatsii.* Retrieved from http://www.scrf.gov.ru/news/448.html

Poslanie Prezidenta Federal'nomu Sobraniiu (2012, December 12). *Prezident Rossii.* Retrieved from http://news.kremlin.ru/news/17118

Putin deplores collapse of USSR (2005, April 25). *BBC News.* Retrieved from http://news.bbc.co.uk/2/hi/4480745.stm

Real'nye ugrozy dlia Rossii, SShA i ES – v nyneshnei nestabil'nosti. (2012, January 12). *Kommersant.* Retrieved from http://kommersant.ru/doc/1848948

Ryabkov, S. (2012, May 23). BRICS is a catalyst for global governance reform. *VIP Premier.* Retrieved from http://rbth.ru/articles/2012/05/23/sergei_ryabkov_brics_is_a_catalyst_for_global_governance_reform_15691.html

Sakwa, R. (2011). Russia's identity: Between the "domestic" and the "international". *Europe-Asia Studies*, *63*(6), 957–75.

Sekretar' Soveta Bezopasnosti Rossiiskoi Federatsii N.P. Patrushev prinial uchastie v zasedanii Komissii po voprosam voenno-tekhnicheskogo sotrudnichestva s inostrannymi gosudarstvami (2012, October 18). *Sovet Bezopasnosti Rossiiskoi Federatsii.* Retrieved from http://www.scrf.gov.ru/

Sekretar' Soveta Bezopasnosti Rossiiskoi Federatsii N.P. Patrushev vstretilsia s vysokimi predstaviteliami stran BRIK, otvechaiushchikh za voprosy bezopasnost. (2010, April 15). *Sovet Bezopasnosti Rossiiskoi Federatsii.* Retrieved from http://www.scrf.gov.ru/

Sofer, S. (1988). Old and new diplomacy: A debate revisited. *Review of International Studies*, *14*, 195–211.

Sovmestnoe kommiunike po itogam vstrechi ministrov inostrannykh del Kitaia, Rossii, Indii i Brazili. (2008, May 16). *Ministerstvo inostrannykh del Kitaiskoi Narodnoi Respubliki.* Retrieved from http://www.fmprc.gov.cn/rus/wjdt/gb/t455696.htm

Sovmestnoe zaiavlenie glav gosudarstv i pravitel'stv stran uchastnits Vtorogo sammita BRIK (Braziliia, Rossiia, Indiia, Kitai). (2010, April 15). *Prezident Rossii.* Retrieved from http://www.kremlin.ru/ref_notes/524

Sovmestnoe zaiavlenie liderov stran BRIK (2009, June 17). *Ministerstvo inostrannykh del Kitaiskoi Narodnoi Respubliki.* Retrieved from http://www.fmprc.gov.cn/rus/wjdt/gb/t568454.htm

Strokan, S. (2013, 13 March). Strany BRIKS vypravili novye dokumenty. *Kommersant*. Retrieved from http://www.kommersant.ru/doc/2155904

Sussex, M. (2011). The impotence of being earnest? Avoiding the pitfalls of "creative middle power diplomacy". *Australian Journal of International Affairs*, *65*(5), 545–62.

Vystuplenie i diskussiia na Miunkhenskoi konferentsii po voprosam politiki bezopasnosti (2007, February 17). *Prezident Rossii*. Retrieved from http://archive.kremlin.ru/appears/2007/02/10/1737_type63374type63376type63377type63381type82634_118097.shtml

Zasedanie sektsii po ekonomicheskoi i sotsial'noi bezopasnosti nauchnogo soveta pri Sovete Bezopasnosti Rossiiskoi Federatsii (2010, November 26). *Sovet Bezopasnosti Rossiiskoi Federatsii*. Retrieved from http://www.scrf.gov.ru/

14. New players, new rules? The BRICS and global economic governance

Mark Thirlwell

These are tough times for global economic governance. According to one assessment, aside from some successful cooperation between central banks, on 'virtually every other important global economic issue, international economic cooperation is stalled, flawed or non-existent' (Frieden, Pettis, Rodrik & Baldwin, 2012). Another judges that 'the system we are supposed to have for coping with the global economy has largely failed' (Beattie, 2012b). A third posits that we now live in 'a world without leaders,' an environment in which 'No one is driving the bus' (Bremmer, 2012). This is also a period marked by a dramatic redistribution of international economic weight driven by the rise of important new economic powers. Prominent among the latter are the so-called BRIC (Brazil, Russian, India, China) or BRICS (BRIC plus South Africa) economies. The two developments are connected.

THE CASE FOR INTERNATIONAL ECONOMIC COOPERATION

There is a long-standing debate over the need for, and appropriate extent of, international economic cooperation (Frieden et al., 2012; Feldstein, 1989). However, to the extent that a case for such cooperation exists, it seems clear that this case is very likely to have *increased* in line with international economic integration and the consequent rise in the potential for international spillovers and externalities. Take for example trade integration. Back in 1960 the ratio of world trade to world GDP was about 24 per cent. By 1980 it had risen to a little less than 40 per cent, and by 2008 it had climbed to about 60 per cent on the eve of the Global Financial Crisis (GFC) (World Bank, n.d.).[1] The increase in financial integration has been even greater. In 1980 the ratio of countries' international financial positions as a share of world GDP was about 60 per cent. By 1990 that ratio had risen to more than 120 per cent, and by 2009 it stood at more than 350 per cent (OECD, 2011).

Trade and financial linkages provide most of the channels through which policy decisions and shocks in one country or region can be rapidly transmitted to the rest of the world. The GFC provided a compelling example of this in action, as a crisis originating in the US housing sector created havoc across the rest of the global economy, with global financial markets and international trade suffering synchronized collapses. The aftermath has left the world economy even more vulnerable to cross-border shocks. We now live in a world of highly correlated asset prices, ubiquitous financial shocks and limited policy space; a world ripe for spill-overs which will have an even greater impact than they would in normal times (IMF, 2012c).

THE GREAT CONVERGENCE AND THE RISE OF THE BRIC(S)

Integration has been accompanied by a major shift in the balance of economic power between the developed and developing worlds. In 1990 developed economies accounted for about 69 per cent of world GDP (measured on a purchasing power parity – PPP – basis), while emerging and developing economies accounted for about 31 per cent. Two decades later the share of developed economies had fallen to 52 per cent, while that of emerging markets had risen to 48 per cent. The IMF estimates that by 2013 emerging and developing countries will account for just over half the world's output (IMF, 2012d). In fact they already account for by far the majority of global growth (IMF, 2012d). This shift in economic power is the product of sustained, rapid catch up growth in some of the world's largest developing economies – a 'great convergence' (Thirlwell, 2010). Some of the leading players have been the BRIC(S) members.

The BRIC acronym was coined by Jim O'Neill of Goldman Sachs, in a paper published in 2001 (O'Neill, 2001). Subsequent work by the same firm saw the term enter into general use (Wilson & Purushothaman, 2003; Tett, 2010). More dramatically, in the following years the four original BRIC economies themselves sought to leverage this growing brand power by constructing an institutional framework around the concept ('The trillion-dollar club', 2010). A stand-alone meeting of BRIC foreign ministers was held on 16 May 2008 in Yekaterinburg and was followed by the first meeting of BRIC economic and finance ministers in November 2008 in Sao Paulo. These meetings culminated in the inaugural BRIC

Summit, involving the heads of state from all four countries, held on 16 June 2009 in Yekaterinburg. On 24 December 2010 the BRICs morphed into the BRICS when South Africa officially became the fifth member of the grouping (Smith, 2011).[2] That Yekaterinburg Summit has since been followed by Summits in Brasilia (16 April 2010), Hainan (14 April 2011), New Delhi (29 March 2012) and Durban (26–27 March 2013).

MULTIPOLARITY AND MULTILATERALISM: THE GOVERNANCE CHALLENGE

Deepening integration has increased the demand for international policy cooperation even as the changing balance of economic power has complicated its supply. More specifically the existing international economic architecture has typically been dominated by the developed world, allocating a much smaller voice for the new players. An optimistic assessment of this shift to a more multipolar world might have assumed that a natural corollary would have been a boost to multilateralism. A greater number and diversity of economic powers would seem to recommend a more multilateral approach to economic governance. In practice, however, the outcome has been 'multipolarity without multilateralism' (Patrick, 2010). An early indication of this came in the context of an inability to complete the Doha Round of multilateral trade negotiations due in part to the successful blocking role played by a coalition of emerging and developing economies known as the (WTO) G20 (Baracuhy, 2012).[3]

To a large extent the difficulties posed by the rise of a multipolar system should not have been surprising. Club theory tells us that expanding the membership of international organizations would make the new organizations unwieldy and less able to meet the preferences of all club members (Kawai & Petri, 2010). Likewise a review of the history of international economic policy coordination indicates that such coordination is most likely to occur and be successful when it: (a) centres on technical issues that are unlikely to raise significant domestic political issues; (b) is institutionalized; (c) is concerned with preserving an existing policy regime as opposed to developing a new one; and (d) takes place 'in the context of broad comity among nations' (Eichengreen, forthcoming). While the last of these conditions may be met in the broad sense that there is no conflict among the major (economic) powers, the new players do have much less in common than the group of developed Western economies comprising the G7. They are also less committed to preserving the status quo.

Moreover although the GFC confirmed the high degree of connectivity in the world economy and hence the need for collective action, it badly tarnished the credibility of developed countries' economic leadership, and also left those leaders grappling with a set of difficult domestic policy issues and a diminishing set of instruments with which to tackle them. For the BRICS and for other emerging economies, this set of circumstances reinforced their claims for a greater voice in international economic governance and their sense that, given its crisis-prone nature, the current system needed some fundamental reforms even as developed economies became more inward-looking and less open to compromise.

WHAT DOES THE BRICS WANT?

Beyond broad ambit claims for a greater say in the system, however, it is less clear what the BRICS wants from global economic governance. Expecting a coherent, consistent position from the BRICS grouping may be unrealistic, given the significant diversity within the membership (IMF, 2012d). The status of the five countries differs significantly in terms of absolute size and level of development, for example (IMF, 2012d):

- The population of the BRICS economies ranges from less than 51 million people in South Africa to more than 1.3 billion people in China.
- Overall economic size ranges from a GDP of roughly PPP$555 billion (US$409 billion) in South Africa to PPP$11 300 billion (US$7298 billion) in China.
- Wealth ranges from a GDP per capita of PPP$3663 (US$1514) in India to PPP$16 736 (US$12 993) in Russia.

Their economic structures (relative share of agriculture, industry and services, and relative dependence on production and exports of manufactures, energy and other resources) are similarly diverse.

Likewise the BRICS has different sized global footprints. China is far bigger than the other members, accounting for about 14 per cent of global GDP in 2011 when output is measured on a PPP basis. India, the second largest of the BRICS on this measure, accounted for less than 6 per cent of global output in the same year, while Brazil and Russia each accounted for closer to 3 per cent (IMF, 2012d). Similarly while China accounted for more than 10 per cent of world merchandise trade in 2011, Russia accounted for less than 3 per cent and India for less than 2 per cent (WTO, 2012).

Differences go well beyond the economic and include a diverse range of political systems, foreign policy alignments and cultures. There are also elements of economic competition between some of the members: as a major agricultural exporter, Brazil has often taken a positive line on global agricultural trade liberalization, while India and to a lesser extent China have tended to be more defensive; both Brazil and India have worried about their manufacturing sectors being squeezed by China's hyper-competitive exporters, and both have fretted about Chinese investment.[4]

Still it is possible to identify elements of a common agenda:[5]

- Demands for a greater voice in the international economic architecture;
- Fears regarding the spillover effects of the current extraordinary measures taken by developed economies' monetary policies ('Quantitative easing');
- Concerns about the potentially destabilizing consequences of volatile international capital flows;
- Concerns regarding commodity price volatility and resource security;
- Concerns about the impact of climate change policy choices for growth and development;
- Infrastructure; and
- Worries about trade (and more recently investment) protectionism of developed countries.

Hence the fourth BRICS Summit in New Delhi in March 2012 saw BRICS leaders pressing for faster progress on the reform of IMF voting rights, and criticizing the monetary policy being pursued by the rich world in an echo of earlier worries about currency wars (Singh, 2012; Gangopadhyay & Kala, 2012). The idea of a BRICS development bank was also canvassed formally at the New Delhi meeting, and received further support at the 2013 BRICS Summit in Durban (Mance, 2012; Beniwal, 2013). The BRICS has also announced that it will start building a financial safety net in the form of a joint pool of reserves that can be drawn on in the event of destabilizing capital flight (Giles, 2012). Reports suggest that the pool of foreign exchange reserves could be up to US$240 billion in size, and there are also discussions regarding currency swap arrangements (Wroughton & Soto, 2012).

The BRICS has to use its financial leverage to push for IMF reform. After repeating their frustration with the lack of progress of IMF reform in New Delhi and threatening to withhold further funding in response, BRICS leaders later held an informal meeting in advance of the Los Cabos G20 Leader's Summit, and agreed to contribute US$65 billion towards the IMF's bailout fund for Europe, with China contributing US$43 billion, conditional on continued fund reform (Fontanella-Khan, 2012; Press Trust of India, 2012).

THE BRICS AND THE G20

Dedicated summits and policy proposals provide some indicators of the implications of the rise of the BRICS for international economic governance. But the most powerful example of the resultant change in the global economic order has been the emergence of the G20 as a peak global economic body. This, despite the fact that some observers have seen the BRICS Summits as a possible alternative to G20 meetings (Halligan, 2011).

The ascent of the G20 began with the elevation of the G20 to leaders' level at the Washington Summit in November 2008, and was followed by the subsequent (self) declaration of the G20 as 'the premier forum for our international economic cooperation' at the Pittsburgh Summit in September 2009.[6] The G20 comprises the established powers of the G7, the new powers of the BRICS and a collection of middle and regional powers.[7] G20 Leader's Summits were a response to the GFC and in recognition of the need to develop a global economic architecture with a bigger role for the emerging powers (Kharas & Lombardi, 2012).

The idea of the G20 embodying a shift in the international economic order was captured in early 2010, when President Nicolas Sarkozy declared that 'The G20 foreshadows the planetary governance of the twenty-first century' (Sarkozy, 2010). The first few Leader's Summits *did* appear to presage a new era of multilateralism. Along with the nature of the grouping itself (with its inclusion of a range of emerging powers), there were promises to reform the governance of the IMF and World Bank and to increase IMF resources, pledges to refrain from protectionism and boost the Doha Round, and the creation of a new and more inclusive Financial Stability Board to replace the older and less representative Financial Stability Forum (Woods, 2010).

Those early summits were marked by a strong sense of collective purpose reinforced by a crisis-induced sentiment of 'hang together or hang separately'. With its US$1 trillion pledge of new resources for the IMF and its US$5 trillion announcement of coordinated fiscal stimulus, some even felt that the April 2009 London Summit could 'go down in history as the most significant summit since the G6/7/8 was formed in 1975' (Bradford & Lin, 2011). The subsequent Pittsburgh Declaration of the G20s pre-eminence seemed to follow on quite naturally from this success. Pittsburgh also brought the launch of the G20s Framework for Strong,

Sustainable and Balanced Growth (FSSBG), aimed at seeking a more balanced pattern of global demand growth, including dealing with the vexed question of global imbalances.

Unfortunately by the time of the Seoul Summit in late 2010, the bloom had well and truly come off the G20. In the time leading up to Seoul there were a series of heated disagreements on international economic policy, including dire warnings of 'currency wars' and rising protectionist pressures. Washington became increasingly critical of Beijing's exchange rate policy, even as China decried the US decision to resume quantitative easing. In theory the G20 should have been the ideal forum to resolve some of these differences. In practice it mainly served to showcase the presence of big divides in the global economy. A *Financial Times* editorial declared 'G20 shows how not to run the world' (2010).

The slump in the G20s credibility reflects mixed progress on some key issues:

- Despite commitments to complete the Doha Round, trade negotiations remain stalled.
- The pledge to refrain from protectionism issued at the November 2008 Summit lasted for less than 48 hours before the first of the G20 member countries reneged. Others followed and within a month, a quarter of the G20 had broken their promises ('Bad start'; 2008).
- Despite the FSSBG, successive IMF reports have emphasized just how far the world economy is from returning to strong and sustainable growth, while the Fund has also judged that progress on addressing global imbalances has been minimal (IMF, 2012b).
- The IMF Board of Governors did approve a fairly significant quota reform in line with G20 pledges in 2010 and if implemented, the changes would see China become the third largest shareholder in the IMF, and Brazil, Russia and India all join the top ten largest shareholders (IMF, 2012a). However, despite pledges to implement the changes by the 2012 IMF/World Bank annual meetings, as of early 2013 they were still not in effect.
- At the London Summit, leaders agreed that 'the heads and senior leadership of the international financial institutions should be appointed through an open, transparent, and merit-based selection process'. But in 2011 the Europeans still appointed a European to head the IMF, and in 2012 the US likewise maintained its grip on the World Bank.

Looking at the intersection between the BRICS objectives, the ambitions set out by the early G20 meetings, and what the G20 was actually able to deliver, there are three areas of overlap: (a) maintaining open markets and avoiding a widespread retreat to protectionism; (b) reform of the IMF and (c) dealing with global imbalances and macroeconomic spillovers. Viewed on this basis, the story is a mixed one:

- On trade, despite the credibility-sapping failure to restart the Doha Round and the embarrassing backsliding by many G20 members (with BRICS members making for prominent examples), there has been no widespread retreat into protectionism.
- On IMF reform, there has been some progress, but it has been slow and partial.
- On imbalances and macroeconomic coordination more generally, there is little progress to point to on many of the issues where the BRICS has expressed concern. Indeed taking the spillover effects of the Euro Area crisis into account, it is possible to argue that conditions have worsened. There has, however, been a shift in IMF policy towards capital controls, where the fund has recently indicated a new willingness to approve the use of capital controls (Beattie, 2012a).

Some of this strictly limited progress is indicative of the general difficulties associated with achieving any kind of international economic cooperation, and some of it reflects the entrenched positions of the developed economies and the limited ability of the new players to force change. But the BRICS itself has also often proved unable to work together to push for the kinds of outcomes they claim to support. A good example of this came in 2011 when a new IMF Managing Director had to be appointed. BRICS countries' representatives on the IMF's board issue a joint statement calling for the promised open and merit-based procedure for selecting a new Managing Director. Yet, when a potentially credible emerging market candidate did appear in the shape of Mexico's Agustin Carstens, the BRICS failed to back him. Indeed other than Mexico, the only G20 members to offer formal support were Australia and Canada (Beattie, 2012b). In practice the BRICS' demands for an emerging market candidate turned out to be almost entirely without substance.[8]

Still, the BRICS has at least been able to exert its new power in order to block initiatives. For example, a Wikileaks cable from a senior US official notes how Brazil, South Africa, India and China have been able to coordinate to either block or play off against each other the US and the EU in the G20 (Wade, 2011). In 2009 the BRICS was able to unite to halt any progress on climate change finance, arguing that the work should stay in the UN Framework Convention on Climate Change (UNFCCC) process

(Bergin, 2009; Friedman 2009). China has also fought a frequently successful campaign to stop the G20 putting it under pressure over exchange rate policy (Flynn, 2011).

CONCLUSION

The rise of the BRICS has created new challenges for global economic governance by generating a period of 'multipolarity without multilateralism'. The diffusion of economic power in the world economy has not yet been matched by equivalent innovations in global economic governance. Instead multipolarity has both increased the need for international economic cooperation and coordination, and made it harder to deliver. In this context the most concrete manifestation of the BRICS' impact on global economic governance to date has not been the BRICS Summits themselves, but rather the elevation in status of the G20 with its explicit recognition of a need for a change in the international economic order. The imperfect workings of the G20 itself are likewise indicative of the imperfect integration of the BRICS into global economic governance, of the challenges this process involves, and of the need to continue with the project.

NOTES

1. By 2011 the ratio was back to 59 per cent.
2. Interestingly, Mr O'Neill is on record as believing that South Africa is 'nowhere near constituting a BRIC' (CNN, 2011).
3. This WTO G20 needs to be distinguished from the G20 discussed earlier.
4. Some Brazilians have complained that China's economic relationship with their country is 'neocolonial' (see, for example, Beattie, 2012b).
5. Derived from the reported agendas and communiqués from past BRICS Summits. On China, see also Huang, Dang & Wang, 2011.
6. The G20 was originally established in response to the emerging financial market crises of the 1990s. It was convened by the G7 and operated at the level of finance ministers and central bank governors. For background on the G20, see Kharas & Lombardi, 2012.
7. The G7 group of rich countries comprises Canada, France, Germany, Italy, Japan, the UK and the US. The G20 comprises the G7 plus the BRICS plus the EU plus Argentina, Australia, Indonesia, Korea, Mexico, Saudi Arabia and Turkey.
8. Although Beijing did manage to emerge from the process with a Chinese national – Min Zhu – installed as IMF Deputy Managing Director.

REFERENCES

Bad start for new Bretton Woods (2008, December 28). *Financial Times*. Retrieved from http://www.ft.com/intl/cms/s/0/593d1b22-d513-11dd-b967-000077b07658.html#axzz2Kd80u2MY

Baracuhy, B. (2012). Running into a brick wall: The WTO doha round, governance gap and geopolitical risks. *Global Policy*, *3*(1), 108–10.

Beattie, A. (2012a, December 3). IMF drops opposition to capital controls. *Financial Times*. Retrieved from http://www.ft.com/intl/cms/s/0/e620482e-3d5c-11e2-9e13-00144feabdc0.html#axzz2Kd80u2MY

Beattie, A. (2012b). *Who's in charge here? How governments are failing the world economy*. Retrieved from http://www.amazon.com/Whos-Charge-Penguin-Specials-ebook/dp/B0076O2W7W

Beniwal, V. (2013, January 9). Contours of proposed bank for BRICS to be finalised in March. *Business Standard*. Retrieved from http://www.business-standard.com/article/economy-policy/contours-of-proposed-bank-for-brics-to-be-finalised-in-march-113010900122_1.html

Bergin, T. (2009, September 9). Climate change funding talks stall at G20. *Reuters*. Retrieved from http://www.reuters.com/article/2009/09/05/us-g20-finance-climatechange-idUSTRE5841RZ20090905

Bradford, C.I. and Linn, J.F. (2011). A history of G20 summits: The evolving dynamics of global leadership. *Journal of Globalization and Development*, *2*(2). Retrieved from http://www.degruyter.com/view/j/jgd.2011.2.issue-2/1948-1837.1239/1948-1837.1239.xml?format=INT

Bremmer, I. (2012). *Every nation for itself: Winners and losers in a G-zero world*. New York: Portfolio Penguin.

CNN (2011, April 5). South Africa an economic powerhouse? 'Nowhere near,' says Goldman exec. *Marketplace Africa CNN*. Retrieved from http://edition.cnn.com/2011/BUSINESS/04/05/jim.oneill.africa.bric/index.html

Eichengreen, B. (forthcoming). International policy coordination: The long view. In R.M. Feenstra and A.M. Taylor (Eds), *Globalization in an age of crisis: Multilateral economic cooperation in the twenty-first century*. Chicago, IL: University of Chicago Press. Retrieved from http://www.nber.org/chapters/c12578.pdf

Feldstein, M.S. (1989). Distinguished lecture on economics in government: Thinking about international economic coordination. *Journal of Economic Perspectives*, *2*(2), 3–13.

Flynn, D. (2011, February 20). Analysis: G20 keeps China onboard but tough talks lie ahead. *Reuters*. Retrieved from http://www.reuters.com/article/2011/02/21/us-g20-analysis-idUSTRE71J2F620110221

Fontanella-Khan, J. (2012, March 29). Brics nations threaten IMF funding. *Financial Times*. Retrieved from http://www.ft.com/intl/cms/s/0/a3b88472-7982-11e1-8fad-00144feab49a.html#axzz2Kd80u2MY

Frieden, J., Pettis, M., Rodrik, D. and Baldwin, R. (2012), *After the fall: The future of global cooperation* (Geneva Reports on the World Economy No. 14). Geneva: International Center for Monetary and Banking Studies.

Friedman, L. (2009, September 11). Still no money for developing nations, new G20 documents show. *The New York Times*. Retrieved from http://www.

nytimes.com/cwire/2009/09/11/11climatewire-still-no-money-for-developing-nations-new-g-20933.html?pagewanted=all
G20 show how not to run the world (2010, November 12). *Financial Times*. Retrieved from http://www.ft.com/intl/cms/s/0/8f33885e-ee90-11df-9db0-00144feab49a.html#axzz2Kd80u2MY
Gangopadhyay, A. and Kala, A.V. (2012, March 29). Brics wants World Bank, IMF reforms. *The Wall Street Journal*. Retrieved from http://online.wsj.com/article/SB10001424052702303816504577311012331186378.html
Giles, C. (2012, June 19). Brics to create financial safety net. *Financial Times*. Retrieved from http://www.ft.com/intl/cms/s/0/bfd6adfe-b9bb-11e1-a470-00144feabdc0.html#axzz2Kd80u2MY
Halligan, L. (2011, April 16). The BRIC countries' Hainan summit could make the G20 redundant. *The Telegraph*. Retrieved from http://www.telegraph.co.uk/finance/comment/liamhalligan/8455956/The-BRIC-countries-Hainan-summit-could-make-the-G20-redundant.html
Huang, Y., Dang, W. and Wang, J. (2011) Reform of the international economic system: What does China want? In J. Golley and L. Song (Eds), *Rising China: Global challenges and opportunties* (pp. 29–44). Canberra: The Australian National University E Press.
IMF (2012a, August 24). *Factsheet: IMF quotas*. Washington DC: International Monetary Fund.
IMF (2012b, July 2) *Pilot external sector report (ESR)*. Washington DC: IMF.
IMF (2012c, July 9) *2012 Spillover report*. Washington DC: IMF.
IMF (2012d, October) *World economic outlook database October 2012*. Washington DC: IMF.
Kawai, M. and Petri, P.A. (2010). *Asia's role in the global economic architecture* (ADBI Working Paper No. 235). Tokyo: Asian Development Bank Institute.
Kharas, H. and Lombardi, D. (2012). *The group of twenty: Origins, prospects and challenges for global governance*. Washington DC: The Brookings Institution.
Mance, H. (2012, September 23). Global shift: A bank of and for the Brics is in the air. *Financial Times*. Retrieved from http://www.ft.com/intl/cms/s/0/63400496-024f-11e2-8cf8-00144feabdc0.html#axzz2Kd80u2MY
OECD (2011, May). *OECD economic outlook No. 89 Vol 2011/1*. Paris: OECD Publishing.
O'Neill, J. (2001, November 30). *Building better global economic BRICs* (Goldman Sachs Global Economics Paper No. 66). London: Goldman, Sachs & Co.
Patrick, S. (2010). Irresponsible stakeholders? *Foreign Affairs*, *89*(6), 44–54.
Press Trust of India (PTI). (2012, June 19). BRICS pledges $75bn to IMF's bailout fund. *Business Standard*. Retrieved from http://www.business-standard.com/article/international/brics-pledges-75-bn-to-imf-s-bailout-fund-112061900142_1.html
Sarkozy, N. (2010, January 27). *Speech at the 40th World Economic Forum* [speech]. Davos, Switzerland.
Singh, R.K. (2012, March 29). BRICS flay West over IMF reform, monetary policy. *Reuters*. Retrieved from http://www.reuters.com/article/2012/03/29/us-india-brics-idUSBRE82S05K20120329
Smith, J.A. (2011, January 21). BRIC becomes BRICS: Changes on the geopolitical chessboard. *Foreign Policy Journal*. Retrieved from http://www.foreignpolicyjournal.com/2011/01/21/bric-becomes-brics-changes-on-the-geopolitical-chessboard
Tett, G. (2010, January 15). The story of the BRICs. *Financial Times*. Retrieved

from http://www.ft.com/intl/cms/s/0/112ca932-00ab-11df-ae8d-00144feabdc0.html

The trillion-dollar club: The BRICs (2010, April 15). *The Economist*. Retrieved from http://www.economist.com/node/15912964

Thirlwell, M. (2010, November 9). The great convergence. *International Economy Comments #4*. Sydney: Lowy Institute for International Policy, 1–4.

Wade, R.H. (2011). Emerging world order? From multipolarity to multilateralism in the G20, the World Bank and the IMF. *Politics & Society*, *39*(3), 347–78.

Wilson, D. and Purushothaman, R. (2003, October 1). *Dreaming with BRICs: The path to 2050* (Goldman Sachs Global Economics Paper No. 99). London: Goldman, Sachs & Co.

Woods, N. (2010). Global governance after the financial crisis: A new multilateralism or the last gasp of the great powers? *Global Policy*, *1*(1), 51–110.

World Bank. (n.d.). *Data*. Retrieved from http://data.worldbank.org/

Wroughton, L. and Soto, A. (2012, November 12). BRICS eye forex reserves pool of up to $240 billion. *Reuters*. Retrieved from http://www.reuters.com/article/2012/11/09/brics-reserves-idUSL1E8M586C20121109

WTO (2012). *World trade report 2012*. Geneva: WTO.

15. BRICS and mortar(s): Breaking or building the global system?

Melissa Conley Tyler and Michael Thomas[1]

As well as its impact on economics and trade, the rise of the BRICS has had a significant impact on international relations and global governance. This is most evident in the rise of the G20 as a forum of leaders to manage issues in the global economy. With the weight of the BRICS, G20 is eclipsing the G7 as the world's 'premier forum for international economic cooperation'.

As the power of the BRICS has increased over the last decade, a debate has arisen over what impact this might have on global governance. One view sees the rise of the BRICS as an assault on the existing systems of global governance and thus, figuratively speaking, as a 'mortar' attack on the foundations of the current global order. Another view sees the BRICS as building institutions for global governance that shore up the basic elements of international order, but in a way that makes it more inclusive and stronger – thus 'bricks and mortar'. These two metaphors – 'mortars' versus 'mortar' – neatly encapsulate the extremes of the debate on the rise of the BRICS in the international system.[2]

This chapter explores the behaviour of the BRICS in the G20 to ascertain whether this is undermining the principles of global governance or promoting constructive reform. The chapter begins by outlining the main arguments used by those who see the BRICS as a threat. It then outlines the counterarguments, particularly focusing on the BRICS Declaration at the 2012 Los Cabos G20 Summit. It concludes that the rise of the BRICS is not necessarily a challenge to global governance, and could in fact strengthen the international system.

BRICS WITH MORTARS?

On 6 September 2011 US Defence Secretary Leon Panetta outlined the current threats to US national security in the lead up to the tenth anniversary of the 9/11 terrorist attacks. He discussed a number of security issues facing the US, including terrorism, cyber warfare and nuclear proliferation. Interestingly he also pointed out that:

> We . . . are living in a world in which there are rising powers, countries like China and Brazil and India, not to mention Russia and others, that provide a challenge to us not only in trying to cooperate with them, but making sure that they don't undermine the stability of the world (Parrish, 2011).

There are two significant aspects to Secretary Panetta's comments. First, he explicitly identifies the four original BRICs members as potential threats to US national security. While he refers to them individually rather than as a group or bloc, by bracketing these four states Panetta suggests that they represent a collective challenge to US leadership in the international system. Second, Panetta considers these nations a threat not just to the US but also to the 'stability of the world'. Not only are these rising powers difficult to cooperate with, they also provide a challenge to the stable world order.

While Panetta only suggests that these countries are a potential rather than a current threat, it is indicative of a broader school of thought in international relations that suggests that the rise of the BRICS poses a danger to international stability. There are three main arguments commonly used by proponents of this view.

1. The Rise of the BRICS Will Cause an Unstable Shift in the International System

This argument rests on two propositions: that the rise of the BRICS will result in an increasingly multipolar international system; and that, historically, multipolar international systems have tended to be more unstable than bipolar or unipolar ones (National Intelligence Council, 2008, p. vi). Drawn together, these propositions can be used to suggest the inevitability of instability and conflict between established and rising powers.

Robert Kaplan sketches the process thus: 'As a great continental nation's economy grows, it begins to trade more with the outside world and develops interests it did not have previously' (Kaplan, 2005). These interests can then conflict with those of the more established powers, whose power is often in relative decline in a number of areas: 'Strategic rivalries are most likely to revolve around trade, investments, and technological innovation and acquisition, but we cannot rule out a 19th century-like scenario of arms races, territorial expansion, and military rivalries' (National Intelligence Council, 2008, p. vi). As established powers band together to attempt to maintain their privileged position, rising powers can also form coalitions to advance their common interests. Proponents of the 'BRICS with mortars' school suggest that this is occurring with the BRICS.

The formation of a common agenda by the BRICS could be seen as an attempt to form a coalition against the established powers, especially the US. Taken together, the BRICS countries occupy more than a quarter of the world's landmass and are home to 40 per cent of its population. The BRICS' combined GDP accounts for almost a fifth of global economic output (Oeheler-Şincai, 2011, p. 32). The Global Financial Crisis (GFC) has exacerbated this trend; while the developed nations are mired in recession, growth in the BRICS, while slowing, shows no sign of failing. The growing economic and geopolitical power of the BRICS thus represents a fundamental redefinition of the international system away from a unipolar system dominated by the US to 'a global multipolar one with gaps in national power continuing to narrow between developed and developing countries' (National Intelligence Council, 2008, p. vi). The question is whether such a change will necessarily cause damaging instability.

Supporters of this argument suggest that not only will the BRICS' combined economic and political weight naturally lead to a more unstable multipolar system, but that this is in fact the goal of the BRICS. They point to pronouncements such as those made at the first BRIC Summit in Yakaterinburg in June 2006, where the BRIC leaders called for 'a more democratic and just multipolar world order', and Dmitry Medvedev suggested that the BRIC nations 'take part in setting the new rules of the game' (quoted in Hounshell, 2011, p. 185). Members of the BRICS have also formed a number of other informal or regional groupings such as the Shanghai Cooperation Organisation (SCO), which includes China and Russia as members and India as an observer, BASIC (Brazil, South Africa, India and China) and IBSA (India, Brazil and South Africa). Through these organizations members of the BRICS are developing a greater degree of cooperation outside a purely economic focus. While to date the SCO has concentrated on local issues, it has nonetheless become an important factor in regional geopolitical calculations and has resulted in reduced Western influence in Central Asia (Hall, 2009, p. 5). Given the rising power of the BRICS, fears are expressed that the BRICS grouping might one day develop into a fully fledged counterbalance to existing powers.

2. The BRICS Members' Economic Policies Undermine the Liberal Principles Underpinning Global Commerce

This argument suggests that the BRICS countries do not adhere to the liberal tenets of the Western-centric world order nor view themselves as beneficiaries of that order (Alexandroff & Cooper, 2010, p. 1). Advocates of this view point particularly to the protectionist behaviour of China and Russia and argue that this undermines the effectiveness of the international economic system. The concern is expressed that rather than embracing the principles of free trade and open markets, the BRICS group instead advocates an economic model that favours state intervention and protectionism (Alexandroff & Cooper, 2010, p. 1).

China, for example, is routinely accused of manipulating exchange markets in order to keep its currency artificially low, most recently by Mitt Romney during the 2012 US presidential election (Branigan, 2012). By buying billions of US dollars, China raises demand and thus increases the price of the dollar. As a consequence, the Chinese currency remains weak relative to the US dollar, making Chinese exports cheaper. The US Treasury considers that such policies 'are highly distortionary and pose a risk to China's economy, its trading partners, and global economic growth' (US Treasury, 2005, p. 2). The artificial manipulation of exchange rates is expressly forbidden by Article IV of the IMF's Articles of Agreement (Goldstein, 2006, p. 143). Some see China's policies as a violation of the norms underpinning the international financial system.

Russia's economic policies are also singled out as contravening the spirit of the international liberal order. The control exerted by the Kremlin over huge state-owned energy corporations like Gazprom has allowed it to use them as a political tool to control prices and influence the policies of neighbouring states, such as Russia's actions in the so-called 'gas wars' with the Ukraine in 2006 and 2008–09, which also affected supplies in Central and Western Europe (Roberts, 2010, pp. 46–7; Smith, 2006, p. 2). Russian subsidies on domestic gas prices also have a distorting effect on global prices, causing Russia's European customers to pay inflated prices (Smith, 2006, pp. 2–3). A key reason for the establishment of global governance institutions like the IMF and WTO was to discourage such nationalistic policies and promote mutually reinforcing trade and financial practices (Goldstein, 2006, p. 142). Russia's actions are seen as undermining these efforts.

Similar criticisms are levelled at the other BRICS members. With the possible exception of South Africa, the other BRICS members also have a long-standing commitment to interventionist economic policies. India, for example, has had a commitment to protectionism that dates back to independence (Sinha & Dorschner, 2010, p. 93). In the last few years, Brazil increased tariffs on more than 100 imports, including steel, petrochemicals and pharmaceuticals, and attempts have been made to keep the real at weak levels against the dollar (Rapoza, 2012). While attempts have been made to liberalize South Africa's economy and open its market,

South Africa's self-conception as the representative of African interests in the G20 has ensured that it has taken a critical stance towards neo-liberal policies, including advocating the implementation of 'fair trade' policies and greater participation by African nations in global financial decision-making (Boulle, 2011, p. 138).

Given that liberal values underpin global economic institutions, the BRICS' lack of support for these principles is thought to make it less likely that the BRICS countries will adhere to the norms of the international financial system – and perhaps may lead them to consider leaving these institutions in search of alternatives more in line with their ideological preferences. If this occurred, it would certainly result in a weakening of global economic institutions.

3. The BRICS Members are Irresponsible International Citizens

Finally, the BRICS is criticized for not contributing sufficiently to the international system. At a G20 Think Tanks Summit in Philadelphia in 2012, one of the authors heard a representative of a leading US think tank express the view that: 'Many countries are interested in the benefits of great power status but not the responsibilities of great power.'

As the BRICS group becomes more vocal in its demands for a greater share of global power, commentators stress the other side of this bargain: that great powers have important obligations to the international community. These obligations include contributing resources to ensure that international organizations can provide global public goods, upholding the basic norms underpinning the international community and guaranteeing global peace and security.

The BRICS countries are criticized for their reluctance to invest significant resources in global public goods. For example, while the BRICS economies made up 19 per cent of the world's GDP in 2012, their combined contributions to the UN amounted to just 6.7 per cent of the UN regular budget. This was similar to the contribution of the UK (6.6 per cent) and around a third of the US (22 per cent) (United Nations, 2012a). As their weight grows, so too will demands that the BRICS countries take on a greater share of responsibility.

Where the BRICS members have committed resources to address global issues, this has been viewed as motivated by narrow national interests rather than by a commitment to the well-being of the international community. For example, 'China moved to buy European debt to bolster an important trading partner . . .. BRICs are willing to combat pirates and help with disaster relief but not shoulder the costs of climate change' (Roberts, 2011, p. 8).

Others point to the BRICS members' foreign policies as evidence of their inability to act responsibly on the international stage. Critics point to the BRICS members' support for regimes condemned by the majority of the international community for violations of human rights. From Russian support for Slobodan Milosevic in Serbia, Chinese support for Omar al-Bashir in Sudan or South Africa's support for Robert Mugabe in Zimbabwe, the BRICS countries have been linked with some of the world's most odious regimes (Roberts, 2010, p. 53; Kaplan, 2005; Sotero, 2010, p. 74). The current humanitarian crisis in Syria is used as a case in point where the BRICS countries have either vetoed (China and Russia) or abstained (Brazil, India and South Africa) when international intervention has been proposed in the UN Security Council, despite overwhelming condemnation of the Syrian regime by the General Assembly (Brütch & Papa, 2012, p. 1). This is criticized as out of step with the wishes of the global community.

The BRICS countries have also been criticized for their own internal policies, including China's treatment of minorities and human rights campaigners (Kaplan, 2005), Russia's increasing authoritarianism (Roberts, 2010, p. 58) and India's refusal to sign the nuclear non-proliferation treaty (Sinha & Dorschner, 2010, p. 75).

According to proponents of this argument, if the BRICS members wish to see their demands for a greater voice in the international community adopted, they must first ensure that they are able to act responsibly as great powers.

BRICS AND MORTAR?

The arguments summarized earlier outline three common explanations why the BRICS group represents a threat to global governance. As discussed further on, others regard these concerns as overblown and question the assumptions involved.

In 2012 the President of the China Institute of Contemporary International Relations, Cui Liru, challenged the negative interpretation of China's rise:

> China intends to realise its national resurgence and modernisation not through violence in a zero-sum game like Fascist Germany or Japan on the eve of and during the Second World War, but through a peaceful path born of a win-win strategy for common prosperity by integrating into or accepting and participating in the existing international system . . . China's peaceful integration into the process of globalisation, thus becoming an integral part of it, should be seen as a matter of creative significance in world politics . . . (Cui, 2012, p. 15).

The key claim in his argument is that China wants to integrate with, rather than disrupt, the existing international system. He explains this through self-interest: China's leadership sees the fulfilment of its long cherished dream of national modernization in 'building a market economy through integration into the outside world in the process of globalisation' (Cui, 2012, p. 14). While he admits that there will be a shift from the dominance of 'US-led Western developed countries' to greater multipolarity, he does not concede that this must cause instability since existing structures can be adapted: 'In light of the objective demand, a search is on for a stable and effective structure of the international system that fits reality' (Cui, 2012, p. 17).

In this view the BRICS members are positive actors engaged in a process of shoring up and constructively reforming the system of global governance in order to maintain stability. Three main arguments are used to support this view:

1. The BRICS Is a Bargaining Coalition, Not an Alliance of Like-Minded Powers

To counter the fears of the 'BRICS with mortars' school that the BRICS is or will become a balancing alliance, commentators note that not only is there a lack of alliance structure but also a divergence of interests that is likely to prevent such an alliance forming.

Unlike fully fledged alliances like NATO which come together in response to common security concerns and shared values, the BRICS grouping was designed primarily as a framework for dialogue (Roberts, 2010, p. 52). The BRICS is a very informal organization; it has neither a permanent secretariat nor a clearly defined agenda or charter. Most meetings have been informal meetings on the sidelines of multilateral conferences. Since 2009, cooperation has expanded somewhat, including meetings between the BRICS ministers for agriculture, finance, health and trade, second track dialogues and business forums, and five formal leaders' summits. Nonetheless there has been no attempt to develop a common security agenda, and the BRICS leaders have stated that their cooperation is based on the principles of 'no alliances, no confrontation' and 'open and transparent cooperation, not aimed at third parties' (Glosny, 2010, p. 110).

Even if it did aim to balance the US and its allies, the BRICS group would not only have to share a commitment to limited common goals but also a broader geopolitical and strategic vision based on common values and interests (Brütch & Papa, 2012, p. 3). This is needed because such balancing 'is costly and requires significant collective mobilization both internally and within interstate coalitions which tend to struggle with mutual suspicions, conflicting interests and distributional concerns' (Roberts, 2010, p. 51). There is little evidence that the BRICS has an overarching common vision.

Aside from their commitment to limited reforms to the global financial system, the BRICS members have relatively little in common. They come from different geographical positions, have massively different economies and population size, have different political systems and cultural values and, at times, conflicting national interests. There are demonstrable differences between the BRICS on most fronts. Are all the BRICS members 'emerging economies'? For Russia, a significant time scale would need to be selected. Are they all 'emerging powers'? China is a genuine power and India is a rising power, but South Africa is never going to have such weight. Are they all 'anti-colonial'? Russia's near abroad might disagree. Are they all non-Western? One of the authors attended a dinner talk given by the author of *No One's World*, Charles Kupchan, where a senior Brazilian mused wonderingly that he had not previously been aware that Brazil is not part of the West. With a history that includes armed conflict and continuing tensions, China and India are not natural allies.

The lack of common cause can be demonstrated by the lack of cooperation between the BRICS members outside the area of global economic governance where their interests converge. For example, attempts by Brazil and India to gain permanent representation on the UN Security Council have not been supported by China and Russia, as this is viewed as detrimental to their interests (Sotero, 2010, p. 78). Even in the economic sphere, the grouping is split between resource-exporters (Brazil, Russia and South Africa) and resource-consumers (China and India), leading to trade disputes between the BRICS members on such issues as access to markets and agricultural protection (Sotero, 2010, p. 78; Roberts, 2011, p. 5).

The BRICS grouping is thus best characterized as a 'bargaining coalition' with limited objectives. States form bargaining coalitions by pooling resources to increase their leverage in negotiations. Bargaining coalitions are therefore utilitarian in nature; members of the coalition do not need to share the same overarching interests, values or priorities, so long as they can agree on limited common objectives (Brütch & Papa, 2012, p. 3). On the evidence of the BRICS joint statement at the last G20 Leader's Summit in Los Cabos in June 2012, a key focus of the bargaining coalition is on reforms to IMF quotas and voting shares (Ministry of External Affairs, India, 2012). Given their conflicting ideals and interests it seems unlikely that the BRICS members will form a united bloc in the near or medium term.

2. The BRICS Members Want a Larger Place in Global Institutions, Not to Undermine Them

One of the key assumptions driving the 'BRICS with mortars' thesis is that the BRICS' preference for statist economic policy will undermine the international system. The obvious first point is that very few countries are complete paragons in their domestic economic policies (just ask low tariff countries like New Zealand, Singapore or Australia whether the US is pro-free trade and anti-protectionist in its own domestic market). It is an area where most countries live in glass houses and should be wary of casting stones.

There is also evidence that integration into the globalized economy has resulted in the BRICS' members modifying their positions and offering greater support for liberal policies. For example, the BRICS Delhi Plan urges 'countries to resist all forms of trade protectionism and disguised restrictions on trade' (BRICS, 2012, Article 15). With Russia's accession to the WTO in 2012, all the BRICS members are now scrutinized to ensure compliance with international trade law and are bound by the decisions of the WTO's Dispute Settlement Body (Elliot, 2012). The BRICS members have attempted to improve their international standing in other areas of contention: for example, China has been more flexible regarding its exchange rate (Brütch & Papa, 2012, p. 13) with the result that the renminbi has increased by 8 per cent against the dollar since 2010 and has increased 24 per cent since 2005 ('China's currency: Enough appreciation for now', 2012).

The bigger issue that this argument fails to take into account is that despite their tendency towards statist economic policies, the BRICS members have benefited greatly from the neo-liberal economic system and have become increasingly integrated into its structure over the past twenty years (Oeheler-Şincai, 2011, p. 40). For the BRICS members, a stable, open and globalized international economy is integral to continued economic growth. In the words of the 2009 Chinese Defence White Paper, 'China cannot develop in isolation from the rest of the world, nor can the world enjoy prosperity and stability without China' (quoted in Glosny, 2010, p. 116). The statements of the BRICS members make it clear that they recognize this. Instead of railing against the international economic regime, their key demand is to be included and given an equitable place in global governance institutions. For example, the Delhi Action Plan states that the BRICS countries 'recognize the importance of the global financial architecture in maintaining the stability and integrity of the global monetary and financial system' (BRICS, 2012, Article 8), and that they are:

> . . . ready to work with others, developed and developing countries together, on the basis of universally recognized norms of international law and multilateral decision making, to deal with the challenges and the opportunities before the world today. Strengthened representation of emerging and developing countries in the institutions of global governance will enhance their effectiveness in achieving this objective (BRICS, 2012, Article 4).

Far from leading to an erosion of liberal values in global governance institutions, increased participation by the BRICS countries in the globalized economy has resulted in them becoming more committed to preserving these values. Realizing the importance of open trade, the BRICS group has made it clear that it advocates reform of the system, not its replacement by a new one. The BRICS joint statement at the G20 Summit in Los Cabos outlined three commitments designed to stabilize the global financial system in the midst of continuing economic uncertainty and sluggish growth throughout most of the developed world. This showed that the BRICS can play a role in contributing to financial stability in the international system.

3. The BRICS Countries Are Contributing to Global Public Goods and Promoting Compliance with International Norms

Proponents of the 'BRICS and mortar' view contest the characterization of the BRICS members as irresponsible actors and point to the ways in which the BRICS countries contribute to the international system and promote compliance with international norms.

In judging the behaviour of the BRICS countries, it is important to employ a reasonable standard. For example, the criticism that the BRICS members are only acting in their national interests when they contribute to disaster relief or anti-piracy efforts (Roberts, 2011, p. 8) is one that could be levelled at any great power. Contributions of global public goods rely on the idea that self-interested action can also provide benefits to others.

The BRICS countries can provide evidence of their contribution to global public goods in a number of areas. For example, the BRICS members are among the most important contributors to UN peacekeeping operations, with four of the BRICS countries ranked in the top twenty contributors to UN missions: India (3rd), Brazil (11th), South Africa (13th) and China (15th). By comparison, the first developed country on the list is Italy at number 25 with around one-eighth of India's contribution (United Nations, 2012b). In determining whether the BRICS countries contribute their 'fair share', it is important to remember that, with the exception of Russia, all the BRICS members are still developing countries.

The BRICS members made an important contribution at the G20

Summit in Los Cabos when they agreed to increase their individual contributions to the IMF (Ministry of External Affairs, India, 2012). China offered a $43 billion contribution to new IMF reserves while India, Brazil and Russia pledged $10 billion each and South Africa $2 billion. This makes it clear that the BRICS group is willing and able to contribute to financial stability, the only condition being equitable voting shares in international financial institutions.

Proponents of the 'BRICS and mortar' view also see the BRICS group as promoting compliance with international norms. They point to the BRICS' bedrock support for the base norm of sovereignty and non-use of force. This can be contrasted with examples where the US and other nations have been willing to breach these principles, as in the case of the 2003 invasion of Iraq.

There is a genuine difference of opinion regarding the application of some norms, such as the Responsibility to Protect (R2P) unanimously adopted at the UN World Summit in 2005. The third pillar of R2P requires the international community to take timely and decisive action when a state has failed in its duty to protect its population from extreme abuses of human rights, such as genocide and war crimes (Bellamy, 2012, p. 15). The BRICS group accepts the principle of RTP; its position is that it is not misused by powerful states to intervene militarily in weaker states.

The BRICS' position on intervention in Syria deserves some analysis. It is true that the BRICS countries have not supported international intervention in Syria: in the UN Security Council, China and Russia exercised their veto and Brazil, India and South Africa abstained to ensure that a resolution imposing sanctions was defeated. However, Brazil, India and South Africa voted in favour of a second resolution which condemned the 'continued and gross violations of human rights and fundamental freedoms by the Syrian authorities' but did not authorize international action (Laidi, 2012, p. 628).

In justifying their position, the BRICS countries have explained that they object to international intervention on the grounds that such intervention might lead to regime change (Aboagye, 2012; Hamann, 2012; Banerjee, 2012). This should be seen in the context of an earlier action authorized by the Security Council, which resulted in the overthrow of the regime of Muammar Gaddafi in Libya. Significantly criticism of the intervention in Libya was not directed at the principles underpinning R2P but in the way they were implemented (Bellamy, 2012, p. 20). Support for the second resolution suggests that Brazil, India and South Africa recognize that the Syrian government deserves censure but are unwilling to support the use of force. Thus 'what remains controversial is not R2P – or even the idea that the international community should become involved in crises involving . . . genocide or mass atrocities – but rather the questions of using force and changing regimes' (Bellamy, 2012, p. 21). This is a disagreement around how two accepted international norms – the non-use of force and R2P – should apply in a particular case.

CONCLUSION

While both offer useful insights, the authors find the 'BRICS and mortar' school matches better with the behaviour of the BRICS in the G20 to date. The BRICS group is an informal grouping of very different countries and currently lacks the institutional framework and common purpose necessary to act as an alliance to challenge the foundations of global governance. Two decades of integration into the globalized economy has bound the BRICS countries to the rules and institutions of global governance. They are active and engaged members of the international community. Looking at the BRICS' behaviour in the G20, they have not used the GFC and continuing instability as an opportunity to topple the international economic system but have consistently attempted to contribute to financial stability.

This is not to say that the BRICS countries are happy with every part of the international regime. Where the BRICS members' interests are not being met, they advocate change – the same as any other countries. However, observers need to be able to distinguish between policy disagreements and attacks on the international system itself. In the realm of global economic governance, the key demand that the BRICS has made over and over again is that it be included and given due weight in global financial architecture; this is very different than wishing to overthrow its basic tenets.

To illustrate how different this might be, it is worth looking outside economic governance to another area. In the case of the various territorial disputes in the South China Sea, China is arguably making a fundamental challenge to the current international regime based on the UN Convention on the Law of the Sea by proposing an entirely different regime, much to the consternation and chagrin of other claimants. This has the potential to result in conflict, as disputes with China's Southeast Asian neighbours become increasingly heated (Hsing, 2012, p. 1). If the BRICS group was questioning whole areas of the international system in this way, it would be a genuine challenge to global governance.

Compare this with the behaviour of the BRICS group at the last G20 Leader's Summit in Los Cabos, where its focus was on how to stabilize the global financial system and find 'cooperative solutions' to resolve the Euro

Area crisis and restore global economic and financial stability (Ministry of External Affairs, India, 2012). The BRICS' statement of solidarity with Europe and the commitment of extra funds to the IMF were well received by G20 members and global markets and enhanced the perception of the G20. Such positive action bodes well for the development of global governance into the future. It may be uncomfortable for the pride of other countries for the BRICS countries to eclipse them in certain areas, but this does not suggest an existential threat to the international system.

The Los Cabos Declaration suggests that should the BRICS group achieve its goal of a greater role in global economic governance, this will not necessarily lead to a weakening of the international system as suggested by the 'BRICS with mortars' school. On the contrary, the responsible and cooperative approach outlined at Los Cabos suggests that the BRICS countries can play an important constructive role – in effect becoming the 'BRICS and mortar' of a more inclusive and effective international system.

NOTES

1. The views expressed in this chapter are the authors' alone.
2. The authors are not the first to use the play on words of 'BRICS and mortar' but may be the first to use mortar in both senses, referring to mortar weapons and construction mortar.

REFERENCES

Aboagye, F. (2012). South Africa and R2P: More state sovereignty and regime security than human security? In M. Brosig (Ed.), *The responsibility to protect – from evasive to reluctant action? The role of global middle powers* (pp. 29–52). Johannesburg: South African Institute of International Affairs.

Alexandroff, A. and Cooper, A. (2010). Introduction. In A. Cooper (Ed.), *Rising states, rising institutions: Challenges for global governance* (pp. 1–16). New York, NY: Brookings Institute Press.

Banerjee, D. (2012). India and R2P: Reconciling the tension between intervention and state sovereignty. In M. Brosig (Ed.), *The responsibility to protect – from evasive to reluctant action? The role of global middle powers* (pp. 91–110). Johannesburg: South African Institute of International Affairs.

Bellamy, A. (2012). R2P – Dead or Alive? In M. Brosig (Ed.), *The responsibility to protect – from evasive to reluctant action? The role of global middle powers* (pp. 11–28). Johannesburg: South African Institute of International Affairs.

Boulle, L. (2011). The Republic of South Africa and the G20: Its political, national interests and priorities as member of the process. In W. Hofmeister and S. Vogt

(Eds), *G20 – perceptions and perspectives for global governance* (pp. 135–46). Singapore: Konrad Adenauer Stiftung.

Branigan, T. (2012, October 23). Mitt Romney renews promise to label China a currency manipulator. *The Guardian*. Retrieved from http://www.guardian.co.uk/world/2012/oct/23/mitt-romney-china-currency-manipulator

BRICS (2012). *Delhi action plan*. Retrieved from http://www.brics.utoronto.ca/docs/120329-delhi-declaration.html#actionplan

Brütch, C. and Papa, M. (2012). Deconstructing the BRICs: Bargaining coalition, imagined community or geopolitical fad? *CRP Working Papers*, *5*, 1–29.

China's currency: Enough appreciation for now (2012, March 12). *The Economist*. Retrieved from http://www.economist.com/blogs/freeexchange/2012/03/chinas-currency#comments

Cui, L. (2012). Peaceful rise: China's modernisation trajectory. *The International Spectator*, *47*(2), 14–17.

Elliot, L. (2012, August 22). Russia's entry to WTO ends 19 years of negotiations. *The Guardian*. Retrieved from http://www.guardian.co.uk/business/economics-blog/2012/aug/22/russia-entry-world-trade-organisation

Glosny, M. (2010). China and the BRICs: A real (but limited) partnership in a unipolar world. *Polity*, *42*(1), 100–129.

Goldstein, M. (2006). Currency manipulation and enforcing the rules of the international monetary system. In E. Truman (Ed.), *Reforming the IMF for the 21st century* (pp. 141–56). Washington, DC: Institute of International Economics.

Hall, M. (2009). *The Shanghai cooperation organisation: A partner for stabilising Afghanistan?* Canberra: Centre for Defence and Strategic Studies, Australian Defence College.

Hamann, E.P. (2012). Brazil and R2P: A rising global player struggles to harmonise discourse and practise. In M. Brosig (Ed.), *The responsibility to protect – from evasive to reluctant action? The role of global middle powers* (pp. 71–90). Johannesburg: South African Institute of International Affairs.

Hounshell, B. (2011). Anthropology of an idea: BRICS. *Foreign Policy*, *185*, 185–6.

Hsing, S. (2012). China and the territorial claims in the South China Sea. *China Studies Centre Policy Paper Series*, *2*. Sydney: China Studies Centre, University of Sydney.

Kaplan, R. (2005). Don't panic about China: Why we should embrace – rather than fear – the next superpower. *The Atlantic*, *10*. Retrieved from http://www.theatlantic.com/magazine/archive/2005/10/dont-panic-about-china/307926/

Laidi, Z. (2012). BRICS: Sovereignty, power and weakness. *International Politics*, *49*(5), 614–32.

Ministry of External Affairs, India. (2012, June 18). Media note on the informal meeting of BRICS leaders ahead of the G20 summit in Los Cabos. Retrieved from http://www.mea.gov.in/media-briefings.htm?dtl/19732/

National Intelligence Council, US. (2008). *Global trends 2025: A transformed world*. Washington, DC: US Government Printing Office.

Oeheler-Şincai, J. (2011). The strategic character of the cooperation relationship between the EU and the BRIC countries. *Romanian Journal of European Affairs*, *11*(2), 31–46.

Parrish, K. (2011, September 7). Panetta assesses national security threats. *American Forces Press Service*. Retrieved from http://www.defense.gov/News/NewsArticle.aspx?ID=65268

Rapoza, K. (2012, May 9). Weak economy pushes Brazil to protectionism. *Forbes*. Retrieved from http://www.forbes.com/sites/kenrapoza/2012/09/05/weak-economy-pushes-brazil-to-protectionism/
Roberts, C. (2010). Russia's BRIC diplomacy: Rising outsider with dreams of an insider. *Polity*, *42*(1), 38–73.
Roberts, C. (2011). Building the new world order BRIC by BRIC. *The European Financial Review*, *February*, 4–8.
Sinha, A. and Dorschner, J. (2010). India: Rising power or a mere revolution of rising expectations? *Polity*, *42*(1), 74–99.
Smith, K. (2006). Security implications of Russian energy policy. *CEPS Policy Brief*, *90*, 1–5.
Sotero, P. (2010). Brazil's rising ambition in a shifting global balance of power. *Politics*, *30*(1), 71–81.
United Nations (2012a). *Assessment of member states' contributions to the United Nations regular budget for 2012*. New York, NY: United Nations Committee on Contributions.
United Nations (2012b). Ranking of military and police contributions to UN operations. New York, NY: United Nations Department of Peacekeeping Operations. Retrieved from https://www.un.org/en/peacekeeping/contributors/2012/Dec12_2.pdf
US Treasury (2005). *Report to the Congress on international economic and exchange rate policies*. Washington, DC: US Treasury Department.

16. China's path to development: Does law matter?

Vai Io Lo

On the world scene, the class phenomenon is replicated. Depending on the level of economic development, there are developed countries, developing countries and the least developed countries. The status of being a developed, developing or least developed country not only signifies a country's wealth and technological advancement, but also conveys how much voice it can have and what impact it can produce in the international arena. Accordingly development is the ultimate goal of many aspiring countries.

In their journey to development, developing and the least developed countries (hereinafter collectively referred to as developing countries) do not travel alone. Unlike other pressing issues facing the world, the goals to lift millions of people out of poverty and to improve the quality of life of the disadvantaged are shared by most, if not all, countries (UNDP, 2000).[1] Developed countries would like to help, whether out of altruistic, resource-seeking, or hegemonic motives. In this connection developed countries, through international financial institutions and development aid offices, have been providing grants, loans and technical assistance to developing countries under the condition that economic, legal and/or political reforms are to be undertaken (Krever, 2011, pp. 291–4; Ohnesorge, 2007b, pp. 305–6; Thomas, 2011, pp. 991–8).[2] The fundamental question is: what kinds of economic, legal or political reforms should developing countries adopt to foster development?

As discussed further on, international financial institutions and development aid offices have espoused development theories and policy directives formulated by economists, legal scholars, international bankers and so forth. However, policy directives derived from development theories, especially some of the Washington Consensus, have been discredited due to the financial crises in various parts of the world (Birdsall & Fukuyama, 2011, p. 46; Ramo, 2004, p. 4). Meanwhile, over the course of three decades, China has transformed itself from an isolated, economically stagnant country into the second largest economy in the world ('China overtakes Japan', 2010). China's 'economic miracle' has confounded advocates of development orthodoxies because China, whose legal system has been extensively criticized,[3] has managed to achieve phenomenal economic success. Indeed China's remarkable economic growth has caused some developing countries to wonder whether the Chinese experience can provide an alternative model (Ramo, 2004, p. 26).

This chapter attempts to trace China's path to development in the past three decades, ascertain the role of law in fostering economic development in China, and identify factors conducive to China's economic growth. Towards these aims the first section provides a succinct account of the theories of development, especially the ebb and flow of the law and development movement. Against those theoretical propositions, the second section outlines China's significant economic developments and concomitant legal reforms since the late 1970s. Following an overview of China's economic reforms and legal initiatives, the third section highlights the essential attributes of China's development course. The concluding section explores what lessons can be learned from the Chinese experience.

THEORIES OF DEVELOPMENT

Since World War II, theories of development have emerged as an eclectic discipline of economics, law, political science, sociology and anthropology. Even so the theoretical underpinning of existing approaches to, or models on, development consists predominantly of economic theories and the advocacy for the rule of law. In fact the emergence of each wave of the law and development movement reflects the rise and decline of the contemporaneous schools of economics and legal-political ideologies.

At the outset Max Weber maintained that a rational system of law played a crucial role in the economic development of the Protestant West because 'formal rationality' enabled individuals to conduct economic transactions with predictability (Weber, 1978).[4] In the 1950s and 1960s the first generation of law and development scholars drew on Weber's theory and defined development as a process in which developing countries were to converge with the developed West, where there were such 'modern' institutions as free market, property rights, political pluralism, democracy, civil rights and an independent judiciary (Davis & Trebilcock, 2001, p. 22). In other words modernization theorists perceived the world as a dichotomy of 'traditional' societies with obsolete institutions and 'modern' societies with progressive institutions. Considering the instrumental role of law in effecting development, modernization theorists believed that legal institutions from the developed world should be transplanted to developing countries to accelerate development and economic growth (Davis & Trebilcock, 2001, p. 22).

Nevertheless since development in many developing countries occurred in the context of complex economic, political and cultural relationships with developed countries, dependency theorists were sceptical of the efficacy of transplanting legal institutions from developed to developing countries (Davis & Trebilcock, 2001, pp. 22–3). Instead they advocated the replacement of capitalist forms of development with socialist ones, such as land and labour reforms, because of their redistributive potential (Davis & Trebilcock, 2001, pp. 22–3). In a similar vein some scholars argued that although development directives and programmes were important, culture played a significant role in effecting development as, for example, Japan with its work ethic had rapidly recovered from its post-war devastated economy (Landes, 2000, p. 10).

In the mid-1970s the first wave of the law and development movement subsided. Trubek and Galanter, the leading figures, concluded that the reform of formal legal institutions had little effect on the socio-economic conditions in developing countries and thus renounced their efforts to promote legal reforms (Trubek & Galanter, 1974). Subsequently with the ascendance of Thatcher and Reagan, the Keynesian welfare state in which moderate government intervention was deemed necessary to ensure redistribution was superseded by neoclassical economics. Neoclassicists were inspired by the Coase Theorem, which argued that, since an efficient market could generate solutions to social harms, the government should refrain from responding with regulatory solutions (Thomas, 2011, p. 978). During that period, free markets without government intervention, trade liberalization and property rights achieved doctrinal importance.

The rise of the New Institutional Economics restored the importance of law in economic development, which gave rise to the second wave of the law and development movement. According to Douglas North, the neoclassical goal of efficient markets only obtains when the transaction cost is zero, and when it is costly to transact, institutions matter (North, 1997, p. 18). Moreover institutions are the 'rules of the game', namely, 'humanly devised constraints that structure human interaction', including formal rules, informal constraints, and the enforcement characteristics of both (North, 1997, p. 23). In this respect property rights, contract law, corporate law, bankruptcy law, competition law, code of conduct and so forth are indispensable institutions.

Nonetheless, since institutions can be used by politicians, bureaucrats and elites for rent-seeking, self-promoting purposes, the legal and institutional environments can either facilitate or hinder market activities and economic growth (Thomas, 2011, pp. 980–81).[5] Because institutional inefficiencies resulting from public choices can continue through path dependency, North advocated good governance based on legal and institutional reforms (1997,

p. 20). Meanwhile advocates of the New Political Economy argued that state-led growth strategies of the developing world were responsible for stifling growth, and endorsed the idea that 'trade openness' was the best determinant of economic growth (Thomas, 2011, p. 984). As a result the New Institutional Economics and the New Political Economy jointly laid the theoretical foundation for the Washington Consensus (Thomas, 2011, p. 979).

The Washington Consensus, which was originally made as a framework for promoting development in Latin America and subsequently debated worldwide, listed ten tenets for development.[6] In particular the Washington Consensus was reminiscent of trade liberalization, property rights, privatization, market economy and deregulation. However, the subsequent discrediting of the Washington Consensus opened another round of debate. For example, the advocates of moderate institutionalism, such as Dani Rodrik, argued for a greater role for the state in regulating economic activities (Thomas, 2011, pp. 985–7). In addition Amartya Sen argued that development was intimately linked with 'human capabilities' (Thomas, 2011, p. 988). According to Sen, since aggregate social development could not happen without a population who could provide the dynamism to fuel economic transformation, development should attend to the protection of civil and political rights as well as social and economic rights (Thomas, 2011, p. 988). In this respect Sen propounded a theory of governance that espoused human rights as the basis for first principles of development policy (Thomas, 2011, p. 988). Consequently, the Post-Washington or Augmented Washington Consensus has such additional elements as good governance, anti-corruption, social security, human rights and poverty reduction.

As an institution, law featured prominently in both waves of the law and development movement. However, Ohnesorge argued that the idealized picture of how law functioned in the developed West was not supported by the roles that law had played in Northeast Asia's successful economies, namely, Taiwan, South Korea and Japan, which experienced high growth under regimes of strong administrative rule and weak law enforcement (Ohnesorge, 2007a, pp. 258–82). Considering the paradox that China has emerged as an economic giant but its legal system has been widely criticized, one inquiry is what kind of role law has played in fostering economic development in China.

CHINA'S ECONOMIC DEVELOPMENTS AND LEGAL REFORMS

In December 1978 the Third Plenary Session of the Eleventh Communist Party Central Committee decided to focus on modernization and adopt the resolution of 'inward reforms and outward opening-up'. Towards this end the subsequent Five-Year Plans were formulated to achieve economic and social developments. Since it is beyond the scope of this chapter to detail the Five-Year Plans and China's economic reforms in three decades, the following discussion will only highlight China's major economic reforms and corresponding legal initiatives.

Economic Developments

The Cultural Revolution brought China's economy to a standstill.[7] To promote economic development, China first adopted the Open Door policy to attract the much needed foreign capital, technologies and management expertise. In the four experimental Special Economic Zones, and subsequently 14 other open coastal cities, foreign and overseas Chinese investors received tax incentives and preferential treatment.[8] Since economic development could not be achieved without the necessary infrastructure for transportation and energy supply, the construction of roads, highways, railways, ports, airports and power plants was concurrently launched.[9] Consequently foreign capital, technologies and management know-how flowed into China through representative offices, branches, equity joint ventures, cooperative joint ventures and wholly foreign-owned enterprises; and export-oriented, labour-intensive manufacturing became the mainstay in China's burgeoning economy.

Apart from the Open Door policy, China de-collectivized agricultural production, decentralized economic decision-making and commenced the reform of state-owned enterprises. Prior to 1979 agricultural production was collective,[10] while industrial production was inefficiently discharged by state-owned enterprises.[11] Inspired by the success story of some farmers,[12] the government allowed farming households to do contracting-out, which resulted in the adoption of the household contract responsibility system nationwide.[13] Regarding state-owned enterprises, the Chinese leadership (1) decentralized economic decision-making, thereby granting enterprises autonomy to make business and production decisions; (2) adopted the director responsibility system to separate management from ownership;[14] and (3) introduced the concept of bankruptcy to close down failing enterprises. These economic reforms led to increased agricultural and industrial productivity, as farming households had income gains and enterprise directors became accountable for profits and losses.

Furthermore, while collectively owned enterprises multiplied in villages and townships since the opening-up, the government permitted individuals to engage in limited entrepreneurial activities with the assistance of his or her household. Later, individuals were allowed to employ a few workers and engage in a larger range of permissible business activities. Even so the private sector of the economy did not prosper due to the absence of formal recognition and the difficulties in securing approvals, loans and raw materials (Lo & Tian, 2002). In 1988 private enterprises were given formal recognition, and certain categories of individuals, such as villagers, the urban unemployed and retired people, were authorized to establish private enterprises.[15] Since then the private sector has made significant contributions to China's economic growth.

The Open Door policy and the reform of state-owned enterprises triggered two other major reforms, that is, tax reforms and labour reforms. The major tax reforms included the imposition of income tax on state-owned enterprises to separate taxes from profits; the imposition of income tax on foreign-invested enterprises; the addition of new tax categories; and the revision of existing tax categories (Lo & Tian, 2009, p. 294). After its accession to the WTO, China furthered its tax reforms to level the playing fields of both domestic and foreign-invested enterprises by adopting a unified enterprise income tax rate and formally ending the preferential tax treatments that foreign investors had enjoyed for almost three decades (Lo & Tian, 2009, pp. 302–3).

On the labour side, the so-called iron rice bowl[16] was smashed to promote the development of a mobile labour market and to remove the financial burden of state-owned enterprises in providing job-based welfare benefits. As a result the employment relationship was to be created through the conclusion of a labour contract, and the dismissal of workers based on misconduct or redundancy became acceptable. More importantly the construction of a social security system entitling workers to receive portable old-age pensions, basic health care, workers' compensation, maternity benefits, and unemployment insurance was launched. In the 1990s the government introduced minimum wages, maximum working hours and overtime pay.

As the reforms of state-owned enterprises intensified and private enterprises increasingly emerged, China undertook financial reforms, namely, banking reforms and the introduction of securities trading. The first banking reform was to dismantle the dual role of the People's Bank of China in being the central bank and a commercial bank. Since 1979 four new banks have been established to assume the role of independent state commercial bank, while the People's Bank of China retains its central bank function (Lo & Tian, 2009, p. 304).[17] In 1994 three policy banks were set up to separate policy banking (lending) from commercial banking (Lo & Tian, 2009, p. 304).[18] Meanwhile other types of financial institutions, such as credit cooperatives and finance companies, were allowed to open. Since 2006 China further liberalized the banking industry by allowing the establishment of equity-joint-venture commercial banks and wholly foreign-owned banks.[19]

The introduction of securities trading commenced with the opening of the Shanghai Stock Exchange and the Shenzhen Stock Exchange in 1990 and 1991, respectively. At the beginning different types of securities, namely, 'A' shares, 'B' shares and 'H' shares were devised for different types of investors.[20] As securities trading expanded and diversified, Chinese investors were allowed to trade 'B' shares using a foreign currency in 2001. Moreover the Qualified Foreign Institutional Investor (QFII)[21] scheme was launched in 2002 to further liberalize the financial market.

In the mid-1990s China began the restructuring of state-owned enterprises. The three major ways of restructuring were merger, corporatization, and management buy-out. First, small and medium-sized enterprises were merged to become large enterprises. Second, large enterprises were listed on the stock exchanges so that part of their stock capital could be purchased by private investors. Third, management and sometimes employees could purchase the shares of their enterprises. In consequence, various corporate forms consisting of a mixture of public and private capital, with the state owning the majority interest, emerged.

Prior to economic reforms China's foreign trade was under strict state control. The state imposed many restrictions on foreign trade, such as the state's monopoly of the right to trade, high tariff rates and various non-tariff trade barriers. At the end of the 1970s China began to liberalize its foreign trade regime by reducing tariff rates and non-tariff trade barriers and offering the right to trade to enterprises. With its accession to the WTO, China has further removed restrictions on foreign trade in terms of the right to trade, tariffs, non-tariff barriers, tariff rate quotas, technical barriers to trade, and designated trading (see WTO, 2001).

As the transformation of its economy progressed, China revised its policies on inbound foreign direct investment and encouraged domestic enterprises to 'go out' or 'go abroad'. With respect to inbound investment, relevant government agencies were to direct foreign investment into 'encouraged industries related to high-technology, modern services, and new energy, energy-saving and environmental protection products' and to the Central and Western Regions; diversify the use of foreign investment; and streamline the regulatory framework for foreign investment.[22]

In the 2000s Chinese enterprises were encouraged to invest overseas, which will enable them to secure the prestige that comes with acquiring internationally known brands, develop advanced technologies or enhance their R&D capability, obtain natural resources, and receive relief from competition at home (Broer, 2010, pp. 1–2). As a result Chinese enterprises have expanded into such international markets as Africa, Australia,

Europe, Latin America and the US. At the same time China embarked on economic integration with Hong Kong, Macau and Taiwan. The consequential free trade areas have further liberalized trade in goods, trade in services, and investment between China and these three economies.

Notwithstanding its economic successes China has acknowledged several key challenges: conflict between rapid economic growth and immense consumption of resources; widening disparities between different regions in terms of social and economic developments; deterioration of the ecosystem; constraints posed by a large population and scarce resources; inconsistencies between existing laws, regulations and policies and the actual needs for sustainable development; and social development lagging behind economic development (NDRC, 2007, part I). Accordingly China is facing the pressing tasks of developing the Middle and Western Regions, undertaking environmental protection, tackling social issues, furthering legal reforms and fostering sustainable development.

Legal Reforms

In the aftermath of the Cultural Revolution, the ascending leadership began to acknowledge the importance of the rule of law. Apart from the enactment or amendment of substantive and procedural laws, China also tried to construct the necessary legal infrastructure by restoring the judiciary, reopening the law schools and reinstating the legal profession. As a result of its opening-up, China has also been internationally active and thus become a signatory to various international treaties.[23] Basically law has facilitated economic development in China in two major ways – promoting and implementing new economic initiatives as well as affirming and regulating experimental economic activities – through statutory enactment and amendment. Since it is beyond the scope of this chapter to provide a full account of China's legal reforms, the following will underscore the major development-related legislation.

To execute the Open Door policy, China has enacted in stages a number of statutes and accompanying implementation regulations that allow foreign investors to establish a presence in China by setting up representative offices,[24] joint ventures,[25] foreign subsidiaries[26] and holding companies.[27] To reform state-owned enterprises and allow the development of the private sector of the economy, China has enacted statutes and regulations to apply the principle of the separation of ownership and management, give formal recognition to private enterprises in the developing market, and introduce bankruptcy procedures to close down failing enterprises.[28]

At the same time China has gradually built a functioning tax system and developed a mobile labour market. Prior to its accession to the WTO,

China promulgated a number of tax laws and regulations to deal with corollaries of economic reforms.[29] In 2007 China enacted the Enterprise Income Tax Law to attain a more uniform treatment of domestic and foreign-invested enterprises in accordance with the principle of national treatment.[30] At the outset China did not have a basic law on employment matters. Since 1994 China has promulgated and revised a number of statutes and regulations to curb the increasing incidents of labour abuse, implement the labour contract system, require both the employer and employee to make contributions to social security, set maximum working hours and overtime pay, and enhance the means of resolving labour disputes by mediation and arbitration.[31]

With the intensification of economic reforms in the 1990s, China passed the Contract Law to unify the previous piecemeal framework dealing with economic contracts, foreign economic contracts and technology contracts.[32] Moreover China enacted three significant pieces of legislation on business entities, which established the regulatory framework for company, partnership and sole proprietorship.[33] After more than ten years of experience, China substantially revised the Company Law and the Partnership Law in the mid-2000s to bring corporate governance more in line with international standards and to diversify partnership for commercial endeavours.[34] In the financial sector China has enacted first provisional legislation and then basic laws to reform the banking industry, introduce securities trading, authorize foreign banks to set up joint ventures, and allow qualified foreign financial institutions to invest in domestic securities.[35] To safeguard competition in an increasingly market-oriented economy, China has enacted the Antimonopoly Law to outlaw monopolistic and anticompetitive behaviour.[36]

In a similar fashion China has gradually improved its regulatory frameworks for property rights and environmental protection. Regarding intellectual property, China has enacted and subsequently amended its laws on patent, trademark and copyright so as to protect the inventions, goodwill and creative works of its nationals and to make its legal norms converge with international standards.[37] More importantly the long-awaited Property Law was enacted in 2007 to affirm unequivocally that lawfully acquired property rights are protected in China.[38] Nonetheless, at early stages of its economic development, China did not pay much attention to environmental protection. Since 2000 China has enacted 28 laws and 39 regulations on resources and environment, and amended a number of relevant laws and regulations, in addition to local regulations and departmental rules (The People's Republic of China, 2012, pp. 75–6).

Outside the mainland, China has signed free trade or cooperative agreements with Hong Kong, Macau and Taiwan to promote economic integration.[39] The free trade agreements with Hong Kong and Macau cover trade in goods, trade in services, and trade and investment facilitation. The cooperative framework with Taiwan reduces customs duties on a number of products over a period of three years and relaxes restrictions on a range of services. To facilitate the 'going out' or 'going abroad' policy, the Ministry of Commerce, State Administration of Foreign Exchange, National Reform and Development Commission and China Banking Regulatory Commission have simplified regulatory requirements to make overseas expansion easier for Chinese enterprises (Broer, 2010, pp. 3–4).

Most of all, the 1982 Constitution, the latest Constitution of China, has been revised four times.[40] The four constitutional amendments are milestones on China's path to development. The 1988 amendment affirmed the legal status of the private sector, stating that it complemented the socialist economy.[41] The 1993 amendment declared that China would put into practice a market economy instead of a planned economy and recognized the household contract responsibility system as part of the collectively owned economy.[42] The 1999 amendment declared that China would implement the rule of law and upgraded the private sector from 'complement' to 'an important component' of the country's economy.[43] In 2004 the Constitution was amended again to include guarantees regarding private property and human rights.[44]

Law and Development

Whether China is a rule-of-law country is quite controversial. For one thing the definition of the rule of law, even in the developed countries, is not devoid of contention (Krever, 2011, pp. 307–11). For another thing, given China's relatively short history of legal reforms, it is understandable that China does not have as well-established a legal system as those of the developed world. Although legal reforms in China have not been as comprehensive or speedy, or law in China has not functioned exactly as intended or expected by the developed world, law has been instrumental in fostering economic development in China. At the very least, law establishes the regulatory framework and provides 'the rules of the game' for economic activities in China's emerging socialist market. Correspondingly the increasing marketization of China's economy enhances China's need for a well-functioning legal system. Hence law and economic development in China is a two-way enterprise.

One may argue that there is no causal connection between the rule of law and economic growth in China, because businesses are willing to take risks despite the absence or limited practice of the rule of law, and informal mechanisms feature strikingly in China's economic development.

Even so law has been enforced by Chinese courts, whether vigorously or selectively, and has been applied by arbitration tribunals.[45] Besides, depending on the particular areas of law, the strength of enforcement in the developed world also varies from country to country. Indeed law plays a significant role in China today because one can often tell what has been happening economically and socially in China by examining the recent revisions of existing laws and regulations or the newly enacted laws and regulations.

As the National Development and Reform Commission explains, China needs to engage in 'capacity building,' including building a legal framework for population, resources and environment; improving law enforcement; and revising relevant laws and regulations in line with market rules and the WTO rules (NDRC, 2007, part III). Accordingly law will continue to occupy a pivotal role in China's development.

A DEVELOPMENT MODEL WITH CHINESE CHARACTERISTICS

China's economic miracle in a span of three decades has engendered much interest in its recipe for success. This section examines the essential attributes of China's development path in terms of approach, guiding principles and strategies.

Concisely China's approach to development is inductive and pragmatic. When China embarked on economic reforms in 1979, it did not adopt any theoretical model or a set of policy directives, nor did it have a detailed plan on how to proceed. The Chinese leadership set out only major directions, such as the Open Door policy and the goal of achieving a 'moderately well-off' society. Without following a predetermined blueprint for development (the so-called 'groping for stones to cross the river' approach), China decided to chart its own course at its own pace and in light of its national circumstances through 'encapsulation of experiences'. Likewise China prefers pursuing multichannelled and multilayered solutions to economic and social problems over resorting to one single, ideal solution.[46] China's adoption of a pragmatic approach reflects a certain sagaciousness learned through hundreds of years of prosperity, poverty, war, peace and natural disasters. In other words, China's approach to development is not deductive and static, but inductive, dynamic and flexible.

Although China does not have a preconceived plan for development, it adheres to four guiding principles – self-determination, economic growth, social stability and sustainability. For historical reasons China does not want to be under the reins of any hegemony, nor does it want to be dependent on any foreign power.[47] Towards the aims of eliminating poverty and achieving a 'moderately well-off' society, China has worked arduously to foster economic growth. Since the late 1970s economic growth has been a top priority on China's national agenda. Even so economic growth is to be achieved under the foremost condition of social stability. China has undergone the Cultural Revolution, so social stability is of utmost importance.[48] As its market economy further develops, China has also begun to strive for sustainable and balanced development.

With respect to strategies, state planning has occupied a central role in China's path to development, as evidenced by the Five-Year Plans and the state's tight control over fiscal and monetary policies. Even so the role of the state and the role of law are not mutually exclusive. Moreover the state's strong role in economic development is not as negative as some critics think because policies and reforms can be carried out quickly, whereas politics in democratic countries cherishing limited state intervention can often take years to effect changes.

Actually China is not as state-driven as some people think because there have been an abundance of grassroots initiatives. As mentioned earlier, the government implemented the household contract responsibility system after the success story of a small group of farmers. To many, China is deemed a land of opportunities. That is, if one has business acumen, one can become rich quickly in China because many innovative commercial activities have not yet been regulated and people can pursue whatever dreams they have as long as those dreams are not outlawed. This is one of the reasons why corrupt and unethical practices have often occurred in China. As such, China needs more regulation rather than deregulation, so that a system is in place to prevent or curb illegal or unscrupulous rent-seeking behaviour.

Furthermore China does not have faith in the so-called shock therapy.[49] Since one erroneous policy will affect millions of people nationwide and result in social instability, China seldom implements economic and social policies and initiatives without first testing them in selected cities or areas. As mentioned previously, China chose four coastal cities in the South to become Special Economic Zones, which served as the precursors to the opening-up of other cities to foreign investment. Moreover China selected two cities as test sites before launching basic health care reforms nationwide.[50] Accordingly experimentation, self-assessment and incrementalism are three key components of China's development strategies.

CONCLUSIONS

Based on their fundamental values and worldviews, developed countries have tried to prescribe a blueprint of development for developing countries, which contains a list of policy prescriptions to be followed without giving much consideration to the national circumstances of individual countries. However, an idealized, value-laden list of policy directives formulated by the developed world may not necessarily work in developing countries. Since immense variations exist among developing countries, the requisite changes for development vary from country to country, and the success of one reform is often built on earlier reforms. Thus each country must set its own programme and pace of development.

Taking heed of its national circumstances, China has chosen to chart its own course of development by selectively and incrementally experimenting with reform initiatives, rather than adhering to every tenet of the Washington-based approaches. Although China has not followed exactly the prescriptive formula for promoting development, such as financial liberalization and deregulation, some of the policy directives, such as the marketization of economy, liberalization of trade, reception of foreign direct investment, recognition of property rights, development of a mobile labour market, and introduction of a social security system, can be discerned on China's path to development. Thus China's experience demonstrates that although it is not necessary to follow the exact blueprint of development espoused by Western liberal democracies, individual policy directives have validity on their own, depending on the state of affairs of the country concerned.

As there is no effective development model that can be applied indiscriminately across the globe, the path to development must be indigenously constructed in light of each country's national circumstances. This understanding may explain why the Seoul Development Consensus for Shared Growth acknowledges that developing countries themselves should take the lead in designing packages of reforms and policies best suited to their needs.[51]

Furthermore the rule of law has been championed as the antidote to the malaise of developing countries. Assuming there is a positive, two-way causal connection between law and development, the definition of the rule of law is often loaded with cultural, political and social values or suppositions. To buttress the argument that China is not a rule-of-law country, the developed world has propounded such reasons as one-party rule, official corruption, lack of judicial independence and suppression of dissenting opinions. However, it can also be argued that their assessment has been influenced by the fact that China's legal system does not converge with their own.

Over the years China has adopted an incremental approach to overhaul its legal system. The enactment and amendment of the Chinese Constitution, statutes and regulations have provided the necessary regulatory framework for economic activities, and have bestowed property rights on natural and legal persons. Apart from legislation, China has taken other steps to promote the rule of law, including judicial reforms, re-opening of law schools and restoration of the legal profession. One may argue that law must be enforced, and since enforcement has been weak, China is not a rule-of-law country. Weak enforcement, however, does not mean that law has not been enforced at all, or that law has not had any impact on China's economic and social developments. Law has played a significant role in China's economic development even though its present legal system has plenty of room for improvement.

Notwithstanding the principle that development policies and programmes should be formulated in light of a country's national circumstances, all developing countries need to tackle one common issue. That is, since the elites in developing countries often amass or appropriate the fruits of development, the crucial question is how to achieve equitable distribution of wealth and improve the quality of life of the majority, if not all, people in the country. This challenging task goes beyond the development plan and should be taken into consideration whenever developing countries try to devise strategies and concrete measures to promote development.

NOTES

1. The Millennium Development Goals pledged by 189 nations in 2000 include: eradicating extreme poverty and hunger, achieving universal primary education, promoting gender equality and empowering women, reducing the child mortality rate, improving maternal health, combating such diseases as AIDS and malaria, ensuring environmental sustainability and developing a global partnership for development.
2. Krever explains the World Bank's role in promoting the rule of law in developing countries; Ohnesorge discusses how international financial institutions have reinterpreted their articles of association to allow them to demand changes to the borrowers' legal systems and to adopt sets of rules that would enshrine the Washington Consensus; Thomas describes how the World Bank introduced structural adjustment programmes as a condition for loans and grants and highlights the fact that the European Bank for Reconstruction and Development stressed the fundamental principles of multiparty democracy, the rule of law, respect for human rights and market economics.
3. For example, Minxin Pei's testimony on the rule of law in China at a hearing before the Senate Foreign Relations Committee on 7 June 2005 listed the lack of judicial independence, fragmented judicial authority and judicial corruption as the weaknesses of the current Chinese legal system.

4. However, the 'English problem', namely, the UK being a cradle of capitalism and having a legal system that did not fit the formal-rational ideal type, posed a challenge to this theory (Ohnesorge, 2007a, p. 227).
5. In his article, Thomas explains the collective action problem in public choice theory.
6. The ten tenets are: fiscal policy discipline, reordering of public expenditure priorities, tax reform, liberalizing interest rates, a competitive exchange rate, trade liberalization, liberalization of inward foreign direct investment, privatization, deregulation and property rights (Williamson, 2004).
7. During the Cultural Revolution (1966–76), Mao and his allies launched a mass campaign to purge counterrevolutionaries, revisionists and 'people on the capitalist road' with the assistance of the Red Guards, who consisted mainly of students and teenagers. Numerous people were persecuted, factories were closed down, education was neglected, and politics was in command.
8. The four Special Economic Zones – Zhuhai, Shenzhen, Shantou, and Xiamen – are southern cities close to Hong Kong, Macau and Taiwan. The 14 other coastal cities open to foreign investment spread across the eastern part of China, such as Dalian, Tianjin, Shanghai, Qingdao and Ningbo.
9. In particular, overseas Chinese, especially those from Hong Kong, were invited to return to the motherland to engage in the construction of railways, highways, utilities and ports.
10. Under a collective system, the agricultural hierarchy consisted of communes, brigades, production teams and individual households. Households were to complete production orders from their production teams and were given grains and other coupons in return.
11. State-owned enterprises were under the supervision of their respective departments-in-charge. Their performance was assessed based on whether or not they had fulfilled the production assignments. Because the government routinely meted out subsidies to loss-making enterprises, many state-owned enterprises suffered from inefficiency and low productivity.
12. In the late 1970s a small group of peasants in the Anhui Province signed a secret pact to divide the farmland of their village to do contracting-out, which led to increased agricultural productivity and the consequential rise of income and improved quality of life.
13. Under the household contract responsibility system, farming households are allowed to contract with their production teams, keep whatever is left after they have fulfilled their production quotas, and engage in sideline production or plant cash crops.
14. Under the director responsibility system, a state-owned enterprise is to be managed through the implementation of the *chengbao* (contracting-out) or *zulin* (leasing) responsibility system. In the contracting-out mode, the enterprise director contracts with the department-in-charge to achieve within the contract term specific goals, such as the amount of profits to be remitted and the completion of technical improvement tasks. In the leasing mode, the enterprise director signs a lease with the department-in-charge and promises to reach the annual business target and remit rents to the lessor.
15. A private enterprise is a for-profit economic organization having private ownership and employing eight or more workers.
16. For decades Chinese workers in state-owned enterprises had enjoyed lifetime employment security and received various kinds of enterprise-based welfare benefits, such as housing and health care, which was commonly referred to as the 'iron rice bowl'.
17. The Agricultural Bank of China, the Bank of China, the Construction Bank of China and the Industrial and Commercial Bank of China were the four commercial banks.
18. The State Development Bank of China, the Agricultural Bank of China and the Export and Import Bank of China were the three policy banks.
19. Prior to 2006 foreign banks established their presence in China by setting up branches.
20. 'A' shares were available only to Chinese investors and were traded only in Chinese currency. 'B' shares were registered shares denominated in Chinese currency and offered to foreign investors and investors from Hong Kong, Macau and Taiwan for purchase

and sale using foreign exchange (US$ or HK$). 'H' shares are registered shares listed on Hong Kong's Hang Seng Stock Exchange.

21. The Qualified Foreign Institutional Investor (QFII) scheme allows foreign institutional investors to invest in the A-shares market if they meet certain requirements and are granted approval from the Chinese government.
22. Several Opinions regarding the Further Improvement of the Work on Utilizing Foreign Investment, promulgated by the State Council on 6 April 2010.
23. For example, China joined such multilateral conventions as the Paris Convention for the Protection of Industrial Property (1985), Madrid Agreement on the Registration of International Trademarks (1989), Berne Convention on the Protection of Literary and Artistic Works (1992) and the WTO Agreements (2001).
24. See the Provisional Regulations of the People's Republic of China on the Administration of Resident Representative Offices of Foreign Enterprises, promulgated by the State Council on 30 October 1980, and the Detailed Implementation Rules on the Approval and Administration of Resident Representative Offices of Foreign Enterprises in China, promulgated by the Ministry of Foreign Trade and Economic Cooperation on 13 February 1995.
25. There are two types of joint ventures – equity joint venture and cooperative joint venture. See the Law of the People's Republic of China on Sino-Foreign Equity Joint Ventures, adopted at the 2nd Session of the 5th National People's Congress on 1 July 1979 and amended at the 3rd Session of the 7th National People's Congress on 4 April 1990 and at the 4th Session of the 9th National People's Congress on 15 March 2001, respectively; the Law of the People's Republic of China on Sino-Foreign Cooperative Joint Ventures, adopted at the 1st Session of the 7th National People's Congress on 13 April 1988 and amended at the 18th Session of the Standing Committee of the 9th National People's Congress on 31 October 2000; the Regulations for the Implementation of the Law of the People's Republic of China on Sino-Foreign Equity Joint Ventures, promulgated by the State Council on 20 September 1983 and amended by the State Council on 15 January 1986, 21 December 1987 and 22 July 2001, respectively; and the Detailed Rules for the Implementation of the Law of the People's Republic of China on Sino-Foreign Cooperative Joint Ventures, promulgated by the Ministry of Foreign Trade and Economic Cooperation on 4 September 1995.
26. Foreign subsidiaries can be a limited liability or a foreign company limited by shares. See the Law of the People's Republic of China on Wholly Foreign-Owned Enterprises, adopted at the 4th Session of the 6th National People's Congress on 12 April 1986 and amended at the 18th Session of the Standing Committee of the 9th National People's Congress on 31 October 2000; the Detailed Rules for the Implementation of the Law of the People's Republic of China on Wholly Foreign-Owned Enterprises, promulgated and amended by the Ministry of Foreign Trade and Economic Cooperation on 12 December 1990 and 12 April 2001, respectively; and the Provisional Rules on Several Issues Concerning the Establishment of Foreign Companies Limited by Shares, promulgated by the Ministry of Foreign Trade and Economic Cooperation on 10 January 1995.
27. The restrictions on setting up foreign-invested holding companies were gradually relaxed through the issuance of supplementary rules and a set of interpretations from the mid-1990s to 2003, when the Provisions on the Establishment of Companies of an Investment Nature by Foreign Investors were promulgated to consolidate the regulatory framework. See the Provisions on the Establishment of Companies of an Investment Nature by Foreign Investors, promulgated by the Ministry of Commerce on 10 June 2003 and amended on 13 February 2004 and 17 November 2004, respectively.
28. See the Law of the People's Republic of China on Industrial Enterprises Owned by the Whole People, adopted by the 1st Session of the 7th National People's Congress on 13 April 1988, and the Provisional Regulations of the People's Republic of China on Private Enterprises, promulgated by the State Council on 25 June 1988. Moreover the Law of the People's Republic of China on Bankruptcy of Enterprises (for Trial

Implementation), adopted by the 18th Session of the Standing Committee of the 6th National People's Congress on 2 December 1986, applied only to state-owned enterprises. Twenty years later, after it had become familiar with issues relating to creditor rights, China enacted the Law of the People's Republic of China on Bankruptcy of Enterprises, which was adopted by the 23rd Session of the Standing Committee of the 10th National People's Congress on 27 August 2006. This statute provides a uniform bankruptcy system for all types of legal-person enterprises in China, such as state-owned enterprises, private enterprises and foreign-invested enterprises, except for the sole proprietorship and partnership.

29. For example, the Provisional Regulations of the People's Republic of China on Value-Added Tax, promulgated by the State Council on 13 December 1993, and the Provisional Regulations of the People's Republic of China on Business Tax, promulgated by the State Council on 13 December 1993.
30. The Enterprise Income Tax Law of the People's Republic of China, adopted by the 5th Session of the 10th National People's Congress on 16 March 2007. However, the Enterprise Income Tax Law does not apply to the sole proprietorship and partnership.
31. For example, the Labour Law of the People's Republic of China, adopted at the 8th Session of the Standing Committee of the 8th National People's Congress on 5 July 1994; the Regulations on Working Hours for Staff and Workers, promulgated by the State Council on 25 March 1995; the Trade Union Law of the People's Republic of China, adopted at the 5th Session of the 7th National People's Congress on 3 April 1992 and amended at the 24th Session of the Standing Committee of the 9th National People's Congress on 27 October 2001; the Decision Regarding the Establishment of a Uniform System of Basic Old-Age Pensions for Enterprise Staff and Workers, promulgated by the State Council on 16 July 1997; the Decision Concerning the Establishment of a Basic Medical Insurance System for Urban Staff and Workers, promulgated by the State Council on 14 December 1998; the Labour Contract Law of the People's Republic of China, adopted at the 28th Session of the Standing Committee of the 10th National People's Congress on 29 June 2007; and the Law on Mediation and Arbitration of Labour Disputes of the People's Republic of China, adopted at the 31st Session of the Standing Committee of the 10th National People's Congress on 29 December 2007.
32. The Contract Law of the People's Republic of China, adopted at the 2nd Session of the 9th National People's Congress on 15 March 1999.
33. See the Company Law of the People's Republic of China, adopted by the 5th Session of the Standing Committee of the 8th National People Congress on 29 December 1993; the Partnership Law of the People's Republic of China, adopted by the 24th Session of the Standing Committee of the 8th National People Congress on 2 February 1997; and the Sole Proprietorship Law of the People's Republic of China, adopted by the 11th Session of the Standing Committee of the 9th National People's Congress on 30 August 1999.
34. The Company Law was amended by the 18th Session of the Standing Committee of the 10th National People's Congress on 27 October 2005. Because the Company Law had been criticized for deficiency on corporate governance, the revised framework included: more protection of shareholders by allowing shareholder derivative suits, shareholders' dissolution of the company by petitioning to the court, protection of minority shareholders in limited liability companies, cumulative voting by shareholders in a company limited by shares, introduction of independent directors, maintaining independence of auditors and piercing the corporate veil. The Partnership Law of the People's Republic China was amended by the 23rd Session of the Standing Committee of the 10th National People's Congress on 27 August 2006. The 2006 revisions created three types of partnership, namely, general partnership, special-general partnership and limited partnership, and directed partners to pay income taxes respectively for partnership gains allocated to them, thereby avoiding the problem of double taxation.
35. See the Interim Measures of the Shenzhen Municipality on the Issue and Trading of Shares, promulgated by the Shenzhen City People's Government on 15 May 1991; the Law of the People's Republic of China on the People's Bank of China, adopted at the

3rd Session of the 8th National People's Congress on 18 March 1995 and amended at the 6th Session of the Standing Committee of the 10th National People's Congress on 27 December 2003; the Law of the People's Republic of China on Commercial Banks, adopted at the 13th Session of the Standing Committee of the 8th National People's Congress on 10 May 1995 and amended at the 6th Session of the Standing Committee of the 10th National People's Congress on 27 December 2003; the Regulations of the People's Republic of China on Foreign Banks, promulgated by the State Council on 11 November 2006; and the Securities Law of the People's Republic of China, adopted by the National People's Congress on 27 October 2005. On 5 November 2002, the China Securities Regulatory Commission and the People's Bank of China jointly promulgated the Provisional Measures on the Administration of Domestic Securities Investment by Qualified Foreign Institutional Investors. On 24 August 2006, the People's Bank of China, the China Securities Regulatory Commission and the State Administration of Foreign Exchange jointly issued the Measures on the Administration of Domestic Securities Investment by Qualified Foreign Institutional Investors.

36. The Antimonopoly Law of the People's Republic of China, adopted at the 29th Session of the Standing Committee of the 10th National People's Congress on 30 August 2007. The Antimonopoly Law applies to monopolies in economic activities inside China and monopolies outside China that have the impact of eliminating or restricting market competition in China.
37. See the Patent Law of the People's Republic of China, adopted at the 4th Session of the Standing Committee of the 6th National People's Congress on 12 March 1984 and amended at the 27th Session of the Standing Committee of the 7th National People's Congress on 4 September 1992 and at the 17th Session of the Standing Committee of the 9th National People's Congress on 25 August 2000, respectively the Trademark Law of the People's Republic of China, adopted at the 24th Session of the Standing Committee of the 5th National People's Congress on 23 August 1982 and amended at the 30th Session of the Standing Committee of the 7th National People's Congress on 22 February 1993 and at the 24th Session of the Standing Committee of the 9th National People's Congress on 27 October 2001, respectively and the Copyright Law of the People's Republic of China, adopted at the 15th Session of the Standing Committee of the 7th National People's Congress on 7 September 1990 and amended at the 24th Session of the Standing Committee of the 9th National People's Congress on 27 October 2001 and at 13th Session of the Standing Committee of the 11th National People's Congress on 26 February 2010, respectively.
38. The Property Law of the People's Republic of China, adopted by the 5th Session of the 10th National People's Congress on 16 March 2007.
39. The Mainland and Hong Kong Closer Economic Partnership Arrangement was signed on 29 June 2003. The Mainland and Macau Closer Economic Partnership Arrangement was signed on 17 October 2003. The China-Taiwan Cross-Strait Economic Cooperation Framework was signed on 29 June 2010.
40. The Constitution of the People's Republic of China, adopted at the 5th Session of the 5th National People's Congress on 4 December 1982 and amended at the 1st Session of the 7th National People's Congress on 12 April 1988, the 1st Session of the 8th National People's Congress on 29 March 1993, the 2nd Session of the 9th National People's Congress on 15 March 1999, and the 2nd Session of the 10th National People's Congress on 14 March 2004, respectively.
41. A new paragraph was added to article 11, which read: 'The state permits the private sector of the economy to exist and develop within the limits prescribed by law. The private sector of the economy is a complement to the socialist public economy. The state protects the lawful rights and interests of the private sector of the economy, and exercises guidance, supervision and control over the private sector of the economy.'
42. Article 15 was amended to: 'The state practises socialist market economy', and article 8 was changed from 'agricultural people's communes, agricultural production cooperatives' to 'agricultural household contract responsibility system'.

43. The paragraph 'The People's Republic of China implements ruling the country in accordance with law and establishes the socialist rule of law' was added to article 5, and article 11 was amended to recognize the 'non-public sector of the economy as an important component of the socialist market economy'.
44. Article 13 was amended to include the sentence, 'The lawful private property of the citizens shall not be violated', and the paragraph 'the State respects and protects human rights' was added to article 33.
45. For example, the parties to a Sino-foreign equity joint venture are governed by Chinese law, regardless of whether their dispute is litigated or arbitrated.
46. For example, to promote the employment of persons with disabilities, China has adopted a 'multi-channel, multi-level, and multi-format' government intervention scheme. See Regulations on the Employment of Persons with Disabilities, promulgated by the State Council on 14 February 2007.
47. In the nineteenth century, China signed unequal treaties with imperialistic and colonial powers. As one of the four ancient civilizations, China does not want to be imposed with Western values and systems.
48. The phrase 'social stability' can be frequently found in China's policy statements, laws and regulations.
49. Simply stated, 'shock therapy' refers to rapid privatization and liberalization of the market.
50. The two pilot cities were Zhenjiang and Jiujiang.
51. In November 2010 the G20 nations held a Summit in Seoul and formally endorsed a development agenda – the Seoul Development Consensus for Shared Growth, which is a set of principles formulated to assist them in working collaboratively with developing countries to boost economic growth and achieve the Millennium Development Goals. The Consensus has six core principles: a focus on economic growth, global development partnership (engaging developing countries as equal partners, respecting their national ownership and recognizing that the most important determinant of successful development is a country's own development policy), global or regional systemic issues, private sector participation, complementarity, and outcome orientation.

REFERENCES

Birdsall, N. and Fukuyama, F. (2011). The post-Washington Consensus: Development after the crisis. *Foreign Affairs*, *90*(2), 45–53.

Broer, W. (2010). China goes global: Examining China's outbound investment. *China Insights*, *January*, 1–8.

China overtakes Japan as world's second biggest economy (2010, August 16). *Bloomberg News*. Retrieved from http://www.bloomberg.com/news/2010-08-16/china-economy-passes-japan-s-in-second-quarter-capping-three-decade-rise.html

Davis, K.E. and Trebilcock, M.J. (2001). Legal reforms and development. *Third World Quarterly*, *22*(1), 21–36.

Krever, T. (2011). The legal turn in late development theory: The rule of law and the World Bank's development model. *Harvard International Law Journal*, *52*(1), 287–319.

Landes, D. (2000). Culture makes almost all the difference. In L.E. Harrison and S.P. Huntington (Eds), *Culture matters: How values shape human progress* (pp. 2–13). New York, NY: Basic Books.

Lo, V.I. and Tian, X. (2002). Property rights, productivity gains, and economic growth: The Chinese experience. *Post-Communist Economies*, *14*(2), 245–58.

Lo, V.I. and Tian, X. (2009). *Law for foreign business and investment in China*. London/New York: Routledge.
National Development and Reform Commission of the People's Republic of China (NDRC) (2007). *Program of action for sustainable development in China in the early 21st century*. Retrieved from http://en.ndrc.gov.cn/newsrelease/t20070205_115702.htm
North, D. (1997). The new institutional economics and third world development. In J. Harris and J. Hunter (Eds), *New institutional economics and third world development* (pp. 17–26). London: Routledge.
Ohnesorge, J.K.M. (2007a). Developing development theory: Law and development orthodoxies and the Northeast Asian experience. *University of Pennsylvania Journal of International Economic Law*, *28*, 219–308.
Ohnesorge, J.K.M. (2007b). On rule of law rhetoric, economic development, and Northeast Asia. *Wisconsin International Law Journal*, *25*(2), 301–12.
Ramo, J.C. (2004). *The Beijing consensus*. London: The Foreign Policy Centre.
The People's Republic of China (2012). *The People's Republic of China national report on sustainable development*. Retrieved from http://www.chinapop.gov.cn/xxgk/gzdt/201206/W020120606366841020010.pdf
Thomas, C. (2011). Law and neoclassical economic development in theory and practice: Toward an institutionalist critique of institutionalism. *Cornell Law Review*, *96*, 967–1024.
Trubek, D.M. and Galanter, M. (1974). Scholars in self-estrangement: Some reflections on the crisis in law and development studies in the United States. *Wisconsin Law Review*, *4*, 1062–1102.
United Nations Development Programme (UNDP) (2000). *Millennium development goals*. Retrieved from http://www.undp.org/content/undp/en/home/mdgoverview.html
Weber, M. (1978). *Economy and society*. G. Roth and C. Wittich (Eds). Berkeley and Los Angeles: University of California Press.
Williamson, J. (2004, September). *A short history of the Washington Consensus*. Paper prepared for the conference From the Washington Consensus Towards a New Global Governance, Barcelona.
WTO (2001). *Protocol on the accession of the People's Republic of China*. Retrieved from http://www.wto.org/english/thewto_e/acc_e/completeacc_e.htm

17. The role of the BRICS in international law in a multipolar world

Muthucumaraswamy Sornarajah

Two tectonic changes occurred in international relations in the last 25 years. The first was the fall of the Soviet Union resulting in the complete hegemony of the US. In this period the world moved towards an order modelled on the preferences of the US, driven by the central themes of democracy and market capitalism (Mandelbaum, 2002).[1] As a result international law came to be used instrumentally to achieve the twin ideological preferences of the hegemonic state. Interventionary norms came to be justified on the basis of promotion of democracy and ending of dictatorships, Iraq being an example. The intervention was originally justified on the grounds that Iraq was manufacturing weapons of mass destruction. The justification was changed as such weapons could not be discovered. It was later justified on the grounds that it was necessary to remove a cruel and unjust dictator. The notion of humanitarian intervention had been used earlier as a justification for NATO's intervention in Kosovo. Market capitalism and liberalization of the flows of trade, capital and investment were the themes that drove the creation of the World Trade Organization (WTO) and the fields of finance and foreign investment. A network of new laws resulted in the areas of trade and investment based on the preferences of the hegemonic power. A hegemonic order was built upon the twin notions of democracy and free market.

The second tectonic change was the apparent collapse of this order.[2] The US hegemony seemed to have overexerted itself through its interventions in Iraq and Afghanistan. The adoption of market economics and the relaxation of state regulation of the economy led to the global crash of 2008.[3] The Western economic collapse was contemporaneous with the rise of the BRICS (Brazil, Russia, India, China and South Africa). The consequence of the rise of the BRICS is the possible emergence of a multipolar world with the decline of the hegemonic power of the US and a sharing of power by the BRICS states with the West. The BRICS leaders announced this change when, in their joint statement in Brasilia, they said: 'We share the perception that the world is undergoing major and swift changes that highlight the need for corresponding transformations in global governance in all relevant areas' (BRICS, 2010, para. 2).

The BRICS states, currently without an institutional base, are nevertheless a powerful group which initially came together for economic reasons. It is well known that the genesis of the idea for the BRICS lies in its identification as such in a Goldman Sach's Report in 2003; that these states would become a much larger force by 2050 if their present rates of growth were to continue (Wilson & Purushothaman, 2003). In 2011 Goldman Sachs confirmed that the states were continuing their advance and were well on track to meet the earlier prediction (Wilson, Burgi & Carlson, 2011). The states have now met for five summits, and there have been other meetings of ministers, officials and academics between the BRICS states.[4] The idea of the existence of the grouping has become a reality. The BRICS nations have gradually emerged as a political force and have stated both political and economic objectives. They can no longer be regarded as a purely economic grouping. Their political objectives will have as much significance in shaping the world order as their economic objectives.

This chapter first sets out the order that was brought about under the US hegemony. It identifies norms that were created through the instrumental use of international law to further a neo-liberal ideology that centred around propagating the ideas of democracy and market capitalism. It then points out that military overreach and the global economic crisis has ended this hegemonic order. Contemporaneous with the decline of US power has been the rise of the economic power of the five states. Their rise portends the coming of a multipolar world and an articulation of norms that stand in contrast to those formulated under the US hegemony. The areas in which cooperation among the BRICS states are possible need to be identified. In these areas, the norms that they put forward will clash with the hegemonic norms that are in existence. This chapter identifies the areas in which a clash and consequent change would occur, bringing about a new world order. Since the political order is dependent on the law, the changes that take place in international law will constitute the basis of this new world order. Studying changes in international law is, therefore, imperative.

THE OLD ORDER CHANGETH

What is described as the old order is actually a relatively new one. It is necessary to describe this US-influenced order so that it is possible to identify the changes that the BRICS states will bring about. In essence, the old order is based on the dominant power of a sole hegemonic state whereas the emergent BRICS states seek to contest this world order, not only on the basis of the countervailing power that they may be able to muster but also on the basis of principles of justice. It is necessary to use notions of justice simply because of the fact that the power of the US will not be displaced for a long time and the collective might of the BRICS states cannot yet provide any countervailing power that is equal to that of the US. Hence appeal to justice-based norms and ideas become significant to make up the shortfall in power.[5] It is necessary to explain the order that the US sought to establish on the basis of power first.

The West has dominated the world for the last 300 years. The colonial period of history was one of dominance of the European states. During this period, there was little doubt that a eurocentric international law was created in order to advance the interests of the colonial powers. Vestiges of the system remain strong to this day. Although colonialism itself was ended through the recognition of the principle of self-determination, the principles formulated during this period in other areas of international law were not displaced. Thus the principal sources of international law, such as notions of territorial jurisdiction and the freedom of the high seas, remain to this day, though changed appropriately in the modern context. The rise of US power began with the end of the Second World War. The role of the US both in the Second World War and in the making of global policy was profound, but its opportunity to shape a new order was restrained by the competing power of the Soviet Union and the Cold War. The US became the sole hegemonic power with the dissolution of the Soviet Union in 1990. It was then able to assert itself in shaping the world order it desired. It is the new order that the US as the sole hegemonic power sought to impose after the Cold War ended and during the last decade of the twentieth century that becomes significant, for within a short period, the US was able to significantly shift the basis of the order that had existed previously.

Until the end of the Cold War, the world had worked on the Westphalian order. The League of Nations and the United Nations did not alter that fact because non-intervention and equality of states continued to be the cardinal rules.[6] The notions under the Westphalian order – that all states are equal and that no state should interfere in the affairs of other states – were particularly appropriate during the Cold War. They enabled the preservation of the spheres of influence of the two parties to the Cold War and protected the sovereignty of the newly liberated states of the Third World. But with the end of the Cold War resulting from the almost sudden collapse of the Soviet Union in 1989, there was an emergence of a new order imposed by the US.

The US emerged as the sole superpower with the ability to impose a new world order on the basis of its preferred norms. Studies of hegemony indicate that every hegemon attempts to bring about a world order it desires, and the law plays an important role in ensuring the articulation of that order and its subsequent maintenance. For example, the instrumentality of the law in formulating principles of justification for the order, the rules of exclusion from the order, the access of the hegemon to resources and markets and the use of force to maintain the order, are visible bases in the history of British colonialism. The civilizing mission or the 'white man's burden' was a justification which enabled conquest and, later, the establishment of mandate systems (Anghie, 2005). The denial of personality to the states of Africa and Asia, on the basis of standard of civilization, enabled the exclusion of large areas of the world from participation in the system and hence their exploitation (Gong, 1984). Principles such as the freedom of the high seas[7] and extraterritoriality[8] enabled access to markets. Force was deemed legitimate in a number of situations, including opening access to markets.[9]

The idea of hegemonic powers using international law to assert rules of a world order that promote their own interests is entrenched in history. The footprints of the Roman and Spanish colonial assertions of power still remain. The US was acting as any hegemon would in seeking to assert its power by indicating its own rules of preference and asserting them through new legal mechanisms it sought to establish during its short-lived period of hegemony (Byers & Nolte, 2003). The US hegemonic order was driven by the political ideology of democracy and the economic ideology of market capitalism. The first was justified as an organizing principle on the grounds that international peace would be assured if states were democratic, as it was assumed no democratic state would go to war against another democratic state. The second was market capitalism, which had proven success in the US and had become the organizing principle of trade, investment and finance for the world.

The US exertion of hegemony in international relations can be seen through the articulation of principles of international law that justified its dominant efforts in coercing states to its will. During the Kosovo crisis, the United Nations was bypassed and NATO forces justified their bombings of Serbia on the grounds of humanitarian intervention. The doctrine of humanitarian intervention is a self-judging notion that a state can use force to prevent atrocities occurring in a third state, on the grounds that such intervention is necessary to save the lives of those at risk from the state. In most historical instances, the doctrine has been used by the intervening state to advance its own political and military interests. Despite its altruistic allure, humanitarian intervention has always been used to procure the interests of the intervening power and seldom, if ever, the safety of the people affected. The intervention in Kosovo was no different. Along with this doctrine, which many weaker states have opposed for the obvious reason that it is capable of justifying improper interventions by stronger states, the US also advanced the rule that the use of force to protect or advance democracy was justifiable. After 9/11, the Bush government announced the notion of preventive force, which diluted the prohibition on the use of force contained in the United Nations Charter (Shue & Rodin, 2010). The US arrogated a right to the first use of force in anticipation of any potential threat, whether from a state or an organization like Al-Qaeda. As such organizations cannot but function within a state,[10] the attack must always be on a state which harbours the terrorist organization.

This new armoury of justifications for the use of force was seen in the intervention in Haiti, where a democratically elected leader was restored with the help of US forces, also the justification given for intervening in Iraq. When the initial reason for the intervention – that Saddam Hussein was manufacturing weapons of mass destruction – failed, the US advanced the reasons for the intervention as the need to spread democracy in Iraq and to overthrow a cruel dictator. Entry into Afghanistan was justified on the preventive use of force as well as on the notion of state responsibility for harbouring terrorists. The practice of such justifications continues with the intervention in Libya, although the intervention can be justified on the basis of a UN resolution. Events in Syria indicate the extent to which the issue is divisive in international relations.

Power has both economic and political aspects: 'The hidden hand of the market will never work without the hidden fist' (Friedman, 1999). One does not exist without the other. The state must keep the conditions necessary for the free market to function. The transference of the free market to the global scene requires the hegemonic power to keep sufficient order to enable the free market forces to work. The US has set out to ensure that the rules of the world in international trade and investment operate in its favour and are based on the free market ideology it practises at home. This is also visible in the manner in which the US exerted its power to bring about global laws on trade and investment.

In the economic sphere, the two institutions dominated by the US and its European allies (the IMF and the World Bank) were at the forefront in ensuring that the Washington Consensus,[11] a set of neo-liberal norms based on market capitalism, became pervasive. It was imposed through attaching conditions to loans and instituting programmes in the developing world that were conducive to the acceptance of the tenets of neo-liberalism. The Washington Consensus involved the purveyance of sets of norms that advanced market capitalism as the organizing idea of domestic and international economic governance. It included liberalization of flows of investment and trade, the recognition of property and contract rights including rights of intellectual property and secure standards of dispute settlement through international tribunals. The programme was sold on the basis that economic success and development was possible only as a result of the adoption of these prescriptions that would bring about market capitalism, with the US being the exemplar of such success.

New institutions were created. The WTO came about largely as a result of the acceptance of the world in this period of the panacea provided by the ideology of neo-liberalism and a passive acceptance of the superior knowledge of economic fundamentals of the US. The norms that resulted, particularly norms that were included in disciplines like the Trade-Related Intellectual Property Rights Agreement (TRIPs) and the General Agreement on Services, were those desired by US businesses.[12] These instruments enable intellectual property to be protected in accordance with US standards, and permit companies in the services sector entry into member countries without hindrance. The WTO has the most effective enforcement situation so far devised in international law. It provides for compulsory litigation of disputes and ensures a mechanism for enforcement of the decisions made by the Appellate Body. A situation of legal hegemony in international trade has been created as a result. Resentment set in and is reflected in the Doha Round, where developing states make a concerted effort to change despite the major hallmarks of the system having been defined.

In the sphere of foreign investment protection, there is a repetition of the same pattern of effective norms of foreign investment flows and protection of such investment. During the 1990s, referred to by Stiglitz as the 'roaring nineties' (2010), a period ruled by individualism and greed generated by neo-liberalism, rules favouring the protection of the assets of multinational corporations were created by an explosive number of investment treaties (around 3000). The provisions of these treaties were given expansionary interpretation to advance the principles of protection. This system created a regulatory chill on the right of states to take measures in the interests of the public, and for a period of time ensured the dominance of investment protection as the central theme of the regime. Again the global financial institutions mandated the maintenance of this order through refusal of loans unless there was compliance.

National self-interest of the US became an all-embracing theme. It became respectable for US academics in international law to argue that international law did not constrain the US, and that the US did not have to follow rules of international law if the law did not coincide with its national interests (Goldsmith & Posner, 2005). An extreme realism dominated such views and provided a cloak for the impermissible exercise of power. The war on terror was conducted in violation of the norms of humanitarian law in respect of the selection of targets, the manner in which suspects were kept and in the torture of suspects. The US kept out of the functioning of the International Criminal Court. But most tellingly, having contributed heavily to the pollution of the world during its industrialization, the US refused to participate in the efforts to reduce the harm caused by climate change, rejecting the Kyoto Protocol. The system was replete with power unconstrained by any notion of justice. The ethical foundations which balanced US policy in the past were dispensed with altogether in favour of an extreme form of realism.

This order was to change. It was an unjust order catering to the interests of the very few, to the disadvantage of the many, both domestically and internationally. Domestically, the rift between the rich and the poor widened. The trickle-down theory simply did not work. Characterized long ago as the 'horse and sparrow theory', the trickle-down theory on which the neo-liberal system worked brought about strains in the social fabric, and much discontent that flowed onto the streets. It was the same at the international level. The meetings of the financial institutions met with popular demonstrations in Seattle, Montreal, Geneva and Dubai, all prosperous cities of the world. Dismay was caused to the poor worldwide as a result of the adoption of the neo-liberal tenets well before the global economic crash of 2008.

In this context, the global financial institutions weakened. The illusion that they possessed some magic economic wisdom could not be maintained. The single panacea for the world that neo-liberalism contained proved erroneous, even for the developed states, and could no longer be accepted as legitimate. The US-led international economic order had been dealt a blow from which it would find it difficult to recover. The standards of governance it enforced through international institutions sounded hollow. Competing techniques of development modes were provided by India, China and Brazil. They differed from each other and, more importantly, from the neo-liberal model. The farcical nature of the situation should not be overlooked. While professing democracy, the West had insisted they should control the global financial institutions on the basis of their financial contributions. A large majority of people in the world found no representation in these institutions. The legitimacy of the system was doubtful. Their technical competence was also doubted. Their ability to ensure recovery seemed slender. The hollowness of their vaunted economic expertise lay exposed. The neo-liberal order had to yield to a new order.

So, too, on the political front, the US has been enfeebled as a result of its imperial overstretch. Its illegal misadventure in Iraq has backfired badly. Its 'war on terror' may have been necessary, but the moral cost in fighting it was great. For a nation that had contributed much to the ethical foundations of the human rights movement, the US treatment of terrorist suspects and the callousness with which they were held in custody caused the US reputation to take a plunge. The war in Afghanistan has proved endless. The drone attacks and the heavy civilian casualties have been unacceptable in human rights terms. The US finds it difficult to extricate itself from the quagmire it has created.

US power will continue. Its economic power is still unmatched. Its military prowess surpasses the collective might of other possible groups, including the BRICS. But its invincibility has been shaken. Its ability to create and maintain a world order has been exposed to doubt. It comes at a time when Europe is also in disarray. The European allies are not able to support the US hegemony. The European economic crisis threatens the fabric of the European community. The carefully built system of regionalism faces economic threats from several weak nations within the region. The PIGS, to use the unappealing acronym (Portugal, Ireland, Greece and Spain) are faced with severe economic crises that have affected the value of the euro currency. So the short-lived old order lies in tatters. Its legitimacy is contested. Its prescriptions are no longer taken seriously. In terms of law, the study of this change is fascinating. The world order, both in its political and economic aspects, was based ultimately on the ability of a single hegemon – the US – to enforce it. Resistance has set in and is displacing many of the norms fashioned during the period of US hegemony. Resistance must lead to change. History has always demonstrated this fact. Resistance to colonialism resulted in the recognition of the norm of self-determination and the independence of the colonies from imperialism. The US hegemonic order is similarly resisted. The old order must yield its place to a new order.

'THE OLD ORDER CHANGETH, YIELDING PLACE TO NEW'

The decline of the US hegemonic order coincides with the rise of the BRICS. There are other contenders for inclusion in the grouping (South Africa being the most recent addition), with Malaysia and Indonesia possible states for inclusion. The characteristics of their cohesion are that they are newly emergent economies and have shared experiences. With the exception of Russia, they were non-aligned states and had experienced colonialism or subjugation of their interests by dominant powers. They perceive existing financial institutions like the World Bank and the IMF to be biased towards the West and consider forming alternative international institutions. They oppose some of the developed country policies of the WTO. They have different views on issues like global poverty, nuclear proliferation and climate change. They are large countries with immense amounts of natural resources. Despite exponential growth, they still harbour a large number of poor nationals because of low per capita incomes. They look to develop large local markets and infrastructure before external markets. Four of the BRICS states are in the non-aligned movement and are leading members who give impetus to Third World initiatives such as the New International Economic Order (NIEO) associated with distributive justice. This sense of justice was displaced by neo-liberalism. There is now an opportunity to recover the spirit that animated these struggles through the BRICS. These characteristics give the BRICS states a certain cohesive sense of having to create a fresh order in which they are not dominated by other powers either economically or politically.

In terms of theory, Western views use globalization towards the construction of a liberal theory of governance that includes interventionary principles such as humanitarian intervention and the rule of law in a neo-liberal guise. In response, the developing states and particularly states like China take refuge in sovereignty and non-intervention, staple notions of the Westphalian order. They are also firmly set against intervention of any type and the imposition of norms from above, or law-making without consent. The notion that international law can be made by non-state agencies that is common among some Western international lawyers would be anathema to the BRICS states. In politics as well as economics, pluralism guides these states rather than the single neo-liberal vision of economics or the neo-conservative vision of politics. In this sense the inclusion of the liberal democracies of Brazil, India and South Africa could well construct a pluralist liberal order that includes Russia and China.

The pluralism is evidenced both in their internal systems as well as in their international outlook. The domestic organization of the internal economy relies to a large extent on state companies, which by definition are monopolists within their sectors. In that sense they are either socialist or mixed economies. They also operate on the international scene through these state corporations, which compete with privately organized multinational corporations, presenting unique problems for law as well as for business. The single-minded pursuit of objectives of large states, now joined together in an organization that could have institutional status, presents different sets of problems. Already the entry of the Chinese state in the natural resources sector has caused anxiety in the US and in

Australia. These anxieties ostensibly take the form of national security, but the greater fear is that the aggressive nature of these state corporations backed by colossal reserves would pose such competitive threats to the multinational corporations of the West that they would be driven out of the countries in which they traditionally operate. Former US Secretary of State Hillary Clinton's tirade about unnamed countries courting the wealth of Africa without having regard to human rights and other values reflects these concerns. It is a sanctimonious concern as the US was friendly with the worst dictators of the world, from Pinochet to Suharto, Idi Amin to Saddam Hussein, in courting markets of resource producing countries.

So the points of unity between the BRICS members have been identified. There are, of course, points of disunity. India and China have border problems. The meeting of the BRICS in New Delhi, 2012 attracted widespread demonstrations from Tibetan refugees in India. The human rights records of the states vary greatly. Yet these have been papered over. The cohesion has been stressed. India and China are the cement which holds the grouping together. The following sections look at specific issues the BRICS may achieve as a group.

International Trade

The BRICS could well be the bridgehead for the second coming of the NIEO. The NIEO was an effort to point out the structural inequities in the international economic order and required the economic order to be restructured to bring about a just solution to the problems of underdevelopment. Its heydays were in the 1970s. It diminished in vigour in the mid-1980s and slowly lapsed without trace. Features of the NIEO were the payment of just prices for commodities, recognition of permanent sovereignty over natural resources and the right to control foreign investment. It was an effort to redraw the rules in a manner that erased the effects of the continuing domination of the West despite the ending of colonialism. It did not succeed. With the onset of neo-liberalism, the NIEO vanished. The NIEO was based on appeals to justice by a group of states without political or economic power. China, India, Brazil and South Africa were strident supporters but did not have the power to carry it through. The failure of the NIEO may demonstrate that a mere appeal to justice may be insufficient, even if the appeal is made by a large group of states, unless they possess significant power.

The claims of the BRICS states, like the NIEO, are advanced on the basis of justice. The reform of the WTO is an area in which they will unite, and this time they are wielders of economic power with a capacity to ensure that they have an impact and an ability to carry out reforms by themselves, if not on a global scale, at least among themselves, and lead the developing states out of a structural situation in which they cannot progress. In trade, the G20 includes the Group of 4 (India, China, Brazil and South Africa). The Group of 4 coincides with the BRICS (excluding Russia). The agenda of the BRICS is to exert pressure to make the Doha Development Round, which represents the interests of the developing countries, a reality. To this extent the BRICS intends to bring about structural changes in the international economy in a manner reminiscent of the NIEO. As the Delhi Declaration refers to the plight of many African states, the Millennium Development Goals (MDG) and the concept of sustainable development, it can be assumed that the BRICS aspire to leadership of the Third World and reinvigorate the notion that there should be a justice-oriented drive that shapes an economic order which would lead the least developed states out of poverty. This altruistic purpose is evident in the declarations and practices that the BRICS states have so far engaged in.

The BRICS would then be in a position to drive the development agenda within international trade that was formulated at the Doha Development Round. It would seek to reduce or eliminate subsidies given to agriculture in the US and Europe, permit better access to agricultural goods in these states, and ensure that the elimination of restrictions on parallel imports of drugs by developing states is permitted and special and differential rights of developing countries are recognized. With Russia in the WTO, the five strong states will be able to play a significant role towards the achievement of these aims. In this sense it can be argued that the NIEO has made a second coming in a more vigorous form, as the states which espouse those norms have considerable economic power behind them.

The International Financial Architecture

The BRICS has expressed dissatisfaction with the architecture of the existing international financial institutions. The World Bank and the IMF reflect the wishes of the West with a European as head of the IMF and an American as head of the World Bank. The two institutions have maintained the neo-liberal ideology reflected in the Washington Consensus. They have ensured that the US dollar remains the currency of exchange, safeguarding the dominance of the financial world by the US. The Global Financial Crisis (GFC) has driven a large hole in their credibility and indicated the need for reform.

The BRICS seek to bring about reform by requiring that leadership of the existing financial institutions be appointed on the basis of merit and not on nationality. They have sought to undermine the present system by announcing that intra-BRICS trade would use the national currency of each of the BRICS states. They have also announced that they would explore the possibility of a Central Bank and establish a Development Bank that will provide for development projects in the Third World.

The inability of the West to recover from the financial crisis is the tenacity of neo-liberal norms, which still continue to dominate the way that governments are run. The powerful elites formed during the era of neo-liberal ascendancy continue to operate, preventing meaningful reform. In this context, it is relevant for the world to have a group of states working out an alternative model.

International Security and the Use of Force

Although in its origin the BRICS was an economic forum, it quickly converted itself into a political forum with a distinctly anti-Western bias. There are several reasons for this bias. Firstly, three of the states – Brazil, India and South Africa (the three members of IBSA) – had colonial experiences and recovered independence after long struggles. China has a deep sense of historical abuse at the hands of Europe. China, being the largest economy of the grouping, may well be a strong influence in shaping political attitudes. Russia has natural inclinations towards such stances. The group's foreign policies are characterized by old animosities. They have interacted closely with each other on separate occasions. India and South Africa had close associations formed when India championed the ending of Apartheid. Mahatma Gandhi had lived in South Africa and provided the model for Nelson Mandela. Russia and India had a long alliance dating from the Cold War era. China and India had participated in the Bandung Conference, and the Five Principles of Co-existence, which were referred to as the Bandung Principles, were first formulated in a treaty between India and China. What China puts forward as the basis of its foreign policy – *harmony under the heavens* – has a strong Buddhist-Confucian flavour. It is easy for the BRICS states to formulate common principles of foreign policy and pursue common norms relating to the international order. There is a remarkable coincidence in their views.

The Delhi Declaration addresses all the important political disputes that exist in current times, including the Arab Spring in the Middle East, the Israel–Palestine issue, the response to the Iranian nuclear programme, the Syrian resistance and Afghanistan. The taking of stances on these political issues indicates that the BRICS wants to emerge as a pressure group in international politics, asserting what could be considered views that most developing states would take. It thus becomes a group that gives leadership to the large majority of the international community. The fact that a group of countries with significant economic power are able to speak for the group may cause their views to be taken more seriously.

The views have been held consistently by all the BRICS states. One reason may be that they have witnessed past incidents of intervention and have memories which continued to shape their views against the acceptance of intervention, whatever it is called. Another is that they value sovereignty. Russia has maintained that international law can only be made through consent of states. The other four BRICS states, having suffered colonialism or Western subjugation, resent the notion that there could be interference with a sovereign state.

Sovereignty is the central theme of the BRICS states. As a result of their past, they resent intervention by third states in domestic politics of their states. While the West believes that, in the liberal order it has evolved, human rights is the central theme, and that a state which transgresses the human rights of its people will justify the intervention of other states to promote a change of regime in that state. Such an interventionary principle is stoutly resisted by every one of the BRICS states. This includes India, which has a strong form of democracy. The doctrine therefore is not considered as having anything to do with democracy. There is an inherent belief that humanitarian intervention as used in the past is not an altruistic doctrine but is a doctrine that has facilitated the advancement of big power's interests. The frequent interventions of the past have demonstrated this simple fact. For example, the UK government believed that humanitarian interests cloaked big power's aims and should not be regarded as lawful until the Blair government changed this long-held view. The fact that it has now emerged in the new guise of responsibility to protect has made no difference. Humanitarian intervention is rejected by the BRICS states individually, though they have not spoken of it collectively.

Well before the formation of the BRICS, the constituent states of the group had expressed reservations about humanitarian intervention. China and Russia voted against intervention in Kosovo so that the intervention had to be carried out by NATO forces. India, in common with the other states, had reservations about the intervention in Iraq and did not accept the legitimacy of the reasoning that intervention might be necessary to overthrow a cruel dictator with a series of crimes against his people. The hollowness of the justification was evident as the intervening states had had past dealings with Saddam Hussein and had contributed through supply of arms to the repression he effected. It was evident that the intervention was grounded in the national interests of the US and its allies rather than for purely altruistic objectives.

Collectively the BRICS states have opposed the intervention in Libya and the current intervention in Syria. The Libyan intervention showed the lack of success of such interventions. Though it did result in the overthrow of Gaddafi, which would probably have been achieved by the uprising against him, the intervention left the state divided between many factions and stability is still to emerge.

As regards the Syrian situation, the Delhi Declaration of the BRICS opposes intervention. The Delhi Declaration deals with Syria as follows:

> We express our deep concern at the current situation in Syria and call for an immediate end to all violence and violations of human rights in that country. Global interests would best be served by dealing with the crisis through peaceful means that encourage broad national dialogues that reflect the legitimate aspirations of all sections of Syrian society and respect Syrian independence, territorial integrity and sovereignty. Our objective is to facilitate a Syrian-led inclusive political process, and we welcome the joint efforts of the United Nations and the Arab League to this end. We encourage the Syrian government and all sections of Syrian society to demonstrate the political will to initiate such a process, which alone can create a new environment for peace. We welcome the appointment of Mr Kofi Annan as the Joint Special Envoy on the Syrian crisis and the progress made so far, and support him in continuing to play a constructive role in bringing about the political resolution of the crisis (BRICS, 2012, para. 21).

The preference is for an internal settlement facilitated by the United Nations rather than for a settlement that is imposed through intervention. The immediate response of the West would be to think of humanitarian intervention or its new guise, 'responsibility to protect'. These are seen by the BRICS as hegemonic responses which would ensure the dominance of the state concerned by the intervening powers, as happened in the case of Iraq.

The long-standing Arab-Israeli conflict attracts attention. The BRICS states take the same stance as they have had in similar situations. It is favourable to Palestine as the long-held view among the grouping is that international law supports the Palestinian position. The Delhi Declaration takes a strong view that a settlement must be reached in accordance with international law principles. It states: 'Thus we confirm our commitment to achieving comprehensive, just and lasting settlement of the Arab-Israeli conflict on the basis of the universally recognized international legal framework including the relevant UN resolutions, the Madrid principles and the Arab Peace Initiative' (BRICS, 2012, para. 20). It calls upon the Security Council to be more active in seeking reconciliation. Again the preference is for solution through the United Nations rather than through the offices of single states or groups of states. There is a clear preference for a world that is based on an inclusive international institutional order rather than a hegemonic order.

There is a commitment to lead Afghanistan to peace. Support is for the global community initiatives represented in the Bonn International Conference on Afghanistan in 2011, rather than for unilateral solutions which the NATO allies seek to enforce. Obviously the security of Afghanistan is important to Russia, China and India. The Bonn Conference was attended by 85 states and international organizations, including the United Nations. The fear of what will happen to Afghanistan after the announced withdrawal of troops in 2014 is a dominating concern.

On the situation in Iran, the BRICS take a stance of conciliation rather than conflict (BRICS, 2012).[13] It recognizes the importance of Iran as a supplier of energy resources to both China and India. It sees the attempted subjugation of Iran as an effort on the part of the West to ensure that a subservient government is instituted there and does not develop into a threat to Israel. Any intervention for this purpose would bring disaster to the region. Conflict avoidance is the better way. The BRICS recognizes the right of Iran to pursue nuclear research for peaceful purposes. Again the BRICS would have a dispute settled through the United Nations rather than through unilateral means or through a Western military organization like NATO. The fear of such intervention motivates the BRICS to take a clear stance on the issue.

On all these issues, there is a clear preference for solutions through the United Nations and through the recognition of the sovereignty of the state concerned. The United Nations assumes importance because two of the BRICS states have vetoes and two of the others (Brazil and India) are aspirants for Security Council membership. Internal sovereignty of all the states in strife – Syria, Palestine, Afghanistan and Iran – is recognized, but the suggested avenue of remedying the difficulties is through assistance given to the states rather than through intervention, so that they can bring about a settlement of their own problems. This is a sovereignty-centred approach which the BRICS states desire for themselves as well as for other states.

It is unlikely that the BRICS states will deviate from this sovereignty-centred approach. They themselves have internal problems (such as Kashmir for India, Tibet and Xinjiang for China and Chechnya for Russia), which may become targets of humanitarian intervention in the future. Without a doubt, the techniques that they have adopted to deal with these internal problems create widespread human rights concerns. The avoidance of such scrutiny and possible intervention is what these states seek. This is not to say that there should be no concern with human rights. In the case of Syria, the BRICS admits its own concern with the human rights situation but believes that it should be settled through consultations among the affected parties with assistance given by third parties to such processes.

Environmental Issues

There is a heavy emphasis on environmental issues in the statements of the BRICS. This concern began with the Yekateringburg Summit and has been maintained through the subsequent summits. The theme that has been taken up consistently is the divergence of the views between the developed and the developing states. Again we see the development of the notion that characterizes the arguments relating to the NIEO, in that what emerges relies on the extent of the environmental depletion that the West has caused as a result of its rapid industrialization, and the methods it has used in bringing about industrial societies. The argument of developing countries and the BRICS is that the major onus for ensuring that further damage will not be caused rests on the developed countries, with developing countries being given a leeway to industrialize themselves. This reflects the separate and differential treatment that developing countries have requested for the least developed amongst them. As is well known, the Kyoto Protocol, which is the first binding agreement on climate change signed by the international community, has met with obstacles and the accusation that the developed countries are not pulling their weight, given the targets for reduction have not been met. The BRICS states have announced that they will actively take measures to reduce carbon emissions. This issue will also lead to the resuming of the North–South divide that has characterized an earlier period. But all parties have agreed that if the problem is not addressed, the whole international community will stand to lose.

Foreign Investment

There is clear evidence that the amount of investment flows between the BRICS states has increased. This is an objective of the cooperation between the BRICS states. The pooling of complementarities involved, such as natural resources, specialized sector-based technology and large consumer markets, has made such cooperation possible. It is interesting that despite the increase in such trade and investment, no formal efforts have been conceived to form a trade grouping through a free trade agreement (FTA). So far such agreements have come about among groups of states, largely on the basis of geographical proximity and in the context of a regional agreement. The obvious instances are the agreements in the European Union, ASEAN and Latin America. The Trans-Pacific

Partnership Agreement (TPP) belies this trend as proximity is not a clear factor behind this projected grouping. Yet bilateral investment agreements are made between states that are distant from each other. Thus neither distance nor absence of a regional context should hinder an FTA with an investment component being brought about between the BRICS states. In any event, Russia, China and India are proximate. Further, in the modern world, proximity is not an obstacle to cooperation, given the easy methods of communication and transport. This would be a novelty, and the commitments they give each other could be the basis on which an institutional structure for economic cooperation could be created, while the same institution could be broadened to include political and security concerns of the BRICS states.

It would be interesting to speculate what the architecture of such an agreement would be. Since the BRICS states fear that the developed world will become more restrictive in its trade policies as a result of the economic crisis, they prefer to conduct open trade among themselves, permitting access of each other's goods to their vast markets. This would also enable them to exploit their complementarities, such as digital technology and services expertise in one country and plentiful natural resources in another. The vast and growing middle classes in all the BRICS states will provide huge markets for the export of manufactured goods, even if the markets of the developed world become protectionist and their buying power diminishes.

It would be beneficial if the BRICS avoided the pitfalls that have come to characterize other FTAs like the NAFTA and the TPP under negotiation. There could be pre-entry national treatment permitted for all BRICS nationals, even though this may promote too much competition between the BRICS enterprises and provoke nationalist sentiments. But the prospects for a BRICS FTA may assist in promoting cohesiveness within the group. It would also be a good idea to rely on the local courts for dispute settlement, again signifying confidence in the systems that have been set up within the BRICS countries. A tribunal staffed entirely by the BRICS nationals could be constituted to iron out difficult situations that may arise, but it should not employ any idea that there are single standards of governance.

The BRICS may be unique in that investments would be made largely by state enterprises rather than by privately held multinational corporations. Sovereign wealth funds controlling vast sums – the Chinese funds are supposed to control over $3 trillion – will bring new dimensions from the perspectives of law as well as economics. It will end the free market notions on the international scene quite conclusively as the vehicles for the investment will no longer be entirely organized on the basis of the free market model. The world will have to get used to two different ideas operating on the international economic scene.

The conclusion of such a partnership agreement, initially for purposes of trade and investment and progressively building it up to include other interests such as those in international security, the environment and international financial services, would be a good start. The projected Central Bank among the BRICS states will also lead to further cohesion.

CONCLUSION

The BRICS states are here to stay. They signify the dawn of a new multipolar order. The areas they have sought to affect are the vital areas of modern international life: international trade, the international financial system, international security, climate change and international investment. The comprehensive views that are slowly being worked out stand in open contrast to the agenda that the US and the West have for the world. There is a set of opposing organizing principles. In that sense a competing order is being built, challenging the existing principles of the world order. The result will hopefully be accommodation of various conflicts through reconciliation of the conflicting principles. A change is clearly visible and the world will have to accommodate the change.

NOTES

1. Michael Mandelbaum (2002) describes a short conquest, if at all, of the two ideas of democracy and free markets.
2. Some writers doubt the collapse of the old economic order. According to Sharma the BRICS is just hype: 'No idea has done more to muddle thinking about the global economy than that of the BRICS' (2012).
3. The crash is described in Joseph Stiglitz's book *Freefall: Free markets and the shrinking of the global economy* (2010).
4. Earlier the leaders had met at the sidelines of the G20 meetings. There have been five summits between the leaders: the first in Yekaterinburg, Russia, on 16 June 2009; the second in Brasilia, Brazil on 15 April 2010; the third in Sanya, China on 14 April 2011; the fourth in New Delhi, India on 29 March 2012; and the fifth in Durban, South Africa on 26 March 2013. The BRICS leaders have also met on the sidelines of other multilateral meetings at earlier times.
5. For such an analysis of the role of justice in shaping international law, see Sornarajah (2006).
6. This was the case despite the creation of the Security Council with the five Great Powers having vetoes. The Security Council was largely hamstrung as a result of the veto.
7. The doctrine of the freedom of the high seas was formulated by Hugo Grotius to enable Dutch naval power to assert itself in Asia.
8. Extraterritoriality was the system imposed in China, Thailand and the areas of the

Middle East for Europeans to live and trade in according to their own national laws, and to exclude the application of domestic laws of the host states.

9. The Opium War against China and the Treaty of Nanjing (1842) which ended it are examples of force being used to open markets.
10. One exception is that in a remote instance, they function on the high seas.
11. The Washington Consensus is so named because the White House, the IMF and the World Bank are located in the US capital. There is an assumed consensus among these three parties that liberalization of trade and investment must be advanced on a global scale.
12. Susan Sell (2005) argues that the extensive lobbying of US pharmaceutical and entertainment industries was the reason for the TRIPs. Equally, the GATS embodies the preferred norms of the US services industries.
13. Paragraph 22 of the Delhi Declaration states (BRICS, 2012): 'The situation concerning Iran cannot be allowed to escalate into conflict, the disastrous consequences of which will be in no one's interest. Iran has a crucial role to play for the peaceful development and prosperity of a region of high political and economic relevance, and we look to it to play its part as a responsible member of the global community. We are concerned about the situation that is emerging around Iran's nuclear issue. We recognize Iran's right to peaceful uses of nuclear energy consistent with its international obligations, and support resolution of the issues involved through political and diplomatic means and dialogue between the parties concerned, including between the IAEA and Iran and in accordance with the provisions of the relevant UN Security Council Resolutions.'

REFERENCES

Anghie, A. (2005). *Imperialism, sovereignty and the making of international law*. Cambridge: Cambridge University Press.

BRICS (2010, April 15). *2nd BRIC summit of heads of state and government: Joint statement*. Retrieved from http://www.brics.utoronto.ca/docs/100415-leaders.html

BRICS (2012, March 29). *Fourth BRICS summit Delhi declaration*. Retrieved from http://www.brics.utoronto.ca/docs/120329-delhi-declaration.html

Byers, M. and Nolte, G. (eds) (2003). *United States hegemony and the foundations of international law*. Cambridge: Cambridge University Press.

Friedman, T.L. (1999, March 28). A manifesto for the fast world. *New York Times*. Retrieved from http://www.nytimes.com/1999/03/28/magazine/a-manifesto-for-the-fast-world.html

Goldsmith, J.L. and Posner, E.A. (2005). *The limits of international law*. London: Oxford University Press.

Gong, G.W. (1984). *The standard of 'civilization' in international society*. USA: Oxford University Press.

Mandelbaum, M. (2002). *The ideas that conquered the world: Peace, democracy, and free markets in the twenty-first century*. New York: Public Affairs.

President Hu dwells on China's peaceful development at BRIC summit (2010, April 16). *English News*. Retrieved from http://news.xinhuanet.com/english2010/china/2010-04/16/c_13254233.htm

Sell, S.K. (2005). *Private power, public law: The globalization of intellectual property rights*. New York: Cambridge University Press.

Sharma, R. (2012). *Breakout nations: In pursuit of the next economic miracles*. New York: W.W. Norton & Company.

Shue, H. and Rodin, D. (Eds). (2010). *Preemption: Military action and moral justification*. USA: Oxford University Press.

Sornarajah, M. (2006). Power and justice: Third world resistance in international law. *SYBIL*, *10*, 19–57.

Stiglitz. J. (2010). *Freefall: Free markets and the shrinking of the global economy*. London: Allen Lane.

Wilson, D. and Purushothaman, R. (2003, October 1). *Dreaming with BRICs: The path to 2050* (Goldman Sachs Global Economics Paper No. 99). Retrieved from http://www.goldmansachs.com/our-thinking/archive/archive-pdfs/brics-dream.pdf

Wilson, D., Burgi, C. and Carlson, S. (2011). The BRICs remain in the fast lane. *BRICS Monthly*, *11*(6). Retrieved from http://www.goldmansachs.com/our-thinking/archive/brics-remain-in-the-fast-lane.html

18. Conclusions: The BRICS – Ascendancy, decline or plateau?

Mary Hiscock and Vai Io Lo

At the beginning of our discussion, we asked whether the BRICS is a loosely formed intergovernmental network or a powerful economic bloc that can effect paradigmatic changes in the world economy, or is it merely a pressure group that can raise awareness of the imperfections in an unbalanced and dysfunctional global political economy? There is no doubt that the BRICS is presently a platform for international cooperation and dialogue with a rich and ambitious agenda, but will it or can it go further?

The BRICS has been greeted with hyperbole, but it already has a history of being unable to deal with real issues, and of not asserting a group interest at the expense of national interest. The failure to support a developing country candidate for the leadership of the IMF, where there was a genuine contest between qualified nominees, is one instance. A further example is the lack of support by Russia and China for Brazil and India to become permanent members of the United Nations Security Council. Coordination is difficult when the BRICS members have critical differences in culture, patterns of development, economic and social systems and stages of economic maturity. To move further as a force for change, the BRICS needs more structure, tighter cooperation and a single strong voice, but it is unlikely to have an alliance based on military or strategic security concerns. Accordingly what could be its tasks as a basis for cooperation? What expectations and objectives can be turned into an agenda?

First of all, the BRICS wants a greater voice in international affairs, especially in global economic governance through the World Bank and the IMF. It has expressed concerns about the monetary policies of the developed economies and about volatile capital flows. Recovery from the global economic crisis, where it has occurred, has been very slow, and the BRICS is feeling the effects of this global slowdown. Moreover the BRICS wants to break the hegemony of the US dollar as the reserve currency, especially given its current weakness and the vast reserves held in the US dollar by China and India. Apart from the rouble, the other currencies are far from being a potential reserve, but the internationalization of the Chinese currency is already irreversible.

Nonetheless the BRICS has had minimal success in global economic reform. There have been some changes through the decisions of the G20, of which all the BRICS countries are members, but with a significant time lag given the Global Financial Crisis (GFC). These changes increased the voting power of the BRICS in the IMF, especially of China. Perhaps to accelerate these changes, the BRICS responded to the requests of the IMF for additional emergency funding, as its solidarity at the G20 meeting at Los Cabos in 2012 testified. There can be no concern that the BRICS seeks to undermine, rather than reform, the global financial and economic system; reform of the IMF is its core aim. Despite the recognition of the strength of these emerging economies, there is no clear match between the economic clout of the BRICS and its representation on the policy and decision-making bodies in Washington.

One reaction of the BRICS at its Summit meeting in Durban in March 2013 was to create the BRICS Development Bank. Preliminary agreements were then signed, but critical details, including the modalities of governance and operation, the exact amount of contributions and its location, are yet to be determined. A lead-in period of two years is presently anticipated before the Bank will be in operation. The BRICS Business Council, with membership from the private sector in each country, was also set up in Durban. The Council stressed the need to recognize trade and investment as the 'two pillars of economic engagement' among the BRICS members (Business Council communiqué). This communiqué foreshadows both continuing pressure for reform of the World Bank and the IMF and simultaneous encouragement of a larger role for the BRICS Development Bank.

At Durban, the BRICS also agreed on a target of US$500 billion in intra-BRICS trade by 2015. There is little common international legal infrastructure outside membership of the WTO. China is the most liberal of the five members in free trade terms, and the others flirt with protectionism, despite the special preferential advantage given to all developing country members of the WTO. The long tradition of socialism, and now state capitalism, is embedded in all except South Africa, where historically the private sector has played a greater role. As a very new WTO member, Russia has some distance to go in meeting the standards imposed by trade rules, and will enjoy a regulatory honeymoon for some time. However, the changing trade patterns of global supply chains are not well suited to WTO concepts, and the BRICS tends to follow traditional modes of trading. As manufacturing declines, the problems of dumping and consequent disputes increase. The BRICS has no dedicated dispute resolution system for intra-BRICS disputes, apart from that given through the WTO. In a curious way, the BRICS countries are limited by being too integrated into the WTO system and not flexible enough by using Preferential Trade Agreements to their advantage. Furthermore Brazil is hindered by its existing commitment to Mercosur, and there are no other relevant agreements.

Like the Association of Southeast Asian Nations (ASEAN), the BRICS members do not have complementary economies. In terms of energy, there is a symbiosis between Russia and Brazil as a major producer of non-renewable resources of oil and gas in the former, and the development of biofuels in the latter. India and China are the major consumers of energy; hence there is a good fit. India, Brazil and China are still largely agrarian states, but due to population size, they must ultimately be net importers of food. This opens up possibilities not only to developing pathways inside the BRICS, but also harmonious and profitable trading and investment relations with non-members. However, until internal and group policies concerning Preferential Trade Agreements are reconsidered, growth will be erratic, though much needed with all members facing weakening economies. Tariff reduction is of little significance. The problems are the non-trade barriers and lack of market access.

Some lessons can be learned from the informality of the Asia-Pacific Economic Cooperation (APEC), and the network of meetings established to date between ministerial officials and business sector players follow that model. The BRICS has a strong resemblance to the ASEAN in its early years, when it was characterized more by what it was against than what it was for. But the ASEAN has evolved almost to the stage of an economic union expected within five years. It has used an informal tiering and mentoring arrangement between the original five members and the subsequent less-developed five members in order to improve the general environment for trade, both internally and externally. Will the BRICS further evolve to resemble the APEC or the ASEAN? The APEC has remained a loosely woven group, but one which has generated ideas and action over a wide range of issues. The ASEAN came into existence for purposes of mutual security, with strong policies of sovereign autonomy and non-intervention, but is now moving closer to an economic union. There has been a long delay between the making of the decision to reach this union and its fulfilment, successively delayed by the currency crises of the 1990s and accelerated by the GFC. Had one asked the future of these institutions at any time in the last 20 years, there would have been very different responses. The future of the BRICS is attended by the same uncertainty.

Each of the BRICS countries ranks poorly in the World Bank's 2012 *Doing Business Index*, with the exception of South Africa, which ranks amongst the top 50. In the area of investment, where there is no global regulatory body as in the area of trade and no agreed customary international law of investment standards, the informal nature of the BRICS relationship is a major disadvantage. Because the BRICS nations are not effectively members of the World Bank's International Centre for the Settlement of Investment Disputes (ICSID), any disagreement amongst themselves or with other countries relating to investment does not have the advantage of access to institutional arbitration or to enforcement. All arrangements must be ad hoc. In this environment, the pervasiveness of corrupt practices is a major disincentive to foreign investment. Again the limited role of the private sector and the major part played by state capitalism are obstacles to extensive private foreign investment, but may provide opportunities for privatization and for public-private partnerships in developing infrastructure. A treaty network amongst the BRICS members would greatly strengthen its position.

The attitude of the BRICS to international law is variable. There has been a number of informal strategic alliances, sometimes with other states, in relation to emerging and controversial areas of international law. One example is the formation of the BASIC (the BRICS minus Russia), a coordinated bloc acting on global climate negotiations. Russia, because of its fossil fuel industries, has remained outside this group. There is no anarchic attitude towards international law, but a strong disapproval and rejection of some aspects deemed as having been settled by major developed countries. However, fundamental stress on the importance of sovereignty and the non-acceptance of external interference are still constant themes of attitudes towards international law, and still mark a division between the BRICS and other developing countries vis-à-vis the majority of the OECD countries.

In many countries, the Washington Consensus has been discredited, and there has been a rejection of the so-called Western values and ideals underlying the developments of the last two decades, especially in trade and investment. In the area of climate change, in promoting the idea of the public good in such areas as health, where entrenched property rights in patents and trademarks have been an obstacle, and in asserting the end of a single dominant world power in favour of multipolarization, the BRICS members are in consensus, and there are some successes not just in blocking undesirable objectives but in achieving their own goals. However, where areas of self-interest appear, as in disputes over the law of the sea and claims to offshore resources, or border disputes and claims to water, then the unity dissolves. As the BRICS both invests and receives investment, much of the sting has gone from earlier disputes about sovereignty over natural resources.

The BRICS has attained a leadership position and a role of influence amongst developing countries, especially in international financial reform and trade policies, but it has not yet attained the status of a paradigmatic force to blast out opposing views, despite its growing and acknowledged economic strength. It is too early to tell whether this will come about, but the position is rapidly evolving and is quickly changed by both internal and external factors. The BRICS certainly has soft power, and often the power to persuade is enough. It has put multipolarity instead of US hegemony on the discussion, if not the action, agenda. However, its most measurable achievement is the extent to which the G20 as a critical policymaker has been strengthened by the inclusion of the BRICS nations as member states.

Index

Aboagye, F. 263
Adem, S. 126, 127, 129
Afghanistan 5, 221, 288, 292, 295, 302
Africa and rise of BRIC countries 123–6, 136, 297, 298
beneficial prospects for Africa 129–32
BRIC's engagement with Africa 125–9
pitfalls for Africa 132–6
African National Congress (ANC) 146, 168
African Renaissance 107–8
African Union (AU) 106, 107, 126–7
Aghion, P. 57
agriculture 56, 131, 201, 244, 260, 298
Brazil 56, 72, 75–6, 143, 165, 245, 310
China 54, 56, 63, 168, 245, 272, 310
Doha Round 74
India 52–64, 72, 144, 167, 245, 310
Russia 166
Seoul Development Consensus 113
Alden, C. 126
Alexandroff, A. 256
Almeida, P.R. de 79
Ancharaz, V.D. 124
Anghie, A. 291
antidumping actions/measures 90, 309
Doha Round 75
risks and pitfalls 86–9
Sino-Brazilian trade 84–5, 89–96
major concerns of Brazil 86–7
South Africa-Brazil dispute 116–17
US 87–8
WTO 76, 88, 90, 91, 92, 95, 96
Arab-Israeli conflict 301
arbitration 211–12, 278
ICSID 115, 211, 311
Arbix, D. 75, 76
Arestis, P. 19
Argentina 72, 73, 90, 213
Ariff, M. 149, 151, 167
Arora, V. 123
ASEAN 174–5, 182, 187, 303, 310
Ashauer, D. 28
Ashok Leyland 128
Asia 124, 187, 234
see also individual countries
Asia-Pacific Economic Cooperation (APEC) 310
Astashin, N. 234, 235
Auboin, M. 213
Audretsch, D.B. 23
Australia 156, 201, 236, 248, 261, 297
Avendano, R. 150
Azambuja, M. 219

Bagchi, I. 205
Bajpai, N. 200
Baldauf, S. 128
Baldwin, R. 155
Bandung Principles 299
Banerjee, D. 263
banks 9, 113, 144, 154, 155, 156, 169
BRICS Bank *see separate entry*
central 4, 19, 157, 213, 273, 299, 305
China 126, 154, 156, 273–4, 276
Baracuhy, B. 243
bargaining coalition 259–60
Barka, H.B. 128, 129
Barro, R. 28, 35, 42
al-Bashir, Omar 258
BASIC group (Brazil, South Africa, India and China) 76–7, 255, 311
Basu, Kaushik 10
Bayoumy, Y. 127
Beattie, A. 241, 248
Bellamy, A. 263–4
Beniwal, V. 245
Bergin, T. 249
Bertazzo, J. 70, 71

Bharti Airtel 128
Bhat, T.P. 144
Bientema, N. 63
Bilateral Investment Treaty (BIT) 110, 212
bilateralism 105, 208–9, 213
  investment treaties 110, 212, 293, 304
Binns, P. 143
Bird, R.C. 215
Birdsall, N. 268
Blair, Tony 300
Bloom, D.E. 13
Botchway, F.N. 125, 126, 127, 132
Boulle, L. 100, 110, 111, 257
Bown, C.P. 89
Bradford, C.I. 246
Bradlow, D.D. 77, 79, 111
Braithwaite, J. 155
Branigan, T. 256
Brazil 11, 12, 24, 67–8, 79–80, 101, 156, 157–8, 163, 237, 310–12
  Africa 123, 124, 125, 128
    South Africa *see below*
  agriculture 56, 72, 75–6, 143, 165, 245, 310
  anti-Western bias 299
  banks 154
  BASIC group 76–7, 255, 311
  BRICS as a bloc *see separate entry*
  China 72, 73, 84–96, 157, 178, 210, 245
  consumption, savings and investment 15–17
  corruption 24, 143, 156, 165, 166
  economic development 68–71
  economic reforms 20, 68, 69, 165
  exchange rate 256
  FDI 71, 192, 195, 204
  foreign exchange reserves 125, 153, 173, 176
  foreign trade 11, 20, 71–6, 77, 79–80, 84–96, 178–82, 196, 200, 204, 213, 231
  GDP 14, 68–9, 72, 73, 143, 165, 173, 244
  global economic governance 77–9, 80
  IBSA group 76, 255
  IMF 110, 247, 263
  India 72
  inflation 19, 68, 69, 143, 165
  institutional investment 153, 154
  intellectual property 214, 215
  IOSCO Board 155
  Mercosur 73–4, 75, 80, 208, 209, 310
  NIEO 297
  pluralism 296
  population 13
  protectionism 256
  Russia 72
  South Africa 72, 105, 108, 116 17
  SWF 151
  state capitalism 143
  Syria 258, 263
  UN peacekeeping 262
  US 72, 75–6, 96, 195, 200
  WTO 75, 76, 90, 91, 92, 95, 96, 116–17
Bremmer, I. 241
Bretton Woods institutions 77–8, 102
  see also IMF; World Bank
BRICS Bank 25, 67, 78–9, 114–15, 213–14, 216, 221, 232–3, 245, 299, 305, 309
BRICS as a bloc 178–82, 186–7
  comparison 169–74
  currency arrangements 174–7
  growth-trade linkages 182–6
BRICS Free Trade Agreement (FTA), potential 73–4, 80, 191, 206–15, 216, 303–5
Broer, W. 274, 277
Brütch, C. 258, 259, 260, 261
Bush, George W. 292
Byers, M. 291

Cagliarini, A. 61
Canada 76, 106, 151, 170, 248
capitalism 156, 157, 288, 289, 291, 292–3
  state *see separate entry*
Cardoso, F.H. 69, 70, 73, 143
Carmody, P. 103, 123
Carstens, Agustin 248
Cass, D. 56
Castel, V. 105, 108
Central Asia 187, 234, 255
central banks 4, 19, 157, 213, 273, 299, 305
Cesar, S.E.M. 74, 75
Chellaney 133, 134

Chenery, H. 53
China 12, 14, 15, 17, 69, 101, 124–5, 156–8, 163, 230, 297, 309–12
  Africa 123, 124, 125–7, 130, 133–5
    South Africa *see below*
  agriculture 54, 56, 63, 168, 245, 272, 310
  anti-Western bias 299
  antidumping actions 84–5, 86–94
  banks 126, 154, 156, 273–4, 276
  BASIC group 76–7, 255, 311
  Brazil 72, 73, 84–96, 157, 178, 210, 245
  BRICS as a bloc *see separate entry*
  Canada 106
  Communist Party 145–6
  Constitution 277, 281
  consumption, savings and investment 17, 41–2
  corruption 24, 156, 168, 279
  development path 268–72, 277–81
    economic developments 20, 168, 272–5
    legal reforms 275–7
  exchange rate 175, 177, 247, 249, 256, 261
  exports/imports 20, 84–96, 147–8, 168, 178–82, 196, 200–2, 231, 274
  FDI 20–21, 173, 183, 204, 274–5, 280
  fiscal policy and economic growth 27–49
  foreign exchange reserves 125, 152–3, 156, 168, 173, 176, 256, 308
  FTAs 208–9
  GDP 12, 24, 40, 44–6, 73, 101, 168, 170, 173, 186, 244
  globalization 258–9, 261
  humanitarian intervention 300, 302
  ICSID 115
  IMF 245, 247, 263, 309
  income inequality 46–7
  India 73, 90, 157, 178, 235, 245
  insurance industry 155
  intellectual property 214, 276
  IOSCO Board 155
  labour mobility 23, 273, 275, 280
  legal system 134, 268–9, 271–2, 275–8, 280–1
  minorities 258, 302
  MFN from US 145
  mutual funds 154
  NIEO 297
  oil price 130
  pension funds 153
  per capita income 15, 27, 48
  population 12–13, 17, 244
  private enterprises 48, 168, 272–3, 275, 277
  protectionism 256
  regional transmission 210
  regulatory issues 155, 156
  renminbi, invoicing in 213
  Russia 73, 157, 178, 200, 201, 234–5, 238
  securities trading 30, 274, 276
  South Africa 73, 103, 108, 110, 146, 157, 178, 210
  South China Sea 264
  SWFs 150–151, 153
  sovereignty 296
  state capitalism 145–6, 167–8
  Sudan 258
  Syria 258, 263
  UN peacekeeping 262
  unemployment 18, 48
  US 127, 145, 201, 247, 296–7
  WTO 20, 85, 90, 91, 95, 96, 145, 168, 211, 273, 274, 278
Chiu, B. 145
Cipla 128
Clark, C. 53
climate change 8, 68, 113–14, 232, 245, 248–9, 257, 296, 303, 305, 311
  BASIC group 76–7, 255, 311
  Kyoto Protocol 294, 303
Clinton, Hillary 297
coal ash waste 223, 225
Coase Theorem 270
Cohen, M. 126
Cold War 128, 129, 290, 299
Collor de Mello, Fernando 69
colonialism 220, 290, 291, 295, 296, 297, 299, 300
commodities 12, 133, 216, 297
  Africa 107, 125, 127, 129–30, 131, 134–6
    South Africa 108, 110, 216
  Brazil 85–6, 94–5, 216

China 125, 127, 157
Brazilian exports to 85–6, 94–5
South African exports to 108, 110
prices 7, 69, 95, 129–30, 157, 245
Russia 129, 144, 178, 216
see also natural resources
Common Market for Eastern and Southern Africa (COMESA) 105
Commonwealth of Independent States (CIS) 205, 209
competition law 270, 276
Confucianism 29, 299
consumer expenditure 6
consumption, savings and investment 15–17, 33, 78
China 17, 41–2, 48
India 167
Contingency Measures (CMs) 89
Cooper, A.F. 99
Cooper, J.M. 163
copyright 169, 214, 276
Corkin, L. 86
corruption 24, 134, 135, 143, 146, 156, 163, 165, 166, 168, 279, 311
Cui, Liru 258, 259
culture 222, 244, 260, 270
Cuneo, D.L. 91
currency swap arrangements 245
Czako, J. 88
Czech Republic 34, 35

Da Silva, Luiz Inácio Lula 69, 70, 77, 128
Dabagian, E. 233
Dailami, M. 79
Das, G. 20
Davis, K.E. 269, 270
de Onis, J. 143
Del Tedesco Lins, M.A. 68, 69, 72, 79
democracy 68, 69–70, 71, 156, 269, 279, 288, 289, 291, 292, 296, 300
Africa 127, 132–3
'new diplomacy' 235–6
Democratic Republic of Congo 133
Deng, Xiaoping 20
development theories 269–71
China 268–9, 271–81
Dispute Settlement Body (DSB) 217, 261
distributive justice 296
Doha Round 6, 74–6, 77, 205, 243, 246, 247, 248, 293, 298
Domar, E.D. 42
Dowling, M. 210
drug trafficking 221, 222
Duruigbo, E. 132, 135

Easterly, W. 28, 35
Eastern European countries 28
economic growth 13, 112, 142, 192, 223, 242, 255, 256, 261
Africa 107, 131
Brazil 19, 20, 143, 165–6, 182–6
China 14, 15, 20, 23, 27–49, 124–5, 168, 170, 182–6, 268–9, 271–81
development theories 269–71
India 20, 23, 25, 52–64, 124–5, 144, 167, 170, 182–6
Russia 19, 20, 166–7, 183
South Africa 19, 20, 169, 182–6
underlying determinants 18–24, 213
economic overview of BRICS 11–25
education and training 20, 23, 24, 187
Africa 131, 135
South Africa 146, 169
Brazil 71, 166
China 27, 33, 34, 47, 48, 131
India 55–6, 63, 163, 167, 169
Russia 163
Egypt 133
Eichengreen, B. 243
Elliot, L. 261
Emerging market economies (EMEs) 5, 7, 14, 20, 21
employment 17, 23, 70, 113, 157
Africa 128, 131, 133–4, 135
energy 6, 7–8, 9, 101, 302
Brazil 70, 72, 310
India 144, 302, 310
Russia 166, 222, 231–2, 237, 310
enlightened shareholder value 157
entrepreneurship 20, 23, 24, 131, 272–3
environmental protection 47, 134, 223–5, 275, 276, 303
see also climate change
Ethiopia 127
Euro Area 14, 20, 24, 248, 264–5, 295
European Union (EU) 24, 69, 103, 115, 158, 174–5, 248, 303
Brazil 75–6, 200

China 90, 200
comparison with BRICS 146–9, 182, 202, 204
supplier of services 196, 200, 201, 207
expropriation 212
Extractive Industry Transparency Initiative (EITI) 133
extraterritoriality 291

Farrar, J. xviii, 3, 149, 151
Feinberg, R.M. 89
Feldstein, M.S. 241
financial crises 107, 154, 166
2008 Global Financial Crisis (GFC) 95, 100, 105, 130, 142, 157, 193, 216, 231, 243–4, 246, 255, 264, 268
ASEAN 310
Brazil 11, 165, 170
China 201
India 11
neo-liberal norms 299
Russia 144, 154, 166, 170
South Africa 169, 170
US hegemony 289
US housing sector 242
weaknesses in regulation 155–6, 288
Financial Stability Board 155, 246
financial transactions tax (FTT) 111–12
Flemes, D. 76
Flynn, D. 249
Fontanella-Khan, J. 246
food security 6, 8, 9, 63, 72, 113, 222
foreign direct investment (FDI) 11, 20–2, 24, 77, 103, 104, 173, 192–5
Africa 107, 126
Brazil 71, 192, 195, 204
China 20–21, 173, 183, 204, 274–5, 280
framing the discourse 112–13
India 144, 167, 192, 204
indirect 194–5
Russia 192, 204
South Africa 105, 109–10, 173, 192
sustainable development 112–13
foreign exchange reserves 77, 150, 151–3, 155, 165, 245
Brazil 125, 153, 173, 176
China 125, 152–3, 156, 168, 173, 176, 256, 308
India 125, 153, 173, 176, 308
Russia 125, 153, 166–7, 173, 176
South Africa 153, 173, 176
foreign policies 101, 163, 221, 230, 235, 236, 238, 244, 258, 299
Forrester, J.W. 220
Foster, V. 125
Framework for Strong, Sustainable and Balanced Growth (FSSBG) 246, 247
framing the discourse 112–13
France 31, 34, 35, 46
Free Trade Agreements (FTAs) 74, 208–9, 211, 214, 276–7, 303–4
BRICS 73–4, 80, 191, 216, 303–5
exclusive or inclusive 206–10, 213, 215
fault lines 210–215
Frieden, J. 241
Friedman, L. 249
Friedman, T.L. 292
Fullerton, D. 28, 33

G7 103, 111, 117, 243, 246, 253
G8 aid commitments 113–14, 129
G20 7, 70, 78, 80, 100, 102, 117, 153, 205, 309
agenda influence 110–1, 112
financial inclusion 112
framing the discourse 113
Group of four 298
rotating chairs 114
South Africa 103, 106
strengthened 111, 222, 246–9, 312
BRICS: breaking or building global system 232, 245–6, 253–65, 309
Gaddafi, Muammar 263, 301
Gadzala, A. 127
Gallagher, K.P. 93
Gammeltoft, P. 193, 204
Gandhi, Mahatma 299
Gangopadhyay, A. 144, 245
Gazprom 256
General Agreement on Trade in Services (GATS) 293

General Agreement on Tariffs and Trade (GATT) 117
Generally Accepted Principles and Pratices of Sovereign Wealth Funds (GAPP) 150, 159
Germany 31, 34, 35, 46, 72–3, 153, 156
Ghana 130
Ghani, E. 23
Ghori, U.H. 210
Giles, C. 245
Gingerich, T. 88
globalization 11, 74–5, 79, 107, 113, 144, 258–9, 261–2, 296
  framing the discourse 113
  spillovers 241–2
Glosny, M. 259, 261
gold 130, 144, 223, 225
Goldman Sachs 5, 6, 162, 163, 165, 169, 192, 289
Goldsmith, J.L. 294
Goldstein, M. 256
Gong, G.W. 291
governance 6, 114–15, 132–3, 163, 169, 241–9, 271, 304
  BRICS: breaking or building global system 232, 245–6, 253–65, 309
  definition 132
gradualism 167
Grant, K. 126
'great power diplomacy' 228, 229–35, 236
Greece 156, 295
Gross Domestic Product (GDP) 6, 13–14, 24, 67, 73, 77, 162, 165, 170, 186, 242, 255
  Brazil 14, 68–9, 72, 73, 143, 165, 173, 244
  China 12, 24, 40, 44–6, 73, 101, 168, 170, 173, 186, 244
  comparing BRICS with EU and US 146–9
  framing the discourse 113
  India 14–15, 52, 54, 167, 170, 173, 244
  Russia 14, 163, 166, 173, 244
  South Africa 108, 169, 173, 244
Gross Domestic Product based annual per capita economic growth (GDPPC) 184
Grossman, G. 57
Growth Environment Scores (GES) 169
Grudgings, S. 128
Gubareva, D.B. 223
Guihai, G. 142
Gulf Cooperating Council (GCC) 182
Guthrie, D. 156–7

Haddad, M. 183
Haiti 292
Hall, M. 255
Hall, R.E. 28, 33
Halligan, L. 246
Hamann, E.P. 263
Harford, T. 132
Harris, J. 59
Harrod, R.F. 42
health 8, 131, 167, 273, 311
  safety standards 133–4
healthcare expenditure 13, 63
  China 33, 34, 35, 47, 279
Hedetoft, U. 143–4
Holman, M. 107
Hong Kong 149, 153, 154, 200, 201, 213, 275, 276–7
Horlick, G. 87
Hounshell, B. 255
Howitt, P. 57
Hsing, S. 264
Hu, Jintao 142
Huang, Y. 132
Hulbert, M. 231
human rights 127, 133, 258, 271, 277, 295, 297, 300, 302–3
  responsibility to protect 263
humanitarian intervention 288, 291–2, 296, 300–1, 302
Hussein, Saddam 292, 297, 300

Iimi, A. 132
income inequality 6, 46–7, 169
incrementalism 279, 280, 281
India 11, 12, 24–5, 101, 124–5, 156, 157–8, 167–8, 230, 297, 310–2
  Africa 123, 124, 125, 128
    South Africa 108, 128, 178
  agriculture 52–64, 72, 144, 167, 245, 310
  anti-Western bias 299
  banks 144, 154

BASIC group 76–7, 255, 311
Brazil 72
BRICS as a bloc *see separate entry*
China 73, 90, 157, 178, 235, 245
Constitution 157
corruption 24, 156
economic reforms 20, 167
education 55–6, 63, 163, 167, 169
employment 17
entrepreneurship 20, 23
exchange rate 167
exports/imports 11, 20, 144, 196, 200, 201, 202, 231
  trade bloc 178–82
FDI 144, 167, 192, 204
foreign exchange reserves 125, 153, 173, 176, 308
GDP 14–15, 52, 54, 167, 170, 173, 244
humanitarian intervention 300, 302
IBSA group 76, 255
IMF 247, 263
income inequality 46
inflation 19, 25
institutional investment 144, 151, 154
intellectual property 214, 215
IOSCO Board 155
Kashmir 302
labour mobility 23
mutual funds 144, 154
NIEO 297
nuclear non-proliferation treaty 258
pension funds 153
per capita income 15
pluralism 296
population 12–13
productivity differences, technology adoption and economic growth 52–64
protectionism 256
Russia 234–5
South Africa 108, 128, 178
SAFTA 208, 209
state capitalism 144–5, 154
sugar cane 72
Syria 258, 263
UN peacekeeping 262
WTO dispute settlement 76

India, Brazil and South Africa (IBSA) 76, 77, 118, 255, 299
Indonesia 12, 103, 118, 157, 158, 210, 295
inequality 6, 46–7, 70, 71, 169, 294
inflation 18–19, 25, 157, 170
  Brazil 19, 68, 69, 143, 165
  China 168, 170
  Russia 19, 166
  South Africa 19, 169
infrastructure 6, 23–4, 35, 79, 208, 212, 245, 296
  Africa 107, 124, 125, 126, 127, 130, 131, 134–5
  Brazil 70, 71, 165
  BRICS Bank 213, 216
  China 29, 31, 42–4, 47, 48, 272
    Africa 126, 127, 130, 131
  India 55–6, 63–4
  South Africa 146
institutional investment 144, 149, 156
  foreign exchange reserves *see separate entry*
  insurance companies 144, 154–5
  mutual funds 144, 153–4, 155
  regulatory issues 155–6
  stewardship values 157
  SWFs *see* sovereign wealth funds
insurance companies 144, 154–5
intellectual property 214–15, 276, 293
  copyright 169, 214, 276
  patents 76, 169, 214–15, 276, 311
interest rates 25, 28, 33
interest group/pressure group 153, 204–6, 215, 299–300, 308
  agenda influence 110–111, 112
  common agenda 245
  framing the discourse 113
International Centre for the Settlement of Investment Disputes (ICSID) 115, 211, 311
International Criminal Court 294
International Investment Agreements (IIAs) 112–13
international law 131–2, 221, 288–9, 311
  law of the sea 264, 291, 311
International Monetary Fund (IMF) 7, 78, 101, 102, 142, 150, 153, 213–14, 296, 308, 309

Africa 125
capital controls 248
contributions 245–6, 263, 265
foreign exchange reserves 155, 256
leadership of 110, 114, 232, 247, 248, 298, 308
Russia 166, 256
voting power and quotas 232, 245, 247, 260, 263, 309
Washington Consensus 292
International Organisation of Securities Commissions (IOSCO) 155
international security and use of force 222, 230–231, 235, 263–4, 299–303
International Working Group on Sovereign Wealth Funds (IWG) 150
intra-BRICS disputes 76, 115–17, 157, 158, 211–13, 260, 297, 309–10
local courts 304
Sino-Brazilian trade and antidumping concerns 84–96
intra-BRICS investment 6, 72, 206–7, 211–13, 303
intra-BRICS trade 6, 9, 25, 72, 73, 79–80, 157–8, 175, 178, 231–2, 304
BRICS FTA, potential *see separate entry*
currencies 213, 232, 299
growth-trade linkages 182–6
Sino-Brazilian trade 72, 73, 84–96, 210
Sino-Russian services trade 201
South Africa 108–9, 110, 185–6, 210
target 309
Investment Agency, proposal for 110
Investment Policy Framework for Sustainable Development (IPFSD) 112, 113
Investment Protection Agencies 113
investment treaties 110, 212, 293, 304
Iran 5, 302
Iraq 263, 288, 292, 295, 300, 301
Ireland 295
Israel 301, 302
Istomina, K. 228–9
Italy 262
Ivanov, S. 233

Jahoda, M. 220
Japan 24, 27, 31, 153, 210, 271
Africa 131
Brazil 72, 200
China 201
culture 270
government expenditure 34, 35
income inequality 46
India 200
trade between BRICS and 73
Jenkins, R. 85
Johnson, R.W. 146
joint ventures 142, 154, 272, 275, 276
Jones, L.E. 28
Joseph, S. 131
judiciary 71, 269, 275, 281

Kahn, M. 103, 105, 107
Kamal, M. 19
Kaplan, R. 254, 258
Karimova, D. 223
Kawai, M. 243
Keeler, D. 72, 73
Kelly, P. 106
Khalid, A. 175
Khan, A. 57
Kharas, H. 246
Khramchikhin, A. 235
Kimenyi, M.S. 123
King, R.G. 28
Kirkby, A. 77
Kobo, K. 125
Kojima, K. 210
Koopmans, T. 56
Kose, M.A. 183
Kosovo 288, 291–2, 300
Kowalski, P. 183
Kragelund, P. 128
Kregel, J. 163
Krever, T. 268, 277
Kuboniwa, M. 183, 186–7
Kukol, E. 237
Kuzmin, V. 233
Kuznets, S. 53
Kyrgyzstan 153

labour mobility 23, 24, 273, 275, 280
labour standards 133–4, 273, 276
Ladurner, U. 70
Lahiri, R. 55, 56, 57, 64

Laidi, Z. 263
Landes, D. 270
Landou, D.L. 28, 42
Laos 210
Larin, V.L. 234
Laryea, E. 130, 131, 132, 135
Latin America 271, 303
see also individual countries
Lavrov, Sergei 221–2
law and development 268–71, 280–1
China 268–9, 271–2, 275–8, 280–1
law of the sea 264, 291, 311
least developed countries 67, 75, 79, 123, 268, 298, 303
Levine, R. 42
Lewis, A. 59
Li, C. 40
Libya 263, 292, 300–1
Lin, J.Y. 24, 143, 154
Lin, L-W.145
Lin, S. 27, 28, 43
Lo, B. 234, 235, 273
Lo, V.I. xviii, 4, 234, 235, 273
Lowenberg, A. 146
Low Income Countries (LIC) 11, 147, 183
Lukyanov, F. 110, 232
Lula da Silva, Luiz Inácio 69, 70, 77, 128
Luxembourg 170
Luzianin, S. 232, 236
Lyman, P.N. 131
Lynch, A.C. 144

Macau 275, 276–7
Macau Forum 95–6
Macfarlane, N.S. 163
McGee, R.W. 87, 88, 89
Mahindra Group 128
Makhov, S.A. 220
Makin, A. 19, 20, 24
Malaysia 118, 147, 149, 295
Mance, H. 245
Mandelbaum, M. 288
Market Economy Status (MES) 91
Mbeki, Thabo 107, 168–9
Mead, W.R. 73
Medvedev, Dmitry 222, 228, 255
Meiden, M. 133
Mencius 29
Meng, X. 23
Mercosur 73–4, 75, 80, 208, 209, 310
Mexico 103, 118, 158, 248
Millennium Development Goals 113–14, 298
Miller, K. 125
Milosevic, Slobodan 258
Mobutu Sese Seko 133
Mokyr, J. 54
most-favoured-nation (MFN) status 145, 152, 206, 210
Moyo, D. 125, 127, 130, 131
Mubarak, Hosni 133
Mugabe, Robert 133, 258
Muller, M. 163
multilateralism 105, 112, 205, 243–4, 246, 249
'new diplomacy' 236
multinational/transnational corporations (MNCs/ TNCs) 75, 130, 134, 157, 193, 211–12, 293, 296–7
multipolar order 6–7, 77, 79, 80, 221, 230, 234–5, 311, 312
international law 288–305
multilateralism and 243–4, 249
unstable 254–5, 259
mutual funds 144, 153–4, 155

Naidu, S. 128, 210
Nehru, Jawaharlal 144
neoclassical economics 270
neo-colonialism 129
neo-liberalism 107, 257, 261, 289, 292, 293, 294, 296, 297, 299
Neri, M.C. 70
Netherlands 72, 134
'new diplomacy' 228, 229, 235–7
New Industrialized Countries (NIC) 200
New Institutional Economics 270, 271
New International Economic Order (NIEO) 131–2, 296, 297, 298, 303
New Partnership for Africa's Development (NEPAD) 106
New Political Economy 271
New Zealand 156, 261
Next Eleven (N11) 158
Nigeria 12, 118, 130, 134
Nolan, P. 157

Nolte, D. 103
Noman, A. 124
Non-Aligned Group 153, 296
North American Free Trade Agreement (NAFTA) 115, 304
North Atlantic Treaty Organization (NATO) 288, 291, 300, 302
natural resources 125, 193, 220, 296, 303, 304
  Africa 107, 127, 131, 135–6
  Brazil 69, 143, 204, 216
  BRICS-based TNCs 211–12
  Central Asia 187
  China 125, 127, 204, 274, 296–7
  expropriation 211–12
  India 204
  large SOEs 208, 211
  permanent sovereignty over 131–2, 297, 311
  Russia 166, 204, 216
  South Africa 105, 216
  see also commodities
North, D. 270
North–South dialogue 153
Norway 151, 200
Noury, V. 108
nuclear energy 8
nuclear proliferation 254, 258, 296
nuclear research 302
nuclear weapons 101
Nugee, J. 151
Nye Jr, J.S. 68

Oeheler-Şincai, J. 255, 261
Ohnesorge, J.K.M. 268, 271
oil 72, 125, 129, 130, 144, 163, 166, 178, 310
Oliveira, M.F. de 76
O'Neill, J. 11, 52, 142, 162, 169, 186, 242
Optimum Currency Area (OCA) 174
Organisation for Economic Co-operation and Development (OECD) 12, 150, 155, 205
outsourcing 209

Pakistan 208–9
Palestine 301, 302
Palmer, D. 214, 215
Panetta, Leon 253–4
Paraguay 73
Parente, S. 55
Parks, K. 213
Parrish, K. 254
patents 76, 169, 214–15, 276, 311
path dependency 270
Patrick, S. 243
Paulino, L.A. 74
Peccei, A. 220
pensions 13, 20, 273
  pension funds 150, 153, 155
per capita incomes of BRICS 15, 16, 27, 48, 147, 244, 296
Pereyra, C. 219
Perkins, D.H. 28
Permanent Sovereignty of States Over their Natural Resources (PSNR) 131
pharmaceuticals 20, 23, 76, 256, 298
  patents 76, 214–15
Philippines 12
Pimental, Fernando 128
pluralism 269, 296
Poland 34, 35, 118
population 11, 12–13, 52–3, 77, 107, 125, 142, 163, 165, 171–3, 244, 255
Portugal 295
poverty 15, 20, 24, 124, 132, 163, 166, 167, 173, 279, 296, 298
  eradication/reduction 8, 63, 68, 70, 131, 268, 271
pressure group *see* interest group
privatization 24, 143, 166, 168, 169, 271, 311
productivity 21, 71
  India: productivity differences, technology adoption and economic growth 52–64
proportionality principle 111
protectionism 245, 246, 247, 248, 256, 261, 304, 309
Prusa, A.C. 68
public goods, global 257, 262–3
Purchasing Power Parity (PPP) 102, 166, 242
Putin, Vladimir 166, 229, 230, 232, 233, 234, 235, 236, 238

quantitative easing 245, 247

Ramo, J.C. 268, 269
Rapoza, K. 68, 256
Ratnasiri, S. 2, 55, 56, 57, 64
Reagan, Ronald 28, 270
Rebelo, S. 28, 57
regime change 263–4
regional transmission 209–10
regionalism 101, 208, 295
  accession of South Africa 103–5
  intentional 105
renewable energy 8, 9, 232, 310
renminbi 27, 175, 177, 213, 214, 247, 249, 256, 261, 309
research and development (R&D) 63, 71, 169, 187, 274
Reserve Bank of India (RBI) vii, 25, 53
reserve currencies 232, 308
responsibility to protect (R2P) 263–4, 300, 301
Roberts, C. 256, 257, 258, 259, 260, 262
Rodrik, D. 27, 271
Romer, P.M. 28, 57
Romero, S. 69
Romney, Mitt 256
Rose, S. 166
Rostow, W. 54
Roubini, N. 164
Rousseff, Dilma 69, 70, 94, 128
Rowley, J. 94
Royal Dutch Shell 134
Russia 12, 101, 142, 156, 157–8, 163–4, 228–9, 309, 310–12
  Africa 124, 125, 128–9
  anti-Western bias 299
  authoritarianism 258
  banks 154, 156
  Brazil 72
  BRICS as a bloc 178–82, 186–7
    comparison 169–74
    currency arrangements 174–7
  Chechnya 302
  China 73, 157, 178, 200, 201, 234–5, 238
  consumption, savings and investment 17
  corruption 24, 156, 163, 166
  economic reforms 20, 166
  exports/imports 20, 144, 166, 196, 200, 201, 204, 231–2
    trade bloc 178–82
  FDI 192, 204
  foreign exchange reserves 125, 153, 166–7, 173, 176
  gas prices 256
  GDP 14, 163, 166, 173, 244
  IMF 247, 263
  India 234–5
  inflation 19, 166
  institutional investment 153, 154
  intellectual property 214
  involvement in BRICS 221–2, 228–9, 237–8
    'great power diplomacy' 228, 229–35, 236
    'new diplomacy' 228, 229, 235–7
  politics and services trade 200
  population 13
  protectionism 256
  Serbia 258
  SWFs 151, 153
  sovereignty 300, 302
  state capitalism 143–4
  Syria 258, 263
  trade and economic growth 183
  WTO 144, 256, 261, 298, 309
Ryabkov, S. 229
Ryumina, L. 220

safety standards 133–4
Sakwa, R. 233, 234, 236
Samake, I. 183
sanctions 133, 168, 263
Santiago Principles 150, 155
Sarkar, J. 144
Sarkozy, N. 246
Saudi Arabia 149, 151, 153
savings and investment 15–17, 33, 78
  China 17, 41–2, 48
  India 167
Schmitt, G. 131, 134
Schneidman, W. 126, 127, 128
Schrijver, N. 132
Secretariat of Foreign Trade Brazil (SECEX) 85, 86, 90–92
Sedelmayer v The Russian Federation 212
Seidman, L. 28, 33
Sen, A. 271
Seoul Development Consensus 113, 280

Serbia 258
Shaffer, G. 75
Shanghai Cooperation Organisation (SCO) 205, 235, 255
Sharma, R. 99, 144, 146, 157
Sharma, S.K. 73, 80
Shasha, D. 126
Shaw, T. 105
Shue, H. 292
Siegle, J. 132
Singapore 31, 34, 35, 149, 153, 261
Singh, Manmohan 10
Singh, R.K. 245
Sinha, A. 163, 256, 258
Slaughter, A. 100, 103
small and medium enterprises (SMEs) 208, 209, 274
Smith, A. 30
Smith, J.A. 243
Smith, K. 256
Smith, W. 24
social welfare: China 33, 34, 47, 273
Sofer, S. 235
soft power 68, 102, 312
Solow, R.M. 42, 56, 57
Sotero, P. 163, 258, 260
South Africa 5, 11, 12, 24, 99, 101, 117–18, 142, 156, 168–9, 310
  accession to BRIC: motivating factors 103, 146
    African Gateway 105–6, 123
    African Renaissance 107–8
    regional power 103–5
    representative agent 106–7
  Africa and rise of BRIC countries 123
  anti-Western bias 299
  banks 154, 169
  BASIC group 76–7, 255, 311
  Brazil 72, 105, 108, 116–17
  BRICS as a bloc *see separate entry*
  BRICs or BRICS 99, 123
  China 73, 103, 108, 110, 146, 157, 178, 210
  consumption, savings and investment 17
  corruption 146, 156
  exports/imports 20, 108–10, 157–8, 197, 202–4
    trade bloc 178–82
  FDI 105, 109–10, 173, 192
  foreign exchange reserves 153, 173, 176
  functions in BRICs 111–15
  G20 256–7
  GDP 108, 169, 173, 244
  IBSA group 76, 255
  IMF contribution 263
  India 108, 128, 178
  inflation 19, 169
  institutional investment 151
  IOSCO Board 155
  membership benefits 108–10
  mutual funds 154
  NIEO 297
  outsourcing 209
  pension funds 153
  pluralism 296
  population 13, 244
  private sector 143, 309
  state capitalism 146
  Syria 258, 263
  UN peacekeeping 262
  unemployment 18, 169
  WTO dispute settlement 76, 116–17
  Zimbabwe 258
South Asian Free Trade Agreement (SAFTA) 208
South Korea 73, 103, 118, 147, 149, 153, 158, 170, 200, 201
  law and development 271
  regional transmission 210
Southern African Customs Union (SACU) 106
Southern African Development Community (SADC) 105, 106, 115
sovereign immunity 212
sovereign wealth funds (SWFs) 78, 149–51, 152, 153, 155, 156, 304–5
sovereignty 221, 263, 290, 296, 300, 302, 311
Soviet Union 127, 128, 129, 154, 230, 234, 288, 290
  see also Russia
Spain 295
state capitalism 142–6, 148, 151, 154, 156, 167–8, 309, 311
state immunity 212
State-Owned Assets Supervision and

Administration Commission (SASAC) 145
state-owned enterprises (SOEs) 24, 148, 150, 208, 212, 304
China 29–30, 38, 48, 145, 151, 154, 156, 168, 204, 212, 272, 273, 274, 275, 296–7
India 144, 154
Russia 143, 204, 212, 256
Stenina, N.G. 223
Stern, N. 78, 79
Stiglitz, J.E. 78, 131, 293
Strokan, S. 233
Sudan 258
Summers, L.H. 28, 33
Summits 7, 165, 215, 243, 259, 289, 303
(2009) Yekaterinburg 164, 229, 232, 242–3, 255, 303
(2010) Brasilia 10, 220, 231, 289
(2011) Sanya 7–8, 220
(2012) Delhi 5, 8, 9–10, 25, 205, 213, 214, 220, 221, 245, 261–2, 297, 298, 299, 301
(2013) Durban 67, 78, 233, 245, 309
supply chains, global 74–5, 309
Sussex, M. 236
sustainable development 6, 79, 112–13, 157, 220, 223, 275, 279, 298
Swan, T. 57
Switzerland 153
Syria 5, 258, 263, 292, 300, 301, 302–3
Szamosszegi, A. 145

Taiwan 149, 153, 210, 271, 275, 276–7
Tata Motors 128
Tautz, C. 78, 79
taxation 20, 71, 111–12, 130, 167, 223
China 27–33, 38, 41, 43, 47–8, 272, 273, 275–6
Taylor, I. 126
Technology Adoption Index (TAI) 60–63
technology adoption, productivity differences and economic growth: India 52–64
technology transfer 21, 135
terrorism 6, 222, 253–4, 292
war on terror 294, 295
Tett, G. 242
Thailand 31, 147
Thatcher, Margaret 270
think tanks 9, 232–3, 257
Thirlwell, M. 242
Thirtle, C. 63
Thomas, C. 268, 270, 271
Timmer, P. 53
Toder, E.J. 28, 33
trade bloc and potential economic bloc, BRICS as 162–4, 186–7
currency arrangements 174–7
growth-trade linkages 182–6
not economic bloc 178–83
overview of BRICS countries 164–9
comparison: BRICS as bloc 169–74
trade, international 11, 20, 24, 74–5, 79–80, 156, 157–8, 241–2
Africa 125–6, 127, 128–9
Brazil 11, 20, 71–6, 77, 79–80, 84–96, 178–82, 196, 200, 204, 213, 231
China 20, 84–96, 147–8, 168, 178–82, 196, 200–2, 231, 274
comparing BRICS with EU and US 146–9
FTAs *see separate entry*
India 11, 20, 144, 178–82, 196, 200, 201, 202, 231
Russia 20, 144, 166, 178–82, 196, 200, 201, 204, 231–2
South Africa 20, 108–10, 157–8, 178–82, 197, 202–4
trade in goods 201–4, 207, 213
trade in services 196–201, 204, 207, 293
US hegemony 292–3
see also intra-BRICS trade; WTO
Trade-Related Intellectual Property Rights Agreement (TRIPS) 293, 306
trade secrets 214–15
trademarks 276, 311
Trans-Pacific Partnership Agreement (TPP) 303–4
transgovernmental networks 100–103, 107
transnational/multinational corporations (TNCs/MNCs) 75, 130, 134, 157, 193, 211–12, 293, 296–7
trickle-down theory 294

Troyjo, M. 74
Trubek, D.M. 270
Truman, E. 150
Turkey 12, 90, 103, 118, 131, 149, 158

Ukraine 256
unemployment 18, 48, 70, 71, 157, 169
United Kingdom (UK) 31, 46, 53–4, 156, 214, 257, 300
United Nations (UN) 222, 290, 291, 301, 302
  budget contributions 257
  force, use of 292
  General Assembly 131–2, 258
  international economic system 131–2
  peacekeeping 262
  responsibility to protect 263
  Security Council 10, 101, 142, 222, 258, 260, 263, 300, 301, 302, 308
  UNCITRAL Arbitration Rules 211
  UNCTAD 112–13, 193–4
United Nations Framework Convention on Climate Change (UNFCCC) 248
United States (US) 11, 14, 20, 24, 25, 27, 53–4, 69, 103, 158, 230, 248
  agriculture 298
  antidumping actions 87–8, 90, 96
  Brazil 72, 75–6, 96, 195, 200
  China 127, 145, 201, 247, 296–7
  comparison with BRICS 146–9, 202
  corruption 156
  dollar 298, 308
  GDP: China catch up with 45–6
  government expenditure 34
  housing sector 242
  income inequality 46
  India 200
  intellectual property 214–15
  international law 288–95, 300
  Iraq 263, 288, 292, 295, 300, 301
  membership directions in BRICS 118
  multinational corporations 157
  national security issues 253–4
  politics and services trade 200
  protectionism 261
  Soviet Union, fall of 288
  taxation 28, 31–2
  trade between BRICS and 73
  UN budget 257
  war on terror 294, 295
Uren, D. 156
Uruguay 73

van Praag, M. 23
Vandenbussche, H. 87, 89
Venezuela 73
Vermulst, E. 88
Vietnam 12, 210

Wade, R.H. 248
Waelde, T.W. 132
Walmart 106
Walter, C. 154
Washington Consensus 102, 145, 157, 268, 271, 292–3, 298, 311
Weber, M. 269
Weiss, T. 132
Wen, Jiabao 156
Wilson, D. 162, 165, 186, 192, 213, 242, 289
Woods, N. 246
World Bank 101, 102, 115, 142, 153, 213–14, 246, 296, 308, 309
  Africa 125, 126, 130
  Doing Business Index 24, 143, 144–5, 146, 158, 310
  leadership of 110, 232, 247
  Washington Consensus 292, 298
  World Trade Organization (WTO) 20, 74, 80, 105, 153, 155, 288, 293, 296, 297–8, 309, 310
  antidumping actions/measures/rules 76, 88, 90, 91, 92, 95, 96
  assisted membership 152
  Brazil 75, 76, 90, 91, 92, 95, 96, 116–17
  BRICS FTA 207
  China 20, 85, 90, 91, 95, 96, 145, 168, 211, 273, 274, 278
  dispute settlement 75, 76, 261, 293
    intra-BRICS 76, 115–17, 211
  Doha Round *see separate entry*
  IBSA group 76, 77
  Russia 144, 256, 261, 298, 309
Wroughton, L. 245

Xiao, Q. 163
Xu, M. 214

Ye, Z. 157
Yeltsin, Boris 166
Yu, G.T. 126, 127

Zagladin, N. 235
Zambia 133–4
Zimbabwe 133, 258
Zimmermann, A. 71
Zongwe, D.P. 127
Zuma, J.G. 114